GÖTTINGER ORIENTFORSCHUNGEN

IV. REIHE ÄGYPTEN 38

Herausgegeben von Friedrich Junge und Wolfhart Westendorf

Classification and Categorisation in Ancient Egypt
Vol. 5

Edited by Orly Goldwasser, Frank Kammerzell and Friedrich Junge

2006

Harrassowitz Verlag · Wiesbaden

Arlette David

Syntactic and Lexico-Semantic Aspects of the Legal Register in Ramesside Royal Decrees

2006

Harrassowitz Verlag · Wiesbaden

Research in the scope of the project „Classification and Categorization in Ancient Egypt", conducted by O. Goldwasser, Hebrew University of Jerusalem, F. Junge and F. Kammerzell, University of Göttingen, under the auspices of the Niedersächsische Ministerium für Wissenschaft und Kunst, Hannover, and the foundation „Niedersächsisches Vorab der Volkswagenstiftung" and the project „Typology and Use of Hieroglyphic Signs".

Bibliografische Information Der Deutschen Bibliothek:
Die Deutsche Bibliothek verzeichnet diese Publikation in der Deutschen Nationalbibliografie; detaillierte bibliografische Daten sind im Internet über http://dnb.ddb.de abrufbar.

Bibliographic information published by Die Deutsche Bibliothek:
Die Deutsche Bibliothek lists this publication in the Deutsche Nationalbibliografie; detailed bibliographic data is available in the internet at http://dnb.ddb.de.e-mail: cip@dbf.ddb.de

For further information about our publishing program consult our website http://www.harrassowitz-verlag.de

Printed on permanent/durable paper.
Printing and binding: Hubert & Co., Göttingen
Printed in Germany

ISSN 0340-6342
ISBN 3-447-05232-5 after 1.1.2007: 978-3-447-05232-0

Table of contents

Foreword

The present research was made possible by the generosity of the Ministry for Science and Education of Lower Saxony (with the Niedersächsische Vorab der Volkswagenstiftung), and the Thyssen Foundation, partners in the joint projects of the Seminar für Ägyptologie und Koptologie of the Göttingen University and the Department of Ancient Near Eastern Languages and Civilizations – Egyptology of the Hebrew University of Jerusalem on the subjects of "Classifiers and Categorization in Ancient Egypt" and "Typologie und Gebrauch der Ägyptischen Hieroglyphenschrift", as well as of the Golda Meir Fellowship Fund (Excellency Grant of the Hebrew University of Jerusalem). Prof. F. Junge, Prof. F. Kammerzell, and my colleagues in Göttingen were a constant source of enthusiastic support, judicious advice, and invaluable logistic help, and provided me with opportunities for which I shall always be grateful.

I am deeply grateful to Dr. Limme, Conservateur de la Section Egyptienne des Musées Royaux d'Art et d'Histoire, for smoothing the path of my research in the rich Antiquity Library of the Cinquentenaire Museum.

I am forever indebted to my teacher, Prof. Orly Goldwasser, for helping me in every possible way to realize my childhood dream and for sharing her advice, encouragement, enthusiasm, and profound insight into Egyptian linguistics and literature, socio-linguistics and semiotics; and I am deeply thankful for the illuminating dialogue with Prof. Ariel Shisha-Halevy whose directives and suggestions opened new horizons for me in structural linguistics.

But it would never have come to fruition without the understanding, patience, constant support, and love of my parents, David, my dear little Lou and Julian.

Il n'est rien sujet à plus continuelle agitation que les lois.
Montaigne, Essais, II, 12.

J'appris de Thémis les lois générales de l'univers, dont toutes les autres lois découlent.
J'appris que la justice, dont elle est gardienne, a pour fonction de maintenir l'équilibre entre les forces antagonistes qui animent tous les actes et toutes les créations.
J'appris que l'ordre n'est que faux ordre qui se fonde sur la contrainte.
Druon, Les mémoires de Zeus, I, Troisième époque.

Introduction

The present work is a study of the syntax and semantics of the Ramesside royal decrees legal register that have survived the test of time. Until now, scholars who have dedicated their attention to legal texts have been concerned mainly with translation and lexicographic analysis, or with a discussion of the legal mechanisms in comparison with modern legal institutions (e.g. Théodoridès, Harari), sometimes adding a syntactic analysis of isolated decrees (Kruchten 1981); but never was this material treated as a closed corpus (coherent, representing an *état de langue*) entitled to a comprehensive syntactical synchronic analysis, a specific period *genre-oriented grammar* (for partial listing and analysis of main legal-carrying constructions, see Lorton (1977) for criminal laws and Morschauser (1991) concerning threat-formulae). Moreover, previous studies never tried to enrich the comprehension of legal terminology through a systematic semantic research into the classifiers used in the legal lexicon.

Typologically, following Werlich (1975: 37), our corpus may be qualified as 'Instruktive Texte'; it forms a *normative genre* (public and written laws) with its specific authoritative/directive content, structures, formulas, stylistics and language. It thus represents a specific type of legal discourse as does modern legislation (Maley 1994: 14-16; Danet 1985: 275-277). Unfortunately, the mere mention of *wḏ*, *wḏ ni-swt*, *wḏ ḥm.f* or *iw wḏ.n ḥm.i/f* does not suffice to indicate that we are dealing with a normative decree. In fact, several types of texts may mention royal decrees[1]:

- *Königsnovelle* or autobiographies, for instance, may include among the royal deeds an order (*wḏ ḥm.f*) that the king gave; they do not belong to the

1 See Vernus (1990) for a distinction among authoritative writings based on fictive (divine, pseudoepigraphic and literary) and 'real' (private monuments, administrative archives, royal monuments and original) decrees. Vernus proposes to consider the *wḏ* as an Egyptian 'genre' that does not fit the ethnocentric definitions of modern researchers, but corresponds to 'un contenu' (authoritative statement) and 'une forme' (one may disagree on this point).

normative genre, show no legal register, the main communicative purpose of the text being other than that of a decree (the same is true for the epistolary decrees);

- a text may mention a (real or fictional) royal decree and add details about its content, without presenting them in the formulaic format original decrees must have had; although the genre of the text is not normative, it may be viewed as embedding a summarized normative text, thus belonging to another genre. But in this case, the register of the decree must be considered with suspicion and treated with caution: are the syntactic forms used to express its content the reflection of the embedding narrative or of the original decree? In the lists of decrees below dating from the Old Kingdom to the Ramesside Period, some texts have not been included since they belong to this problematic category;
- an isolated and brief mention of a king's order may constitute an enacting clause and thus a normative text. Although the Egyptian format of the clause (a perfect inherited from Old Egyptian, see *infra*) expresses a report of a royal order commemorating or awaiting its execution, it provides essential elements (authority, object, beneficiary, applicability conditions) that justifies our classifying it as a normative genre (the main communicative purpose of the text is to publish the decree) with a legal register. Furthermore, if normative documents are not, *a priori,* narrative texts, a certain 'narrative' flavour cannot be totally discarded for certain textemes composing them. As Bal (1997: 220) observes: 'Not everything 'is' narrative; but practically everything in culture has a narrative aspect to it, or at the very least, can be perceived, interpreted as narrative.';
- a text containing detailed dispositions of a decree in a format that appears to be extremely close to its original but that is preceded or followed by a totally different register (eulogy, for instance) endowing it with a politico-religious apparatus, must be considered normative. The main communicative purpose of the text is still the decree, with a propagandist value attached to it, the legal dispositions being expressed in the legal register. See *infra* under (g);
- finally, the decree may constitute an original document or its precise monumental copy, fully representative of the genre and composed in the legal register.

This issue must be examined in our corpus: the various textemes in play in the decrees are of a specific nature and must be studied with reference to modern narratology in order to relate them to the syntactic material covered.

Royal documents belonging to the epistolary genre have been added for the sake of comparison, being qualified as *wḏ ni-swt* (royal decree) in their opening formula and containing direct orders to officials (authoritative statements expressing a royal command, 'énoncé d'auctoritas,' not 'énoncé normatif,' see Vernus 1990: 239[2]). These

2 See also Menu (1990: 234) 'l'ordre royal, émission de volonté issue de l'autorité suprême, l'institution pharaonique étant expression terrestre de Maât'; Trapani (1992: 2-3 and 1993: 537-538).

are not normative acts but personal commands (private sphere) expressed by letters in another dialect, and they have no legal register.

The study is limited to the *legal register* of the decrees, excluding other registers (represented in the prologue, eulogy, cultic and historical parts) of the same texts that form an exterior propagandist apparatus, not exclusive to royal decrees. To identify the royal decrees' legal register, a simple test was conducted: the only dispositions selected for analysis were the norms whose main function was regulating relationships between people, as well as goods' and property's fate[3], even when reduced to a laconic enacting clause awaiting practical elaboration and execution (see the commission decrees).

Divine decrees are not included in the corpus as they constitute a separate genre.

I. The corpus

The corpus of texts under scrutiny consists of the following decrees[4]:

a. Normative genre

Specific protection/criminal law decrees[5]

1. **Nauri decree** (*Stẖy* I[6], Year 4);
2. **Hermopolis decree** (*Stẖy* I);
3. **Kanais/Wadi Abbad or Mia/Redesieh decree** (*Stẖy* I, Year 9);
4. **Armant decree** (*Rˁmss* II);
5. **Karnak decree** (*Stẖy* II);
6. **Elephantine decree** (*Rˁmss* III);

Specific endowment decrees

7. **Two Buhen decrees** (*Rˁmss* I, Year 2; *Stẖy* I, Year 1);
8. **Four West Silsileh decrees** (*Stẖy* I, *Rˁmss* II Year 1, *Mrnptḥ* Year 1 & *Rˁmss* III Year 6);
9. **Deir el-Medineh decree** (*Rˁmss* II, Year 9);
10. **Abydos decree** (*Rˁmss* II);
11. **Medamud decree** (*Rˁmss* III, Year 2);

3 Norms which answer to the 'two basic functions of law: the ordering of human relations and the restoration of social order when it breaks down' (Danet 1980: 449).

4 For a partial list, see Trapani (1992: 10 & 29 and 1993: 544) (on p. 537, the decrees are classified in two main categories: 'the administrative and the letter decrees').

5 The decrees are named, for convenience only, after the location of their known public record(s). They were obviously issued in the administrative unit of the royal palace.

6 From the 19th dynasty, the spelling *Stẖ* is adopted alongside the earlier *Stẖ* and *Stš* (*EG*, 460) for the god's name (*Wb* IV, 345); it is the orthography adopted here. Note that all Egyptian proper names are given in transliteration; the more popular vocalized and/or Greek form of the king's names appearing in our text are the following: Sethos or Seti for *Stẖy*; Ramesses for *Rˁmss*; Merneptah for *Mrnptḥ*.

12. **Medinet Habu decree** (*Rˁmss* III, Year 4);
13. **Three Karnak (Temple of Amun) decrees** (*Rˁmss* III, Years 6, 7, 16);
14. **Fayum/Herakleopolis decree** (*Rˁmss* III);
15. **Qantir decree** (*Rˁmss* III);

Specific commission decrees

16. **Brooklyn 69.116.1 and Fayum decrees** (*Sty̠* I, Years 1 & 2);
17. **East Silsileh decree** (*Sty̠* I, Year 6);
18. **Assuan decree** (*Sty̠* I, Year 9);
19. **BM 1665 decree** (*Sty̠* I);
20. **West Silsileh** (*Rˁmss* II, Years 33-34, 40, 42 & 45)**, Bigeh** (*Rˁmss* II, Years 36-37), **Armant** (*Rˁmss* II, Years 54, 57, 60, 63, 66?) and **El-Kab** (*Rˁmss* II, Year 57 & *Rˁmss* III, Year 30) **decrees**;
21. **Tanis decree** (*Rˁmss* II, "Year 400");
22. **Saqqara (*Wnis, D̠sr, Wsrk3f* Pyramids, *Špssk3f* Tomb), Abusir (*S3ḥwrˁ* Pyramid) & Abu Gorab (*Niwsrrˁ* Sun Temple) decree** (*Rˁmss* II);
23. **West Silsileh decree** (*Mrnptḥ*, Year 2);
24. **Medinet Habu & Deir el-Bahari decree** (*Mrnptḥ*, Years 2 & 3);
25. **Tod, Karnak, Edfu, Elephantine & El-Kab decree** (*Rˁmss* III, on basis of a Year 5 decree, Edfu being Year 15);
26. **Heliopolis decree** (*Rˁmss* III?, Year 15);
27. **El-Kab decree** (*Rˁmss* III, Year 29?);

b. Epistolary genre

Epistolary warning and instruction decrees

28. ***pAnastasi* IV. 10,8 – 11,8 decree** (*Sty̠* II);
29. ***pCairo ESP (B)* decree** (*Rˁmss* IX, Year 2);
30. ***pTurin* 1896 r° decree** (*Rˁmss* XI, Year 17).

The state of language revealed by these royal decrees spans about 220 years, a fact that may explain a certain lack of homogeneity in the corpus, besides variations in object, medium, intent or in original/copy character (engraved stone associated with propagandist records for most normative decrees, papyrus for the – model or real – epistolary decrees). The decrees mutual affinities or variances should be examined in the light of their thematic and chronological[7] repartition (bearing in mind that some peculiarities should be explained by a marked tendency towards archaism):

7 The following reign years are based on Baines & Málek (1981: 16-7).

19th dynasty:	*Rꜥmss* I (-1307-1305)	Year 2 *Buhen decree*
	Stḫy I (-1306-1290)	Year 1 *Buhen decree*
		Year 4 *Nauri decree*
		Year 9 *Kanais decree*
		Year 9 *Assuan decree*
		? *Hermopolis decree*
		? *West Silsileh decree*
	Rꜥmss II (-1290-1224)	Year 1 *West Silsileh decree*
		Year 9 *Deir el-Medineh decree*
		Years 33-34 *West Silsileh decree*
		Years 36-37 *Bigeh decree*
		Year 40 *West Silsileh decree*
		Year 42 *West Silsileh decree*
		Year 45 *West Silsileh decree*
		Year 54 *Armant decree*
		Year 57 *Armant decree*
		Year 57 *El-Kab decree*
		Year 60 *Armant decree*
		Year 63 *Armant decree*
		Year 66? *Armant decree*
		Year 400! *Tanis decree*
		? *Armant decree*
		? *Saqqara, Abusir, Abu Gorab decree*
		? *Abydos decree*
	Mrnptḥ (-1224-1214)	Year 1 *West Silsileh decree*
		Year 2 *West Silsileh decree*
		Years 2-3 *Medinet Habu & Deir el-Bahari decree*
	Stḫy II (-1214-1204)	? *Karnak decree*
		? *pAnastasi* IV.10,8-11,8
20th dynasty:	*Rꜥmss* III (-1194-1163)	Year 2 *Medamud decree*
		Year 4 *Medinet Habu decree*
		Year 5 basis *Tod, Karnak, Elephantine, Edfu* (Year 15) *& El-Kab decree*
		Year 6 *West Silsileh decree*
		Year 6 *Karnak decree*
		Year 7 *Karnak decree*
		Year 15 *Heliopolis decree*?
		Year 16 *Karnak decree*
		Year 29 *El-Kab decree*
		? *Elephantine decree*
		? *Fayum/Herakleopolis decree*
		? *Qantir decree*

Rˁmss IX (-1131-1112)	Year 2 *pCairo ESP (B)*
Rˁmss XI (-1100-1070)	Year 17 *pTurin 1896 r°*

Obviously, the state of language during the reigns of *Rˁmss* I and *Stẖy* I is closer to that of the language at the time of *Ḥrmḥb* (18th dynasty, -1319-1307; for his *Karnak decree* see Kruchten 1981) than during the reign of *Rˁmss* XI.

These decrees must also be examined from a diachronic perspective, their genre spanning Old, Middle, and New Kingdoms as well as the Late Period. The complete list of remaining royal decrees might be similar to the following:

a. Old Kingdom and First Intermediate Period

- dynasty 4, *Špssk3f* (Shepseskaf)*: Giza* endowment decree (Goedicke 1967: Abb. 1);
- dynasty 5, *Nfrỉrk3rˁ* (Neferirkare)*: Abydos* protection/criminal law decree (*Boston* 03.1896, Goedicke 1967: Abb. 2);
- dynasty 5, *Ỉssỉ* (Izezi)*:* 6 *Abusir* nomination decrees (*JE* 97348, Posener-Kriéger 1985: fig. A-F); 2 *Giza* tomb eulogy epistolary decrees to *Snḏmib* (*Urk.* I, 60 & 62); *Saqqara* tomb eulogy epistolary decree to *Rˁšpss* (*Urk.* I, 179); *Abusir* protection (?) decree (*Louvre E* 25416a v°, Posener-Kriéger & de Cenival 1968: pl. LXXII A, LVIII A and p. 23);
- dynasty 6, *Ttỉ* (Teti)*: Abydos* response to complaint/protection decree (*BM* 626, Goedicke 1967: Abb. 3);
- dynasty 6, *Ppy* I (Pepy I): *Coptos A* protection decree (*JE* 41890, Goedicke 1967: Abb. 4); *Dashur* protection decree (*Berlin* 17500, Goedicke 1967: Abb. 5);
- dynasty 6, *Mrnrˁ*? (Merenre): *Giza* endowment? decree (Goedicke 1967: Abb. 6);
- dynasty 6, *Ppy* II (Pepy II): *Abydos* endowment decree (Goedicke 1967: Abb. 7); *Dakhla* nomination decree (*IFAO* 3153, Pantalacci 1985: 247); *Assuan* tomb epistolary instruction decree to *Ḥrḫwf* (*Urk.* I, 128-131); *Coptos B, C & D* protection/criminal law decree (*JE* 41893; 41491; 43052 & *MMA* 14.7.10, Goedicke 1967: Abb. 8, 9 & 11); *Coptos G* protection? decree (*JE* 41892, Goedicke 1967: Abb. 10); *Giza* protection decree (Goedicke 1967: Abb. 12); 2 *Saqqara* fragmentary decrees (Goedicke 1967: Abb. 13 & 14);
- dynasty 6, ?: *Saqqara* protection decree (Goedicke 1967: Abb. 15);
- dynasty 8, *W3ḏk3rˁ*? (Wadjkare): *Coptos H* fragmentary decree (*MMA* 14.7.14, Goedicke 1967: Abb. 16);
- dynasty 8, *Nfrk3wḥr* (Neferkauhor): *Coptos L* epistolary upon stela instruction decree (*JE* 41895, Goedicke 1967: Abb. 17); *Coptos I, J, O, M, N, Q, S/T* nomination (notification) decrees (*JE* 43053; *MMA* 14.7.13; *MMA* 14.7.11; private collection; private collection; *MMA* 14.7.12; ?[8], see Goedicke 1967: Abb. 18-22, 24, 25); *Coptos K* foundation decree (Goedicke 1967: Abb. 27);

8 Goedicke does not mention its location.

- dynasty 9?, *Dmḏibtȝwy* (Demedjibtawy): *Coptos R* criminal law decree (*JE* 41894, Goedicke 1967: Abb. 28).

b. Middle Kingdom and Second Intermediate Period[9]

- dynasty 12, *Snwsrt* I (Sesostris or Senwosret I): *Abydos* epistolary upon stela decree to *Mnṯwḥtp* (*CG* 20539 II); *Sinuhe* B, 178-179 fiction epistolary decree of *Snwsrt* I in a document dating of *Ỉmnmḥȝt* III (Amenemhet III) reign (*pBerlin* 3022, Blackman 1932: 31-32);
- dynasty 12, *Snwsrt* III (Sesostris or Senwosret III): *Deir el-Bahari* endowment decree (Naville 1907: pl. XXIV); *pBerlin* 10071 epistolary decree to *Ḥrmsȝf*? (Kaplony-Heckel 1971: 33); epistolary upon stela instruction /eulogy decree to *Ỉiḫrnfrt* (*Berlin* 1204, Schäfer 1904: 70-71);
- dynasty 13, *Ḫwtȝwyrʿ Wgf* (Khutawyre Wegaf): *Abydos* protection/criminal law decree (*CG* 35256, Leahy 1989: 42);
- dynasty 13, *Sbkḥtp* II? (Sebekhotpe II): *pBrooklyn* 35.1446 epistolary instruction decrees to *ʿnḫw* (Hayes 1955: pl. V (B) & VI (C));
- dynasty 13, *Sbkḥtp* IV (Sebekhotpe IV): *Karnak* endowment decree (*JE* 51911, Helck 1969: 199-200);
- dynasty 17, *Nbḫprwrʿ Ỉntf* (Nubkheperre Inyotef): *Coptos* response to complaint/criminal law decree (*CG* 30770, Petrie 1896: pl. VIII);
- dynasty 17, *Rʿḥtp* (Rahotpe): bow dedication decree (*Moscow* I.1.a.1804, Berlev 1975-76: 32).
- dynasty 17, *Ỉʿḥḥtp* (Ahhotpe): *Dra Abu el-Naga* endowment/eulogy decree (*Cairo* without number, *Urk.* IV, 45-46).

c. New Kingdom (18th dynasty)[10]

- *Ỉʿḥms* (Ahmose): *8th Karnak pylon* endowment/eulogy decree (*CG* 34001, *Urk.* IV, 14-24);
- *Ḏḥwtyms* I (Tuthmosis I): *Wadi Halfa & Kuban* epistolary upon stela instruction decrees to *Twri* (*CG* 34006, *Buhen stela* 9 & *Berlin* 13725, *Urk.* IV, 79-81); *Sehel* commission decree (*Urk.* IV, 89-90);
- *Ḏḥwtyms* III (Tuthmosis III): *pBerlin* 3049, v° XVIII-XIX public health protection decree (Vernus 1979: pl. I); *North Karnak* endowment decree to *Snmwt*, corrected by *ȝḫnitn* (Helck 1960: 24-25 and 1975: 122-126); *Karnak Ptḥ* temple commission/publication/endowment decree (*CG* 34013, *Urk.* IV, 763-72); *Buto* endowment/eulogy decree (Klug 2002: 96-105); *Heliopolis* commission decree (*Berlin* 1634, *Urk.* IV, 832); *Karnak* publication/foundation ritual decree (*CG* 34012, *Urk.* IV, 833-8); *Sehel* commission decree (*Urk.* IV,

9 See Berlev (1975-76: 36-37) for further references. There might be yet another text to which Möller (1909:14) alludes as a law from Illahun, belonging to a papyrus lot dispersed between Berlin, Cairo and a private collection.

10 See Klug (2002) for royal stelae from *Ỉʿḥms* to *Ỉmnḥtp* III reigns.

814-5); *Buhen* commission/endowment decree (*BM EA* 1021, *CG* 34014, *Urk.* IV, 820-1); *Sai* commission decree (Klug 2002: 191-2);

- *Ỉmnḥtp* II (Amenophis II): *Semneh* epistolary upon stela instruction decree to *Wsrstt* (*Boston* 25.632, *Urk.* IV, 1343; Helck 1955: 23; Cumming 1982: 45-46); *West Karnak* 8th pylon eulogy/protection (?) decree (*Urk.* IV, 1319-21); *Elephantine* ritual/endowment decree (*Wien ÄS* 5909 & *CG* 34019, *Urk.* IV, 1287-99); *Turah* commission decree (*Urk.* IV, 1448);
- *Ḏḥwtyms* IV (Tuthmosis IV): *Nbimn* tomb n. 90 *Thebae* eulogy & protection decree (*Urk.* IV, 1618);
- *Ỉmnḥtp* III (Amenophis III): *Medinet Habu* 21st dynasty copy of his protection/criminal law decree (*BM* 138, Robichon & Varille 1936: 2-4; Varille 1968); two *Turah* commission decrees (*Urk.* IV, 1680-1);
- *Ꜣḫnitn* (Amenophis IV or Akhenaten): *Karnak* endowment decree (Saad & Manniche 1971: pl. XXI);
- *Twtꜥnḫimn* (Tutankhamun): *Upper Egypt?* taxation and endowment decree (*Liverpool E* 583, Amer 1985: 18);
- *Ḥrmḥb* (Haremhab): *Karnak* protection/criminal law decree (Kruchten 1981).

II. The framework; terminology

a. Structuralist syntactic analysis

The structuralist textual-analytic approach has been favored at the Hebrew University since H. J. Polotsky taught linguistics there (the Polotskyan Jerusalem School), and it is the reference framework adopted here (see Shisha-Halevy 1998: 10-12). As for the terminology used, some central concepts related to (socio-) linguistics have been too often misunderstood, and it is of crucial importance to define them properly (for an in-depth presentation of the ambiguity and problematic nature of some of these concepts, see Junge 1989). The definition of key words used to describe syntactic forms and constructions is to be found in Shisha-Halevy (1988 and 1998) and in his numerous books and articles on Egyptian, Coptic, and other languages. For the sake of clarity, a basic glossary is provided hereunder (see Shisha-Halevy 1988: 261-277):

- *actor*: 'noun or pronoun expressing the carrier-out of an active action, the undergoer of a passive action, or the one who is in a state ("grammatical subject")', e.g. <u>The postman</u> always rings twice;
- *adjunct/expansion/modifier/satellite*: optional or secondary structural element, extending or qualifying another (adnominal; adverbal; adnexal; ad-pattern), e.g. It's <u>always</u> <u>fair</u> weather;
- *adnexal*: 'verb form attaching a rhematic element to a clause or phrase', e.g. Some like it <u>hot</u>;

- *adnominal*: expansion or modifier of a nominal element, e.g. The man who knew too much;
- *aorist*: conjugation form expressing general, natural, or habitual atemporal action, e.g. Gentlemen prefer blondes;
- *augens*: reinforcer modifying a nominal form and containing a pronominal element referring (mostly back) to this nominal form, e.g. I myself;
- *converb*: verb form of adverbial status and function, e.g. Some came running;
- *deictic*: pointing out, indicating, e.g. This property is condemned;
- *delocutive*: pertaining to the 3rd person, e.g. She couldn't take it;
- *determinator*: 'marker of a noun with respect to specificity and definiteness', e.g. All the Vermeers in New York;
- *focus*: 'center or highlight of the communication stretch' (macrosyntactic information), e.g. It was only to see you that he came by;
- *interlocutive*: pertaining to the 1st - 2nd persons, e.g. You can't cheat an honest man;
- *locutive*: pertaining to the 1st persons, e.g. I hate actors;
- *marker*: formal characteristic, e.g. in Egyptian, the plural grapheme ııı for number;
- *marked:* 'term of an opposition that is positive with regard to the presence of a specific linguistic feature', e.g. un chien et une chienne, for gender;
- *nexus*: 'the special interdependence and link of theme and rheme' (microsyntactic, nominal, adverbial, verbal), e.g. My name is nobody;
- *nucleus*: grammatical center of a phrase that defines its paradigm, e.g. Lost angel;
- *quantifier*: marker of quantity or number in a noun phrase, e.g. Another 48 hours;
- *rheme*: structural constituent conveying the message about the theme (microsyntactic information), e.g. Where were you when the lights went out?;
- *texteme*: subtextual signaled and bounded unit presenting a distinctive system of grammar, e.g. dialogue, narrative, exposition, report;
- *theme*: structural constituent containing given or presupposed information (microsyntactic information), 'what is being discussed', e.g. Where were you when the lights went out?;
- *topic*: (con)textual information discussed (macrosyntactic, extraclausal information) that signals, maintains, and affirms textual thematic continuity and cohesion, and relates to the entire theme + rheme nexus, e.g. A good movie, that's entertainment.

b. Socio-linguistics analysis of register, genre and dialects

Concerning socio-linguistics aspects of language and literature, the basic definitions used in the present study are to be found in Even-Zohar (1990), Hasan (1973: 253-292), Bakhtin (1981), Gregory (1967: 177-198) and Goldwasser (1990 and 1999). Again for the sake of clarity, the definition of the main terms used is provided hereunder:

- *dialect*: variety of language, idiom;
- *diglossia*: 'use of two varieties of a language in the same speech community', one of them being regarded as superior to the other by the speakers (prestige associated with abundant written literature and higher education) (Ferguson 1964: 429);
- *genre:* recurrent textual form associated with a specific language, subject, style, communicative purpose (for example, the legislative genre). See Hodge & Kress (1988: 7); Bhatia (1993: 13-16) ('each genre is an instance of a successful achievement of a specific communicative purpose using conventionalized knowledge of linguistic and discoursal resources'); Jackson (1995: 90-92);
- *heteroglossia:* 'internal stratification of any single national language into social dialects, characteristic group behavior, professional jargons, generic languages, languages of generations and age groups, tendentious languages, languages of the authorities, of various circles and of passing fashions, languages that serve the specific sociopolitical purpose of the day, even of the hour', differentiated by various social pressures and contexts (Bakhtin 1981: 262-263);
- *idiolect:* variety of language, idiom associated with a specific individual, 'the individual who speaks and writes (…). The individual is, so to speak, the smallest dialect unit: each speaker has his own IDIOLECT.' (Halliday, McIntosh & Strevens 1964: 94-95);
- *register:* 'variety of language distinguished according to use (…). The crucial criteria of any given register are found in its grammar and lexis.' (Halliday, McIntosh & Strevens 1964: 87-88); for the factors correlating with a register (subject-matter, situation type, participant roles, mode and medium of discourse), see Hasan (1973: 271-272) and Goldwasser (1990: 212-214; 1991: 133). 'Written legal language may be considered a particular register of the "grapholect"' (Jackson 1995: 111);
- *repertoire:* 'aggregate of laws and elements (either single, bound, or total models) that govern the production of texts' (Even-Zohar 1990: 17); 'a combination of "grammar" and "lexicon" of a given "language"' formed of individual elements (morphemes, lexemes), syntagms and models ('combination of elements + rules + the syntagmatic ("temporal") relations imposable' on the text (*ibidem*, 39 & 41);
- *sociolect:* variety of language or idiom associated with a particular social class or status group (Hasan 1973: 255-258 'social dialect');
- *technical dialect:* variety of language or idiom associated with a particular profession or occupation;

- *temporal dialect:* variety of language or idiom isolated in terms of time (Gregory 1967: 180-182);
- *topolect:* variety of language or idiom associated with a specific geographical unit;
- *vernacular:* colloquial language ('Low dialect", see Hodge & Kress 1988: 87, 108; Goldwasser 1999), sometimes 'educated vernacular' and even 'standard or normative vernacular' (that underwent a process of canonization or legitimization by the dominant circles);
- *written as if spoken* (Hasan 1973: 280): 'texts that might be defined as those "attempted to be written as if spoken" could be the closest parallel to the term "spoken language" of modern linguistics' (Goldwasser (1990: 203-204), on the basis of Gregory (1967: 191) 'the speaking of what is written to be spoken as if not written').

c. Forensic discourse analysis

Legal texts are the object of interdisciplinary researches in philosophy (Austin's 1970 and his followers' Speech Act theory), sociology (sociolinguistics, ethnography of communication), literature (stylistics), cognitive psychology (conceptual analysis, psycholinguistics), semantics, pragmatics, and linguistics (text linguistics - texts typological research - and discourse analysis, the study of the legal discourse in a lexical, syntactic, pragmatical, rhetorical, prosodic and functional perspective); see Danet (1980: 453-470) and Bhatia (1993: 3-12). Forensic (legal genre) discourse analysis centered upon the modern legislative genre, as practiced first by Mellinkoff (1963), then by Bhatia (1993, 1994), Crystal & Davy (1969), Danet (1980, 1984, 1985, 1990), Charrow *et alii* (1982), Gunnarsson (1984), Gustafsson (1984), Jackson (1995), Kurzon (1984, 1986), Maley (1994) *inter alii*, is of prime importance in establishing whether there are constants in legal registers of various cultures and times and a transcendent legal repertoire in terms of geography and time. See also David (2004).

d. Narratologic analysis

As for narratologic concerns, our attempt to qualify the textemes in play in the royal decrees is based on Mieke Bal's seminal work (1997) as well as various concepts and definitions borrowed mainly from structuralist studies. This identification has never been precisely made in legal Egyptian texts, although it will prove to be a useful instrument in the comprehension of the structure and the syntactic strategy of the forensic discourse. The following terminology has been used (see Prince 1987):

- *alethic modality:* qualification of a statement by a possibility, impossibility or necessity modal operator, e.g. You <u>can't</u> win them all;

- *catalysis:* 'A satellite; a free motif; (...) not logically essential to the narrative action' (Prince 1987: 11), e.g. in the story of a trial for murder, a digression about the courtroom's architectural history;
- *deontic modality:* qualification of a statement by a permission, prohibition or obligation modal operator, e.g. You may sleep on the sofa, if you want;
- *external focalization:* 'A type of focalization or point of view whereby the information conveyed is mostly limited to what the characters do and say and there is never any direct indication of what they think or feel.' (Prince 1987: 29), e.g. The soldier went to town, entered a bar, sat on a chair and asked for a drink. The barman brought him a full glass of whiskey. The soldier drank, paid, and left;
- *isotopy:* 'The repetition of semiotic features that institutes the coherence of a text. (...) In its more restricted acceptation, (...) the repetition of semantic units in a text (...). In its broadest sense, (...) the repetition of units at any and all textual levels (phonetic, stylistic, rhetorical, syntactic, prosodic, etc.).' (Prince 1987: 47), e.g. 'Everybody was beautifully dressed. John and Mary were led to a magnificent table in the middle of a splendidly decorated room and were offered champagne' or Signed, sealed, delivered, I am yours;
- *tag clause:* 'A clause (...) accompanying a character's discourse (...) and specifying the act of the speaker or thinker, identifying him or her, and (sometimes) indicating various aspects of the act, the character, the setting in which they appear, etc.' (Prince 1987: 95), e.g. He said that he was on the verge of a significant breakthrough;
- *tagged direct discourse:* 'A direct discourse accompanied by a tag clause.' (Prince 1987: 96), e.g. – Are you coming tonight? she asked full of hope.

e. Neo-Egyptian registers

The classification of Neo-Egyptian texts as 'literary' or 'administrative' (based on the syntactic forms from which the language they represent is built) used by Černý and Groll (*LEG*)[11] was not adopted in this study, as it presents numerous conceptual difficulties.

First of all, each text may contain several segments representing different registers; secondly, the terminology used confuses genre and dialects, as a text written in a 'literary' language is not always a 'literary' piece (see most royal decrees), and the 'administrative' language is not always used in administrative documents (see the *Wenamun* controversy[12]); moreover, several texts are composed of elements belonging to both languages, but in various dosages or 'stages' of development. Although the concepts of 'literary' and 'non-literary' texts have not been unanimously adopted, Groll's (1975) seminal article distinguishing the Neo-Egyptian verbal formations ('pure

11 See Goldwasser (1990) on this issue.

12 See for instance Scheepers (1992); Satzinger (1997); Goldwasser (1999: 17-8); Baines (1999).

Middle Egyptian', 'specific literary Late Egyptian' and 'non-literary') has paved the way for the analysis by various scholars of Neo-Egyptian diglossia. Following Vernus (1979), Winand (1992)[13] has proposed a model of three 'registres d'expression' ('néo-égyptien partiel', 'mixte' and 'complet'), based on morphologic and orthographic signifiers, on an axis between the 'égyptien de tradition' (an artificial language based on Middle Egyptian) and the 'néo-égyptien' (the diachronic 'written as if spoken' language). This model constitutes the basis of our attempt to find an instrument of analysis applicable to any text written between the 18th and the 20th dynasty, whatever its genre, registers, purpose, medium, and script. We have adapted it and it has been divided into four degrees of basic changes vis-à-vis the 'classical' language of Middle Egyptian (degree 0) represented by its two central prototypes, the tale of *Sinuhe* and the *Coffin Texts* (note that the same dialect is represented by central members belonging to different genres). Each degree is associated with syntactic, lexicographic, morphologic, and/or orthographic criteria; the model may be further refined by dividing each degree into sub-degrees corresponding to more specific precisions. Within a limited time/genre corpus, the model must be applied to each register composing the texts (each register within a text may attain another degree of Neo-Egyptian, which means that a text may include several degrees of Neo-Egyptian).

Our Neo-Egyptian text analysis model for distinguishing dialectal features:

a. **degree 0**: syntactic, lexicographic, morphologic, and orthographic forms present in Middle Egyptian 'classical dialect' (reference: *Sinuhe, CT*) [conservatism];
b. **degree 1**: lexicographic, morphologic, and orthographic variance from the degree 0 introduced during the New Kingdom [adaptation];
c. **degree 2**: degree 0 forms + degree 1 adaptations + some new (sometimes transitory[14]) syntactic forms [innovation];
d. **degree 3**: very few degree 0 forms (with degree 1 adaptations) + maximum new, finalized syntactic forms composing a different system, probably closest to the vernacular of the period during which the text under consideration was composed (reference: *Wenamun*) [autonomy].

Degree 3 was not reached in our corpus, as we shall see. The decrees various textemes have been examined and presented in the following chapters so as to distinguish 'Neo-Egyptian characteristics' (degree 1, 2, or 3 features), ''classical' degree 0 forms used' (Middle Egyptian forms), and 'general dialectal features' summarizing the results of the two preceding kinds of forms by assigning a degree of Neo-Egyptian nature to the entire texteme (for example, in the case of a texteme constituted by some Middle Egyptian constructions, morphologic New Kingdom

---

13 See Junge (1996: 22, rem.).

14 Forms that will disappear from Neo-Egyptian written texts and be replaced by other forms. For instance: the *ḥnᶜ ntf sḏm* form of conjunctive disappears totally by the 19th dynasty (*Mrnptḥ*), replaced by *mtw.f sḏm* (see Gardiner 1928; Winand 1992: 466-8 and table p. 473).

adaptations of Middle Egyptian forms and a few new Neo-Egyptian forms, the texteme would be qualified as degree 2 Neo-Egyptian in the general dialectal features rubric).

Note that the progression from degree 0 to 3 is not simply a matter of time, but of genre and register also. The use of specific forms belonging to a particular degree is conditioned by the texts purpose and corresponds to a deliberate strategy (see Goldwasser 1990, 1991, 1999; Jansen-Winkeln 1995). The language of any Neo-Egyptian text is the result of a skilful blend of ancient and new, prestigious and expressive, conservative and dynamic modes of expression.

f. Semiotics, cognitive linguistics, and categorization

The theoretical framework of the script classifiers study (the old-fashioned terminology 'determinatives' does not reflect their classificatory function) is provided by Rosch (1978), her school (Lakoff 1986; Taylor 1989), and Goldwasser (1995, 1999b, 2002, pioneering studies of the categorization system of Egyptian script). It may not be superfluous to resume the theoretical context of this research, already delineated in a previous study of the [INFERIORITY-PERTURBATION] category (David 2000: 31-33). Classifiers in the hieroglyphic system represent iconic elements having no phonetic value, but assigning lexemes to semantic classes (the hieroglyphic script has other pictograms associated with other values and reading strategies: phonograms or paronomasia devices, logograms or word-signs, and repeaters[15] constituting pictorial tautologies). Classifiers may stand in a taxonomic relation with the lexeme (hierarchical set-inclusion in a superordinate - basic level - subordinate type of system), a schematic - metonymic - contiguity relation (of the part/whole; stuff/object; container/contained type) or metaphoric/alternative or even ad hoc relation (based on the comparison of a less prototypical member of the newly created ad hoc category to one of its prototypical members) (see Goldwasser 2002: 10-35). Thus hieroglyphic classifiers reflect a system of knowledge-organization and their icons represent the 'politically correct' (reflecting dominant class ideology), conventional 'prototype elect' mental images for the category they represent (Goldwasser 2002). In Rosch's cognitive linguistics theory, a system of categorization is conceived to provide 'maximum information with least cognitive effort' (principle of cognitive economy) so that 'the perceived world comes as a structured information' (principle of anthropocentricality) in a precise space/time context (Rosch 1978: 28). In each category, members show various degrees of membership, certain members representing prototypes (best members/examples and cognitive reference points), usually not unique. Most abstract domain superordinate categories have no clear-cut boundaries and their members may entertain several types of relations with the classifier that represents them (see for instance the 'bad bird' in David 2000); their complexity justifies also the presence of more than one classifier that refers to several categories. A semantically complex lexeme usually belongs concomitantly to several categories (double or even quadruple classification).

---

15 Goldwasser, forthcoming.

g. Legal norms and terminology

Before scrutinizing the chosen corpus, the issue must be raised of the nature of the royal decrees; genuine *legal* documents or merely expressions of an ideological intent (on this issue, see Vernus 1983: 78 and 1990). Most of them were engraved upon strategically placed stelae or public parts of monuments in a richly adorned form, preceded by the eulogy[16] of the reigning king and a pictorial scene with religious significance. Commission decrees are usually no more than a mention of a royal command, a commemorative note of a past order (the enacting clause) and its execution[17]. In this case, one may argue that there is no real legal register to study, that no Ramesside public law texts have escaped the ravages of time. In fact, we may not possess original texts of law (probably papyrus or leather decrees filed in the royal administration as well as in the temple archives), but rather copies[18] of those texts introduced and followed by literary formulas or mentions of the royal order intended to present the king's positive actions to restore or follow Maat. Nevertheless, if we examine the legal dispositions, we might observe a substance and organization very close to the original legal norm[19].

Finally, an important remark must be made when dealing with lexis and ancient institutions that we might be tempted to compare with our own legal mechanisms and terminology. As Menu (1990: 235) puts it: 'Il n'est pas certain (...) que le vocabulaire du droit européen soit apte à définir les catégories et concepts juridiques de l'ancienne Egypte.' (see our discussion of *wḏ*, *hp*, requisitions, etc.). For Théodoridès (1971: 291), Egyptian legal documents make use of 'only a few technical terms, and even these had several applications and were frequently imprecise.' (polysemic lexemes belonging to several linguistic sub-ensembles). Although their imprecision may be the result of our ignorance, non-legal-specific lexemes indeed represent the vast majority of terms used in legal texts to qualify legal mechanisms and tools.

---

16 See Posener (1956: 18); Bleiberg (1985-86: 9) 'If propagandistic texts were used as scripts for public readings, they must have been easily accessible to people.' The question remains whether the public was able to read them or they had to be read aloud in public, but they still belong to the category of 'written to be spoken' texts (Gregory 1967: 192-3), a common feature with the liturgical genre. Compare for the Old Kingdom with Goedicke (1964: 37 and 1967: 6); for the publication of a private law document during the 17th dynasty, see Lacau (1949: 2-3) (*Stèle juridique de Karnak*).

17 Brevity is not a serious argument, some modern laws showing but very few and brief articles, sometimes meant to be enforced and detailed by more extensive dispositions.

18 See *LÄ* VI, 380.

19 See also Kruchten (1981: 216-218), about *Ḥrmḥb*'s 18th dynasty decree; Grandet (1994 II: 31).

As a brief but explicit introduction to the material covered by our corpus, the following excerpt from *Rꜥmss* III (20th dynasty) posthumous panegyric, *pHarris* I, summarizes various domains covered by the Ramesside decrees: posting and protection of temple personnel and propriety against abusive requisitions, endowments, public work commissions, renewal of rituals and survey/inspection of temples. Note that all the translations in this work are ours, unless otherwise indicated.

> (59,8) *ỉry.i ꜣḫw ꜥšꜣt m Kmt wrt m-bꜣḥ ỉt.i Ḥr-ḫnty-ẖty ỉry.i smꜣwt ỉnbw n ḥwt-nṯr.f ḳd ỉrw m mꜣwt* (59,9) *ꜣꜥꜥ nḳꜥ ḳ(ꜣ)b(.ỉ) n.f ḥtpw nṯr m ỉmnyt n ḥr.f mryt r-tnw dwꜣwt mst.ỉn.f ỉnw m ḥmw ḥmwt ḥḏ nbw sšr nỉ-swt šmꜥ nfr nḥḥ* (59,10) *snṯri bỉt ỉꜣw rnnw ỉry.i n.f mnmnt m mꜣwt m ỉꜣwt ꜥšꜣt r smꜣꜥw n kꜣw.f pꜣ sr wr ḥn.i pr.f špsy ḥr mw tꜣ ỉrw* (59,11) *m wḏwt ꜥꜣyw ḥr rn.f r nḥḥ dỉw.i ḥmw-nṯr rwḏw n pr.f ḥr ḏrt.w r sḥnt smdt.f r ḫrpw r pr.f rwy.i ṯꜣty ꜥḳt* (59,12) *m-ẖnw.w nḥmw.i rmṯ.f nb wn m-ꜥ.f dỉw.i sw mi rw-prww ꜥꜣyw m tꜣ pn ḫwyw mkw r nḥḥ ẖry ḏdwt ỉn.i rmṯ.f nb* (60,1) *wnw ḫnry m-ꜥ rmṯ nb rwḏ nb dỉw r ỉr ḥnty.sn m pr.f špsy*
>
> *pHarris* I 59,8-60,1 (hieroglyphic text from Erichsen 1933: 69)

(59,8) I have made a multitude of beneficial actions in *Kmt wrt*, in front of my father *Ḥr-ḫnty-ẖty*; I have done renovations of his temple walls, rebuilt, made anew (59,9), ornamented (and) engraved; I have doubled for him divine offerings, as daily offerings, for his beloved face, each morning; I have brought him presents consisting of male (and) female servants, silver, gold, royal linen, good fabric, oil, (59,10) incense, honey, cattle (and) youngs (of their species); I have made for him anew a large cattle to present for his sustenance, this Great Magistrate; I have equipped his august temple on water (and) land, made (59,11) by (= in execution of) long decrees with (= bearing) his name forever; I have let prophets (and) agents for his temple with their (free/own) handling to command its personnel, to control his temple; I have impeached (the) vizier to enter (59,12) into (= to dispose of) them; I have withdrawn all of its people who had been in his (the vizier's) possession; I have made it like (the) great temples in this land, retained (and) preserved forever under what has been instructed; I have brought (back) all of its people (60,1) who had been restrained in (the) possession of any person, any agent, placed to execute their service in his august temple.

1. Specific protection/criminal law decrees

I. *Nauri decree*

Some royal decrees are public laws designed to prevent and punish criminal behavior (mainly on the part of the administration), to settle conflicts of authority (protecting an institution's property and staff[1] by forbidding 'le détournement entre administrations rivales' - civilian, military and the temple's[2] -, abusive practices and arbitrary 'requisitions'[3]). In fact, they constitute administrative law dispositions determining the competence of specific services and state employees and regulating cases of incompetence *ratione materiae* by prohibiting state servants from exceeding their powers by using ('rerouting') reserved resources (usually not to serve a private interest, but to ensure the functioning of their service) by enticing temple staff away from their service or displacing temple goods from their original allocation. Such interventions by the central authority have been known in Ancient Egypt since the Old Kingdom[4] and

1 An early case of legal personality (*LÄ* I: 1039; Théodoridès 1971: 294; Harari 1990: 226)? It may not include notions such as 'immunity' or 'exemption', because the document prohibits specific practices but does not reveal anything about the duties of the temple (an issue beyond its scope). We might have a case of 'exemption' from civil/military administrative branch interference, but not from general taxation, the 'atélie', of goods, lands or services, for instance; see Warburton (1997: 193) and Haring (1997: 18); compare with Old Kingdom decrees, especially *Dashur Ppy* I decree in Goedicke (1967: Abb. 5 and 244-247) and in Théodoridès (1982). It is worth mentioning that the king is still responsible for the temple's foundation and the decree endowing the temple with some privileges, and that it is his own cult that is essentially protected; for Kemp (1972: 659) 'the person ultimately responsible for the management of temple economic affairs is the vizier, at least in Upper Egypt'. For the complex relationships between central administration and the temples, see Haring (1997: 380-383, 392-396). See also *LÄ* I: 1040-41; Trapani (1993: 538, 543-544); Spalinger (1991: 26, 29-30); *LÄ* III: 151-152; Harari (1950: 23-24, 28, 1987: 96 and 1985: 226); Edgerton (1947: 219, 230); *LÄ* VI: 379-381; Gardiner (1948b: 202 & 1952: 32); Otto (1968: 56); Lorton (1977: 25-27); Helck & Otto (1970: 84-85).

2 For Kruchten (1981: 207 and 1979: 523-525), 'pénurie de main-d'œuvre' explaining the need for decrees protecting the temple's personnel against 'débauchage' or 'détournement au profit des domaines rivaux'. But 'Le temple égyptien n'est pas autonome, car sa structure doit représenter le pharaon, qui reste le seul prêtre autorisé, confirme chaque nouvelle nomination sacerdotale et contrôle, en dernière analyse, l'utilisation des biens du temple. Le temple n'est qu'une branche de l'administration' (Donadoni 1993: 310). See also De Buck (1942: 577); Menu (1971: 569); Spalinger (1991 : 33) notes that the protection is organized against state officials, not the temple's or other temple's personnel, but this must be moderated when general formulations such as 'anybody' are used, or in the case of the *Hermopolis* and *Karnak decrees*.

3 Théodoridès (1981: 642, n. 60) speaks of 'abus de droit de coercition, ou de réquisition, commis par des fonctionnaires' (about *Ḥrmḥb*'s decree); the qualification of the text proposed by Davies (1997: 277) as a series of measures 'to prevent corruption within the civil administration' is too hasty (see *infra*). Note Menu's (1981: 60) qualification of this type of decree as 'documents de nature *administrative*', sanctioning 'des délits d'ordre économique'.

4 See for instance 5th dynasty *Nfrirkꜣrꜥ*'s *Abydos decree* for the protection of the prophets and personnel of the nome temples.

they are 'specific' regulations because they are not intended to protect all the temples in the country but only specific sanctuaries[5]. Among Ramesside examples of such decrees that have survived, the *Nauri decree* (*KRI* I, 45-58 n.24 and corrigenda I, 416 n.180[6]; prior text edition: Sander-Hansen 1933: 13-24) is the most complete document of its kind in our possession[7]. It dates from the fourth year of *Stẖy* I's reign (19th dynasty, *c.* 1302/1291 B.C.[8]) and concerns the personnel and property of *Stẖy*'s Abydos funerary temple[9]. It was issued in Memphis (line 29), carved on a hill 'in full view of anyone traveling in the region', 'intended for future bureaucrats' serving in Nubia (Spalinger 1991: 31)[10]. Its study complements the material found in other Ramesside royal decrees (of *Hermopolis, Elephantine, Karnak*, and *Armant*, for example) as well as in its famous predecessor, *Ḥrmḥb*'s decree, a few decades before[11]. For Groll (1987: 154-166), the *Nauri* and *Kanais decrees* (see *infra*) are representative of a 'Kūbban dialect' (although the decree of which the *Nauri* inscription is an elaborate copy was probably drafted in Memphis).

I.1 Composition[12]

The text is a continuum without section/paragraph markers[13], as is customary in ancient legal texts (Maley 1994: 24):

a. Pictorial scene
b. Pre-material (identificative and backgrounding aetiologic texteme):

---

5 Seidl (1951: 21); Helck & Otto (1970: 84); in Bedell's opinion (1973: 18), 'Although these decrees were restricted to a particular area and a certain group of people, in the New Kingdom they showed a great similarity which could almost be called standardization.' Nevertheless, the isolated examples of 5th dynasty *Nfrirkȝrʿ*'s *Abydos decree* and 9th (?) dynasty *Dmḏibtȝwy Coptos R decree* cover a larger territorial area (all the nome temples for the first and Upper Egypt for the second); *Ḥrmḥb*'s *Karnak decree* (18th dynasty) is apparently the sole decree to survive that concerns the entire Egyptian territory, protecting any individual in the situation it describes (see Kruchten 1981: 209-210, 225). See also the remarks made *infra* about *Rʿmss* III *Elephantine decree*.

6 Following Helck (1973: 212-214).

7 Roeder (1960: 295) 'Die Inschrift dieses Denksteins ist eine der gröβten literarischen Kompositionen, die in hieroglyphischen Inschriften erhalten geblieben sind.' (although inserted in a 'literary' frame, the decree's main dispositions cannot be qualified as a 'literary composition', see *infra*).

8 *RITANC* I: § 95, p. 52 and Kitchen (1979: 454, note 17).

9 See Griffith (1927: 205-6) about the identity of the temple concerned. *Contra*: *RITANC* I: § 96, p. 53.

10 Kemp (1989: 238) 'the Nauri version was only one copy' of the decree in an administrative system of 'decision-petition of complaint-redress'.

11 Following Baines & Málek's chronology (1981: 16-17), about 15 years at most before; for Kruchten (1981: 64 & n.183), about forty years before (based on Drioton & Vandier's computation).

12 For the structure of modern statutes, see, for instance, Maley (1994: 19): 'pre-material' with 'long title, year and number, short title [optional], preamble [optional] and an enacting formula'; then the 'body of the statute' 'divided into numbered sections, subsections and paragraphs' with optional 'larger units' such as definitions, substantive and procedural parts, in an invariable sequence.

13 Although recurrent enacting clauses and preambles *sensu stricto* act as section dividers (see *infra*).

b.1 **date** (line 1): the decree is precisely dated, as would any modern legal document. The date format is based on the classical model[14] in use, and it is placed at the beginning of the decree pre-material.

b.2 **authority**: the king's titulary (lines 1-2). The exact formula used is # *ḫr ḥm n* + king's titulary # (under the majesty of the king), as in other Second Intermediate Period and New Kingdom decrees (17th dynasty *Nbḫprwrꜥ Ỉntf Coptos*, 18th dynasty most of *Ḏḥwtyms* III decrees, *Ỉmnḥtp* III *Medinet Habu* (21st dynasty copy) and *Twtꜥnḫimn Upper Egypt (?) decrees*). Old Kingdom decrees are apparently always introduced by the formula # king's Horus name + *wḏ ni-swt* + addressee(s) # (which remains in use as late as the 18th dynasty, but has disappeared, for instance, in the decree noted in *Nbỉmn*'s tomb, under *Ḏḥwtyms* III's reign). This formula is perhaps still in use in all 18th – 20th dynasties original normative decrees (papyrus or leather acts kept in administrative archives), but, unfortunately, no example of these has been discovered. The lexeme *ḥm* is already in use in the body of the 5th dynasty *Giza decree* of king *Ỉssi*.

b.3. **eulogizing aetiologic/narrative background** (lines 2-29): general preamble[15] of the decree, with a 'sacralisant' purpose, also mentioning the main concerns of the legal provisions (the Abydos temple and its property, cattle, service of priests, prophets, slaves, herdsmen and fleet to be protected) and the establishment of a cadastre register[16] (line 24). Mention is also made of a decree (reference to *Nauri's decree* as Kitchen[17] believes it?[18]) in lines 25-27, enforced throughout the country, the purpose of which is to protect the temple's personnel and property, wherever it is, from any interference (not only from Nubian intervention):

---

14 *EG*, 203.

15 For Vernus (1990: 243), this composition respects the original decree but inserts it in an ideological apparatus. Compare with the situation during the Old Kingdom, when lapidary versions of decrees appear to be limited to the original dispositions and to respect the archived text layout, free of eulogy pre-material, and generally addressed to specific individuals, as in epistolary rescripts (Goedicke 1964: 33 *et passim*). See also, for instance, 17th dynasty, *Nbḫprwrꜥ Ỉntf*'s *Coptos decree* which represents the copy upon stela of an epistolary answer to the complaint of the temple priestly staff, specifying criminal dispositions against offenders and any king or official asking the criminal's pardon. No such 'criminal law' epistolary decree has yet been discovered for the Ramesside Period.

16 Where any transmission act is registered; see Pirenne (1934: 243); Spalinger (1991: 32); Warburton (1997: 167 & 190).

17 *RITANC* I: § 93, p. 50.

18 It could also be a reference to a previous and more general legal text to be executed by the current decree or of which the *Nauri decree* is a monumental copy placed in a specific region as a means of publication or reminder. Gardiner (1952: 32) notes: 'The passage just quoted perhaps does not refer directly to the Nauri decree, since that deals only with the Nubian possessions of the Abydos temple, but it undoubtedly defines the thought underlying any charter of the kind.' We cannot completely adhere to his opinion, as it is stated (lines 30-32, for instance) that the scope of the decree consists of the whole territory of Egypt, as well as any property or personnel belonging to the temple, wherever it is (see also *LÄ* I, 1040).

(25) (…) *i͗r.w w{ꜣ}ḏt ḥnt* (26) *mrt.s ḫt ṯsw šmꜥw mḥw rmṯ.s nb ḫwy mky mi͗ smnw ḥr wḏbw n ꜣbb.sn ḥnt.sn nbt mꜣꜥ* [*n*] *kꜣ.f ḥr spꜣt wrt mr.n.f nn thmw.tw.w i͗n kꜣwy nn wn tht.tw r.sn* (27) *m sꜣ* [*n sꜣ s*]*mn ḥr ḥn.sn r ḏrw ḥnty nḥḥ*

(25) (…) (The/a) decree has been made/drawn up (or shall be executed) posting (26) its (*ḥwt:* the temple's) farming corvée subjects[19] throughout (the) districts[20] of Upper and Lower Egypt, so that all its people are retained (and) preserved, like geese on river-banks of which they are fond, when all their services are offered [to] his *kꜣ*[21] in (the) great nome that he (always) had loved. They ought not to be interfered with by others, nor shall be ones transgression against them, (27) from son [to son][22], when/since confirmed in their service to (the) ultimate limits of eternity[23].

* Neo-Egyptian characteristics:

- *i͗r.w w{ꜣ}ḏt:* an independent (formally marked as syntactically autonomous, not preceded by a linking marker, see Shisha-Halevy 1988: 268), in a delocutive context, passive and affirmative *sḏmw*.N form. It follows a series of *sḏm.n.f* narrative forms (the actor being the king) of the narrative eulogizing and aetiologic background texteme, and although a passive independent prospective is syntactically and semantically acceptable (that could justify the notion of execution and be in tune with the following modal prospective and existential compound), a Neo-Egyptian passive 'perfect' (with undetermined nominal actor that avoids the naming of the decree's 'author', for centrality is now granted to the act itself, see *infra*) corresponds better to the context (see the king's declaration following in line 27, assuming that he has already organized the protection of the temple's personnel). The spelling is consistent with the 19th-20th dynasties usage (*i͗rw*.N in *BM* 10052, 1, 13; *BM* 10383, 1, 4; *BM* 10403, 3, 10; *pLeopold-Amherst*, 3, 19; Winand 1992: § 476, 478). The 'perfect' is a

19 *mrt*: for Moret (1912: 77) 'agents d'exploitation des domaines immunitaires' (already in *Ppy* I's *Coptos A decree*); Korostovtsev (1947: 169) 'esclaves des propriétés sacrées'; Goedicke (1967: 30) and Hafemann (1985: 7) 'Hörige'; Théodoridès (1982: 82-86) 'occupants des terres du temple', and they are free; Lorton (1995: 351) 'tenants on nonroyal lands, perhaps including usufruct lands'; Haring (1997: 49-50) 'personnel of low status in general'; Moreno Garcia (1998 and 1999: 268) 'Egyptiens qui effectuaient leur prestation périodique en travail pour l'Etat, et qui étaient recrutés dans les villages proches à l'endroit où ils prêtaient leurs services' (temporary work), and remaining in the same status during the New Kingdom (1998: 79-80).

20 For Théodoridès (1962: 60 n. 49), *ṯsw* is to be understood as '« personnel » d'un domaine (…) synonyme de *rmṯ* (…) ; ailleurs, *smdt* est employé avec le même sens, dans le même *Décret de Nauri* (l. 38)'.

21 *LÄ* I, 1040: these services are devoted to Osiris' *kꜣ*, which means to the temple.

22 Théodoridès (1964: 53-54); Helck (1974: 126 (g)); Berlev (1975-76: 38-39) 'formule héréditaire'. The formula is already in use in Old Kingdom decrees (6th dynasty *Ppy* II *Coptos D* and 9th (?) dynasty *Dmḏibtꜣwy Coptos R decrees*); the *Coptos D decree* may present the ancestor of the decree's object description (*i͗w wḏ.n* king *ḫwt m*[*kt*] foundation *ḥnꜥ mrt nb* […] *ḫr* […] *nb ḥ*[*n*]*ꜥ sꜣ* [*n*] *sꜣ nb*).

23 The position adopted by Gardiner (1923: 6) about translation is the one followed in the present study: 'I have, with few exceptions, preferred to be literal at all hazards, and if the result be inelegant, I would point out that my purpose has been linguistic and psychological, rather than aesthetic.'

report time in narrative context in Neo-Egyptian (rctrospective discourse); but its passive form is limited in Neo-Egyptian: Frandsen (1974: § 17) notes that 'In L.E. the perfect passive *sḏm.f* is found exclusively in judicial texts (...) as vestiges of an older usage, in a manner analogous to modern officialese.' (same remark in Junge 1996: 161-2, who coins the *sḏm.f* 'Präteritum', 'eine neutrals Kennzeichnung für Aussagen über die Vergangenheit', translated as a perfect, or even as an 'Imperfekt/Erzähltempus'). For Warburton (1997: 191, n. 575), *ir.tw* has to be restored. The form marks a ceasure with the two preceding independent *iry.n.f* (lines 24 and 25, the king being the actor), with the change of diathesis, and with the following locutive passage; it introduces the whole legal content of the decree, the actor of the form being the central *w{ꜣ}ḏt*. The use of the passive voice pervades the legal register in our corpus, as it does in modern forensic discourse, often without an expressed agent, see Charrow (1982: 182-183) for bureaucratic language; Charrow, Crandall & Charrow (1982: 176-177); Finegan (1982: 118-119) in modern wills; Danet (1985: 283); Jackson (1995: 119).

- *w{ꜣ}ḏ:* spelling probably due to a phonetic 'confusion' (quite common in the later New Kingdom, as stated in *RITANC* I, § 9, p.5). In fact, this spelling already appears in *Iꜥḥḥtp*'s 17th dynasty decree.
- *thmw.tw.w:* the sole syntactic element surely Neo-Egyptian in this passage of the decree, the delocutive plural suffixed actor *w* in *thmw.tw.w*.

* 'Classical' degree 0 forms used:

- *ẖwy mky*: stative doublet ('binomial', see *infra*), rheme of a dependent adverbial nexus with purpose/consequence nuance.
- *ḥr wḏbw n ꜣbb.sn* is 'classical' Middle Egyptian: adverbial adjunct # preposition + ø noun + [*n* (relational expansion marker) + abstract, atemporal, nominal and geminating, 'non-emphatic' synthetic relative *sḏm.f*] relational (type qualification) noun phrase #. See *pWestcar*, 21: *wnm.k špssw n didi ni-swt, ḏfꜣw n wnmw šmsw.f* ("you shall eat rich food of (the kind) the king gives, provisions of (the kind) his suite eats"). The noun is the object of the verbal (pronominal actor) form in nominal function. Concerning the terminology used instead of the Greco-Latin-centric 'genitive' in a context ignoring *casi*, see Sisha-Halevy (1986: 18 and note 17). Compare with the following.
- *mr.n.f:* 'classical' Middle Egyptian synthetic past relative *sḏm.n.f* form with pronominal actor (and a noun antecedent followed by its adjectival modifier) in an adverbial adjunct. Kitchen (*KRI* 24, p. 43), Gardiner (1952: 32) and Ford (1995: 62) translate it as a present, and only Griffith (1927: 199) as a past expression. It may be a habituative form ("that he always loved"), due to the verb's semantics, as viewed in *EG* § 389.3 (*mri* to love 'implying continuity' but sometimes equivalent to 'wish' 'as definite occurrences resulting from 'having (...) conceived a wish'. So even in reference to the present'), see also Polotsky (1965: 2) and Vernus (1997: 69). But it is also possible to understand it as expressing anteriority, especially when applied to Osiris' *kꜣ* (death connotation).

- *nn thmw.tw.w:* 'predicative negative' *nn* (which is also a macrosyntactic marker of independent status), here followed by a *sḏm.tw.f* form, passive of the independent nominal and prospective *sḏm.f* (theme) whose pronominal actor has a Neo-Egyptian form, instead of the 'classical' *.sn;* see Gilula (1970: 211); Gunn (1924: 119); Ford (1995: 62). Another option could be the one of an infinitive (Gilula 1970: 210 in a circumstantial phrase of which the actor is the same as that of the 'main' sentence, *rmṯ* in this case; Gunn 1924: 155) + Neo-Egyptian direct object pronoun *tw.f* (*LEG* § 2.5), but the existence of this pronoun is not generally recognized (see Borghouts 1980: 99-109; Winand 1992: 98-100; although it is present in the rare *m.k tw.ỉ r/ḥr sḏm*, see infra *Kanais decree*, line 12). Concerning the radical *thmw*, see Polotsky (1976: 23-24) 'graphie pleine du "*sḏm.f*" prospectif', for instance after the negation *n*(*n*). The negative prospective has a modal prohibition value ('they ought not to be interfered'); the use of impersonal or passive forms has a generalizing effect. Note that the directive tone of the decree is rendered by a deontic modality, not an imperative ('do not interfere'), nor a performative ('I command you not to interfere'). In modern forensic language, indicative future may be found, for Villey (1974) the main solution in criminal law, or deontic sentences (Guastini 1994: 2075 'deontic sentences can be taken as the standard, although contingent, formulation of rules.'). Of course the essence of a criminal disposition is its preventive, dissuasive purpose that conveys in itself a 'deontic' message, even if not always formulated as such. Concerning the difficulty of distinguishing if an utterance expresses a performative, see Jori (1994: 2092-7) and *infra*.
- *nn wn tht.tw:* 'classical' *nn wn sḏm.f* independent negative complex form (*nn wn* existential negation + *sḏm.f* modal prospective), see Gunn (1924: 124); Gilula (1970: 211) who does not observe any difference from *nn sḏm.f*; Vernus (1985: 167 n.86); Goldwasser (2001: 128-129) who notes its presence in the non-literary dialect of the 19th dynasty. The fact that it follows *nn thmw.tw.w* could mean that it has the same value or that it is opposed to the preceding (they belong to the same substitution category). Note also the prosodic and lexical parallel between *thm* and *thi* (for prosodic features of modern legal dialects, see Danet 1985: 284). The members of this paradigm are: # *nn sḏm.tw.f* + agent # and # *nn wn sḏm.tw r.sn* #; the unspecific actor-offender and the patient-victim appear in chiastic relationship. An interesting parallel may be drawn with the construction used in 13th dynasty *Ḥwtꜣwyrʿ Wgf Abydos decree*, where the *ḥwt mkt* protection of a sacred abydean zone is followed by the construction *n wnt rdỉt ḫnd rmṯ nb* (translated by Leahy 1989: 43 as 'forbidding anyone to trespass'), protection and interdiction being associated, as in our preamble, to expose the decree's object. As for the *t* preceding the classifiers 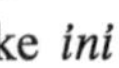 and the suffix *tw*, its reason could be **morphosyntactic**, some verbs, like *ỉnỉ* and *ỉw*, getting a final *t* when prospective, even in Middle Egyptian (see *EG* § 450.4; Doret 1980: 39; Polotsky 1964: 269-272; Frandsen 1974: 25), and perhaps also some other weak verbs (Ford 1995: 20). There are other instances of the same

form (lines 31, 33, etc.) after *rdit*, implying a dependant prospective *tht.tw* (but note also the occurrence of *rdit th.tw*, line 36). The option of an infinitive is dubious because of the impersonal suffix *tw* (*EG* § 47 and 306.2; Groll 1992: 87). But **phonetic** (*RITANC* I: 52), **lexical** (nominal marker), **stylistic** (archaism) and **calligraphic** (filling a blank) reasons should not be rejected. For a general discussion of the infinitive and other forms final *t*, see Winand (1992: 90-95, esp. n. 172): 'Cela signifie que la forme avec *–t*, qui est historiquement la marque de l'infinitif, a été réinterprétée par les scribes comme faisant partie intégrale du radical verbal', which is dubious, as we have seen it with *ini* and *iw*'s prospective. Note in *Rꜥmss* II's *Hittite Treaty* (*KRI* II, 225-232, line 13) another formulation of a similar idea, but with a circumstantial aorist and full identification of the offender and the victim (active diathesis): *iw bw ir*.N *thi r*.Egypt *r-nḥḥ r iṯꜣ nkt im.f* ("when N can never commit a transgression against Egypt to seize valuables from it").

* General dialectal features: degree 1 or 2 (in case of a perfect *ir.w w{ꜣ}ḏt*).

* Legal terms:

w{ꜣ}ḏt – classifier: (decree: the papyrus/leather document). For general remarks about decrees, see *LÄ* I, 678-679; for Pirenne (1934: 234 ff. and 1957: 27), decrees during the Old Kingdom represent laws from the Horus court creating a new 'état juridique', or 'arrêtés publiés par le Roi en vertu de son pouvoir exécutif' that ensure the application of the law, or administrative dispositions based on the king's instructions; as the probable 'transcription of a verbal statement', see Goedicke (1964: 35) and Grandet (1994 II: 30-31 (130)); for Middle Kingdom, see Blumenthal (1970: 397-400). The classifier , V12 in *EG*'s list is a 'band of string or linen', 'det. papyrus-book'[24]. It appears to stand in a metonymic relationship to the lexeme it classifies (schematic or contiguity relation of the type instrument/activity, see Goldwasser (1999b: 57 and 2002: 16, 33-35) on partonomy and meronymic relations). The emphasis is laid upon the binding (a rolled up document is bound for filing in the royal and temple archives), a feature that is implied but not especially emphasized by the more general classifier (the one that classifies in our corpus another lexeme, *wḏ* as a command or "to decree", with zero-classifier exceptions). The [ABSTRACT] category is a superordinate one, while the [BINDING] category is more of an intermediate level category. The [BINDING] category classifier also appears in lexemes such as *hp, wḫꜣ, imy-pr, spy wr* in our corpus (see *infra*), whether the document is closed for archiving or for reasons of privacy, being intended for its addressee only. A central member of the [BINDING] category is probably the lexeme *ꜥrḳ* (binding, *EG*, 523). An interesting comparison with the situation during the Old Kingdom must be added to the discussion: following Goedicke (1964: 34 and 1967: 10-12), the decree document (a substantive) is a ,

24 See Théodoridès (1967: 134 and n.104); for Kruchten (1981: 217, n. 63), 'Ce lacet, qui servait à tenir fermés les feuillets d'un texte, apparaît fréquemment à l'époque ramesside comme déterminatif pour les termes désignant des documents sur rouleau'.

written with the classifier, in contrast with the verb 'to command' that lacks any classifier. No example of the classifier is reported during the Old Kingdom. The earlier examples of the classifier in royal decrees seem to belong to *pBerlin* 10071 (12th dynasty, *Snwsrt* III epistolary decree) and *pBrooklyn* 34.1446 (13th dynasty, *Sbkḥtp* II? epistolary decree), when it follows meant as the epistolary decree, but it is never used when a monumental inscription opens with 'royal decree to...' (or) because it represents the verbal command. The importance of archive rooms and administrative registers is emphasized in texts belonging to the New Kingdom (see *The Admonitions of an Egyptian Sage*, 6,5-6,11; *The Installation of the Vizier*, 18, for instance). We may see in this example a general tendency of the Egyptian categorization system towards specialization: during the Old Kingdom, few classifiers are used; from the Middle Kingdom on, development of the superordinate classifying system; during the New Kingdom, multiple classification and tendency to refer to more 'specialized' categories.

iri (*w*{*3*}*ḏt*) – classifier: ø (to conceive, draw up or execute a decree). Concerning the lexical value of *ir* in a legal context with *hp* (to execute, enforce the law), see Gardiner (1952: 30), Otto (1956: 151) and Kruchten (1981: 46-47 but 109).

ḥn – classifier: (to post, to allocate personnel/property, provide or 'desservir'; passive: to be endowed/equipped with personnel/property attached to a service, or 'être desservi'). Ford (1995: 61) proposes the translation 'to confirm the rights of' which seems a long paraphrase for 'protect' (as it is understood by Spalinger 1991: 32, for instance). For Harari (1974: 61-64; 1981-82: 24, 27; 1990: 227), it is a matter of posting or 'affectation', as for Menu (1971: 564) 'constituer un ensemble économique indépendant et en prévoir le fonctionnement' and (1981: 72) 'affectation permanente à une tâche en vertu d'une disposition organisatrice'; Vernus (1975: 23) 'organiser', 'pourvoir' and his references; Grimal (1986: 643) 'prescriptions'; see also Grandet (1994 II: 32 (131)). The idea of defining someones functions or the nature of ones service (posting) is confirmed by the semantics of the substantive *ḥn*(*wt*) (service – see Spiegelberg 1907: 56) and the expression *ir ḥn* (to carry out ones functions). Note also the intimate link between the lexemes *ḥn, ḫwi, mki, mrt, wḏ* significantly appearing together in criminal decrees and other texts (see for instance *Rʿmss* IV Cairo stela *JE* 48831 (Korostovtsev 1947: 158 & 162), line 14: *ḫw.i n mri nt niwt.k mky.i n dmi.k iry.i wḏw r ḥn r-pr.k m sḏ3w nbt* 'I have retained your city's tenants, I have preserved your town, I have done decrees to provide your temple with every treasure'; *ḥn* is here followed by the papyrus roll classifier, as in the *Kanais decree*). The categorizing element of the word *ḥn* (line 26) is for Griffith (1927: 198) but for Kitchen (*KRI* I, 50, line 4), a choice confirmed by the *Wb* as customary in 19th and 20th dynasties papyri as in *pHarris* I 26, 9 for instance, and by line 27 of the *Nauri decree*. The relation between the lexeme and its classifier is complex. Usually, *ḥn* does not take a classifier (the icon, Gardiner's V36 sign '*ḥn* (*ḥnt*?), name of a receptacle given to a temple', is a phonetic classifier[25] only). In two cases in our corpus (compared with 9 without classifier and 2 with the [ABSTRACT] category 𓏛 classifier, see *infra*), it is followed by the superordinate 𓀁 classifier. The pictogram A2 in *EG*'s list, following Gardiner's definition, classifies activities such as to 'eat, (...) drink, (...), speak, (...) think, (...) feel', essential activities of the living organism, apparently all linked to the mouth and the belly in Egyptian imagery; see Goldwasser (2002: 5-6) and her references to 'the belly denoting man's innermost soul, the seat of his intelligence, thoughts and emotions'[26]. The temple may be viewed here as a complex body needing to be fed with property and personnel, and properly organized in order to function; being an essential link in the Ramesside economy, it may also be considered as one of the state's sustenance providers (Helck 1960b I: 790-791 notes that economic dependency is expressed by *sḏf(ꜣ)* "to feed", "to provision one institution by another", another alimentary metaphor); see also *Kanais decree*, line 15; Finnestad (1985: 121-125) for whom the temple is a symbol of the divine body, an icon of the divinity; Frandsen (1997: 82) 'the body as a whole served as an important metaphor for conceptualizing the cosmos (...), or the land of Egypt or the temple'. The relation between *ḥn* and its classifier 𓀁 may thus be in the nature of a *simile* ("to allocate personnel/property to a temple is like feeding an organism"), allowing the lexeme to be classified in the rather abstract [MOUTH LINKED ACTIVITIES] superordinate category (the less prototypical member *ḥn* being compared to a prototypical and more concrete member of the category as *wnm*, to eat). The metaphor emphasizes a salient characteristic of *ḥn* (feeding activity) and associates it temporarily to the category represented by 𓀁. For the category represented by this superordinate classifier, Goldwasser (1999: 52), following Wiesmann's views (1922: 73-77), proposed the definition '[ACTIONS OF MOUTH (feelings?)]', revised as '[SENSES AND EMOTIONS]' (2002: Introduction), suggesting an interesting corroboration in the fact that the infant first apprehends the world during his oral stage of development, 'Taste may be thus defined as the "Ur-emotion".' It seems that a fixed spelling of *ḥn* was difficult to attain; in most of its occurrences it was left without a classifier due to the complexity and far from obvious relation to any semantic category, but was sometimes classified metaphorically with the 𓀁 classifier or with the even more abstract papyrus roll. In previous decrees (Old and Middle Kingdom), the absence of a classifier is the rule; *Ỉmnḥtp* III (21st dynasty copy) *Medinet Habu decree* uses the 𓀜 or 𓂡 classifiers of the [COERCION] category once each with *ḥn*, another entry being left without a classifier. In the *Wb* III, 101, *ḥn* ('belegt seit Pyr') is written without a classifier for the Old Kingdom, without or with the papyrus roll for the Middle Kingdom.

25 Concerning this notion, see *EG* § 54: an icon summarizing the phonetic value of a lexeme already established by previous phonograms (the opposite function to the 'phonetic complements').

26 The mouth is also conceived as a door (*rꜣ*, *Wb* II, 390-1), which means a passage, a *locus* of exchange, the body's main opening (*LÄ* IV, 222-3).

ḫwy – classifier: 𓏤 (to reserve, retain). The *ḫwy mky* duo is the subject of an abundant literature, *inter alii*: Spiegelberg (1907: 55); Gardiner (1912: 264, note 33) 'to reserve and consecrate'; Moret (1912: 76-77) 'réserver'; Gunn (1927: 222-223) 'to reserve and protect'; Kuentz (1929: 105) 'réserver et préserver', 'privilégier et protéger'; De Buck (1937: 154 & 160 and 1942: 576) 'consacrated and exempted', 'tabu', 'exempted from ordinary life and work'; Bennett (1939: 10, 13) 'protected and preserved'; Korostovtsev (1947: 169) 'immunité accordée aux propriétés sacrées'; Caminos (1952: 56) 'protection against external interference'; Goedicke (1967: 246) for whom *ḫwi* represents the exemption of a basic imposition and *mki* of a special one in Old Kingdom decrees; Kruchten (1979b: 47-48) 'exemption de tout travail à fournir à l'extérieur du domaine pour quelque autorité que ce soit'; Harari (1987b: 89) 'inviolabilité'; Spalinger (1991: 22-23, 30) 'to exempt and protect.' ; Grandet (1994 II: 195 (804)). The doublet *ḫwy mky* might be satisfactorily translated by retain and preserve, a translation that implies that the institution's property and personnel are devoted to its service only and kept this way (it suits quite well, for instance, the 22nd dynasty *Bubastis W3s3irkn II relief*, about which Van Siclen III (1973: 297) sensed the inadequacy of the term 'exemption'). Note that in Old Kingdom protection decrees, *ḫwi* alone is used in the beginning (*Nfrirk3rʿ* and *Tti Abydos decrees*, *Ppy* I *Coptos A* and *Dashur decrees*, *Ppy* II *Abydos* and *Coptos B decrees*), without a classifier (or with the 'phonetic classifier' 𓂡 D43[27] in Gardiner's list; Edel 1955-64: § 574; Goedicke 1967: 53); *mky* (no classifier) is associated to *ḫwi* from *Ppy* II *Coptos C decree* on. It appears to be a fixed collocation, one of the legalese doublets that also pervades modern forensic language (e.g. *all or any*, *error or omission*, *full and complete; nul et non avenu, violences ou voies de fait*), composed of two or more lexemes syntactically, semantically and prosodically related, and termed 'binomials' by Malkiel (1959: 113-160); see Raymondis & Le Guern (1976: 16 & 33) for French legal language; Charrow (1982: 185); Danet (1984: 143-172 and 1985: 283); Jackson (1995: 121-122). For Gustafsson (1984: 129), most of English legal binomials appear in the rhematic (and adverbial) part of the sentence, 'a linguistic device which is used for the conveyance of new and additional information towards the end of the sentence.' The semantic relation between the two lexemes is of a synonymous, contiguous, or complementary type (gradation). In Egyptian royal decrees, *ḫwi* appears first in time and is always the first member of the later binomial; it may already have had an archaic flavor by the time of *Ppy* II (6th dynasty), when *mky* was adjoined for precision, and conveyed a certain ritualistic authority (diachronic couple, see Mathieu 1996: 92, n. 308). In fact, the legal English 'retained and preserved' (Gustafsson 1984: 138) may well be close to our *ḫwi-mky*. Other binomials appear regularly in the

---

27 Or D36 𓂝 (in *Nfrirk3rʿ Abydos decree*, for instance), or even D40 𓂡 (*Tti Abydos decree*) and 𓂢 (*Ppy* I *Coptos A decree*), probable archaic imprecision or corruption.

decree, such as *šmꜥw mḥw* (Upper and Lower Egypt, always in the same sequence), *m sꜣ n sꜣ* (from son to son), *ḥr mw ḥr tꜣ* (by water and by land, irreversible), etc. (see *infra*); a fixed order seems to be one of their characteristics. As for the superordinate category classifier, in *EG*'s list Y1, it is for Gardiner a 'papyrus rolled up, tied and sealed (…) Det. writing and things written (…) also abstract notions' (see also Wiesmann 1922). We may add that the written document is to the Egyptian cultivated mind the prototypical product of a finalized mental human activity symbolized and dominated by the recording scribe. The classifier has a basically metonymic relation of the type instrument/activity or substratum/contents to the lexeme it follows (the reserve right must apparently be recorded). Furthermore, as Gardiner suggested, the category of [WRITTEN THINGS] may have been extended so as to encompass any mental activity or abstraction (see the example of beauty, goodness). For Goldwasser (1995: 87-88), the use of for abstractions that are not represented in writing is probably due to 'a metonymic extension or ad hoc categorization'; the process involved is complex, and such complexity will be observed in respect of several classifiers used in the legal register. It is impossible to analyze the precise nature of the relation between some of the legal register lexemes and their classifier, for it would lead us far beyond the scope and bounds of the present study; but one must be aware of the fact that 'Metaphoric thinking (…) operates at every level of cognition' (Fauconnier & Turner 2002: 17), so that it must surely interfere in the process of creation and extension of conceptual categories. For us, *ḫwy* shows at least a double appurtenance to the [ABSTRACT] category, being probably viewed as an abstract right confirmed in writing, when legal matters, sophisticated mental activities, and writing are processed by the learned scribe and always result in an inscribed document. Note also that the classifier follows the lexeme *ḫwy* for the first time in a royal decree in *Ḏḥwtyms* III *pBerlin* 3049 (18th dynasty).

mky – classifier: ø (to preserve).

ḥn(t) – classifier: ø / (services). The lexeme is already used in Middle Kingdom decrees, without a classifier (see *Nfrḥtp* I usurpation of *Ḫwtꜣwyrꜥ Wgf* decree, line 6).

thm – classifiers: (to interfere). The double classifiers represent limbs. The first one, (*EG*'s D56 'leg, foot') is sometimes associated with movement (when coupled to), the second (*EG*'s D40 'forearm with hand holding stick') implies constraint, coercion[28], authority, effort, use of force (but not necessarily *ultra vires* or illegitimate violence), epitomized by the king's epithet *nḫt-ꜥ* 'strong of arm' (where *nḫt* is also classified by). The classifier represents, in an abbreviated form of , a superordinate category of activities implying the use of constraint [COERCION], the relation between the classifier and the lexeme being of a metonymic organ+instrument/activity nature. For Goldwasser (1995:

28 Curzon (1988: 76) 'the use of physical or moral force in an attempt to interfere with the exercise of free choice.'

88), the 'strong arm' [D40] denotes aggression, 'a pictorial synecdoche, emphasizing the limb responsible for the aggression', and she mentioned its metaphorical value (1995: 19) (in 2002: 19, she calls the superordinate category represented by [D40] '[ACTION OF FORCE]'). The arm alone does not represent coercion as effectively as an armed hand or one empowered by virtue of a function/status symbol such as the crook or stick/scepter. It is the combination of the limb and the symbolic attire of power that forms the perfect image. The hooked stick was perhaps once used by shepherds to direct their herds and it gained the status of symbolic authority. Nevertheless, in the case of *thm*, the stick is not an instrument with which the interferer exerts coercion (metonymy), but a symbolic designation of 'who's in charge' (as for the D43 [D43] hand with flail, D44 [D44] hand with *ḫrp*/*ʿbꜣ*/*sḫm* scepter etc.). Perhaps the simile 'coercion exerted by an interferer is a scepter in an empowered authority's hand' represents the category (people holding scepters perform an office that entitles them to use coercion). Again, we are faced with a complex relation between the lexeme and its classifiers. The abundant use of the [D40] strong arm classifier in our legal register, when appended to lexemes expressing the administration's actions, recalls the eternal truth that 'law is the monopoly and codification of authorised and organised violence.' (Goodrich 1987: 174) and the opinion of those who reduce law to coercive rules (Pintore 1994: 2102); but obviously, the legal register lexicon of our corpus cannot be reduced to the [COERCION] category. As for the leg [D56] classifier, the lexeme *thm* is often classified by [D56] only, with or without *EG*'s D54 [D54] (walking legs) classifier (and later by [D40] alone or with the crossed sticks Z9 × classifier, see *Wb* V, 321). As we will note *infra*, [D56] is also used with [D54] to classify *thi* and *tkn*, two lexemes associated with specific offenses; it seems unlikely that [D56] and [D54] cover precisely the same semantic field. If it is not a movement of both legs (e.g. walking) but the foot/leg itself or another leg state/action that is emphasized, one may wonder if we are not confronted by another image of power based on the symbolic trampling of the defeated opponent (as in the expression [hieroglyphs] 'under the feet'[29] and the numerous representations of an Egyptian king trampling corpses in battle or placing his feet upon a low stool decorated with captives). The [LEG] category represented by the [D56] classifier seems extended in this case so as to include the concept of ascendancy (most of the lexemes classified by [D56] being linked physiologically to the limb or implying control). See *thi infra*.

thi *r* – classifiers: [D56][D54] (to transgress). For Griffith (1927: 200), it means an interference; Gunn (1927: 228), also to disobey orders; Edgerton (1947: note 11), a wrong doing; see also Meeks (1980: 420, 1981: 415-416, 1982: 326); Parant (1982: 154-155); Goedicke (1984: 44 & 61) who evokes to trespass, overstep about an allowance in *Ḥkꜣnḫt*'s first letter; Grimal (1986: 644) 'construction prépositionnelle', 'dévoyer', ' "détourner" des biens affectés';

29 See Théodoridès (1972) 'mettre des biens sous les pieds de quelqu'un' is to assign them to someones use or possession.

Spalinger (1991: 32) a violation; Morschauser (1991: 55-59). The expression 'transgression of an order' is already in use in *PT* 1024 (although *thi* does not get a classifier at this stage). The lexeme is also used in the concrete sense of crossing boundaries (*thi r t3š,* see *infra*), trespassing[30]. The same image of *passage* is used in several languages to express a crime: see, for example, Hebrew עבירה and English/French *transgression* from the Latin *transgressus*. In *EG*, Gardiner notes that the double classifiers (𓂾 and 𓂻 D54 'Legs walking (...) Det. movement (...) also lack of movement') are used to determine various verbs expressing movement', assimilating apparently 𓂾 and 𓂻 semantics. If the icon 𓂻 is used to represent movement (schematic/metonymic relation organ/activity), one must admit that no real movement is involved here. Combined with the 𓂾 classifier (which again has a 'trampling down' or 'taking over' connotation), the group relates metaphorically to the lexeme, when 'trespassing is walking all over someone' (transgression of moral/legal limits, overstepping of limits/rights, contravention, infringement, abuse, suggesting that the offender possess some rights but is using them for an unlawful purpose or to an unlawful extent, or that he does not have any right in the first place, as in an administration's *ultra vires*[31] action or misuse of authority). It is not clear in our document if the transgression nature is incompetence ('lack of legal qualifications or fitness to discharge the required duty'[32]) or abuse within the scope of the transgressor authority, except in the case of robbery (*m ḥwrʿ*). About the same issue in *Ḥrmḥb*'s decree, Kruchten writes (1981: 209) that the transgression must be understood as 'formes particulières d'abus de pouvoir, qui résultent soit de l'intervention dans un processus administratif d'une autorité non compétente (...), soit de l'absence de fondement réglementaire à l'action dénoncée'. 'Corruption' is the term used by Polaček (1974: 93) and Leprohon (1985: 100-102). Compare a similar process with the lexeme *ʿḥʿ* (classified by 𓂻) in Lacau (1949: 35) 'c'est « se présenter en justice ». Le même lien sémantique se retrouve dans notre mot technique « ester » en justice, de « stare, se tenir debout ».' (where 𓂻 expresses the dynamics of the upward position, the firm physical stance implying both physical and moral position at the 'stand' in the court room, the same image being used in Hebrew לעמוד לדין). Note that twice in our decree *thi r* gets only the 𓂻 classifier and thrice 𓂾𓂡. In earlier decrees, 𓐍𓈖𓂡𓂾 is used (*Ḫwt3wyrʿ Wgf* 13th dynasty decree) but *thi* in *Imnḥtp* III *BM* 138 decree (21st dynasty copy) is followed by 𓀜𓂡.

[*s*]*mn* – classifier: ø (to confirm, establish). See Moret (1916: 304) 'le mot technique qui caractérise la fondation, *l'établissement* d'un bien' (see in 6th dynasty *Ppy* II

30 Curzon (1988: 444): 'An unjustifiable interference with possession' and p. 445 'trespass to goods', 'trespass to land' ('Unjustifiable, direct and immediate interference with anothers possession of land'), 'trespass to the person'; Deebank (1989: 292) 'Unlawful infringement of a personal right.'

31 Beyond the powers. *CDL*: 425 'the exercise of an administrative power in a modern legal system is *ultra vires* not only if unauthorized in substance, but equally if (...) it is procedurally irregular, improperly motivated, or in breach of the rules of natural justice.'

32 Gifis (1984: 224-225).

Coptos G decree, also without classifier); Blumenthal (1970: 124); Grimal (1986: II 13:1) 'établir', 'désigne surtout la capacité juridique du roi en tant que législateur' and (1986:III 5) 'confirmation juridique d'un acte'. Otherwise, it gets the papyrus roll classifier (see the perpetuation commission decrees *infra*).

* Legal formula: *ỉr.w w{ꜣ}ḏt* (legal document) + *ḥnt* (content measure) + *ẖt* (territorial application) + *rmṯ nb* (general protection) + *ḫwy mky* (decree objective) + *nn sḏm.tw* (general interdiction) + *m sꜣ [n sꜣ]* (hereditary formula) + *[s]mn ḥr ḥn.sn r ḏrw ḥnty nḥḥ* (unlimited duration of the legal right)

c. legal provisions (29-119).
d. epilogue (119-128).

I.2 The legal provisions

The legal provisions are introduced by a heading statement about the decree's **proclamation** in the Palace on the same day (perhaps as part of its promulgation process), the specification of the proclamation's **addressees** (lines 29-30), and a brief **introduction** of the decree's content.

The legal provisions sequence conforms to the following scheme:

- **enacting clauses**: exposition of the commanding authority, the decree's object, its beneficiary, and its applicability. The enacting clauses act as section dividers between various categories of offenses;
- **preambles *sensu stricto***: expose the negative and positive intents of the decree, the protection of several categories of possessions and individuals in order to prevent a crime being committed by a category of offenders ('exposé des motifs', 'de l'abus' for Kruchten 1981: 10-11 in *Ḥrmḥb*'s *Karnak decree*)[33]. Along with the enacting clauses, the negative intents provide a frame for the crimes and penalties subsequent dispositions; in modern legislation, backward reference (by way of indicating the number/letters affixed to the articles referred to) is used, but here internal intertextuality remains implicit;
- **operative parts, purviews**[34]: *casi* of crimes and their punishment, following the preamble *sensu stricto* negative intents sequence (as for the category of offenders who shall commit the crime [referred to in the preceding part and the way described], the law will be enforced on them in the prescribed way). The systematic way in which crimes and penalties are presented reflects the Roman principle *Nullum crimen sine poena*, but it is impossible to establish if the principle of a

33 The structure of the legal dispositions is slightly different in *Ḥrmḥb*'s *Karnak decree* (18th dynasty), with an 'anecdotal' relation of the abuse (motivation of the measure), followed by its formal condemnation (as in 6th dynasty *Ppy* II decrees), the interdiction (negative order) or the king's positive order to put an end to the abuse, sometimes an administrative measure suppressing the crimes' opportunity, and the more formal and 'archaic' expression of the crime and its sanction; see Kruchten (1981: 222-223 *et passim).*

34 Gifis (1984: 378) 'body of a statute as distinguished from other parts of it, such as the preamble.'

written criminal law (*Nullum crimen, nulla poena sine lege*) pervades the Ramesside legal system[35].

I.2.1 The decree's proclamation to the Administration (heading texteme)

(29) (…) *w{ꜣ}ḏt ꜣwy[t]w m ḥm n stp-sꜣ ꜥnḫ wḏꜣ snb m [hrw] pn n ṯꜣ[ty] srw*[36] *smrw ḳnbwt sḏmyw sꜣ ni-swt n Kš ḥryw pḏt*[37] *imy-r nbw*[38] *ḥꜣty-ꜥw*[39] *ṯs[w?] wḥywt*[40] *nw šmꜥw mḥw kꜣḏnw ḥryw iḥw ṯꜣy-srywt*[41] *rwḏ nb* (30) *n pr ni-swt*[42] *rmṯ nb hꜣbw m wpt*[43] *r K[š]* (...) (29) Decree proclaimed/issued/handed over in (the) majesty of (the) palace[44], L.P.H., on this [date], to (the) viz[ier], magistrates/civil servants, courtiers, courts of hearers, Viceroy of Kush, troop/bowmen commandants, superintendents of gold, mayors, tribe commanders of Southern and Northern lands, officers, stable masters, standard-bearers, any agent (30) of (the) king's estate, anybody sent on a mission to K[ush]

* Neo-Egyptian characteristics:

- *w{ꜣ}ḏt ꜣwy[t]w:* same formulation as in the *Elephantine decree* (line 3) although *ꜣwyt* stands there without the final *w*, confirming the vocalizing nature of this sign (a Ramesside characteristic, see *LEG* § 1.1.2 & 1.2.3; Junge 1996: 1.1.1) in a feminine participial[45] or stative form (Winand 1992: 123, 145-146), the preceding noun being undetermined. On the 'attributive' use of the stative instead of passive participles, see *EG* § 317 and 353 Obs.; Lefebvre (1955: § 353 & 355-357); Polotsky (1976: 29-30); for Vergote (1955: 338-361), the

35 *Contra*: Théodoridès (1967: 134); Kruchten (1981: 219).

36 See Théodoridès (1971: 311-312); Bedell (1973: 42-47); Kruchten (1981: 32); McDowell (1990: 65-69) 'any government official, regardless his rank (…) to whom some portion of the royal authority had been delegated', 'magistrates', sometimes having only an administrative role; Lorton (1995: 351) 'administrator'.

37 See Warburton (1997: 190, n. 583). Note the abbreviated spelling in line 42, as for *ḥryw iḥw*.

38 See Vercoutter (1959: 137).

39 See Gardiner (1947: 31); Kruchten (1981: 101). Treated here as a compound (the plural mark is appended to the end of the compound and not to its first member).

40 See Gardiner (1947: 31); Lorton (1977: 21-22, n. 100).

41 Compound, as in line 42.

42 The royal palace representing the central administration, see Théodoridès (1981: 632).

43 See Steindorff (1939: 31); Blumenthal (1970: 396-397) in Middle Kingdom 'Auftrag des Königs', 'bereits im AR analog zu *wḏ* als Rechtsdokument behandelt, das die Legitimation durch den Königs enthält'; Valloggia (1976); Théodoridès (1982: 111-112, 117-118 in note 232); Goedicke (1964: 39-41) about Old Kingdom Sinai inscriptions titled *wpt (ni-swt) hꜣbt ḥnꜥ*, with the 𓏛 classifier, understood as a royal mandate. It may imply that in Ramesside decrees, the 'mission to Kush' is executed by an official detaining a 'pouvoir letter' from the central administration.

44 Memphis, the authority; see references in Vernus (1975: 22).

45 See also Hayes (1955: 35) on *pBrooklyn* 35.1446 and *Nauri* decrees.

stative in its 'attributive' function has a descriptive role and may be discarded from a sentence otherwise complete, as opposed to the participle in the same function, which has a 'determinative' role and cannot be omitted without 'killing' the sentence (although some of his examples of 'indispensable' participles are rather unconvincing); see also Barri (1975: 209-220), following Damourette & Pichon, for the distinction between 'épicatathètes' (creating a distinctive entity with specific signified) and 'épanathètes' adjectives (descriptive); Jansen-Winkeln's demonstration (1993: 7 ff.) of the origin of the stative, an ancient perfect passive participle, a nominal form used in adverbial rhematic functions[46] confirms an intuition shared by many other authors ('pseudoparticiple'). On the distinction between adnominal (attributive) and adnexal expansions (rhematic), see Shisha-Halevy (1981: 323 for Coptic); for Shisha-Halevy (1998b: 595), the stative is always rhematic. Note that the proclamation statement has a heading nominal turn, and constitutes a distinct texteme. For earlier examples of the same formula[47], see *Ḏḥwtyms* IV protection decree of *Nbỉmn: w{ꜣ}ḏwt ꜣwyt m ḥm n stp-sꜣ* L.P.H. *m hrw pn n*... and *Ḏḥwtyms* III *Karnak decree*: *wḏ ꜣw r ḥwt nṯr n ỉmn* (...) *m hrw pn*. In contrast, it is worthwhile to note that Old Kingdom decrees are generally addressed to specific individuals by means of the formula # Horus king name + *wḏ ni-swt* + addressee(s) #, although their monumental copy is intended for public communication. During the Middle Kingdom, the preposition *n* is inserted before the addressees (see *supra*). Note that the main actor and leading strand of the decree is the decree itself and not the king or his speech act; after the king's (primary author) utterance of the decree and its redaction by the royal scribes (secondary authors of the decree), it is the document that is designated as the narrator and actor (see *infra tꜣ w{ꜣ}ḏt m ḏd* 'this decree is saying').

- *kꜣḏnw:* syllabic script of a Semitic word, 19th dynasty; see Albright (1934: 61); Groll (1983: 238); Hoch (1994: 341) *ku=ḏ=n* 'charioteer'.

* 'Classical' degree 0 forms used:

- *rwḏ nb:* of some interest is the semantics of *nb*'s distribution which could refer to *rwḏ* only (without plural marker, a determinative relational expansion following *nb*) or to the preceding list of first hand addressees[48] taken as a whole (but containing nouns number-marked and unmarked, some obviously singular

46 Note the large substitution property of nominal and adverbial forms: 'virtual relative clause' (rhematic expansion of an undetermined noun), substitution of *nfr sy* to the stative in adverbial nexuses (*EG* § 374 *in fine*; Lefebvre 1955: § 356-357), perhaps also the various N *sḏm.f* syntagms, and also circumstantial thematisations in cleft sentences (Shisha-Halevy 1978: 51-67).

47 As we shall see, the corpus studied is of a highly formulaic structure, as are modern legalese and administrative documents (Crystal & Davy 1969: 194 'much legal writing is by no means spontaneous but is copied directly from 'form books' (...) in which established formulae are collected.').

48 They are the proclamation's addressees, but the decree's final addressees constitute a much more general public (including the temple staff): the implications of the propagandist aim of the stela public exposition are much wider and constitute the publication of the act, perhaps as an essential part of its promulgation.

as *s3 ni-swt n Kš*). We prefer the first option, due to the presence of the relational expansion. For the contrast between # plural noun + *nb* # (totalizing value with specifying determinator: 'all the X') and # singular noun + *nb* # (distributive value with non-specifying quantifier: 'any/every X', as here), see Shisha-Halevy (1987: 162) for Coptic and (1989: 43) for Demotic. Furthermore, # *rmṯ nb* + attributive expansion # is meant to encompass even the less significant state employee or any uncovered category of operators in Nubia (in a 'diminishing progression'[49] type of administrative hierarchy list). Although *rmṯ* already represents a collective/generic[50] entity (hyperonym marked by a fixed, non-pertinent, plural classifier whose quantifier is not marked for gender and number), the syntagm *rmṯ nb* could function semantically as a more abstract concept than 'any person', exactly as 'anybody' or 'anyone' is a further stage of abstraction, marked by the cohesion between 'any' and 'body' and the choice of 'body/one' instead of 'person'. A further issue to be addressed is if *rmṯ nb* represents 'anyone of a similar nature' to the ones preceding it, or 'anyone, even not belonging to the state's officials hierarchy.' It seems that the first alternative must be taken into account, mainly because of the limitative function of the following *h3bw m wpt r K*[*š*]. But see also for modern legal register Davison (1980: 238-239) 'General words, such as *other*, *the like*, and *et cetera* are often limited by previous discourse.'; and note also the legal principle *ejusdem generis* still used in courts ('in a list of two or more items, followed by a more general term that includes the prior items, the more general term is limited by the prior items', Charrow, Crandall & Charrow 1982: 185; Crystal & Davy 1969: 214). Note the fact that in sentences where *nb* is repeated in our text (lists), it is never gender-number marked. The list formula is thus # [singular or plural nominal lexemes (hyponyms), with or without attributive/determinative expansions] + [singular lexeme + distributive *nb* + determinative expansion] + [hyperonym *rmṯ nb* + attributive expansion] #. We will see *infra* that the type of list # noun + noun + noun + hyperonym *nb* # where lexemes follow one another without distributive *nb* (which is appended mostly to the sole hyperonym) concern addressees, objects or victims of the offenses, whereas offenders lists are always of the type # noun *nb* + noun *nb* + noun *nb* + hyperonym *nb* #.

- *h3bw*: participle in attributive function, written *h3btw* in a similar proclamation sentence of the *Elephantine decree* (line 4) but *h3b* in the other instances of # *rmṯ nb h*(*3*)*b*(*w*) *m wp*(*t*) # in the *Nauri decree* (lines 34, 36, 42, 48). It cannot be

49 See Fischer (1973: 5, 7) 'progression relating to (…) (3) rank, i.e. superior to lesser status'; Groll (1983: 235) 'hierarchical order, descending from highest to lowest'.

50 In *EG* § 77.4, Gardiner postulates that in Middle Egyptian, *rmṯ* may be either the singular and masculine 'man', the plural 'men', or the collective and feminine 'people' (because of instances of *rmṯ nbt* and *rmṯt nbt*). In our decree, officials sent on a mission to Kush must have been exclusively male; but when dealing with temple personnel, *rmṯ* must be understood as male and female staff (see the precision, line 31 for instance, *m ṯ3y ḥmt*). In this case, *nb*'s absence of concord is the rule in our text, denoting an abstract category or simply due to its general absence of concord, except for *ḫt nbt*.

a stative (rhematic, adnexal form), because of the preceding noun determination by *nb*.

- [*ḥrw*] *pn: LEG* § 3.1.1.1. Specific, anaphoric (the date has already been established) and proximal, archaic demonstrative (temporal deixis), in a formulaic nominal phrase never expanded. Compare with Simpson (1996: 29-30) for the Ptolemaic sacerdotal decrees (in Demotic). Archaism of anaphoric expressions is also a characteristic of modern legal register, see for instance, for French criminal law language, Raymondis & Le Guern (1976: 14). Of course, the demonstrative is not to be transliterated *pnn*, because the *n* following *pn* is the preposition introducing the addressees.

* General dialectal features: degree 1.

* Legal terms:

w{3}ḏt - classifier: 𓏛 (decree, the papyrus/leather roll).

3wy - classifier: 𓂡 (to proclaim, issue, hand over). See Lacau (1949: 38-39) for the *Stèle juridique de Karnak*, line 22; Hayes (1955: 35-36); Helck (1974: 127 (b)); Spalinger (1991: 32) 'the physical transfer of a papyrus from one individual to another'; *CLEM*, 274; Vernus (1975: 22). Proclamation is a matter of 'public announcement giving notice of an act done or to be done' (Gifis 1984: 369); it belongs in modern societies to the promulgation formalities. Its exact value in the Ramesside society is a matter of conjecture, but it is reasonable to suppose that a decree became effective as soon as the king pronounced it; the notice given to the king's officials may not automatically indicate that publication is required to give it legal effect. Furthermore, the proclamation at issue could concern the original utterance by the king of the decree (or at least of its outline), its verbal birth, the moment of its simultaneous writing by the royal scribes (who may later elaborate it in precise dispositions). Again, the lexeme is classified by 𓂡 in the [COERCION] category, implying the constraining and authoritative character of the document. In *pBrooklyn* 35.1446 (insertion C, line 7), 𓂡 is used as classifier of *3w*.

rwḏ - classifier: 𓂡 (agent detaining a 'parcelle d'autorité'). See Gardiner (1947: 32) controller managing 'estates on behalf of far distant temples that own them', (1948b: 82-83) for *pWilbour* and (1952: 26 & 28); Théodoridès (1962: 75, n. 107); Janssen (1981: 64) 'Vertreter'; Groll (1983: 238-239): agricultural supervisors; Kruchten (1979: 517-525) 'autorités au sens large des domaines qui devaient demeurer la plupart du temps au siège même de ceux-ci et qui ne participaient pas directement au processus de production' or 'agents locaux au sens strict' 'en liaison étroite avec la gestion domaniale', 'agents subalternes intervenant lors de la collecte des ressources du domaine et vivant presque exclusivement à la campagne'; Kruchten (1981: 72); Menu (1981: 73) 'sortes de contrôleurs ou des fondés de pouvoir'; McDowell (1990: 59-65) 'anyone exercising authority on behalf of others'; Spalinger (1991: 30) in a 'specific connection to the state and not to the temple', as appears from the expressions *rwḏ nb n pr ni-swt* in *Nauri decree*, lines 30 and 36 and *rwḏ n p3 t3 n Kš* in line

38. The lexeme apparently appears for the first time during the 18th dynasty (*Wb* II, 413). The 𓂡 classifier implies the use of constraint by and the authority of state agents (schematic/metonymic relation of an organ/activity nature and complex relation with the symbolic instrument of authority), the lexeme belonging to the superordinate [COERCION] category.

ḳnbwt sḏmyw - classifier: 𓀀 (courts of hearers). See Labib (1948: 477); Otto (1956: 157); Lurje (1971: 57-62) 'Behörde der Verhörenden'; Bedell (1973 : 9-10); McDowell (1990: 69 & 143 ff.) 'we do not know exactly what constituted a *ḳnbwt* or what degree of formality or ceremony was involved' and court "of hearers" stresses 'that the court was functioning in its judicial capacity rather than in some other, administrative, capacity'. The 𓀀 classifier of the superordinate taxonomic [MALE-HUMAN] category represents the prototypical image of a short-haired, short-skirted seated Egyptian male, of which the lexeme must be a basic-level member (see Goldwasser 1995: 31 & 87). The reason why a sitting man represents the prototypical image of the category [MALE-HUMAN] may reside in the fact that most human activities must have been accomplished in this position (the movement of the arms implies a dynamic upper body, but the worker is comfortably seated to allow for long-term activity). Compare, for example, the end of Old Kingdom/First Intermediate Period models of men at work in the same position (e.g. *CG* 245 Meir 6th dynasty painted wooden statuette of a man roasting a duck, from *Niʿnḫppy*'s tomb). The classification of the lexeme into the superordinate [MALE-HUMAN] category implies the centrality of the human vis-à-vis other possible classifications such as 𓏴 or 𓂡.

* Legal formula: *w{ꜣ}ḏt ꜣwyt* (decree proclamation) + *m* (location) + *m* [*hrw*] *pn* (date) + *n* (list of addressees)

I.2.2 Introduction of the content (tag clause)

(30) (…) *tꜣ w{ꜣ}ḏt m ḏd* (...)
(30) (…) This decree is stating: (...)

* Neo-Egyptian characteristics:

- *tꜣ w{ꜣ}ḏt:* use of the gender/number characterized (feminine singular referent, but not sole gender marker or determinator, see the noun's *t* suffixed nucleus), anaphoric (*prius notum*, line 29: ø *w{ꜣ}ḏt* = referate, and referring to the present decree in general), specific demonstrative identificative (*EG* § 112; Kroeber 1970: 1-30), for the first time in our register, with a prominent genus (theme of a brief adverbial nexus of a durative present value) contextually identifiable. The prenominal *pꜣ/tꜣ/nꜣ* appear moderately in the text (absence of automatic, or so-called generalized/grammaticalized 'article') and are generally phoric, so that each entry of the demonstrative or 'articloid' must be weighed separately. The position adopted by us in the following study is to consider that a selective use of a mainly phoric (referential) morpheme cannot be assimilated to an 'article'. This intermediate stage will be coined 'articloid', following Löfstedt (1981); it is to be related to the register analyzed and its value cannot be inferred from the use of *p3/t3/n3* in other registers of the same period. Furthermore, 'noun determination is not synonymous with "article".' (Shisha-Halevy 1987: 160). Compare with Simpson (1996: 29) for the Ptolemaic sacerdotal decrees in Demotic, with one instance of the demonstrative *p3y* in '*p3y wt* "this decree"', referring to the subject of the preceding text, as well as to the physically present document under the eye of the reader and also 'self-referential (…) to the linguistic material in which it itself exists.' On other ancient languages article emergence, see Rosén (1988: 21-62) for Greek; Löfstedt (1981: 269-279) and Rosén (1994: 129-150) for Latin; Epstein (1993: 111-134) for Old French and modern Jamul Diegueño. For Demotic, Coptic and terminology, see Shisha-Halevy (1985: 97-102, 1987: 159-163 and 1989b: 429-430). On the absence of article as a syntactical archaism in French criminal law 'locutions lexicalisées' recalling the 14th – 15th centuries state of French, see Raymondis & Le Guern (1976: 17-20).

* 'Classical' degree 0 forms used:

- *t3 w{3}ḏt m ḏd:* tag clause introducing a quotation, with adverbial nexus placing the decree itself ahead as theme and actor, origin of the speech act (*ḏd* is the *verbum dicendi*). The pattern is Middle Egyptian, as we have seen that *t3* is still deictic here. It denotes a process of abstraction, which is the essence of a quotation from written material: the origin of the norm is viewed, from the beginning, as the document itself, detached from its verbal transmission by the king (it is already the third significant occurrence of the lexeme in our register). Note the absence of *ỉw* ahead of the clause. The rheme (converb *m ḏd*) is durative as a process detached from the transitory, mortal, and specific person of the regnant king. It may also highlight the fact that the text following is not precisely the original written version of the decree, but an excerpt or summarized transmission of its substance (limited quotation or paraphrase). For other examples of quotation from written material using *ḏd*, see Sweeney (2001: 27-28). The introduction of the decree's content by *t3 w{3}ḏ m ḏd*, is already known from *Dḥwtyms* IV's decree for *Nbỉmn* (*w{3}ḏ* without feminine suffixed nucleus).

* General dialectal features: degree 1.

* Legal terms: *w{3}ḏt* - classifier:  (decree: the papyrus/leather roll).

* Legal formula: *t3 w{3}ḏt m ḏd* (introduces the decree's content).

I.2.3 Enacting clause (authority, object, beneficiary, applicability)

(30) (…) *iw w{ꜣ}ḏ.n ḥm.f rdit ḥn.tw tꜣ ḥwt nt ḥḥw m rnpwt ni-swt bity Mnmꜣꜥtrꜥ ib hrw m ꜣbdt ḥr mw ḥr tꜣ ḫt spꜣwt šmꜥw* (31) *mḥw*

(30) (…) his Majesty has decreed to cause that be endowed/equipped the temple of millions of years of (the) King of Upper and Lower Egypt '*Mnmꜣꜥtrꜥ*'s heart is contented in Abydos', on water (and) on land, throughout (the) districts of Southern (and) (31) Northern Egypt,

* Neo-Egyptian characteristics:

- *tꜣ ḥwt nt ḥḥw m rnpwt ni-swt bity Mnmꜣꜥtrꜥ ib hrw m ꜣbdt:* every time the name of the Abydos temple is mentioned, it appears with *tꜣ* (feminine gender/number marked determinator). It is the only temple proper name mentioned in this document and this is its first occurrence in our decree. *tꜣ* has a cataphoric function with a noun expanded by *nota relationis*. This nominal syntagm functions as actor of the passive verb (or direct object of the impersonal form). As for the composition of the temple's name (appellative + proper name), there are probably two main ways to see it:
  - *tꜣ ḥwt* (cataphoric determinator + appellative) + determinative expansion [*nt ḥḥw m rnpwt ni-swt bity*] + proper name [*Mnmꜣꜥtrꜥ ib hrw m ꜣbdt*]: the determinative expansion (with relator *nt*) gives the type of temple (royal memorial or 'funerary' temple, see *RITANC* I: 53; Haring 1997: 20-24 for whom temples of millions of years are characterized by an 'emphasis on the person of the founding king himself in connection with the principal local deity'), its name following in apposition. The question of its syntax may be resolved by seeing the owner of the heart (*Stḫy* I) in honorific transposition, as Roeder (1960: 316) does 'das Gehöft von Millionen von Jahren (namens) « das Herz des Königs von Ober- und Unter-Ägypten (Men-Maat-Rê) ist zufrieden in Abydos »', although *ni-swt bity* may be viewed as belonging to the preceding determinative expansion (here without *nota relationis* marker, but with it in line 80) as well as a link with the proper name, as the abbreviated *tꜣ ḥwt Mnmꜣꜥtrꜥ ib hrw m ꜣbdt* used almost every time in our text confirms the reading[51]. Note the concord of the relator *nt* (archaism);
  - *tꜣ ḥwt* + determinative expansion [*nt ḥḥw m rnpwt*] + owner [*ni-swt bity Mnmꜣꜥtrꜥ*] + proper name [*ib hrw m ꜣbdt*]*:* in this option adopted by Griffith (1927: 200), Edgerton (1947: 221) and Haring (1997: 6), the owner is in direct juxtaposition ('loose composition' without relator) with *tꜣ ḥwt nt ḥḥw m rnpwt,* and the syntax of the proper name is slightly problematic because of the absence of a suffix pronoun after *ib* and of the attributive exocentric compound *hrw-ib* (as erroneously viewed by Spalinger 1991: 32). Note that

51 See, for example, inscribed upon *CG* 42056 (statue of *Ḏḥwtyms* III) a similar way of expressing the proper name of the statue: [*twt*] [*Mnḫprrꜥ ḥnk rnpwt n Ỉmn m Ỉpt-swt*].

this solution works in the case of *ḥwt Wsrm3ʿtrʿ Mryỉmn ḫnmt nḥḥ m pr Ỉmn ḥr ỉmntt W3st* (*Rʿmss* III Medinet Habu temple), where the feminine *ḫnmt* is obviously in concord with *ḥwt* (see Haring 1997: 26). The proper name in this alternative may be viewed as adverbial (theme + stative rheme '[the] heart is happy'), a noun in direct juxtaposition + participial attribute ('of [the] happy heart') or an exclamatory rheme following a topicalized theme ('[the] heart, may it be happy'). For Warburton (1997: 191), it has to be rendered as 'the Mansion of *Mn-M3ʿt-Rʿ*, Heart's Ease in Abydos', which seems syntactically unjustifiable.

- *3bdt: 3bḏw*. The form *3bdt* is always used in the decree, except for one instance of *3bdw* (line 34) and one of *3bd* (line 78).

* 'Classical' degree 0 forms used:

- *ỉw w{3}ḏ.n ḥm.f:* independent (after the introductive tag clause with *m ḏd*), inherited from Old Egyptian, perfect (see Shisha-Halevy 1989c: 252-253), a delocutive complex form with *ỉw*, deictic status marker of independence, auxiliary grammeme, and a prominent nominal actor (the king is a central actor in the eulogy), still a common form during the 19th dynasty (Winand 1992: 180), although the middle '*n*' might already not have been pronounced (Winand 1992: 185). On the form *ỉw wḏ.n ḥm.f* in royal decrees, see Menu (1971: 564); Goedicke (1960: 66-68 and 1967: 235) 'Kodifizierung einer Verbaldeklaration' which explains in Old Kingdom decrees the use of the past formula and (1975: 678); Helck (1974: 117); for Doret (1986: 105-6), a perfect describing 'a royal order still valid in the present when the decree was written' in Old Kingdom decrees; Trapani (1993: 543-544). It opens the quotation of the decree's content, and again it is the prominent (auxiliated) lexeme *w{3}ḏ* that leads a new section of the document. The formula *ỉw w{3}ḏ.n ḥm.f rdit ḥn.tw* appears four times (lines 30, 55, 82-83, 98-99) to express the object of the decree, the 'organisation (des possessions)' of the temple (Grimal 1986: 642). The first instances of *ỉw wḏ.n ḥm(.ỉ)* appear during the 6th dynasty (see *Ppy* I *Dashur* and *Coptos A decrees*), alternating with the form *ỉw wḏ.n (.ỉ)* in *Coptos A*. The *Coptos A decree* is also the first one to be preceded by the illustration of the main concerned protagonists, as in Ramesside decrees; the construction belongs to the reserve *ḫwt* clause and is followed, as here, by negative forms (*n rdỉ ḥm*) (see *infra*). It also lacks several formulas taken from the original papyrus decree, as in our case; therefore, it may constitute the first example of a document of the kind we observe during the Ramesside Period. Before the New Kingdom, the formula uses either *ḥm(.ỉ)* or *ḥm* + royal proper name as actor, but never *ḥm.f* (already used during *Ḏḥwtyms* III and *Ỉmnḥtp* II reigns[52]). In *Ḏḥwtyms* IV decree for *Nbỉmn*, the beginning of the text is parallel to our *Nauri decree*: date + *w{3}ḏwt 3wyt m ḥm n stp-s3 ʿnḫ wḏ3 snb m hrw pn n* + titles of *Nbỉmn* + *t3 w{3}ḏ m ḏd w{3}ḏ.n ḥm.ỉ ʿnḫ wḏ3 snb* (without *ỉw*). *ỉw wḏ.n ḥm.f* is an archaism in

52 Even earlier, the form *ỉw grt wḏ.n ḥm.f* is used in *Ỉʿḥms' Karnak 8th pylon decree*, with the enclitic particle *grt*.

Ramesside decrees, a feature tending to add to our text a 'touch of formality', as is the case with archaisms used in various modern legal dialects (Crystal & Davy 1969: 208). In *Ḥrmḥb*'s decree, *iw wḏ.n ḥm* appears after the condemnation of the criminal administrative practice, as in some Old Kingdom decrees, alternating with the interdiction of the crime (*m rdi ir.tw m-mitt*), as in line 19 (*iw wḏ.n ḥm.i dit s3 r.f* 'My Majesty has decreed to put an end to it'), line 31 (*iw wḏ.n ḥm.i tm di ir.tw m-mitt grw š3ᶜ m p3 hrw* 'My Majesty has decreed not to let one do likewise again, from this day on'), and line 36 (*iw wḏ.n ḥm.i di.tw s3 r.*[*sn*]). Finally, we must try to assess if we are in the presence of a performative, if an enacting clause is 'an explicit performative utterance' and not a simple identification of the authority behind the act (Hancher 1980: 253-254) or at least an 'implicit performative' (Kurzon 1986: 12 on legislation acts close to our decree, for instance the German statute opening with the formula 'Der Bundestag *hat* mit Zustimmung des Bundestages das folgende Gesetz *beschlossen*' where 'the verb in the formula is perfect to report the fact that the legislature *has decided* to pass a law'[53])? As Austin (1970) put it, the performative represents 'How to do things with words'; for instance, a promise exists when the words 'I promise' are uttered. 'The statement is the act' for Charrow, Crandall & Charrow (1982: 181), about the performative in legal language. The issue is a delicate one. The enacting formula (promulgation) opens statutes, identifies the authority behind the act, and 'provides the frame of power, distance and status which endows legislative texts with their formal, imperious quality' (Maley 1994: 20 on modern English statutes and their enacting formula 'Be it enacted by the Queen's Most Excellent Majesty, by and with the advice and consent of the Lords Spiritual and Temporal, and the Commons, in this present Parliament assembled, and by the authority of the same, as follows:', a passive iussive). For Jackson (1995: 58-60), the enactment formula represents a convention, 'the legal community accepts at face value the statutory force of appropriately printed volumes which carry this enactment formula.' Now the formula used in our text neither appears 'in the canonical first-person' form (*ḥm.f* instead of *ḥm.i* may represent an enallage) nor in a simple present ('I command'); the locutive simple present formula must have been pronounced earlier by the king (his verbal order being a performative)[54].

---

53 Kurzon adds (1986: 12): 'All those cases may be considered implicit performatives, since it is only the situation – the promulgation of a law – not the linguistic form, that allows for a performative interpretation.'

54 But the Old Kingdom negative formula appearing sometimes after headings is probably performative ('I (or My majesty) forbid'), which is not past, but atemporal and locutive: see 4th dynasty *Špssk3f Giza decree* (*n rdi* (*.i*)), 5th dynasty *Nfrirk3rᶜ Abydos decree* (*n rdi.n*(*.i*)), and 6th dynasty *Ppy* II *Coptos B/C/D decrees* (*n rdi.n ḥm*(*.i*)). They are analyzed by Edel (§ 542) as 'Präsentisches Perfekt', although Allen (1984: § 354 and 436) notes that in the Pyramid Texts, *n sḏm.f* expresses an independent aorist and *n sḏm.n.f* is usually a 'generic negation' (sometimes also a past negation), and Shisha-Halevy (1989c: 253) mentions that '*n sḏm.n.f* is tense-indifferent' in narrative textemes of Old Egyptian. The performative is used even in monumental copies of decrees because of their extreme resemblance to the original during the Old Kingdom.

What we have here is an account (a 'constative' in Austin's terminology), a record of this original speech act that was not addressed to the general public (the perfect relates the past royal order to the present situation)[55]; see Goedicke (1967: 12, 235). We are not even in the presence of the original written version of the decree, but of a copy/excerpt in a propagandistic apparatus, and even if its content is normative, we have already seen that the context is a narrative one (see the eulogy). Even the authentication or sealing formula that was usually present in Old Kingdom lapidary versions of decrees (*ir/ḫtm r-gs ni-swt ḏs* + date) is absent here. What we have is a verb (*w{ꜣ}ḏ*) with a 'performative flavor (...) used in nonperformative utterances' (Jori 1994: 2092). But 'it is often difficult to say whether an utterance expresses a performative or not' (Jori 1994: 2092), and when Austin (followed by some later authors) finally introduced the locutionary/illocutionary/perlocutionary acts distinction, he was in fact establishing 'that all utterances have, after all, a performative character, [which] is the same as saying that none has' (Jori 1994: 2092); gradation is a key element in performativity. The performative *sḏm.n.f* in Middle Egyptian (Gunn 1924: 68-74 'synchronous present'; Vernus 1985b: 307-316) is in fact a locutive form (*sḏm.n.i͗*), never preceded by *i͗w* (which may be opposed to an *i͗w sḏm.n.i͗* form as in *Urk.* IV, 290 lines 1-9, see Vernus 1985b: 313). The Old Egyptian perfect thus occurs in our register in a delocutive report texteme, as its Neo-Egyptian form occurred earlier in the aetiologic part of the eulogy narrative (but in a passive diathesis with an archaic value).

- *rdit*: infinitive, nominal object of *i͗w w{ꜣ}ḏ.n ḥm.f*.
- *ḥn.tw*.N: dependant passive prospective, nominal object of *rdit*.
- *ḥr mw ḥr tꜣ:* irreversible binomial, see *Wb* II, 50. For general linguistics, see Malkiel (1959: 121) 'military's long-standing dualistic formula *on land and on sea'*. He notes on p. 143 that the sequence of the two nouns is irreversible in each language that uses it (land + water in English, Greek and French, but water + land in German and Spanish). It is followed here by another doublet: *šmꜥw mḥw*. Concerning the binomial 'in heaven and on earth' in Neo-Egyptian narrative context, Hintze (1950: 107) notes the absence of explicit coordination ('Asyndeton') in poetic texts (as well as the absence of articloid), but its presence ('Syndeton') in other stories as *m tꜣ pt ḥnꜥ pꜣ tꜣ*. The legal register is also on that level closer to 'poetic' registers.

* General dialectal features: degree 1.

* Legal terms:

w{ꜣ}ḏ - classifier: 𓏛 (to decree, to command). See Grimal (1986: 642). The superordinate [ABSTRACT] category classifier is used instead of the binding element because it is another *signified* that is expressed by this lexeme (the verbal uttering of an order that may afterwards be translated into a document, but has at this stage nothing to do with the medium). See Goedicke (1964: 35)

55 See Polotsky (1965: 17 and 1976: 35-6).

for the process of law during the Old Kingdom (the king's verbal issuing of order (law), the original transcription by the chancery, the sealing and the execution of copies) and the absence of a classifier in the case of the lexeme 'to command' (Goedicke 1967: 10-12).

ḥn - classifier: ø (to allocate personnel/property, post or 'desservir' – passive: to be endowed/equipped with personnel/property attached to a service or 'être desservi').

* Legal formula: *iw w{ꜣ}ḏ.n ḥm.f* (source of the decree) + *rdit* (the executive power has to implement the King's order) + *ḥn.tw* (nature of the measure: allocation) + beneficiary + *ḥr* (the decree's territorial application)

I.2.4 Preamble *sensu stricto* (negative intents) – part 1

(31) (…) *r tm dit tḥt.tw r rmṯ nb n [t]ꜣ ḥwt nt ḥḥw m rnpwt ni-swt bity Mnmꜣꜥtrꜥ ib hrw m ꜣbdt nty m tꜣ r ḏr.f m ṯꜣy ḥmt*

r tm rdit tḥt.tw r ḫt nbt n (32) *pr pn nty m tꜣ r ḏr.f*

r tm [rdit iṯꜣ.tw rmṯ nb] n pr pn m kfꜥw m w n w m bꜣrti m bḥw n skꜣ m bḥw n ꜥwꜣyw in sꜣ ni-swt nb (33) *ḥry pḏt nb ḥꜣty-ꜥ nb rwḏ nb rmṯ nb [hꜣb m] wpt [r] Kš*

r tm rdit šnꜥ.tw im(w).sn ḥr mw in šnꜥy nb

r tm rdit tḥt.tw r ꜣḥwt nb n tꜣ ḥwt (34) *Mnmꜣꜥtrꜥ ib hrw m ꜣbdw m sḫt [r smnmn tꜣš]w.sn*[56] *in sꜣ ni-swt nb ḥry pḏt nb rwḏ nb n pr rwḏ n pr ni-swt [rm]ṯ*[57] *h(ꜣ)b m wp r Kš*

r tm dit iṯꜣ.tw 𓃒[58] (35) *ꜥꜣ šꜣw ꜥnḫw tp n iꜣwt [nb n tꜣ ḥwt nt] ḥḥw m rnpwt n ni-swt bity Mnmꜣꜥtrꜥ ib hrw m ꜣbdt m ḥwrꜥ r-pw m sḫr n wstnw in sꜣ ni-swt nb ḥry pḏwt nb ḥꜣty-ꜥ nb* (36) *kꜣḏn [nb ḥry i]ḥw nb ḥry Nḥsyw nb rwḏ [nb n pr ni-swt] rmṯ nb hꜣb m wp r Kš*

r tm rdit th.tw[59] *r wḥꜥw*[60] *nb n tꜣ ḥwt nt ḥḥw m rnpwt n ni-swt bity Mnmꜣꜥtrꜥ* (37) *ib hrw m ꜣbdt ḥr šꜣw.f n grg ḥr swnnw.f n ḥꜣmw ḥr sḫt r nwt*[61] *n.f*

r tm rdit tkn.tw wḥꜥ rmw nb n tꜣ ḥwt Mnmꜣꜥtrꜥ ib hrw m ꜣbdt (38) *ḥr s[w]nnw.f n ḥꜣm nty m pꜣ tꜣ n Kš r ḏr.f in sꜣ ni-swt nb ḥry pḏt nb ḥꜣty-ꜥ nb rwḏ nb n pꜣ tꜣ n Kš r ḏr.f*

r tm rdit tḥt.tw r smdwt nb n tꜣ ḥwt (39) *nt ḥḥw m rnpwt n ni-swt bity Mnmꜣꜥtrꜥ ib hrw m [ꜣ]bdt nty m pꜣ tꜣ n Kš m ṯꜣyw ḥmwt m ḫwyw ꜣḥwt rwḏw bityw ꜥḥwtyw kꜣmwyw*

---

56 See line 51 for the restitution.

57 Without *nb*.

58 "Phonetically enigmatic' logogram, susceptible of representing several lexemes (a 'high intermediate covert category [bovine]' or its subspecies), see Goldwasser (2002: 82-83).

59 Compare with line 38, for instance: *r tm rdit tḥt.tw*.

60 Graphic doublet, explained by *ḥr šꜣw.f n grg ḥr swnnw.f n ḥꜥmw*.

61 See *RITANC* I, 54.

k3ryw (40) *iswt wsḫw ḥr nʿw* (?) *n g3wt šwtyw*[62] *n ḫ3st ḳwrw* [*n*] *iʿ nbw wḫrw irr nb ḥnwt.f m t3 ḥwt nt ḥḥw m rnpwt n ni-swt bity Mnm3ʿtrʿ ib hrw m 3bdt*

(31) to prevent ones transgression against/in respect of[63] any person of [t]he temple of millions of years '(the) King of Upper and Lower Egypt *Mnm3ʿtrʿ*'s heart is contented in Abydos', who is (anywhere) in (the) entire land, being man (or) woman[64];

to prevent ones transgression against/in respect of any material property[65] of (32) the aforementioned temple that is (anywhere) in (the) whole land;

to prevent [that be seized any person] of the aforementioned temple by coercion(,) from a district to (another) district, by (submission?) contract, by/as a forced labor (corvée) of ploughing (or) by/as a forced labor of harvesting, by any Viceroy (33), any troop commandant, any mayor, any agent, anybody [sent on] a mission to Kush;[66]

to prevent that be detained their boat on water by any executive force;

to prevent ones overstepping of any field of the temple (34) '*Mnm3ʿtrʿ*'s heart is contented in Abydos' in (the) countryside [to shift] their [boundarie]s by any Viceroy, any troop commandant, any agent of (the) Agent(s) Department of the King's House, (or) [perso]n sent as messenger to Kush;

to prevent that be seized bovine(s) (35), donkey(s), pigs, goats, [any] head/kind[67] of livestock [of the temple of] millions of years '(the) King of Upper and Lower

62 For Spalinger (1991: 33), independent or temple-employed traders who receive 'surplus from a temple in return for needed goods'; see also Reineke (1979: 5-14, esp. note 24 p. 9), temple employees 'Handelsagent'.

63 Gardiner (1952: 28): it is ultimately Osiris, lord of people and goods, who is wronged.

64 Note that *m ṯ3y ḥmt* precise *rmṯ nb* (hyperonymous, superordinate) in an effort to be cautious. Also a binomial expression, with typical sequence male + female, decreasing hierarchy (see *supra* the remark about progression in lists).

65 Gardiner (1952: 26).

66 The oldest decree containing criminal dispositions to survive is *Nfrirk3rʿ*'s *Abydos decree* (5th dynasty). It contains a parallel disposition: *n rdi.n(.i) sḫm s nb m*
iṯt ḥmw-nṯr nb ntw m sp(3)t ntt.k im.s (…))
f3t h3t n k3t nb r) *3ḥt nṯr nb*) *r r3-ʿwy ḥnʿ k3t nb nt sp3t*
iṯt mrt nb ntt ḥr))
"I do not give any man power to seize any prophets who are in (the) nome you are in, to impose a corvée of any (kind of) work upon, (or) to seize any farming corvée subject who is in, any god's field, for the domain work and any work of the nome".

67 *tp n* + appellative*:* represents either a *unit in a group*, which may be superior (archetypic: 'first/best of' as in the title *tp n sš* (*Urk.* I 69,2 & 190,7)), or a specimen in a category including similar items (paradigmatic: 'any/example/item of' as in 'head of cattle' (*contra*: Gardiner 1952: 31) or in *Buhen Sthy* I decree, line 6: *tp n w3ḥ* (example/item of endowment?)), perhaps even a species in a category including different species (typologic: 'a particular kind/sort of'); or a *group* (generic: 'notion name representing the entire category', as for Nims 1936: 51-54 ('in the Abydos decrees (…) the group had already come to be treated as one word, and to have the general meaning of 'animal') and Gardiner 1952: 30-31(any kind of – 'generalizing')). See also the expression *tp-ḏrt* (' "head-tax" (?)' in Haring 1997: 18). But in lines 55-56, we find: *t3 mnmnt* (herd, flock) + species (bovines, goats, donkey, pigs, fowls) in a list closed by *t3 mnmnt i3wt* (*i3wt* being apparently classified by *EG*'s list E8 icon of a kid  'Det. small cattle, exx.  *ʿwt* 'flocks', 'goats';  *mnmnt* 'herds'.'). Consequently,

Egypt *Mnm3ʿtrʿ*'s heart is contented in Abydos', by robbery or in arbitrary plan by any Viceroy, any troops commandant, any mayor (36), [any] off[icer], any stab[lemaster], any commander of Nubians, [any] agent [of the King's House], anybody sent as a messenger to Kush;
to prevent ones transgression against any fisherman/fowler of the temple of millions of years '(the) King of Upper and Lower Egypt *Mnm3ʿtrʿ*'s (37) heart is contented in Abydos', (one) in his marshes for hunting, (the other) in his fishing pounds in (the) countryside, to rouse[68]/annoy[69] (?) him;
to prevent that be approached[70]/molested[71] any fowler/fisherman of the temple '*Mnm3ʿtrʿ*'s heart is contented in Abydos' (38) in his fishing ponds that (are anywhere) in the entire land of Kush, by any Viceroy, any troop commandant, any mayor, any agent of the entire land of Kush;
to prevent one's transgression against any staff members[72] of the temple (39) of millions of years '(the) King of Upper and Lower Egypt *Mnm3ʿtrʿ*'s heart is contented in [A]bydos', who are in the land of Kush, whether men (or) women, guardians of fields, beekeepers, cultivators, gardeners, vintners (40), crews of barges conveyors (?)[73] of dues/tribute, desert/foreign traders, staff [of] gold-[w]ashers, wharvesmen (?)[74], anyone who accomplishes his service in the temple of millions of years '(the) King of Upper and Lower Egypt *Mnm3ʿtrʿ*'s heart is contented in Abydos'.

* Neo-Egyptian characteristics:
- *t3 ḥwt*
- *p3 t3:* occurs thrice in a construction functioning as an adverbial adjunct:
(a) line 38: # noun determined + **relative phrase *nty m p3 t3*** expanded (by a relational noun phrase with ø country name + augens *r ḏr.f*) #
(b) line 38: # noun(s) determined (by *nb*) + **relational noun phrase *n p3 t3*** (expanded by a relational noun phrase with ø country name + augens *r ḏr.f*) #
(c) lines 38-9: # *t3 ḥwt* (expanded) + **relative phrase *nty m p3 t3*** (expanded by a relational noun phrase with ø country name) #.
In fact, we always have the same scheme: a determined name expanded by *nota relationis n* or relative phrase (adverbial rheme) with determined formal place

it seems that in our decree, *i3wt* represents the generic 'cattle' (a group) and *tp n i3wt* a unit in the group as in the modern expression 'head of cattle'.

68 *RITANC* I: 54.

69 Griffith (1927: 201).

70 Griffith (1927: 201), to approach unto, with 𓂻 classifier.

71 *RITA* I: 45.

72 Caminos (1958: 56); Vernus (1975: 23) and his references; Théodoridès (1982: 85, note 53) 'subalternes'; Spalinger (1991: 32) 'staff of workers'; Haring (1997: 6), non-priestly staff.

73 *nʿi*: to convey (see *KRI* I: 416 and Helck 1973: 213). The puzzling construction # *ḥr* + infinitive + *n* + object # seems to be a shortcut between an adverbial and a nominal expansion, because the object of this verb is not usually introduced by the preposition *n*, which leaves us with a *nota relationis*. But it could also be a misreading of a damaged line (see also the classifiers).

74 *RITANC* I: 54; Griffith (1927: 201) 'boat-building or joinery'; Edgerton (1947: 222) 'carpenters'.

lexeme + appurtenatively related name identifying country (for the same construction in Coptic, see Shisha-Halevy 1989d: 81).

On the other hand, *p3* is absent in the frequent, fossilized syntagm # *m t3 r ḏr.f* # (see line 31, for example, and also in *Ḥrmḥb*'s *Karnak decree*, see line16) (d) and systematically when the name of the country is not preceded by *t3* 'land of' (sent to Kush) (see line 34, for example) (e).

In occurrences (a, b, c) of the determinator *p3,* the articloid (Löfstedt (1981) terminology, see *supra*) has a cataphoric referentiality with the non-specific *t3* (the land of Kush). The proper name *Kš* being unique, autoidentifiable (determined *per se*), it does not require a determinator (as for (e)). Compare with Simpson (1996: 35) for the Ptolemaic sacerdotal decrees (in Demotic), with an example such as *t3 m3y(t) n S3lmyn3* 'the island of Salamis (Cyprus)', a 'non-phoric definite article indicating relation-dependent identity'. In (d), Egypt is meant by *t3*, a clear signified for any Egyptian (identifiable species).

- *r tm* (*r*)*dit*: negative intent-list preamble formula, conceived as an adjunct to lines 30-31 sentence, the negative intent statements always being introduced in our text by # *iw w{3}ḏ.n ḥm.f rdit ḥn.tw*.N # (lines 30-31, 55, 82-83, 97-98). In *EG* § 341 and 348 Middle Egyptian examples, *rdi* ('negatival complement' considered adverbial by Gardiner but surely nominal, see Gilula 1970: 212) appears instead of *rdit* after the infinitive *tm* (verb with negative *signifié* but affirmative *signifiant*) as in *Ỉmnḥtp* III decree (21st dynasty copy) to *Ỉmnḥtp*, son of *Ḥp* (*r tm di*, the negative counterpart of preceding *r dit*). In *EG* § 344, Gardiner notes that "In Late Egyptian the infinitive is regularly used after *tm* in place of the earlier negatival complement. Examples are found already in Dyn. XVIII and even earlier.' Interestingly enough, he mentions as an early example of this feature another royal (but Second Intermediate Period) decree (king *Nbḫprwrˁ Ỉntf*'s *Coptos decree*, line 10: *tm rdit in.tw s nb*). See also *LEG* § 11.5.1. (v) on this construction. One must note the non-significant substitution of *dit* with *rdit* (and restricted infinitive constituency) in the causative construction, a stylistic variant to relieve monotony or dictated by the space left on the stela, since the use of *dit* increases towards the end of the decree ('economizing script')[75]. For Winand (1992: 77), *dit* is more widely used during the 19th dynasty, but in the *Nauri decree,* we counted 8 occurrences of *rdit* against 9 of *dit*. Negative purpose is expressed in Old Kingdom decrees by *nfr n* + *sḏm.f*/N nominal form (in *Coptos B & C Ppy* II decrees, for instance, with *nfr n ṯss.sn*) as Gilula (1970: 214) noted: 'in Middle Egyptian *tm* assumed almost all the uses of *nfr n*'. Mention must also be made of prohibitions in those decrees, usually expressed by *n rdi.n ḥm(.i)* (as early as in the 5th dynasty *Nfrirk3rˁ Abydos decree* where it immediately follows the heading and is a locutive performative *n rdi.n*(*.i*) 'I forbid') and preceding the 'retain (-preserve)' clause. Although not formulated

75 The same phenomenon is to be observed in the spelling of *hrw* in the temple's name (see *infra*).

as negative purposes[76] but as a performative, this prohibition might be an earlier parallel (in another syntactic form) to our *r tm rdit* sentences, sole systematic negative expressions in Ramesside royal decrees. Note also the presence of the formula in *Rꜥmss* II's *Hittite Treaty* (*KRI* II, 225-232, line 9: *r tm dit ḫpr ḫrw*). The repetition of *r tm (r)dit* has a cohesive function in the text. Isotopy is characteristic of legal discourses (also modern ones), which share prosodic features with religious discourses. For modern forensic register, see Crystal & Davy (1969: 207-208); Charrow, Crandall & Charrow (1982: 181) who quote Prof. Fred Rodell's definition of legal language as a 'high class mumbo jumbo'.

- *tht.tw:* dependant prospective as nominal object of *(r)dit* (impersonal *sḏm.f* or *sḏm.tw*.N passive), expressing the nature of the crime to prevent, with an intrusive *t* before *tw* in almost every instance (see line 37: *th.tw*). See preceding note about the same verb in line 26.
- *Kš*: for *Kꜣš* (*Wb* V, 109: from 18th dynasty on).
- *bꜣrti*: earliest example of this Semitic word in an Egyptian text, see Gardiner (1952: 28); Görg (1977: 28); Kitchen (1979: 454). Note that the segment *m kfꜥw m w n w m bꜣrti m bḥw n skꜣ m bḥw n ꜥwꜣyw* is a typical case of multinominal sequence enumerating contiguous terms for precision and all-inclusiveness as in modern legalese, see Danet (1985: 284); Bhatia (1994: 142-144). Note also its prosodic features, including binomials and repetition.
- *iꜣwt*: typical Ramesside (Middle Egyptian: *ꜥwt*), see *Wb* I, 29 and Nims (1936: 51-54).
- *kꜣmwyw*: 18th dynasty lexeme (for plurals in –*y*(*w*), see *LEG* § 4.1.2.a). The precise meaning of the words *kꜣmy* and *kꜣry* (and even *kꜣny*) is not clear in *CD*, 284 and *Wb* V, 106-108, due to the same vine classifier. It could in fact be the same word, with slight diachronic phonetic/orthographic changes (an Old Kingdom *kꜣny*, followed by *kꜣry* by the end of the Middle Kingdom and *kꜣmy* from the 18th dynasty on). But here, the two words are used, though *kꜣmy* does not get the vine classifier. For Gardiner (1952: 29 & 1947: 96*-97*), *kꜣmy* is related to vineyard-keepers (exclusively used in wine-jar inscriptions) and olive-tree tenders, but could be the Lower Egypt dialect of the older *kꜣny*, *kꜣry*, its Upper Egypt counterpart (although usually employed in relation to vegetables and flowers). See also Vercoutter (1959: 127) and Haring (1997: 243-245 & 348 (4)).
- *wstnw*: Ramesside spelling (*LEG* § 1.1.2).
- *ḥwrꜥ:* Neo-Egyptian (*Wb* III, 56).
- *hb*: Neo-Egyptian for *hꜣb* (*LEG* § 1.6; Winand 1992: 33).
- *ḳwrw* [*n*] *iꜥ nbw:* see *Kanais decree* and Gunn & Gardiner (1917: 247, n. 3).

* 'Classical' degree 0 forms used:

---

76 Shisha-Halevy (1989c: 253): *n sḏm.n.f* is 'tense-indifferent; in past cotext, it has past reference or is circumstantial: *iw gr rdi.n ḥm.f… n gr rdi.n ḥm.f*, *Urk.* I 283.6 ff.)' which is *Coptos B decree* of *Ppy* II. But see the line after the address and the object of the decree: *n rdi.n ḥm*(.*i*) is the performative '(My) majesty forbids'.

- *ḫt nbt:* gender concord of the determinator (as of the relator, see *supra*) is limited in our text to the lexeme *ḫt*, and is not strictly observed, as it disappears from line 92 on (*ḫt nb*) probably to economize on space. The use of archaisms has already been signaled as a common feature of Ramesside and modern statutes.
- 𓃒 *ꜥꜣ šꜣw ꜥnḫw tp n iꜣwt* [*nb*] (lines 35-6)*:* rather puzzling is the issue of singular/plural noun use in lists, as here with the plural 'goats' (and 'pigs'?) after singular species nouns (inconsistency in plural marking?), and the possible 'collective' or generic nature of some (or all) of the lexemes (the value of the presence/absence of the exponent of number ׀׀׀ or *w*). The question is further complicated by the probable presence of *nb* (as in line 58 that reads: 𓃒 *ꜥꜣ šꜣ* [*ꜥ*]*nḫ*[*w*] *tp n iꜣdw nb im.sn*, see *infra*), which could be related to *tp n iꜣwt* only, to cover any species not expressly mentioned (followed by its determinative expansion), or to the whole group of species. Groll notes (*LEG* § 4.1.2a) that in Late Egyptian, it seems that 'the ending *.w* was, in general, lost in pronunciation' and that 'In most cases, therefore, no ending is written' and even the plural determinative may be omitted. The value of singular *nb* is distributive; it has an unspecific and decontextualised value corresponding to the aim at generality of the decree. Based on the reading of lines 58, one may assume that bovine(s), donkey(s), pig(s) and goats are generic categories or represent an undetermined number of animals seized, while the sole *tp n iꜣwt* unit is determined by a distributive *nb*. Again, as noted before for the list of addressees, we are faced with the type of list adopted when the listed items are not offenders. As is the case with and modern criminal laws, the rule is 'both general and detailed' (Maley 1994: 31), with general terms, detailed lists, specificity expansions (e.g. by robbery or in an arbitrary manner), phrasal repetition. The other list formulas of this section are the following:
    - lines 32-33: [singular nominal lexemes, with or without expansion + distributive *nb*] + [all-inclusive hyperonym *rmṯ nb* + expansion].
    - line 34: [singular nominal lexemes, with expansions[77] + distributive *nb*] + [all-inclusive hyperonym *rmṯ* (without *nb*) + expansion].
    - lines 35-36: [singular nominal lexemes, with or without expansions[78] + distributive *nb*] + [all-inclusive hyperonym *rmṯ nb* + expansion].
    - line 38: [singular nominal lexemes, with or without expansions[79] + distributive *nb*].
    - lines 38-40: [collective noun + distributive *nb* + expansion] + [*m* + sexe] + [*m* + plural nouns (members of professions covered by the collective noun) + all-inclusive participle + distributive *nb*)].

77 In one instance, the relational expansion follows *nb* instead of the lexeme it expands (open juncture nucleus/satellite): *rwḏ nb n pr rwḏ n pr ni-swt*. It may also indicate that at least two lexemes + *nb* are expanded by the relational satellite.

78 *Idem.*

79 *Idem.*

We may therefore assume that in our text, two types of lists are used in specific conditions:

- # noun + noun + noun + hyperonym *nb* # concerning addressees, objects or victims of the offences in the Proclamation, Preamble and Crimes textemes; usually the last item (hyperonym) is followed by the distributive *nb* (*rmṯ nb*; participle *nb*; *tp n i͗3wy nb*; *ẖt nb*, see *infra*); the lexemes may be of singular or plural number, or generic; the list is conceived as a catalogue with a cohesive structure, each item being individually unimportant;
- # noun *nb* + noun *nb* + noun *nb* + hyperonym *nb* # for lists of offenders in the Preamble or the Crimes textemes; hierarchically ordered as a diminishing progression, usually the all-encompassing last item (hyperonym) is followed by the distributive *nb* (*rmṯ nb*); the lexemes are usually of singular number (for exceptions, see lines 41-42 and 58); each offender being important as he may be the unique individual affected by the disposition, the list structure is less cohesive and each lexeme is followed by *nb*.

- *r tm:* preposition + infinitive (purpose).
- *(r)di͗t* + dependent prospective, nominal object of *rdi͗t*.
- *h3b*: see above. Note the spelling *hb,* line 34.
- *pr pn:* anaphoric proximal determinator, already archaic in the Ramesside context, used with limited lexeme constituency, in the syntagm # noun *nb n pr pn* # (it never appears with *t3 ḥwt* and complete name of the temple). See *LEG* § 3.1.1.2; in French, 'dudit + noun', as an archaic anaphoric, relational determinator used in modern legal register (along with other similar forms, see Danet 1985: 283; Kurzon 1986: 55-56; Raymondis & Le Guern 1976: 27). For Haring (1997: 27 & 32), it is the only case in which a memorial temple may be referred to by *pr* instead of *ḥwt* (general word for building, temple, estate, or royal foundation).
- *r-pw:* Middle Kingdom disjunction marker between two adverbial adjuncts #(preposition *m* + noun) *r-pw* (preposition *m* + noun expanded) #; see *EG* § 91.2; '*r3-pw*: Substantivische Partikel' for Junge (1996: 91); *Wb* II, 396-7: in Neo-Egyptian, also between nexuses. The decree shows other instances of the marker: lines 59, 68-70, and 111. Compare with *Rˁmss* II's *Hittite Treaty* (*KRI* II, 225-232, line 16), introducing a new disposition.
- *i͗rr nb:* geminating participle, used substantively.

* General dialectal features: degree 1.

* Legal terms:

r tm (r)di͗t – classifier: ø (to prevent).

thi r - classifiers: (to transgress).

ẖt – classifier: (material property). The use of the superordinate [ABSTRACT] category classifier to categorize material property allows for the inclusion in the same category of a large range of assets (land and movable property). It also refers to the document listing the goods and perhaps constituting the legal title (for the written *ỉmy(t)-pr* attesting such a title, see, for example, the *Stèle juridique de Karnak* in Lacau 1949: 7-9; *Kanais decree*, line 18). Interestingly, when the goods involved are of a more specific nature, the papyrus roll may be dropped in favour of the image of the goods concerned (see for instance *Wb* I, 124.5 'Speisen'), which proves the advantage of the all-encompassing and abstract nature of the papyrus roll where undetermined types of assets are concerned. Writing, legal processes, counting, and listing being prototypical activities that lead to a written record and account (as well as a primary concern for the bureaucratic Egyptian society), their involvement will usually lead to the use of the [ABSTRACT] category papyrus roll classifier[80].

m kfꜥw – classifier: 𓂡 (by coercion). Known from 18th dynasty (*Wb* V, 121). The translation 'requisition'[81] could be misleading, because it implies a specific administrative prerogative that does not lead to a permanent deprivation of property, a service or goods request, of the type for which our text uses the lexeme *ỉṯꜣ*. The word *kfꜥw* could simply imply the use of constraint (implied by 𓂡), not exclusively in a requisitive procedure, and not automatically with the use of violence or *ultra vires*. Edgerton (1947: 221) and Griffith (1927: 200) translate it 'capture', Harari (1990: 232) ' « par la force », donc par violence, ou par contrainte lésionnaire, parce que (…) par des personnes abusant de leur capacité juridique', Kitchen (1979: 455) and Spalinger (1991: 32) alternate between the use of 'requisition' or 'press-gang', Kruchten (1981: 62-63) 'opérer une réquisition de main-d'œuvre'; Warburton (1997: 191) 'forcefully'. Precisely how was a regular procedure of 'requisition' conceived, by which the Egyptian administration requested a service, or any kind of performance from a person or an institution? The practices following *m kfꜥw* in our text may elaborate on this expression, or imply other situations, perhaps opposed to *m kfꜥw*. Lines 43, 45, 67 and 100 use the same terms (or some of them), and Gardiner (1952), followed by Kitchen (1979: 456), distinguishes the four practices on the basis of the presence of the 'explicit disjunctive locution' *r-pw* in line 68 between *m kfꜥw* and *m w n w*: capture (forced), transfer (not forced? or subcase of capture?), contract (probably not derived from consensus) and land forced labour (forced, but specific). The 𓂡 classifier represents by metonymy (the armed organ for the activity) and a possible metaphorical process (a hand holding a crooked stick symbol is empowered with a coercive authority) the category [COERCION]. *m kfꜥw* denotes administrative practices involving coercion (moral or physical) and, during the Ramesside Period, perhaps one of the prototypical members of the category. Even *bꜣrti* is once written with 𓂡, which may imply that consent is forced upon the Administration's contractor (see *infra*). Note that the word *ỉṯꜣ* is

80 Naming, counting, classifying, listing, and labelling are major concerns for scribes (from onomastica to Deir el-Medineh records examples abound of all kinds of lists).

81 Théodoridès (1981: 633) uses 'réquisition' for *ṯsi*, a lexeme understood by Harari (1957: 341) as a definitive recruitment.

a better candidate for 'requisition' because it is decribed by the other expressions, but it is not exclusively applied to the administrative procedure of appropriation.

m bꜣrti – classifier: ø (by (submission?) contract). See Kitchen (1979: 454). For Hoch (1994: 108-109), *bi=ra=ta* represents an 'obligatory service; treaty of submission', and not a freewillingly agreed (by mutual consent) convention, noting the (usually present, but only once in the *Nauri decree*) classifier of the superordinate [COERCION] category as proof of his assertion (based on Görg 1977: 29 'nötigendes Verhältnis', who notes that later occurrences of the word show the or + classifiers). The semantic borderline between *m bꜣrti* and *m bḥw* is thus difficult to distinguish (it could be a question of duration, or *m bḥw* could be an illustration of *bꜣrti*, when determined, as in our text, by adnominal expansions, ploughing and harvesting). See also Warburton (1997: 192, n. 584).

m bḥw – classifier: (by forced labor - corvée). See Théodoridès (1981: 633) for *kꜣt*, a synonym (?) and Janssen (1961: 30) who compares it to *hꜣ* (perhaps a forced labour during the Old Kingdom, but some kind of temple service during the 19th dynasty). The superordinate [COERCION] category classifier again adds the picture of the essential coercion component of the action (imposed upon the subject).

rwḏ - classifier: (agent).

šnʿ - classifiers: (to detain); see Janssen (1961: 100). The classifier of the superordinate [MOTION] category is used to represent the 'missing quality', the most salient characteristic of detention being movement restriction (Goldwasser 1995: 92-93 and 2002: chapter I, as in *idi* 'deaf', classified by the 'ear' icon), in a schematic reversed relation to the lexeme (to detain is 'not to let go'). The classifier refers to the 'restrictive' semantics of the lexeme *šnʿ* (see *supra* for *thm, thi, ẖnd*), classifying it in the [LEG] category.

šnʿy - classifiers: (member of the executive police force). Interestingly, the lexeme, although built on the same root as the preceding, is not classified by the same icons (which could be preserved along); the main message delivered by *šnʿy*, as chosen by the scribe, is the idea of a man using coercion (superordinate [COERCION] + taxonomic superordinate [MALE-HUMAN] categories), the agent, and not the motion he restricts. The purpose of this coercion suddenly becomes of less importance than the fact that the detention is exerted by a person invested of a certain authority. The pleonastic use of the root *šnʿ* could also have saved the scribe a second mention of the classifiers. Compare the *Elephantine decree* (classifier).

pr rwḏ - classifier: (agents department?).

iṯꜣ – classifiers: (to seize, take possession, appropriate), following Kitchen's reconstitution (lines 43, 44 and 45, for instance). At least four lookalike forms may have the same meaning: *iṯi*, *iṯꜣ*, *ṯꜣw* and *ṯꜣi*. The lexeme *iṯꜣ* already appears in *The Eloquent Peasant* B1, 192 with the classifiers, but the *Wb* I, 150 notes that the lexeme belongs to the New Kingdom; Théodoridès (1970: 145, note 4) mentions 'to take' but in relation to other words, forming specific expressions; Borghouts (1980: 101) adds that it is 'probably a LEg alloform of older *iṯi* which itself appears to be quite rare in LEg'). For *iṯi,* see Goedicke (1967: 26), Lorton (1974: 78-82), and Harari (1957: 341-342) 'requérir pour une corvée temporaire' (opposed to *ṯs*, definitive recruitment); McDowell (1990: 38); Morschauser (1991: 47); Simpson (1963: 56) 'to take as ones rightful possession' (in the context of *iṯi tꜣwy, iṯi iwꜥt tꜣwy* and *iṯi st nt it.f*). The classifiers used are usually of the superordinate [COERCION] category and the finger from the New Kingdom on (metonymic organ/action relation between the lexeme and the classifier, as one needs grabbing fingers to seize); but in Old Kingdom decrees, *iṯi* is written, for instance in *Nfrirkꜣrꜥ Abydos decree*, as (the walking rope).

m ḥwrꜥ - classifier: (by robbery). A sure case of *ultra vires* action, with the 'strong arm' classifier of the superordinate [COERCION] category. Thus the [COERCION] category covers legal as well as illegal practices.

m sẖr n wstnw – classifiers: for *sẖr* and for *wstnw* (in an arbitrary way, at someones discretion). See Kruchten 1981: 40-41 (*sẖr*: plan, project, intention, premeditation) and p. 68 (*wstn*: liberty of action, arbitrariness). Being either the product of a mental process or a totally abstract concept, *sẖr* belongs to the superordinate [ABSTRACT] category. The superordinate [MOTION] category classifier of *wstnw* may be due to the fact that this lexeme is also used in the sense of 'travel freely' (*CD*, 69 and *Sinuhe* B 115 with) or in several other expressions indicating an unhindered will or freedom of movement; again, a schematic relation leading to a complex extension process may be observed here, where 'freewill is liberty of movement'.

tkn - classifier: (to approach unto, molest). Here, the superordinate [MOTION] category prototypical members involving simple dynamics are again joined by a less prototypical member with hostile semantics (to come near; as in French, for instance, 'marcher' and 'marcher sur (l'ennemi)'). Again, the classifier expresses the original metonymic expression of movement but applies also to metaphorically related notions (as with *thi* and *wstnw*). Note that the *Wb* V, 333 adds that *tkn* is found 'ganz selten auch' with the or classifiers.

iri ḥnwt - classifier: ø (to accomplish a service).

* Legal formulas: - *r tm (r)dit* + *sḏm.tw* (offender) + *r* (victim)
- *r tm (r)dit* + *sḏm.tw*.N (victim) + *m* (method) + *in* (offender)

I.2.5 Preamble *sensu stricto* (positive intent): part 1

(40) *wp-ḥr wnn.sn* (41) *ḫwy mky iw s nb im.sn ḥr irt ḥnwt.f irt <m> [t]ꜣ ḥwt nt ḥḥw m rnpwt n ni-swt bity Mnmꜣꜥtrꜥ ib hrw m ꜣbdt iw nn rdit ḏꜣy.tw tꜣ r.sn in sꜣw ni-swt* (42) *n*

Kš nb ḥry pḏt nb srw nb kꜣḏn nb ḥry iḥw nb ṯꜣy-srywt nb wʿw[82] *nb n mšʿ rmṯ nb hꜣb m wp r Kš*

(40) In contrast, it is (41) retained (and) preserved that they are/will be, so that each man among them is doing/will do his service carried on <in> [th]e temple of millions of years '(the) King of Upper and Lower Egypt *Mnmꜣʿtrʿ*'s heart is contented in Abydos' while not allowing that will be interfered against them by any Viceroys (42) of Kush, any troop commandants, any civil servants, any officer(s?), any stable masters, any standard-bearers, any soldier of (the) army, anybody sent as messenger to Kush.

* Neo-Egyptian characteristics:

- *tꜣ ḥwt*
- *iw nn rdit: iw* and *nn* being mutually-exclusive in Middle Egyptian, it is a Neo-Egyptian construction, a particular case of # *nn* + noun #. For Gilula (1970: 210, esp. note 4), 'Beginning with Late Egyptian the negation of the circumstantial phrase is carried out by addition of the circumstantial converter *iw* (...) to the negative phrase. This phenomenon already exists in the Eighteenth Dynasty' (as in *Urk*. IV, 751, 9). Thus we are faced with the syntagm # circumstantial converter *iw* + *nn* preverbal negator + causative infinitive (deontic) #. See *EG* § 307.I on the use of *nn* + infinitive 'to express the non-performance or non-occurrence of some verbal action' and § 308 Obs. qualifying *nn* as the 'existential predicate', the infinitive being the 'subject'; Gunn (1924: 155) 'Infinitival Negative Clause' and p. 158 *nn rdit sḏm.f* 'not being allowed'; Gilula (1970: 211) '*nn* is a predicative negative', 'an existential negation' and *nn* + infinitive has a circumstantial meaning 'When the 'actor' of the circumstantial phrase is the same as that of the main sentence then the circumstantial phrase (...) will be negated by *nn* + infinitive.' (pp. 210, 212); Junge (1996: 181) 'adjektivischen Negation' (that will be replaced by *bn* in Neo-Egyptian) with a noun, often an infinitive, and 'nach den Verfahren des Neuägyptischen in der Regel explizit durch *iw* untergeordnet'; Shisha-Halevy (1998b: 596) considers that 'nexal theme-rheme structure does not apply to existential statements: they are in fact *pre*-predications, introducing nominals into discourse, and thus preparing predicational terms of reference' like 'presentative deictics'. An earlier instance of a similar disposition in a royal decree is to be found in *Ḫwtꜣwyrʿ Wgf* 13th dynasty *Abydos decree* (lines 1-3): *wḏ ḥm.i ʿnḫ wḏꜣ snb ḫwt mkt* + object + beneficiary + *n wnt rdit ḫnd rmṯ nbt*. In place of *iw nn rdit* after the retained (and) preserved disposition we notice *n wnt rdit*, also a deontic causative of an earlier stage of Egyptian (see Vernus 1985: 153, n. 1). A later narrative formulation appears in 18th dynasty *Ḏḥwtyms* IV's decree in favour of *Nbimn*: *ʿḥʿ.n w{ꜣ}ḏ.n ḥm(.i)* (nomination and attribution (*ḥn*) of staff and

82 See Vandersleyen (1971: 28-29), simple soldiers; Groll (1983: 238) ' "ordinary soldier", but in the El-Amarna letters it apparently means "garrison commander"'; Spalinger (1991: 35) 'military official'.

material property) *nn rdit ḏꜣ tꜣ r.s in rwḏ nb n ni-swt*. In *Rꜥmss* III's *Elephantine decree*, line 6, the construction *n rdit ḏꜣ.tw* is used. These formulations obviously belong to the same paradigm. We can probably trace the evolution of the motive from *n wnt rdit ḫnd* (13th dynasty *Ḫwtꜣwyrꜥ Wgf*), *nn rdit ḏꜣ tꜣ r.s* (18th dynasty *Ḏḥwtyms* IV), *iw nn rdit ḏꜣy.tw tꜣ r.sn* (19th dynasty *Štḫy* I), to *n rdit ḏꜣ.tw* (20th dynasty *Rꜥmss* III). Note *Ḥrmḥb*'s *Karnak decree*, line 25 *iw bn wꜣḥ dḥr*, where *bn* replaces *nn* with the infinitive in another expression.

* 'Classical' degree 0 forms used:

- *wp-ḥr wnn.sn ḫwy mky iw*.N *ḥr irt*:
  - on a *microsyntactic* level, # *wp-ḥr* (proclitic contrastive particle following the negative intent *r tm* preamble *sensu stricto*) + thematic nominal that-form *wnn.sn* + stative binomial rhemes[83] # is an adverbial (statal) nexus, followed by another adverbial nexus # theme *iw*.N + rheme *ḥr irt* #.

    As for *wp-ḥr*, Gardiner regarded it as a 'compound preposition' ('but') followed by a *sḏm.f* (?) form (*EG* § 179.3). It is a proclitic particle introducing an independent sentence (not a dependence 'subordination' conjunction), marking a contrast between the preceding negative exposition of crimes to prevent and the positive protection hereby enunciated; see Sottas (1913: 97) 'exception est faite'; Parant (1982: 87-93) who refers to the etymology of *wp*, 'to separate'.

    As for *wnn.sn ḫwy mky,* it is a contrastive cleft sentence, reinforced by the use of *wp-ḥr*, focalizing the blessed situation (stative, durative) of those affected by the decree. The alleged 'simple futurity' (*EG* § 326) implied by *wnn.sn* (although fitting the view that the decree regulates a situation from its utterance or enactment on) is only a factor of context, the nominal auxiliary having no time value *per se;* see Polotsky (1965: note 19 & § 48 and 1976: 3.8.1, 3.8.3.2); Shisha-Halevy (1978: n. 43) 'forme emphatique (presque un convertisseur déprédicatisant aux temps duratifs)'; Vernus (1982: 85-89, 1983: 75-76 and 1982-1983: 119) qualifying *wnn* as a 'morphème de substantivisation'; Neveu (1985: 50). The durative aspect of the form is induced by the use of the stative that also appears in Neo-Egyptian, but in rare instances; see Satzinger (1976: 89 & 94) on *LRL* 31, 13, non dynamic form.

    Concerning *iw*.N *ḥr irt*, the adverbial nexus may have an independent or circumstantial value in Middle Egyptian (see examples of both in *EG* § 323), whereas in Neo-Egyptian it may be a circumstantial 'first present' with relative time value or a narrative sequential form (*LEG* § 38 and 40 'non-initial main (past or future) clause'; Frandsen (1974: 85, 102): succeeding action in a non-initial main sentence preceded by a clause with which it forms a 'syntactically coherent (complete) and closed complex' referring to past or future time; Satzinger (1976: 100, 242 & 247) 'Narrativ', neither

83 Clearly not infinitives.

initial, nor subordinated but continuative, 'zeit neutral' but somctimes expressing present or future; Polotsky (1985: 157-161): a narrative past or preterit, sequential non-durative; Junge (1986): a circumstantial first present inherited from Middle Egyptian; Winand (1992: 443-457) 'séquentiel'). See *infra*.

- On a *macrosyntactic* level, the *wnn.f*/N *sḏm iw.f*/N *ḥr sḏm* construction has mainly been studied from two points of view: its temporal value with and without the proclitic *ḥr* (Baer 1965; Frandsen 1974: 184-192) and its epistolary Neo-Egyptian use as the *wnn tꜣy.i šꜥt spr r.k iw.k* (*ḥr*) *sḏm* formula[84] (*LEG* § 55.2; Bakir 1970: 80-81; Frandsen 1974: 185-186). The construction *wp-ḥr wnn.sn ḫwy mky iw*.N *ḥr irt* may theoretically be viewed in our text as:
  - two independent nexuses ("In contrast, it is retained (and) preserved that they are. Each man among them is doing his service");
  - an independent sentence followed by a dependent one ("In contrast, it is retained (and) preserved that they are, so that each man among them is doing his service"), the focus of the cleft sentence being the statives. Note that in the *Kanais decree*, lines 16-17, only *wpw-ḥr wnn*.N *ḫw mkw* appears, without following *iw.f ḥr sḏm*, in the same type of preamble *sensu stricto*, which could mean that in a similar texteme, the focus is on the stative. This is the option adopted here (see also hereunder the origin of the construction in royal decrees), although the adverbial vedette could also be found in the second nexus ("In contrast, it is when each man among them is doing his service, that they are retained (and) preserved"), the entire circumstantial clause being focalized as in Polotsky (1976: 3.8.9) translation of *The Eloquent Peasant* B1, 83-84 *wnn.k ḥr rdit di.tw n.f ꜥḳw nn rdit rḫ.f ntt ntk rdi n.f st* 'que-tu-fais-continuellement lui donner des provisions soit caractérisé par la circonstance de ne pas permettre qu'il sache que c'est toi qui les lui a données';
  - another option postulates a protasis-apodosis link between the two nexuses and the head position of the circumstantial member; see Vernus (1981: 80-81); Neveu (1985: 50); Shisha-Halevy (1995: 307-308) 'in the protasis-apodosis complex, both constituents are nexally interconnected (and interdependent) as high-level topic-theme and rheme'. For many authors, in Neo-Egyptian, the first nexus is not an independent one, with subtle nuances: 'subordonnée virtuelle' for Kruchten (1981: 14); main clauses, 'semantic equivalents of an English temporal clause' for Baer (1965: 138); 'subordinated clause of time' in *LEG* § 55.2; 'initial clause conjugations and not main sentences functioning as virtual subordinate clauses' for Frandsen (1974: 185); see also Cassonnet (2000: 97). The

84 Here the alleged construction is of a *wnn.N* (*ḥr*) *sḏm iw.k* (*ḥr*) *sḏm* nature. For Satzinger (1976: 95) *ḥr* + infinitive is dynamic or progressive in contrast with the stative.

apodosis may be viewed as a rhematic event, focalized and circumstantial, as in "In contrast, when it is retained (and) preserved that they are, each man is doing his service" or "In contrast, as soon as they are retained (and) preserved, each man is doing his service" ('contiguity' effect with inversion of logical sequence and concomitant 'no sooner than', see Polotsky (1957: 114-115 and 1965: § 21, in note 19 he adds that for Neo-Egyptian, *wnn.f* in an initial *wnn.f ḥr sḏm* is 'emphatic' and 'often refers to the future', and the following *ỉw.f ḥr sḏm* 'is circumstantial and expresses concomitance with the preceding sentence'); Depuydt (1993: 117-200); Shisha-Halevy (1995: note 51); Junge (1986: 122-124 and 1996: 288-291) 'closed complex' 'Wechselsatz mit *wnn*' 'temporale Abhängigkeits-beziehung' 'sobald dies, dann das'); Wente (1961: 122, note j). Another option is to view the apodosis as sequelling with the use of a narrative sequential form as do Satzinger (1976: 100) and Shisha-Halevy (1978: 59) as in the case of an apodotic-sequelling *ỉw.f ḥr sḏm* after a circumstantial temporal *ỉw.f ḥr sḏm*/stative. For Vernus (1981: 80-83), in Middle Egyptian, *wnn*.N, second tense of the protasis, has a circumstantial function (it belongs to an adverbial paradigm) in a system whose apodosis, never containing the adverbial nexus of the second tense, never has a circumstantial form; the second tense is not the theme of an emphatic turn of phrase but, as a nominal form, it assumes the circumstantial role as in "In contrast, when they are retained (and) preserved, each man among them is doing his service"; see also Neveu (1985: 50).

Concerning the origin of the construction in royal decrees, it may be traced to a pattern of the type # *ỉw.f*/N *ḫww* + *m ꜣww ḏt*/*mỉn mꜣʿwy* (temporal precision) + *n*.N (beneficiary) + *m wḏ* king (conformity/legality) #, probably of an explanatory/contrastive value, following the prohibition clause, already present in the second protective royal decree to survive (5th dynasty *Nfrỉrkꜣrʿ Abydos decree*) and in *Ppy* II *Coptos B/C decrees*. In fact, the damaged formula of the decree of *Špsskꜣf* (4th dynasty), also following a prohibition clause, is to be reconstructed for Sethe as [*ỉr.n ḥm nw n-mr*]*wt nḫt wʿbw.f m* [*ꜣwt ḏt*] (*Urk*. I, 160; Goedicke 1967: 16 & 20 (17)), a cleft sentence (*nḫt* as synonymous with *ḫwỉ*?) found also in a 6th dynasty *Dashur decree* of *Ppy* I. In *Ppy* II *Coptos C decree*, the formula # *ỉw wḏ.n* king *ḫw.t.sn mk.t.sn n* (beneficiary) *m ꜣwt ḏt* # is to be found after the above mentioned one (see also *Ppy* II *Coptos D* and *Giza decrees*, and 6th dynasty unknown king *Saqqara decree*), probably as a general protection affirmation. The protective contrast with *wp-r* (not *wp-ḥr*) is expressed for the first time in the *Coptos D decree* as an exception to a prohibition # *wp-r ḫwt.s*(*n*) *mkt.sn* #; see Goedicke (1967: 141-142 (28)) correcting Hayes (1946: 9 & pl. 2). In another context, the segment # *wp-r wnn.f snḥyw nṯṯyw* # appears in the 9th dynasty *Dmḏỉbtꜣwy*'s *Coptos R decree*, a contrastive formula on the same basis as our sentence, but this has nothing to do with the 'retain (and) preserve' clause.

In view of all the facts uncovered, the disposition's value as counterpart of the negative intents and the origin of the disposition, we chose to consider the first part of our formula as a cleft sentence (the use of *wnn.f* is here evidently polemic-contrastive), with the focus on the special status (statives) of the temple personnel/goods imposed by the decree (a fact that may justify the use of the future in the translation, as in a 'from now on' measure). The second nexus is a dependent, circumstantial one, the practical consequences of the retained-preserved status of the temple's staff and property (omitted in the *Kanais decree*, for instance). The repetition of this construction in our text has a cohesive effect, emphasizing the protective purpose of the decree. The construction *wnn.f* (*ḥr*) *sḏm* – *iw.f* (*ḥr*) *sḏm* obviously covers several patterns to be analyzed separately in context.

- *ḥnwt.f irt:* noun + attributive participle (the option of an adnexal stative is to be excluded because of *ḥnwt*'s determination by *.f*).
- *ḏ3y.tw*: dependent prospective object of *rdit.*
- *s3w ni-swt n Kš nb:* usually, the text opts for the singular 'any viceroy', referring to a position fulfilled by a unique representent of the King in Nubia. But it may also concern any person who will be Viceroy, encompassing all the subsequent officers who will occupy this position in the future. Note the relational expansion's place, before distributive *nb* (with *n* relator). The list's formula is: [singular/plural nominal lexemes, with or without expansion + distributive *nb*] + [summarizing hyperonym *rmṯ nb* + expansion].
- *h3b*

* General dialectal features: degree 2.

* Legal terms:

ẖwy - classifier: [𓂡] ? (to reserve).

mky - classifier: 𓂡 (to preserve). See *ẖwy supra.*

irt ḥnwt - classifier: ø (to accomplish a service).

ḏ3y t3 r - classifier: 𓊛 (to interfere with/violate). See Caminos (1958: 57) literally 'to cross the land for, *or* concerning, *or* against'; Menu (1971: 564); Gardiner (1912: 203) (metaphor); Harari (1974: 66) 'violation d'une relation juridique'; Théodoridès (1962: 61, note 51) and Kruchten (1981: note 307) 'faire opposition'; Lacau (1949: 14-15) 'faire obstacle' and Spalinger (1991: 30) note that the formula *nn ḏ3 t3 r.s* is also used in private contracts and wills (*Stèle juridique de Karnak*, line 7) and in 22nd dynasty *Bubastis W3s3irkn* (Osorkon) II relief (Van Siclen III 1973: 295). *EG*'s P3 𓊛 classifier represents a 'sacred bark', 'Det. divine boats (…). Also det. sail, when divine journeys are meant, ex. (…) *ḏ3i* 'cross' sky, said of Rēʿ'; the boat classifier being the vehicle of passage, it stands in a metonymic relation with the [CROSSING] category's basic level member *ḏ3y* 'to ferry'. Here used in an abstract way, literally 'crossing land against', the image of *passage* recalls *thi* and its negative signified. The expression *ḏ3y t3* could be one more boat metaphor implying a certain power (see Goldwasser 1980: 21-22), here the fact of committing an abuse. Note that in the *Stèle juridique de Karnak*, line 7, and *Sinuhe* B 304, the classifier used for *ḏ3i* is the crossed sticks × icon; see Lacau (1949: 14-15, esp. note 1) and *infra* for the × classifier discussion.

* Legal formula: contrast proclitic particle *wp-ḥr* + *wnn.f ḫwy-mky* (protection) + *iw nn rdit ḏ3y.tw t3 r.sn* (exclusion of interference) + *in* (offenders).

I.2.6 Operative part: the crimes (part 1 – requisition of temple staff in general)

(42) *in* (= *ir*)[85] *s3 ni-swt n Kš nb ḥry pḏt nb ḥ3ty-ʿ nb* (43) *rwḏ nb rmṯ nb nty iw.f r iṯ3 rmṯ nb n t3 ḥw*[*t*] *Mnm3ʿtrʿ ib hrw m 3bdt m kfʿw m w n w m b3rti m bḥw n sk3 m* (44) *bḥw n ʿw3yw*

m-mitt p3 nty iw.f r iṯ3 st-ḥmt nb rmṯ nb n t3 ḥwt Mnm3ʿtrʿ ib hrw m 3bdt m-mitt n3y.sn ḥmw m kfʿw r irt wpt nb (45) *nty m t3 r ḏr.f*

m-mitt k3ḏn nb ḥry i[*ḫ*]*w nb rmṯ nb n pr ni-swt h3b m wpt nb n pr ʿ3 ʿnḫ wḏ3 snb nty iw.f r iṯ3 rmṯ nb n t3 ḥwt Mnm3ʿtrʿ ib hrw m 3bdt* (46) *m w n w m b3rti m bḥw n sk3 m bḥw n ʿw3y m-mitt r irt wpt nb*

(42) As for any Viceroy of Kush, any troop commandant, any mayor (43), any agent, anyone who will seize any person of the temp[le] '*Mnm3ʿtrʿ*'s heart is contented in Abydos', by coercion(,) from a district to (another) district, by (submission?) contract, by/as a forced labor (corvée) of ploughing (or) by/as a (44) forced labor of harvesting;

likewise, the one who shall seize any woman of/or anybody of the temple '*Mnm3ʿtrʿ*'s heart is contented in Abydos' (and) as well as their servants, by coercion, to execute any mission (45), who (are anywhere) in the entire land[86];

likewise, any officer, any sta[b]le master, anybody of (the) King's House sent on any mission of Pharaoh, L.P.H., who will seize anybody of the temple '*Mnm3ʿtrʿ*'s heart is contented in Abydos' (46) from a district to (another) district, by (submission?) contract, by/as a forced labor (corvée) of ploughing (or) by/as a forced labor of harvesting, as well as to perform any mission,

* Neo-Egyptian characteristics:

---

85 Griffith (1927: 201) 'scribal error' (idem *KRI* I, 52: 13a). There are other instances of the same variation (confusion?) between *ir* topicalizer and *in* focus marker: Kammerzell (1993: 18 Ex. 6), who insists on a universal tendency to link question and conditional protasis (see, for example, Hebrew 'האם'). In the diverse stages of Egyptian, *in* focus marker is also an interrogative particle and *ir* topicalizer a conditional one.

86 Because of the insertion of the method by which the subjects will be abducted, the relative *nty m t3 r ḏr.f* has been pushed back to the end of the sentence, far from its multiple antecedents (*hyperbaton*). It is a common feature of modern legal register to disrupt the natural order of the sentence by inserting multiple precisions (see, for instance, Bhatia 1994: 148-149).

- *t3 ḥwt*
- *# ir + [nouns + nb] + nty iw.f r iṯ3 #:* topicalized categories of offenders (legal subjects of the provision, see Bhatia 1994: 149) followed by an attributive, adnominal relative expansion composed of the relative adjective and the Neo-Egyptian future ('third future' for most Neo-Egyptian grammars, but we will not use an unjustifiable terminology for this state of language) with its delocutive actor pronoun (singular and masculine, as its resumptive *r.f* in the following penalty disposition, referent to masculine singular antecedents and to *rmṯ*). The non-modal future (see Vernus 1990b: 27 'true future tense') usually still retains its prepositional *r* during the 19th dynasty, but it disappears by omission during the 20th dynasty; see Winand (1995: 196, k). In Middle Egyptian (*EG* § 107,2; 328 Obs. and 468,4), *iw* is avoided after *nty*, but this construction becomes common in Neo-Egyptian. Gardiner cites one example belonging to the 18th dynasty (*Tarkhan* I, 79, 47: *nty iw.f r rdit*); see also *Ḥrmḥb*'s *Karnak decree* (line 27: *ẖr ir ʿnḫ nb n mšʿ nty iw.tw r sḏm*); Kroeber (1970: 136-138) who gives other examples belonging to the 18th dynasty; Winand (1992: 769) 'futur III relatif'. The presence of relative clauses in the topicalized list of offenders is characteristic of the criminal law register, see, for example, the analysis of modern corporate attorneys' language in Arena (1982: 143-154); nevertheless, it is not an exclusivity of legal Neo-Egyptian provisions (see *LEG* § 53.11.1; 53.13.6). Concerning the role of the simple future tense in modern criminal laws, see Villey (1974: 40-41); in our decree, the future is the mark of legal non-retroactivity, although for Shisha-Halevy (verbal communication), protases are generic, they do not express a 'true future' (see below our characterization of the texteme as 'casuistic-logic'). Nevertheless, as Villey (1974: 41) notes: 'il s'agit (...) de juste *positif*, c'est-à-dire créé par la loi, et qui par définition même *n'existera* qu'une fois la loi promulguée. (...) Si le législateur a conscience de promulguer un droit nouveau, il le marque par le futur. (...) le Code pénal, monument de droit positif par excellence, s'exprime au futur'. Concerning the offenders, they are presented in lists achieving generality in a 'comprehensive', hierarchical, diminishing progression of hyponyms, each lexeme followed by the distributive *nb*, culminating in the last *rmṯ nb*, the final hyperonym, all-inclusive 'anybody'. Generality is one of the objectives the law strives for, see Maley (1994: 22); for instance, in the Belgian 'Code Pénal', art. 447: 'Le prévenu d'un délit de calomnie pour imputations dirigées (...) soit contre les dépositaires ou agents de l'autorité ou contre toute personne ayant un caractère public, soit contre tout corps constitué'. The distributive value of *nb*, the enumerations and other similar features observed, are related to the all-inclusiveness, generality, 'impersonal and decontextualised' character of legislative texts, an 'attempt to refer to every conceivable contingency within their model' (Bhatia 1994: 136-137). On decontextualisation of the legal discourse, see Goodrich (1987: 167 & 175); for its claim to universality and its distanced quality, *ibidem* (p. 175). Topicalizers are also widely used in modern legal discourse (Charrow, Crandall

& Charrow 1982: 177 'Phrases beginning with "as to"'). Concerning the lists' formulas, they are the following:

- lines 42-43: [singular nominal lexemes, with or without expansion + *nb*] + [hyperonym *rmṯ nb* + attributive relative expansion] topicalized; the adnominal relative clause following the noun syntagm containing *nb* has singular reference (*iw.f*), which implies that *nb*'s value is of a non-defining distributive quantifier. Compare with Demotic in Shisha-Halevy (1989: 43).
- lines 45-46: [singular nominal lexemes, with or without expansion + distributive *nb*] + [hyperonym *rmṯ nb* + determinative /attributive/relative expansions] topicalized (the methods of seizing are also presented as a list in line 46).

As for the decree's formula, it constitutes for Lorton (1977: 53-59) a 'stipulation' formed by *ir* + noun + attributive syntagm with future reference where the topicalized object (the offender) constitues a protasis expressing 'conceptually' a condition. Indeed *ir* "if" is the homonym of the preposition *ir* "with regard to"' (conservatism of a non-verbal (pseudo)conditional element in frontal extraposition that will be supplanted by genuine conditional protasis in vernacular usage but not in royal legislation during the 19th dynasty[87]). This is not an uncommon phenomenon, as 'Conditionals are topics' (Haiman 1978: 564-589), a conditional clause/topic being 'the framework which has been selected for the following discourse'. Eventual condition is an essential part of criminal law, as it is of contracts, for many clauses are 'contingent (...) on the unknown circumstances of an uncertain future time.' (Finegan 1982: 116-117); see also Kevelson (1982: 123-124) on English law; Crystal & Davy (1969); Bhatia (1994: 150). Repressive laws have an inherent anticipative direction (principle of non-retroactivity of criminal laws). For Egyptian texts, see Lacau (1949: 16) on the *Stèle juridique de Karnak,* 'éventualité très générale d'une intervention dans l'avenir'; Lurje (1971: 166); Morschauser (1991: 3-16) on topicalized themes; Satzinger (1976: 203) on the absolute character of the future tense in relative clauses; Nordh (1996: 81) in curses; Junge (1996: 269-270) on 'topikalisierte Nominalphrase'. Compare with Old/Middle Kingdom formulas in royal decrees, as in Lorton (1977: 53-55): for the Old Kingdom, # (*ir*) N (*nb*) *sḏm.t(y).f(y)* # (apodosis: *sḏm(.tw).f*/N or condemnation *wꜣ m mdw sbit pw* or *msḏḏ ni-swt pw mꜣꜥ mꜣꜥ*); for Middle Kingdom, *idem* or # *ir rf nty ṯw nb r sḏm.f* # (apodosis: *sḏm.tw; ḫr.tw sḏm* or *wd pꜣ hp ḫr.f* in *Ḫwtꜣwyrꜥ Wgf* 13th dynasty decree, representing for Lorton (1977: 54) an example of vernacular dialect); for Second Intermediate Period *Nbḫprwrꜥ Ỉntf Coptos decree* # *ir* N *nb nty r sḏm* # (apodosis: *nn sḏm.f,* a curse, or *ꜥḥꜥ sḏm(.w)*.N followed by embryo-conjunctive *ḥnꜥ (tm) rdit*). The analytic form of the relative clause (instead of the synthetic *sḏm.ty.fy*), apart from belonging to a later stage of language, seems to increase the clarity of the disposition: in modern English public documents,

87 'Real' conditions with *ir sḏm.f* in private legal documents and oaths, see Lorton (1977: 57-58).

'comprehension is often found to be better when relative pronouns ("who", "which") and complementizers ("that", "for-to") are added to sentences with embedded clauses' (Campbell & Holland 1982: 162). Note that the topicalized offender is not the actor of the following penalty, but its indirect object (*ir.tw hpw r.f*). As for the criminal dispositions texteme, it cannot be strictly qualified as narrative, although these dispositions foresee a case, a hypothetical scenario (often on the basis of actual cases encountered), the eventuality of the fulfilment of certain conditions and their necessary consequences. It has the logical structure of a mathematical function: if A does x, A must be punished (the legal action); see Crystal & Davy (1969: 203); Guastini (1994: 2077) 'In their deep logical structure most (perhaps all) legal rules can be construed as conditional sentences having the standard form: 'If *p*, then *q*.' The protasis refers to a certain class of facts (*p*) as a condition while the apodosis provides some legal effect (*q*) as a consequence of such facts.' Because it is casuistic (cases description, see Bhatia 1993: 110; Thiem 2000: 284 on *Ḥrmḥb*'s *Karnak decree* 'eine Zusammenstellung von Präzedenzfällen'), it corresponds to a list of possible scenarios that are micro-narratives (evenemential, related to past events, but exclusively considered in the future), fictions (indetermined, hypothetical), fabulas[88] with minimal treatment and context, operating with a fixed scheme, a high level of abstraction, a strict chronology, the actors being assimilated to functions without distinctive characteristics or feelings (external focalization[89]), we propose to coin the texteme as 'casuistic-logic'. The casuistic presentation allows the scenario that corresponds to the facts presented to the judge (probable function of the topicalizations) to be found relatively easily, in the order of their brief introduction in the preamble *sensu stricto* (negative intents).

- *pꜣ nty iw.f r iṯꜣ:* commutes with the preceding. Frandsen (1974: 236) classifies this construction with the patterns in which the pronominal actor of the relative clause is coreferent to the antecedent. *pꜣ* is expanded by a relative clause and acts as a substantivizer (*LEG* § 53.6), being the nexus that establishes the nominal status of the syntagm, 'the one who', 'celui qui' (instead of the preceding 'any X who'). See Shisha-Halevy (1989: 41) about Demotic: 'non specific reference role of the determinator *pꜣ*- with *nty*- ("anyone that", "such [a person] as"), which is nonetheless definite'. In Middle Egyptian, a (future) participle would have been used ('the natural method of expressing the same meaning' for *EG* § 201; see *Urk.* IV, 1800, 8 & 12). Again, we notice a marked preference for an analytic construction (Kroeber 1970: 195-198). See Jackson (1995: 113) on modern forensic language, and, for example, a similar formulation in art. 439 of Belgian 'Code Pénal': 'Sera puni d'un emprisonnement de quinze jours à deux ans (...), celui qui, sans ordre de l'autorité (...), se sera introduit dans une maison (...)'. Note the absence of *nb* in

88 Bal (1997: 5) 'A *fabula* is a series of logically and chronogically related events that are caused or experienced by actors', the material of the story told by a narrative text.

89 *Ibidem*: 142-161 on focalization (see also our introduction for terminology).

this syntagm; in the *Nauri decree,* the relative clause expands either nominal lexemes + *nb*, or the determinator *p3*, or is substantivized with a colon-enclitic quantifier *nb* (as in line 66 *ir nty nb r tht*).

- *n3y.sn:* Neo-Egyptian possessive determinator, although it actually appears in 'non-literary' texts of the Middle Kingdom (*LEG* § 3.2; *EG* § 113.1; Kroeber 1970: 1). The possessor supposedly refers to *rmṯ nb* (and perhaps also to *st-ḥmt nb*), the resumption being plural. See Frandsen (1997: 78-79 and notes) for the use of the prenominal determinator instead of the suffixal in Neo-Egyptian, the suffix being retained for 'inalienable' possession (mainly parts of the body); see also Shisha-Halevy (1986: 237) on 'inalienable possession' terminology. The language of royal decrees being still extremely close to 'classical' Middle Egyptian, the suffix is still the main possession vehicle. In this case the *possessum* belongs to the human category and may be the object of a contract.

* 'Classical' degree 0 forms used:

- *m-mitt*: *idem*. Introduces sub-articles (see Neveu 1985: 152[90]; Cassonnet 2000: 36, n. 128), hereby translated 'likewise', other defenders who will incur the same penalty, avoiding the repetition of the topicalizer *ir* as it begins the sentence and has a cohesive effect. It is also used instead of other sentence parts (translated 'as well as'), in the middle of a disposition (instead of a nexus, in front of the object, or introducing another type of adjunct).
- *r irt*: preposition + infinitive for purpose.
- *h3b*

* General dialectal features: degree 2.

* Legal terms:

iṯ3 – classifiers: (to seize, appropriate, abduct).

m kf'w – classifier: (by coercion).

m b3rti – classifier: or ø (by (submission?) contract). Kitchen (1979: 454, note 18): 'The striking-arm determinative denotes merely action or activity'; but 'action' *signifieds* are not systematically followed by this classifier, as stated above, the classifier denoting constraint practices (superordinate [COERCION] category).

m bḥw – classifier: (by forced labor - corvée).

* Legal formulas: - *in* (= *ir*) + offender *nb* + *nty iw.f r sḏm* + crime's object + *m* (method)[91].

- *m-mitt* + offender (*nb* or *p3*) + *nty iw.f r sḏm* + crime's object + *m* (method) + *r* + infinitive (purpose of the crime)

90 *m-mitt* 'intervient ainsi comme particule à deux niveaux hiérarchiques différents :
- pour introduire les chapitres,
- pour introduire les sous-paragraphes,

tandis que la particule *ḫr* est réservée à l'introduction des paragraphes' in the *Nauri decree*. 'On ne peut qu'être frappé par la construction rigoureuse de ce texte et par l'emploi hiérarchisé de différents morphèmes pour le subdiviser en chapitres et paragraphes.'

91 Bhatia (1994: 146-149) 'Most legislative provisions are extremely rich in qualification insertions within their syntactic boundaries'; they 'make the provision extremely restricted.'

I.2.7 Operative part: the penalties (part 1)

(46) (...) *ir.tw hpw r.f m ḥwitw.f m sḫ* 200 *wbnw sd* (47) 5 *ḥnꜤ šdw b3kw n p3 rmṯ n t3 ḥwt Mnm3ꜤtrꜤ ib hrw m 3b*[*dt*] *m-di.f m hrw nb nty iw.f r ir.f m-di.f didiw r t3 ḥwt Mnm3ꜤtrꜤ ib hrw m 3bdt.*

(46) (...) (the) rule will have to be enforced against him by beating him with 200 blows, (47) 5 open wounds[92], and confiscating (the) revenues/work's product of/from the person of the temple '*Mnm3Ꜥtr*Ꜥ's heart is contented in Aby[dos]' in his possession, for every day that he (= the offender) will use him (= the victim) in his (= the offender's) detention, given (= the revenue or the victim) to the temple '*Mnm3Ꜥtr*Ꜥ's heart is contented in Abydos'.

* Neo-Egyptian characteristics:

- *t3 ḥwt*
- *p3 rmṯ: p3* is here anaphoric to the victim mentioned in the crime's definition, and cataphoric to the relational expansion *n t3 ḥwt*. The determinator is masculine and singular (again an abstract category of members belonging to the two sexes represented by *rmṯ*), as is the resumptive *iw.f.*
- *m ḥwitw.f:* preposition + nominal form (infinitive) + suffix pronoun (object of the infinitive), an adverbial adjunct of *ir.tw hpw* representing the method applied for punishment. Characteristic of Ramesside spelling is the final *w* (see above). For Winand (1992: 39 and 90-101), among several cases of *tw* closing different lexemes, one of the best known is the 3[ae] inf. infinitive.
- *m-di.f:* typically Neo-Egyptian compound preposition, expressing possession or origin. See *Wb* II, 45 and 176; Spiegelberg (1925: 59-61); Gardiner (1930: 229); Černý (1937: 188-189); Edel (1967: 74-75), for whom the Semitic יד (hand) is at the lexeme's origin; Théodoridès (1970: 139-154) notes that *n* expresses property and *m-di* a temporary, sometimes illegitimate, possession[93]; *LEG* § 7.3.1; Borghouts (1980: 65-78); Kruchten (1981: 53, 229). It represents an illicit detention twice in the present disposition.
- # noun + *nb* + *nty iw.f r ir.f* #: relative future (see above); note the infinitive of *ir* without *t*. The pronominal object in *ir.f* is coreferent to *p3 rmṯ*. Compare *Ḥrmḥb*'s decree in Kruchten (1981: 65 'fragment 2 de Bouriant') *m hrw nb irr.f*, 'tournure plus classique' with geminated synthetic relative form (not temporal, contrary to *nty iw.f r ir.f*). The verb *iri* probably has here the idiomatic meaning 'to use'.

92 As Gardiner notes (1952: 28), it is strange that this extreme punishment is applied throughout the entire administrative hierarchy, to any minor officer as well as to the Viceroy!?

93 Curzon 1988: 335 'Concept based on a degree of physical control and involving: *corpus* (that which is possessed) and *animus possidendi* (...). May be prima facie evidence of ownership. Defined variously as, eg, "physical detention coupled with intention to use the thing detained as one's own" (...); "continuing exercise of a claim to the exclusive use of some material object"'.

- *didiw:* Neo-Egyptian distinctive form of the stative of *rdi*, variant of *diw,* for Gardiner (*EG* § 310 and 1952: 30), and Winand (1992: 149), on stative of *rdi* during the 19th dynasty with 3 occurrences of *didiw* compared with one of *diw.* A geminating participle (attributive or substantivated) is also possible, and even a relative geminating *sḏm.f* with Neo-Egyptian delocutive plural pronominal suffix *w* (but whose reference is inexplicable). As for *didiw*'s reference, it may be referring to the offender[94] (administrative degradation, see Gardiner 1952: 30, although *rdi r* + lower function would probably have been used), the victim (retrocession of personnel), or the revenue (compensation for working days lost). Thus, *didiw* may be used as a distant adnominal expansion to *b3kw* or *rmṯ* (both of them being determined, in which case it must be a participle) or another adverbial penalty method after *m ḥwitw.f* (rhematic stative, although the offender's determination would seem to exclude this). The issue of the 'geminating stative' is a crux (Groll 1970: 203, 218-219): gemination belongs to non-predicative forms (Polotsky 1944: 92), but a geminated stative could reinforce Jansen-Winkeln's view (1993: 5-28) of the stative being a passive participle with a rhematic function. Nevertheless, gemination occurring with imperfective forms contradicts his 'perfective' passive participle explanation (although it could be a Neo-Egyptian development that does not take into account the past origin of the form). Compare lines 50, 52 (*didiw*) but lines 73, 77, 108, 118 (*diw*); the transition to a more concise form could be the result of spatial 'economizing script' requirements (as in the case of the spelling of *hrw*, see *infra*).
- *m ḥwitw.f... ḥnᶜ šdw b3kw:* adverbial adjunct of *ir.tw hpw*, the second infinitive (see line 93 *šditw*) with *w* ending + direct object (*EG* § 171.3; Gardiner 1928: 87) being coordinated without repeating the preposition *m*. For Lorton (1977: 55-56), *ḥnᶜ/m-ᶜ šd* introduces the 'continuation of the prospective *sḏm.f* [*ir.tw hp*] in the apodosis'. On the infinitive form *šdw*, see *pBoulaq* 15, a 7; *Ḥrmḥb Karnak decree*, line 27 (*ir.tw hp r.f m ḥw.f m sḫ* 100 *wbn sd* 5 *ḥnᶜ šd p3 dḥr iṯ.n.f m-di.f m ṯ3w*); Gardiner (1928: 87) 'at a period where the omission of *t* does not count for much (…) this verb, ending in *d*, would be particularly prone to omit its *t*'. The coordination of two adverbial adjuncts is the very first step towards the atemporal sequelling conjunctive (see Shisha-Halevy 1995: 305 ff.). See Gardiner (1928: 86-96) for the evolution *ḥnᶜ sḏm – ḥnᶜ sḏm ntf – ḥnᶜ ntf sḏm – ntf sḏm – mtw.f sḏm*, with examples from 3 Ramesside and *Ḥrmḥb*'s *Karnak* decrees; Kroeber (1970: 140-170, esp. 161) '*ḥnᶜ sḏm* (*ntf*) manifestiert sich in Zeugnissen der nicht-literarischen Sprache des MR, sowohl in Texten der Umgangssprache, v.a. in Briefen, als auch in Texten mit technischer Sprache, d.h. in juristischen, medizinischen und bürokratischen Texten' and p.169: 'Zeitliche Überschneidungen mit anderen Etappen der Konjunktiv-Geschichte sind sowohl nach oben wie nach unten möglisch: im gleichen Text kommt *ḥnᶜ*

94 Although this is usually expressed in our text by *rdi r* + function with which the degradation is associated, *ᶜḥwty* for example.

sḏm neben *ḥnꜥ ntf sḏm* vor (…), ebenso kann *ḥnꜥ ntf sḏm* neben *mt.f sḏm* stehen' (same remark in Gardiner 1928 : 93); Winand (1992: 457-473); Shisha-Halevy (1995: 306, note 29); Kruchten (1981: 90). We will see that other forms of conjunctive appear in our decree: relative future forms + *ḥnꜥ ntf sḏm* (line 90) or *mtw.f sḏm* (lines 48-49, 67, 94, 116) in the enunciation of the crime, as is the case in *Ḥrmḥb*'s *Karnak decree* (where *ḥnꜥ ntf sḏm* is the rule and *mtw.f sḏm* the exception). Note in lines 50, 54 and 93 *m ḥwitw.f... m-di šdw* in the same penalty context (a 'synonym' for Gardiner 1928: 95). This means that in our text, the coordinating structure in the context [*ir.tw hpw* + *m* + infinitive + object] is achieved with [*ḥnꜥ/m-di* + infinitive + object], the lexeme constituency of those infinitives being limited to *ḥwit* for the first infinitive and *šdw* for the second. This 'embryo-conjunctive' (it is not a nexus at this stage) is used here to join a '"verbal abstract", infinitival atemporal predication' (Shisha-Halevy 1995: 301; see also Shisha-Halevy 1986: 185-214) to another infinitive used to express the modalities of the penalty applied to the offender in the casuistic-logic texteme.

* 'Classical' degree 0 forms used:
    - *ir.tw hpw:* independent passive or impersonal prospective following the topicalized enunciation of the crime. The modal value of the prospective is prescriptive (deontic modality; 'volitive future' for Vernus 1990b: 27 and Winand 1992: 214), an inevitable punishment being applied whenever the criminal behaviour is bound to take place (indetermined future, posterior to the decree that is the *terminus post quem*). See Lorton (1977: 53-56); Morschauser (1991: 20-21); Nordh (1996: 81-82) for curses, the prospective 'expresses volition as well as wish and exhortation'. For Satzinger (1976: 263, n. 13) and Cassonnet (2000: 36, 215), *ir.tw hpw* is a second tense, 'expression de l'injonction', with the impersonal pronoun for a 'mise à distance' (Winand (1992: 316) calls it a 'forme emphatique prospective (*i.)sḏm.tw.f*)[95]. There is a noted absence of gemination during the 19th dynasty, apart from some formulaic uses (Winand 1992: 264-265); at the beginning of our text,  could pass for the geminated form, but  that follows could not (the observed tendency to abbreviate the script in the course of the text would probably not go so far as to mask gemination). The absence of the final 'double *yod*' of the Neo-Egyptian prospective (*iry.f*) cannot be used as a criterion to validate the 'emphatic' thesis because *ir.f* is still in use in 19th dynasty texts (see Winand 1992: 212); the *prothetic yod* is also largely missing in 19th dynasty examples of *sḏm.tw*.N (*ibidem*, 316). Due to the fact that earlier decrees apparently use the prospective, not an emphatic form, in the absence of clear gemination[96], and the lack of convincing motivation for the use of an emphatic tour (no polemic justification, no interclausal delimitation, no explicative, parenthetic or descriptive value), we

95 Frandsen (1974: 154) notes that the that-form '*isḏm.f* var. *rsḏm.f*, which refers to future time (…) is likely to be the LE. prospective that-form.'

96 Except for one instance: the first part of the curse in *Imnḥtp* III *Medinet Habu decree*, line 7 (*wnn.f m ḥb n Imn*), but a curse may theoretically be expressed by another construction.

reject this solution in favour of the modal prospective. See the use of the modal *shall* (as in 'shall be liable to be punished'), 'obligatory consequence of a legal decision' in modern English legislation in Crystal & Davy (1969: 206); Kurzon (1986: 16 & 21-22) sees in the modal *shall* of English/American statutes an 'implicit performative'; Maley (1994: 21) notes that 'Performativity and modality are the linguistic means which express the institutional ideology of the rule relationships involved in legislative rule-making. In themselves, they have no role in achieving certainty. However, since it is assumed that the rule once uttered is forever speaking, the rule acquires continuity and permanence as an authoritative text, a major contribution towards certainty.' Goodrich (1987: 175-183) insists on the monologic quality of the 'imperative and axiomatic', modal legal discourse (and its characteristics such as objectification, depersonalization, generalization, abstraction, pseudo-objectivity and distance to legitimize the discourse, give it authority, as a 'strategy of persuasion' 'presenting a discourse as a species of science'). But for Villey (1974), Latin and modern law never use the imperative in statutes, the function of the norm being to indicate reality, to state what is everybody's lot, not to 'prescrire une conduite', which is the reason why the indicative, present or future, is used: Villey does not believe that deontic propositions are addressed to the general public, to the judges, or to the executive power by means of statute in Roman and modern societies. As Jori (1994: 2096) puts it, indicative mode gives an 'impression of ineluctability (...), a future indicative tense is often used to reinforce this effect even further.' Concerning the imperative, it is perhaps not used in statutes because of the indetermination of a potential-only offender (see Finegan 1982: 115-116, for modern wills); note that imperative or modal verbs are used in moralistic texts such as the Bible. Our corpus, however, presents rare examples of a non-modal penalty expressed by the future (*Karnak decree*, lines 16-17; *Elephantine decree,* line 9). The repetition of *ỉr* + *hpw* in the legal register has a cohesive function. Note that during the Old Kingdom, the prospective is already in use in the penalty context in *Nfrỉrk3rꜥ Abydos decree* (*m3ꜥ.k*), but that a simple condemnation may sometimes appear instead of a penalty, as in *Ppy* II *Coptos B* (*w3 m mdw sbỉt pw*: "it is a participation to a criminal act") and *Coptos C* (*msḏḏ ni-swt* [*pw*] *m3ꜥ m3ꜥ*: "it is really really what (the) king hates"). The first appearance of the lexeme *hp* as actor or object in the penalty formula is in 13th dynasty *Ḫwt3wyrꜥ Wgf Abydos decree* (*wd p3 hp ḫr.f*); see Leahy (1989: 42); Lorton (1977: 18, 54). Actually, the formula used in the *Nauri decree* is already in use during the 13th dynasty in *pBrooklyn* 35.1446 r°, "d" entries, which are copies or summaries of a series of directives about fugitives; see Hayes (1955: 47); Lorton (1977: 55)[97]. Compare also *Ḥrmḥb*'s *Karnak decree*, for instance line16: *ỉr.tw hp r.f m sw3 fnḏ.f diw r Ṯ3*[*rw*], and line 27 quoted above. In the

97 'It was issued to the Great Prison (in) regnal year [...], month [...] of [...], day [...], to release his people in (= from) the law-court, being (an order) issued in order to execute against him the law (*ỉrt hp r.f*) pertaining to one who deliberately deserts for 6 months'.

case of *Rʿmss* II's *Hittite Treaty* (line 15), the prospective is also used in the injunctions (*ỉr*.N) after the exposition of each problematic situation the parties may be confronted with (*ỉr sḏm*.N). The passive diathesis and the omission of the agent are characteristic features of the legal register, the agent being, of course, the royal administration; see Goodrich (1987: 180) for the same features in modern forensic language. For Finegan (1982: 118-119), the agentless passives in modern wills allow a focusing on foreground information and a downplaying of background information. In fact, it is an instrument of narrative suppression (or at least minimization), the avoidance of narrative concurring with the generalization tendency already observed; see Jackson (1995: 120-121 & 138). Note also the resumptive function of *r.f* referring to the topicalized offender.

* General dialectal features: degree 2.
* Legal terms:

ỉr r – classifier: ø (to enforce/apply (the law) against, to execute a sentence). See Otto (1956: 151); Théodoridès (1967: 125); Kruchten (1981: 46-47); Menu (1995: 107, n. 23).

hpw – classifier: (norm, rule). For Kruchten (1981: 217-222), *hp* was the leather or papyrus roll containing the extensive, original normative measure that became, by extension, a 'règle juridique' *par excellence*; it is opposed to *wḏt*, the stone stela that enunciates the abbreviated version of the measures (but see *wḏt*'s classifier in line 29). For Lorton (1977: 60-61), *hpw* are 'the stipulations of the royal decrees', a 'legal provision which is written' and '*wḏ* cannot be an Egyptian term for "law code".' Menu (1981: 69-70) notes that *hp* is a 'disposition réglementaire, d'ordre religieux, statutaire, administratif ou juridique', 'tout dispositif juridique destiné à être appliqué', *wḏ* being a legal disposition, a royal decree (legislation being the king's prerogative). It seems reasonable to see in *wḏ* any 'énoncé d'auctoritas' as Vernus (1983: 78 and 1990: 239-246) calls it, 'ce qui ne signifie pas nécessairement un énoncé normatif'; see also Grimal (1986: 641) 'ordonnance' with 'caractère réglementaire'; *hp* represents the more abstract 'juridic norm', 'le droit'[98] (*M3ʿt* or *lex naturalis*, coutume, legislation, doctrine, jurisprudence) and its (papyrus/leather) support. This interpretation of *hp* is also more consistent with the texts when considering, for instance, the examples offered by Théodoridès (1967) as proofs of the existence of 'laws'. The classifier of the basic level [BINDING] category probably relates to the fact that the norm is archived (metonymic relation between the classifier and the lexeme). Kruchten (1981: 217) notes that prior to the 19th dynasty, *hp* is always classified by . The lexeme is absent from the Old Kingdom lexicon (Théodoridès 1967: 129) and probably appears during the Middle Kingdom (*Wb* II, 488-489; Nims 1948: 243; written in 13th dynasty *Ḫwt3wyrʿ Wgf Abydos decree* and *pBrooklyn* 35.1446, but also in *The*

98 For many examples in Demotic, see Nims (1948).

Instruction of Ptahhotep, 6, *The Admonitions of an Egyptian Sage*, 9, *The Installation of the Vizier*, 5 and 20 and *Ḥrmḥb*'s *Karnak decree* II, 4-5, e.g.). As seen previously with *wḏt*, the classifier is not used during the Old Kingdom and used before is more general. See also Otto (1956: 153); Bedell (1973: 11-12); Allam (1984: 447-453); *LÄ* II: 570-571. Binding is also implied by codification (assembling and organizing legal texts), but although the filing of legal documents by region or object is probably already achieved during the Old Kingdom (Posener-Kriéger 1985: 195 and Helck 1964: 36), only Persian and Greek sources mention codification in Egypt (*pBN* v° 215 'Demotische Chronik'; Spiegelberg 1929 and Reich 1933) and the only 'code' actually preserved is the *Hermopolis Code* of the Ptolemaic Period about various real estate matters (Mattha 1975).

šdw – classifier: (to exact, confiscate); see Helck (1974: 132 (vv)) and his references; McDowell (1990: 29). We observe that here again, it is a legal measure enforced upon the offender (deprivation of property by seizure), and that the [COERCION] category covers the legitimate as well as the illegitimate use of constraint. The lexeme *šdi* is already in use in the Pyramid Texts (without classifier), the or classifier being a Middle Kingdom addition (*Wb* IV, 560).

b3kw – classifier: (work yield/product). See Kruchten (1981: 64, n. 182 and p. 73) 'valeur du travail qu'ils auraient pu exécuter au bénéfice de la fondation s'ils n'avaient été arbitrairement retenus'; Lorton (1977: 25) 'replacement of the work-days lost'; Warburton (1997: 237-257, esp. 248), and his references, 'products of activity (working) or tasks'; Haring (1997: 15, 51) 'regular/internal' temple revenue. The classifer represents the superordinate [ABSTRACT] category (calculations, written account registered in the temple).

* Legal formulas: - law enforcement: *ir.tw hpw r.f* + *m* + infinitive (method) (types of penalties coordinated by *ḥnꜤ*)

- confiscation: *šdw b3kw n* + victim *m-di.f* (object) + *m hrw nb nty iw.f r ir.f m-di.f* (quantification). Compare with *Ḥrmḥb*'s *Karnak decree*, line 23, as reconstructed by Kruchten (1981: 61, 65), only *m hrw nb irr.f* being actually preserved.

I.2.8 Operative part: the crimes (part 2 – requisition of shipping property)[99]

(…) *ḫr ir* (48) *s3 ni-swt nb ḥry pḏt nb ḥ3ty-Ꜥ nb rwḏ nb sr nb rmṯ nb h3b m wpt r Kš nty iw.f šnꜤ* boat *nb n t3 ḥwt Mnm3ꜤtrꜤ ib hrw m 3bdt m-mitt* boat *nb n rwḏ nb n pr pn mtw.f* (49) *mni.f m wꜤ n hrw wꜤtwy r-ḏd iw.i r iṯ3.f m nḥm r* [*wp*]*t nb n pr-Ꜥ3 Ꜥnḫ wḏ3 snb im.f*

99 Compare with boat protection measures in *Ḥrmḥb*'s *Karnak decree*, lines 13-16 and 16-21.

(...) And as for (48) any Viceroy, any troop commandant, any mayor, any agent, any civil servant, anybody sent on a mission to Kush who (shall) detain any boat of the temple '*Mnmȝ*ʿ*tr*ʿ's heart is contented in Abydos' as well as any boat of any agent of this temple, and (49) moor it for (even) one single day saying: 'I shall seize it as commandeered for any [missio]n of Pharaoh L.P.H. with it',

* Neo-Egyptian characteristics:

- *# ḫr ir* + [nouns + *nb*] + *nty iw.f šn*ʿ *#:* topicalized categories of offenders expanded by a relative future (omission of the preposition *r*) (see above). The list of offenders is constituted of [singular hyponyms + distributive *nb*] + [hyperonym *rmṯ nb* + expansion], and the adnominal relative clause following the list has singular reference (*iw.f*). For Gardiner (*EG* § 239), *ḫr* 'indicates what comes next in order, and may be translated 'and'' (see Winand 1992: 231 'particule de liaison'); it may be followed by a sentence with adverbial, nominal or adjectival predicate; Hintze (1950: 64-66) notes along the coordinative function of *ḫr* (as in *ḫr ir*), an 'adversativer Bedeutung' in Neo-Egyptian. For Kruchten (1981: 103), this locution marks the beginning of a statement and highlights one of its terms. Neveu (1985: 82, 152) notes that *ḫr* is used for paragraph coordination only, for coordination and demarcation (1985: 141, 1988). See also Frandsen (1974: 285, n. 24); Satzinger 'freies *ḫr*'(1976: 258); Junge (1996: 92) 'Partikel der "Kontingenz"'. *ḫr ir* can be found in texts without any legal implication (see *The Tale of Two Brothers*, 1, 1 for example). In the context at hand, the first crime category appearing after each preamble *sensu stricto* is introduced by *ir* only (*in* for *ir* in line 42) as in lines 66, 89, and probably 102. The next categories of crimes following the same preamble are introduced by *ḫr ir* (lines 47, 50, 53, 74, 80, 94), *m-mitt* (lines 52, 71), *mi* (line 76), or even *ḫr swt ir* (line 103) and *iw(?) swt ir* (line 114). For *ḫr ir* introducing a new article, see *R*ʿ*mss* II's *Hittite Treaty* (*KRI* II, 225-232, line 19).
- *tȝ ḥwt*
- *nty iw.f šn*ʿ*... mtw.f mni.f:* a full-fledged, Neo-Egyptian delocutive conjunctive rhematic (adnexal) *mtw.f sḏm.f* annexing a relative future protase (retrospective relation) in the casuistic-logic texteme of crimes and associated penalties. It is not exactly the fact of detaining the boat that constitutes the offense, but *if* it is detained, to moor it with a certain motivation (expressed by the direct speech). See Gardiner (1928: 91-96); Hintze (1950: 61) for the quasi-absence of the conjunctive in narrative but its abundant use in dialogue; *LEG* § 42; Frandsen (1974: 112-152); Junge (1996: 246-254). The grammemic base *mtw* is followed by the verbal nexus (*f sḏm.f*), forming a 'sequelling finite converb', an adverbial rheme; see Shisha-Halevy (1995: 300-314). The relative sentence has an eventual quality (devoided of a 'fixed formal temporal anchoring point', Shisha-Halevy 1995: 301) that perfectly suits the conjunctive and its crime descriptive value. For the same construction, see 21st dynasty copy of *Imnḥtp* III *Medinet*

Habu decree: *ỉr* N *nty ỉw.f sḏm… mtw.f sḏm*; note that in *Ḥrmḥb*'s *Karnak decree*, two forms of the conjuctive also coexist (*ḥnʿ ntf sḏm* and *mtw.f sḏm*).

- *wʿtwy:* intrusive *w* – a Late Egyptian spelling (*Wb* I, 278).

* 'Classical' degree 0 forms used:
  - *h3b*
  - *m-mitt*: idem. Marker of connectedness of the two objects of *ỉw.f* (*r*) *šnʿ* (boats with different expansions).
  - *ỉw.ỉ r ỉṯ3.f:* independent adverbial nexus or Neo-Egyptian future in a locutive embedded texteme that we propose to qualify as an illustrative pseudo-quotation or constructed quotation, introduced by *r-ḏd* ('direct indicator of initiality' for *LEG* § 17.1.2.g; tagged speech marker). It is a catalysis segment that may be a declaration of intentions, the background or circumstances of the crime described and that gives a dynamic, real-like aspect to the crime's description by throwing light on the offender's motivation (he acts deliberately but is not motivated by personal interest). Note that *r-ḏd* may imply an interior monologue and that the quotation may also indicate the use of a false pretext and of the king's name in a criminal intention (aggravation) or, on the contrary, his *bona fide*. The change of texteme corresponds to a sudden concretizing movement: it may perhaps be compared to recent propositions for the drafting of modern statutes by illustrating abstract statutory norms with short narrative cases (see Jackson 1995: 133 and note 24). Although the general scheme of the legal provisions tends to achieve a high degree of decontextualized abstraction, in some cases a short illustrative direct speech is inserted in the crime's qualification (see *infra*). Constructed quotation textemes are already in use in *Ḥrmḥb*'s *Karnak decree*, probably for the first time in a royal decree, in lines 23, 29 and 32 (after *r-ḏd*) and 26 (after *m-ḏd*), in the crime's enunciation or description of its circumstances. See Peust (1996: 20-21) on constructed direct speech. Note that the official short speech is apparently classical Middle Egyptian, even the preposition is retained in *ỉw.ỉ r ỉṯ3.f*.

* General dialectal features: degree 2.
* Legal terms:

  šnʿ – classifier: 𓂻 (to detain). Note that only the 'walking legs' are used to classify the lexeme, without the 𓂾 classifier used in line 33.

  ỉṯ3 – classifiers: 𓂝 𓂡 (to seize).

  nḥm – classifier: 𓂝 (to commandeer). See Helck 1974: 129 (y) 'konfiszieren'. The lexeme already appears in 8th dynasty *Nfrk3wḥr Coptos J decree*, with 𓀜 classifier. Legal constraint expressed by the superordinate [COERCION] category classifier.

* Legal formula: *ḫr ỉr* + ø offenders *nb* + *nty ỉw.f r sḏm* (+ conjunctive) + object of the crime (+ illustrative direct speech *r-ḏd ỉw.ỉ r sḏm*).

I.2.9 Operative part: the penalties (part 2)

(49) (…) *ỉr.tw hpw r.f m* [*ḥwỉtw.f*] *m sẖ* 200 *wbnw sd* (50) 5 *m-dỉ šdw bꜣkw n pꜣ* boat *m-dỉ.f m hrw nb nty ỉw.f r ỉr.f mnỉ dỉdỉw r tꜣ ḥwt Mnmꜣꜥtrꜥ ỉb hrw m ꜣb*[*d*]*t*.

(49) (…) (the) rule will have to be enforced against him by [beating him] with 200 blows, (50) 5 open wounds, and confiscating (the) service yield of the said boat in his possession, for each day that he will use her mooring, to be given (= boat or revenue) to the temple '*Mnmꜣꜥtrꜥ*'s heart is contented in Aby[d]os'.

* Neo-Egyptian characteristics:
- *tꜣ ḥwt*
- *pꜣ* boat: *pꜣ* is here an anaphoric prenominal articloid, referring to the boat *prius notum* in the crime's definition, a prominent noun (functions as origin of the direct object *bꜣkw*), not identifiable *per se* but by the context and by *m-dỉ.f*.
- [*m ḥwỉtw.f*]
- [*m ḥwỉtw.f*]... *m-dỉ šdw bꜣkw:* coordinative role of the Neo-Egyptian compound preposition *m-dỉ* (instead of *ḥnꜥ* as in line 47) in another version of the 'embryo-conjunctive' (*m-dỉ sḏm* – see Gardiner 1928: 95). See above and Hintze (1950: 105) on the *m-dỉ* ''Syndeton'.
- *m-dỉ.f:* typically Neo-Egyptian compound preposition (*LEG* § 7.3.1).
- *nty ỉw.f r ỉr.f mnỉ:* relative future (see above). *ỉrỉ* may be viewed as the *Hilfsverb* + auxiliated lexeme as infinitive (the masculine infinitive of *mnỉ* is noted by *EG* § 285), an analytic form (*EG* § 485; Kroeber (1970: 180-195); *LEG* § 10.4; Junge (1996: 100-101)), a phenomenon already present in Middle Egyptian. But it may also be a homonym thematic *ỉrỉ* that belongs to another paradigm ('to use'), as in line 47 (*m hrw nb nty ỉw.f r ỉr.f m-dỉ.f* about a staff member diverted from his duty). In this case, *mnỉ* must be adverbial and rhematic (stative with a 'verb of incomplete predication'). *ỉrỉ* is deprived of its feminine infinitive *t* suffix.
- *dỉdỉw*

* 'Classical' degree 0 forms used:
- *ỉr.tw hpw:* independent passive or impersonal prospective following the topicalized enunciation of the crime, see above. See also Kruchten 1981: 71-73 for the parallel with *Ḥrmḥb*'s *Karnak decree*, lines 13-16 and 16-21 and the distinction between direct (confiscation of the boat) and indirect damages (loss of profit resulting from deprival of the work instrument).

* General dialectal features: degree 2.

* Legal terms: *ỉr* – classifier: ø (to enforce).
hpw – classifier: (norm, rule).
šdw – classifier: (to confiscate).
bꜣkw – classifier: (service yield).

* Legal formula: - law enforcement: *ỉr.tw hpw r.f m* (method) + infinitive (types of penalties coordinated by *m-dỉ*)
- confiscation: *šdw b3kw n* + noun (object) + *m-dỉ.f* + *m hrw nb nty ỉw.f r ỉr.f mnỉ* (quantification).

I.2.10 Operative part: the crimes (part 3 – encroaching upon boundaries)

(50) (…) [*ḫ*]*r ỉr sr nb ỉmy-r 3ḥwt nb n pr pn* ⌜*my*/⌜*3my*[100] (51) *sk3 nb rwḏ nb nty ỉw.f r tht r t3š n 3ḥwt n t3 ḥwt Mnm3*ʿ*tr*ʿ *ỉb hrw m 3bdt r smnmn t3šw.sn*

(50) (…) [An]d concerning any civil servant, any overseer of fields of this temple, any riverbank/Asiatic (?) (51) plough(man), any agent who will overstep (the) limit of fields of the temple '*Mnm3*ʿ*tr*ʿ's heart is contented in Abydos' to shift their boundaries,

* Neo-Egyptian characteristics:
- # [*ḫ*]*r ỉr* + singular nouns + *nb* + *nty ỉw.f r tht #:* topicalized offenders expanded by a relative future (see above, also about the list of lexemes formula, same remark concerning singular reference and the value of *nb*).
- *t3 ḥwt*

* 'Classical' degree 0 forms used:
- *pr pn*
- *r smnmn*: preposition + infinitive (purpose).

* General dialectal features: degree 2.

* Legal terms: *thỉ r t3š* – classifiers: 𓂾𓂡 (to trespass, overstep, encroach upon boundaries). Here the 𓂻 classifier has been replaced by the 'strong arm' expressing [COERCION], but the idea of [LEG] (and control) is retained with the 𓂾 classifier.

* Legal formula: *ḫr ỉr* + offender + *nty ỉw.f r sḏm* (the crime) + *r* + infinitive (crime's purpose).

I.2.11 Operative part: the penalties (part 3)

(51) (…) *ỉr.tw hpw r.f m sw3 fnd.f msḏrwy.f* (52) *dỉdỉw r* ⌜*ḥwty m t3 ḥwt Mnm3*ʿ*tr*ʿ *ỉb hrw m 3bdt*

(51) (…) (the) rule will have to be enforced against him by cutting off his nose (and) his ears (52), (when) reduced to a cultivator in the temple '*Mnm3*ʿ*tr*ʿ's heart is contented in Abydos';

100 Spiegelberg (1906: 201) 'Rinderhirt'; Griffith (1927: 202) and Edgerton (1947: 223) 'keeper of plough-oxen'; Roeder (1960: 322) 'Asiaten (Kriegsgefangener als Landarbeiter) des Pflügens'; *RITANC* I, 54: 'mud-man of ploughing'?; Warburton 1997: 192 'plough herdsman'.

* Neo-Egyptian characteristics:
- *t3 ḥwt*
- *didiw:* almost the same sentence is to be found in *Ḥrmḥb*'s *Karnak decree*, line 16: *ir.tw hp r.f m sw3 fnḏ.f diw r Ṯ3*[*rw*], although the form used in that case is not geminated.

* 'Classical' degree 0 forms used: *ir.tw hpw:* independent passive or impersonal prospective.

* General dialectal features: degree 1.

* Legal terms:

ir – classifier: ø (to enforce).

hpw – classifier: ⌒ (norm, rule).

rdi r – classifier: ø (to reduce someone to an inferior position). See Bedell (1973: 178) 'forced labor'. The literal meaning of the lexeme is, of course, 'to place someone in (a position)', a position that may be superior (as for instance in *Beni Hasan* I, pl XXV, lines 13-17: *iw rdi.n wi ḥm n Ḥr* (…) *r iry-pˁ(t) ḥ3ty-ˁ imy-r ḫ3swt i3btt*); but all instances of *rdi r* in our corpus are of the degrading type representing penalties. Compare the *Bilgai stela*, lines 5-6 (…) *mtw.f* [*ṯ3i*] *rmṯ im.s r ditw.f r ky h3w* "and who will [seize] a man in it to reduce him to another corvée".

* Legal formula: *ir.tw hpw r.f m* (method) + infinitive (type of penalty).

I.2.12 Operative part: the crimes (part 4 – disturbing fowlers/fishermen in their work)[101]

(52) (…) *m-mitt rmṯ nb nty m t3 r-ḏr.f nty iw.f r hd wḥˁ nb n t3 ḥwt Mnm3ˁtrˁ ib hrw m 3bdt* (53) *ḥr š3w.f n grg ḥr swnnw.f n ḥ3mw*

(52) (…) likewise, anybody who (is anywhere) in (the) entire land who shall assault[102] any fowler/fisherman of the temple '*Mnm3ˁtrˁ*'s heart is contented in Abydos' (53) in his hunting marshes (or) his fishing ponds;

* Neo-Egyptian characteristics:
- # *m-mitt* + noun + distributive *nb* + relative adverbial rheme + *nty iw.f r hd* (relative future) #: see above. Concerning the frontal presence of the marker of connectedness *m-mitt*, it appears instead of the previously encountered (*ḫr*) *ir* (stylistic variation). Note that in modern legalese also, 'adverbials tend typically to cluster at the beginning of the sentence, although they are not confined to that position' (Crystal & Davy 1969: 204). The two relative clauses have a restrictive effect 'by including a statement which distinguishes it from other members of its category' (Simpson 1996: 55); two relative adjectives are used to form the

101 See also the same type of crime against herdsmen, lines 80-82.

102 Or drive off, see Griffith (1927: 202); Gardiner (1952: 30); *RITANC* I, 54. This must be paralleled with line 37 (*tht, nwt*).

relative expansions, as in lines 80-81, although another solution is preferred in lines 89-90 (a relative clause followed by a conjunctive).
- *tꜣ ḥwt*

* 'Classical' degree 0 forms used:
- *m-mitt*: *idem*. Replaces the topicalizer at the beginning of a new category of crime.
- *šꜣw.f n grg, swnnw.f n wꜣḫmw:* relational expansions, undetermined, expressing a typological association, or preposition *n* (for) + noun expressing advantage.

* General dialectal features: degree 2.

* Legal terms: *hd* – classifiers: 𓂣𓂡 (to assault, attack, drive off); see McDowell (1990: 28); = *hꜣd*. Already used in *Sinuhe* B119 (with classifier 𓂡). *EG*'s list classifier D41 𓂣 'forearm with palm of hand downwards' 'det. various actions involving movement of arms' completes the image of [COERCION] implied by 𓂡, perhaps in the same way as ʃ completes 𓂻, the category represented by 𓂣 being the [ARM MOTION] category (schematic relation with the lexeme *hd*). It probably emphasizes the physical character of the assault (note the absence of accessory in the hand).

* Legal formula: *m-mitt* + offender + *nty iw.f r sḏm* + victim + *m* (crime's location).

I.2.13 Operative part: the penalties (part 4)

(53) (…) *ir.tw hpw r.f m ḥwitw.f m sḫ* 100 *wbnw sd* 5
(53) (…) (the) rule will have to be enforced against him by beating him with 100 blows (and) 5 open wounds;

* Neo-Egyptian characteristics: *m ḥwitw.f*

* 'Classical' degree 0 forms used: *ir.tw hpw*

* General dialectal features: degree 1.

* Legal terms: *ir* – classifier: ø (to enforce).
hpw – classifier: 𓏛 (norm, rule).

* Legal formula: *ir.tw hpw r.f m* (method) + infinitive (the type of penalty).

I.2.14 Operative part: the crimes (part 5 – requisition of material property)

(53) (…) *ḫr ir rmṯ nb nty iw.tw r gmitw.f* (54) *ḥr ṯꜣwt ḫt nbt n tꜣ ḥwt Mnmꜣˁtrˁ ib hrw m ꜣbdt*

(53) (…) And as for anybody one will catch (54) seizing[103] any material property of the temple '*Mnmꜣꜥtrꜥ*'s heart is contented in Abydos',

* Neo-Egyptian characteristics:

- *# ḫr ir* + noun + distributive *nb* + *nty iw.tw r gmitw.f ḥr ṯꜣwt #:* topicalized noun expanded by a relative impersonal future. The addition of the semi-vowel *w* after the feminine infinitive ending and before the suffix pronoun designating the object of the infinitive could be considered to be the Neo-Egyptian 'object pronoun' *tw.f* (*LEG* § 2.5), but the alternative spelling (line 72: *iw.tw r gmit.f*) seems to prove this option wrong. *gmitw.f*'s rheme is completed by the converb *ḥr* + infinitive (verbal form of adverbial function), expressing the fact that the offender is caught in the act perhaps not by an official. To permit this precision, the impersonal *tw* is used for the first time in the exposition of the crimes.
- *tꜣ ḥwt*

* 'Classical' degree 0 forms used: *ḫt nbt*

* General dialectal features: degree 2.

* Legal terms: *gmi ḥr* + infinitive – classifier: ø (to catch in the act).
ṯꜣw – classifier:  (to seize).
ḫt – classifier: ø (material property).

* Legal formula: *ḫr ir* + offender + *nty iw.tw r gmit.f* + *ḥr* + infinitive (object of the crime).

I.2.15 Operative part: the penalties (part 5)

(54) (…) *ir.tw hpw r.f ḥwitw.f m sḫ* 100 *m-di šdw pꜣ nkt n* (55) *tꜣ ḥwt Mnmꜣꜥtrꜥ ib hrw m ꜣbdt m-di.f m ṯꜣwt iw* 100 *m-sꜣ wꜥ*

(54) (…) (the) rule will have to be enforced against him (by) beating him with 100 blows and confiscating the share/valuables of (55) the temple '*Mnmꜣꜥtrꜥ*'s heart is contented in Abydos' in his possession, with a fine when 100 (is) after 1 (= of 100 to 1).

* Neo-Egyptian characteristics:

- *(m) ḥwitw.f:* preposition omission (see line 53, for example) + infinitive with intrusive *w* + suffix pronoun, object of the infinitive.
- *tꜣ ḥwt*
- *pꜣ nkt:* cataphoric use of the articloid with prominent noun (the goods in the offender's possession). *Nkt* is a generic collective noun, masculine with fixed (non pertinent) plural strokes marker (*Wb* II, 347: in Neo-Egyptian, with *pꜣ*).

103 Stealing for McDowell (1990: 38, n. 142), although it may represent the seizing by an official for a public use when he diverts the goods from their original purpose, but not for his personal benefit.

- (*m*) *ḥwitw.f... m-di šdw:* see line 50.
- *m-di.f*
- *ṯ3wt:* Neo-Egyptian lexeme; *m ṯ3wt* could be seen as a converb on the same level as <*m*> *ḥwitw.f* and *m-di šdw,* or as an adverbial adjunct of *m-di.f*; but the absence of an object of *ṯ3wt* and the presence of the adnexal expansion *iw* 100 *m-s3 wꜥ* would appear to cancel those options.

* 'Classical' degree 0 forms used:

- *ir.tw hpw*
- *# m ø ṯ3wt iw* 100 *m-s3 wꜥ #:* undetermined noun + circumstantial rhematic adnexal expansion (*iw* + quantifier + preposition + quantifier).

* General dialectal features: degree 2.

* Legal terms:

ir – classifier: ø (to enforce).

hpw – classifier: 𓍢 (rule, legal norm).

šdw – classifier*:* 𓂡 (to confiscate).

nkt – classifier*:* 𓏛 (share, valuables). 'Share' may link the double semantics of the lexeme in Egyptian, low quantity and *res* (literally, something, but 'this something' is not a sound translation). See Helck (1956: 85-86) for valuables; Kruchten (1981: 102 and note 329) 'petit rien', 'A l'origine, certainement un euphémisme pour designer une contribution, peut-être, volontaire, limitée à des événements exceptionnels.'; Allam (1987: 24) for *res*. Note in *Rꜥmss* II's *Hittite Treaty* (*KRI* II, 225-232, line 13): *iw bw ir.*N *thi r.*Egypt *r-nḥḥ r iṯ3 nkt im.f* 'N will never commit a transgression against Egypt to seize valuables from it'. The superordinate [ABSTRACT] category 𓏛 classifier implies countable goods that may appear on a written statement. But note that *nkt* takes the crossed sticks classifier 𓏴 in line 106, as it does in *Stẖy* II *Karnak decree* (see infra), although it is sometimes written with the 'bad bird' 𓅪 classifier during the New Kingdom (see David 2000: 6 and 109).

ṯ3wt – classifier*:* 𓂡 𓏛 (fine). See Černý (1937: 186-189) 'represents the amount of the fine only, quite apart from the original stolen object'; Gardiner (1952: 30); Bedell (1973: 179-183); Kruchten (1981: 91); McDowell (1990: 29 and 230-231); the root (*i*)*ṯ3* (' a seizure') explains the classifiers.

* Legal formulas: - law enforcement: *ir.tw hpw r.f* <*m*> (method) + infinitive (types of penalties coordinated by *m-di*)
- fine: *m ṯ3wt iw* 100 *m-s3 wꜥ* (basis of computation).

I.2.16 Second enacting clause (authority, object, beneficiary, applicability - protection of the herd)

(55) (…) *m-mitt iw w{3}ḏ.n ḥm.f rdit ḥny.tw t3 mnmnt* 𓃒 *t3 mnmnt* (56) *ꜥnḫw t*(*3*) *mnmnt ꜥ3w t3 mnmnt š3w t3 mnmnt 3pdw t3 mnmnt i3wt n t3 ḥwt Mnm3ꜥtrꜥ ib hrw m 3bdt ḥr mw* (57) *ḥr t3*

(55) (…) Likewise, his Majesty has decreed to cause that the herd of cattle, the flock (56) of goats, the pack of donkeys, the herd of pigs, the flock of fowls, the stock of animals be attached to the service of the temple '*Mnmꜣꜥtrꜥ*'s heart is contented in Abydos', on water (and) (57) on land,

* Neo-Egyptian characteristics:

- *m-mitt:* textemic transition recalling that the texteme it opens begins previously in the text.
- *w{ꜣ}ḏ*
- *tꜣ ḥwt*
- *tꜣ mnmnt:* list of actors or objects of *ḥny.tw,* closed by the hyperonym *tꜣ mnmnt ỉꜣwt n tꜣ ḥwt* (interestingly classified by basic level , although the superordinate classifier is used in the decree for *tp n ỉꜣwt*). This part of the text refers to lines 34-35 of the preamble *sensu stricto*, using for the first time the lexeme *mnmnt* (not *per se* identifiable, generic-collective, with fixed plural strokes marking, concrete, probably prominent as a central valuable possession of the temple). As *mnmnt* is on each occasion determined by an adnominal expansion (the species), *tꜣ*'s function is cataphoric. Note that adnominal expansions of a 'bare' *mnmnt* (without classifier) are used instead of a 'reverse classification' consisting of several icons of prototypical species covered by *mnmnt* (as in Middle Kingdom examples, e.g. *Beni Hasan* fig. 4-8a.). In fact, the expansions play the role of classifiers (and in the case of and , they actually function as classifiers). For an extensive study of the intermediate taxon *mnmnt* ('the moving ones' or 'walking property'), an 'administrative' category, not a 'natural' one, used in the context of traxation, see Goldwasser (2002: 72-78).

* 'Classical' degree 0 forms used:

- *ỉw w{ꜣ}ḏ.n ḥm.f:* independent perfect in delocutive report of enacting clause texteme, acting as a section divider.
- *rdỉt ḥny.tw tꜣ mnmnt:* infinitive (object of *w{ꜣ}ḏ*) + *sḏm.tw*.N passive or impersonal, dependent prospective (object of *rdỉt*). Note the spelling *ḥn.tw* in line 30.

* General dialectal features: degree 1.

* Legal terms: *w{ꜣ}ḏ* - classifier: ø (to decree).
ḥn - classifier: ø (to allocate, attach).

* Legal formula: *ỉw w{ꜣ}ḏ.n ḥm.f* (source of the decree) + *rdỉt* (the executive power's implementation) + *ḥny.tw* (nature of the measure: allocution) + object + *n* (beneficiary) + *ḥr* (the decree's territorial application).

I.2.17 Preamble *sensu stricto* (negative intents) – part 2

(57) (…) *r tm rdit tht.tw r tp n i3dwt nb im.sn*
r tm dit tht.tw r mniw.sny
r tm dit iṯ3.tw [hieroglyph] *ꜥ3* (58) *š3* [ꜥ]*nḫ*[*w*] *tp n i3dw nb im.sn m nḥm m wstnw*
r tm rdit iṯ3 imy-r [[hieroglyph] *nb*] *imy-r* [*mni*]*w nb mniw nb n t3 ḥwt* (59) *Mnm3ꜥtrꜥ ib hrw m 3bdt* [hieroglyph] *ꜥ3 š3 ꜥnḫ n t3 ḥwt Mnm3ꜥtrꜥ ib hrw m 3bdt* [*r dit m šb*] *n ky*[104] *r-pw dit* (60) *m3ꜥ.f n ky nṯr iw bn* (61) *m3ꜥ.f n Wsir p3.sn nb m t3.f* (62) *ḥwt šps ir.n ḥm.f*
r tm dit hd.tw mniw (63) *nb n t3 ḥwt Mnm3ꜥtrꜥ ib hrw m 3bdt ḥr p3.f smw* (64) *n* [hieroglyph] *in sr nb ḥ3ty-ꜥ nb imy-r* [hieroglyph] *nb* [*r*]*wḏ nb imy-r ꜥ3 nb rmṯ* (65) *nb nty m t3 r-ḏr.f*
[*r*] *tm dit iṯ3.tw n3y.sn ḥmwt* (66) *n3.sn b3kw kfꜥw m wpt nb n Pr-ꜥ3 ꜥnḫ wḏ3 snb*

(57) (…) to prevent ones transgression against any head/kind of livestock among them (the herds);
to prevent ones transgression against their herdsmen;
to prevent that be appropriated bovines, donkey(s) (58), pig(s), [g]oat[s], (or) any head/kind of livestock among them, by seizure/order (or) in any arbitrary manner;
to prevent [any] overseer of [cattle], any superintendent of [herds]men, any herdsmen of the temple (59) '*Mnm3ꜥtrꜥ*'s heart is contented in Abydos' to seize an ox, a donkey, a pig, a goat of the temple '*Mnm3ꜥtrꜥ*'s heart is contented in Abydos' [to exchange] (it) with/for another, or cause (60) its offering (that he will offer/ it be offered) to another god, while not (61) offering it to Osiris, their lord, in his (62) august temple that his majesty has made;
to prevent that be assaulted any herdsman (63) of the temple '*Mnm3ꜥtrꜥ*'s heart is contented in Abydos' in his cattle pastures (64), by any high official, any mayor, any cattle overseer, any [a]gent, any donkey overseer, anybody (65) who (is anywhere) in the entire land;
[to] prevent that be seized their wives (66), their servants, (when) compelled (to be) on any mission of Pharaoh, L.P.H.;

* Neo-Egyptian characteristics:

- *t3 ḥwt*
- *tht.tw:* dependent prospective (*sḏm.f* impersonal or *sḏm.tw*.N passive) with an intrusive *t* before *tw* in each instance.
- *mniw.sny:* the suffix pronoun has an uncommon ending, previously reserved for dual forms, but also appearing in *Rꜥmss* III's *Elephantine decree*, lines 4 (boat.*sny*) and 5 (*n.sny*). See Griffith (1927: 202, n. 8) and Ford (1995: 68) for whom the final *n* had probably already disappeared in pronunciation and the phonetic change was consequently marked by the addition of *y*.
- *iw bn m3ꜥ.f: iw bn sḏm.f* is composed of # circumstantial converter *iw* + Neo-Egyptian preverbal negator *bn* + *sḏm.f* #. This negative syntagm follows the

104 Used without nominal expansion, unlike the following *ky nṯr*. See also on line 76.

affirmative (*r*) *dit m*ꜣꜥ*.f* (infinitive + dependent prospective), with the same lexeme constituency, and seems to have an 'although/but not' value. Several issues are subject to discussion regarding this construction. First, the nature of the *sḏm.f* form: either prospective with delocutive actor (*LEG* § 21.3 and 37.4; Goldwasser 1987: 136-137; Winand 1992: 219-220) or an infinitive and its object expressed by the suffix pronoun, for Frandsen (1974: 15) 'the prospective *sḏm.f* cannot be preceded by converters' (note 1 recognizes an exception on p. 178, Ex. 23: with *wn* + *sḏm.f*, and p. 205 'no examples of the prospective *sḏm.f* preceded by *iw* have been noted'); Kruchten (1981: 85) '*iw* + proposition non-verbale (*nn*/prédicat + infinitif/sujet)'. Polotsky (1964: 271) and Gilula (1970: 211) have established that *nn sḏm.f* is composed of a negator and a that-form and is used to negate the independent prospective; Groll (1970: 118, Ex. 254) gives one example of the form *iw bn sḏm.f* (*pTurin* P/R 1880, *RAD* 49, 5-6: *w*ꜣ*ḥ Ỉmn w*ꜣ*ḥ p*ꜣ *ḥḳ*ꜣ ꜥ*.w.s. iw bn diw.i* 'By Amun (and) by the Ruler L.P.H. it does not exist that I should give') in her discussion of *bn sḏm.f* and concludes (p. 120) that '*bn* indicating non-existence (...) can precede only nouns or noun equivalents (...) the initial Prospective *stp.f* is a 'that' form'. Frandsen's objections to a prospective cannot easily be dismissed, although obviously we are not always in the presence of an infinitive with its suffixed object. See, for instance, previously quoted *pTurin 1880*; with Middle Egyptian negator *nn*, the examples quoted by Frandsen (1974: 288), *Doomed Prince* 4,6 (*iw nn pri p*ꜣ *ẖrdw*) and *The Tale of Two Brothers* 7,4 (*iw nn sḏm.k r.i*); Winand 1992: 220 (he has noted 9 examples in his corpus); line 11 of the *Elephantine decree* also shows a finite *sḏm.f* form following *bn*: *iw bn di.i n.f ḫt nb* (*ḫt nb* is *di*'s object). We prefer the option of a *sḏm.f* that-form proposed by Polotsky and Gilula as it suits the paradigmatic axis. The next question that has to be solved is linked to the 'circumstantial inexistence' expressed by the pattern. Thetic statements of the kind have been analyzed as composed of a rhematic negator + a thematic noun; see for instance Gilula (1970: 211) and Vernus (1985: 168) 'dans *bn sḏm.f* (...) sa [*bn*] valeur prédicative qui est à l'origine de ces tours en Moyen Egyptien (négation de la phrase) tend à s'estomper dans la synchronie du Néo-égyptien de la pratique'. *Nn* (and *bn*) is the 'Ausdruck der Nichtexistenz' (Polotsky 1964: 271); see also *supra* the discussion of line 41 (*iw nn rdit ḏ*ꜣ*y.tw*), where the pattern is # *iw nn sḏm* # (with an infinitive), a 'lesser degree' Ramesside form with the Middle Egyptian negator *nn*. But we have already noted that existence statements are 'prepredications', devoid of a nexus (Shisha-Halevy 1998b: 596). What does not exist is the fact of offering the animal to Osiris (there is actually an offering made to another god), literally 'when there is not the fact that he offers it to Osiris'. The non-existence pattern introduces or presents not only the that-form, but the entire relative segment.

- *p*ꜣ*.sn, t*ꜣ*.f, p*ꜣ*.f, n*ꜣ*y.sn, n*ꜣ*.sn*: Neo-Egyptian possessive nuclear determinators (see above). Note that of all its occurrences in the second preamble *sensu stricto*, only one instance is the 'complete' form *n*ꜣ*y.sn*. Again the possessed is either human or inanimate and the reason for the use of the pronominal possessive instead of the suffixal one cannot be clearly assessed.

- *tp n i͗ꜣdwt* and *i͗ꜣdw:* spelling variants of *i͗ꜣwt*: line 35, *i͗ꜣwt*; line 58, *i͗ꜣdwt/i͗ꜣdw*; line 70, *i͗ꜣwt*; line 75 *i͗ꜣt*; line 79 *i͗ꜣt*. See Nims (1936: 51-54) for Middle Egyptian *ꜥwt*, Neo-Egyptian *i͗ꜣwt*; Gardiner (1952: 30-31) on *i͗ꜣwt* 'The etymology cannot be disputed on the ground of the presence of [*d*] in the writing, this having a perfect counterpart in the well-known Late-Egyptian spellings [*i͗ꜣdt*] for [*ꜣt*] 'moment' (...)'; *CD*, 8 for *i͗ꜣwt* 'Later wtg. of *ꜥwt* 'small cattle'; Goldwasser (2002: 70-72) concerning *ꜥwt* already used during the Old Kingdom for cervines, 'intermediate taxon' and 'collective term' for herbivorous quadrupeds in the Middle Kingdom (when *i͗ꜣwt* becomes a variation of it), and also used for birds during the New Kingdom. Nevertheless, one may tentatively propose that *i͗ꜣwt* could be an example of 'fusion' between two distinct lexemes, *ꜥwt*-cattle and *i͗dr*-herd (reproduction animals for Moret 1912: 81 & 110; 'something bound together', for Goldwasser 2002: 73).

* 'Classical' degree 0 forms used:

- *r tm (r)di͗t* + object (dependent prospective).
- *i͗r.n ḥm.f:* relative synthetic *sḏm.n*.N, durative and expressing anteriority. Its prominent actor probably explains the use of the classic form.
- *r-pw*: see above. The disjuncter is used here between [*r di͗t m šb*] *n ky* and *di͗t mꜣꜥ.f n ky nṯr*, without repetition of the probable initial preposition.
- # singular or plural nouns + *tp n i͗ꜣdw* + distributive *nb i͗m.sn* #: list comprising species or indefinite number of typical animals followed by the addition of an all-encompassing '(or) any unit among the preceding species or animals' (see lines 34-35). Compare with lines 64-65 list # [singular hyponyms + distributive *nb*] + [hyperonym *rmṯ nb*] + *nty* + adverbial rheme (relative expansion) #.
- *kfꜥw*: passive participle, adnominal expansion of determined *nꜣy.sn ḥmwt nꜣ.sn bꜣkw*.

* General dialectal features: degree 2.

* Legal terms:

r tm (r)di͗t – classifier: ø (to prevent).
thi͗ r - classifiers: (to transgress).
i͗ṯꜣ – classifiers: (to seize, appropriate).
m nḥm - classifier: (by seizure/order).
m wstnw – classifier: (in arbitrary manner).
di͗t m šb – classifiers: [×] in *KRI* I, 55 for the corrupted text, but in complete line 76, only × is used (to exchange). See Peet (1928: 71 n.8); Green (1980: 46). The lexeme *šbi͗* is related to the New Kingdom by *Wb* IV, 436 'belegt seit D. 18'. The presumed × classifier (*EG*'s list Z9 'two sticks crossed' 'Det. break (...) divide (...) actions involving something crossed or encountered', usually situations in which a physical or mental division/reunion is concerned), may evoke here two-sided obligations, a synallagmatic relation (with mutual duties and rights), rendered by the image of two sticks lying crossed (metaphoric

relation between the classifier and the lexeme: 'an exchange is formed of two intertwined deeds as two crossed sticks'). For Grapow (1911: 116-119), the primary meaning of the × classifier is related to a breaking, later applied to other semantic fields as counting, for example. The crossed sticks classifier appears in various lexemes, such as *gmgm, wpi, psš, ḫbi, t3š, ḥsb, ḥdi, nkt,* etc., and is already in use during the Old Kingdom (see *EG*'s list Z10 ⤫; Dreyer 1987: 99 (b) and 103 for *ḥsb*, end of the 3rd dynasty; *PT* § 282 for *sk3t*). Bur we should investigate cases of crossed objects in the Egyptian imagery to try to understand the meaning of the icon. Crossed items appear as early as the Predynastic period in relation to the goddess *Nt* (Neith) *ḥmwst* fetish of crossed arrows upon a shield (*LÄ* IV, 392-394) on numerous seals and impressions (e.g. Kaplony 1963: Abb. 75, 201 in names, 823 without the shield), representing metonymically her warrior temperament, as a very early example of an icon that will appear later upon chivalry blazons (motive of 'sautoir' or crossed swords). In numerous cases commonly translated as *Nt*, the icon used is limited to two crossing traits (e.g. Kaplony 1963: Abb. 12, 52, 107) or larger items, one extremity of which being appreciably thinner, perhaps due to the medium used (e.g. stela *Berlin* 18137 from Abydos in Dreyer (1998: Abb. 57)), both taken perhaps as a more cursive writing of the weapons. The same image of crossed weapons appears on chariots in the form of two crossing quivers (see e.g. *Rꜥmss* II in Ramesseum's second pylon scene or his Qadesh relief of Abu Simbel; satirical *pTurin* 55001, on the mouse's chariot, reproduced e.g. in Brunner-Traut 1955: taf. III) and in the 'crossing of swords' (staves) scenes of wrestlers or (e.g. Deir el-Medineh ostracon *Louvre E* 25309; Peck & Ross 1978: n. 87). Besides these contentious instances, crossed items appear in other contexts: probably related to the signified 'to unite' (as in *dmḏ*), their expression in the script is summarized by the hieroglyph S23 of *EG*'s list, representing 'knotted strips of cloth' (e.g. *Twtꜥnḫimn* mummy arms position in his tomb painting of the 'opening of the mouth' ritual; Osiris' crossed red wrapping bands in *Ḏḥwtyms* IV and *Twtꜥnḫimn* tombs; the crossed scepters upon royal or Osiriac funerary images and 18th to 20th dynasties royal mummies). All the cases mentioned of crossed items/weapons are of united whole objects rather than broken pieces; union (and its contrary, division, or even conflict) may be implied by the cross icon. The *crux decussata* (x shaped cross) must also be distinguished from the + shaped cross with vertical and horizontal strokes as it appears in the hieroglyph , for instance. It has an entirely different value (compare with Western modern ideography in Liungman 1991: 50). The x shaped cross, because of its cutting diagonals, has a more dynamic, conflictual semantics than the +-shaped, although the two are representations of two opposed lines united at an intersectional point (note that in hieroglyphic script many signs have a vertical or horizontal axis static version, and an oblique one indicating motion, for example classifying *sbty* 'rampart' and classifying *whn* 'to overthrow'). Interestingly, as crosses are extremely common icons in many different cultures (see for pre- and non Christian religions Ries 1985: 295-314), it seems that they often have, beyond their multivalence, the same fundamental 'union of opposites' meaning (Cirlot 1962: 65-68; Chetwynd 1982: 317-318; Biedermann & Cazenave 1996: 177). For an interesting parallel with the semantics of the crossed forms category (*gilimmû*) in Assyriology 'which relate as a rule to conflict, hostility, and confusion', see Whittaker (2001: 24). The classifier × thus represents the superordinate category of [UNION/DIVISION], see David (2003). In the case of the presence of an erased classifier, it is also referred to the [ABSTRACT] superordinate category, for an abstract contract involving accounted goods and perhaps confirmed in writing.

hd - classifier: (to assault, use violence). Note the absence of the [COERCION] category classifier present in line 52.

kfꜥw - classifier: (coercion).

* Legal formula: *r tm (r)dit* + [*sḏm.tw* (offender) + *r* (victim) (+ *in* + offender)] or [*sḏm.tw*.N (victim) (+ *m* (method))]or [*sḏm*.N (offender) + object (victim)]

I.2.18 Operative part: the crimes (part 6 – requisition of herdsmen)

(66) (…) *ir nty nb r tht* (67) *w{ꜣ}ḏ tn mtw.f iṯꜣ mniw n tꜣ ḥwt Mnmꜣꜥtrꜥ ib hrw m ꜣbdt m* (68) *kfꜥw m r-pw m w n w m wpt nb m*[*tw*] *pꜣ mniw ḏd ir ḏr iṯꜣ wi* (69) *pꜣ mn iw ꜣḳw ḥr ḫpr m pꜣy idt m wꜥ tp n iꜣt r-pw* 2 *r-pw* 3 (70) *r-pw* 4

(66) (…) As for anyone who will transgress (67) this decree and seize a herdsman of the temple '*Mnmꜣꜥtrꜥ*'s heart is contented in Abydos' by (68) coercion or from district to district on any mission, [and] this herdsman will say: 'since this so-and-so has seized me (69), a loss of one head/kind of cattle or 2 or 3 (70) or 4 results in this/my herd';

* Neo-Egyptian characteristics:

- *nty nb r tht... mtw.f iṯꜣ:* full-fledged conjunctive (see above) with suffix thematic coreferent to *nty nb* after future *r tht,* in the relative clause. Probably also *m*[*tw*] *pꜣ mniw ḏd* (conjunctive *mtw*.N *sḏm*) as Griffith seems to have regarded it (1927: 203), to compare with *ntf ḏd* (*Elephantine decree*, line 7).
- *tꜣ ḥwt*
- *pꜣ mniw:* anaphoric (*prius notum,* see referate *mniw,* line 67) specific prenominal identificative, gender/number characterized, with prominent noun (actor of *ḏd*).
- *pꜣ mn: mn* is already in use in Old Egyptian. Edel (1955: § 380) does not define its nature ('Anhang zum Adjektiv'), but indicates that it appears in place of a noun ('nur substantiviert vorkommt') when it is impossible or unwanted to give a precise name (in *PT*, instead of the king's name). See also *CD*, 107 and *Wb* II,

64-65. Could be the statal verb *mnỉ* (to be established) substantivated, used to replace a proper name for a more general formulation ('untel'); the formula is widely used in illustrative constructed quotation textemes. *mnỉ* is not part of the fictional verbal declaration by the victim (as for *r-pw* + quantifier), but belongs only to the written text. The formula expresses the legal discourse tendency to generality (conventionalized way of generalizing an expression in which specificity is important), see *supra*, with parallel between *nty nb* and *pꜣ mn*. Here preceded by *pꜣ*, definite and deictic (even if not named in the decree, the offender is probably pointed out by his victim). See Shisha-Halevy (1989d: 43, 54) in Coptic 'non-phoric i.e. really *paradigmatic* counterpart of PNs [proper names]: *nim* "so-and-so" (...). (Here the conventional term "indefinite" is certainly inapt, considering that both pro-forms are as specific as proper names, if without actually spelling them out).'

- *ỉr ḏr ỉṯꜣ*. N: here placed after *m[tw]*.N *ḏd* tag clause that opens the 'direct speech' consisting of an illustrative pseudo-quotation, a constructed soliloquy or catalysis denunciation that uses passive forms to throw light on the nature of the loss, giving a truth-like aspect to the case. The damage suffered by the herdsman is the consequence of his forced departure and his herd being thus left unattended, a specific damage that needs a more graphic account to reveal its nature (note that the material loss of an animal due to the herdsman's forced absence is not reflected by the preceding preamble *sensu stricto*). Compare with line 49 where the same technique is used to communicate the offender's motivation; characterization is achieved by the constructed quotation. The backgrounding topicalized circumstantial *ỉr ḏr sḏm*.N (*ỉr* topic + adverbial form) generally expresses the origin or cause of a situation ('temporalis', see Satzinger 1976: 20-21); it is expressed in Middle Egyptian by *ḏr sḏm.f* (EG § 176), the preposition + 'forme substantive personnelle du prospectif' for Polotsky (1976: 24) who notes that 'quand l'événement est situé dans le passé, [son emploi] doit probablement être considéré comme « relatively future » (envisagé du point de vue du terme initial), (...) et non comme « relatively past » (par rapport à la principale).' (1944: 189). In Middle Egyptian, *ḏr sḏm.f* does not appear to occur ahead of a sentence, and is thus never topicalized by *ỉr*[105]. The *sḏm*.N form used after *ỉr ḏr* in our text is a prospective for Frandsen (1974: 22-23, 166), Winand (1992: 256) and Loprieno (1995: 230), a 'subjunktivische Form' for Satzinger (1976: 21 and 265, note 7, apparently in the 'Stories', not in a narrative context, and in 'nichtliterarischen Texte', the context being either narrative or not) and Junge (1996: 107, 239), but a 'perfectif' for Kruchten (1981: 105-106), and 'perhaps the circumstantial' for *LEG* § 32.2 (explaining a *m-ḏr sḏm.n.f* occurrence). Note also Hintze's (1950: 71) remark that the form is probably time-indifferent in a Neo-Egyptian narrative context ('synchron oder präterital'); of course, nominal forms have only a relative relationship to time. The issues are

105 Although there are other instances of topicalized circumstantial clauses in Middle Egyptian, see *EG* § 149.2 (*ỉr m-ḫt* N); Loprieno (1995: 151 (41) *ỉr m wn.ỉ*).

the fact that prepositions are followed by nominal forms (prospective or other abstract that-form) but that conjunctions can precede various nexuses, and while any type of nominal form may follow a preposition, it may not be the 'subjunctive prospective'. We may be faced with a type of cleft sentence consisting of a circumstantial 'syntagme conjonctionnel' 'thématisé' with *ἰr* as theme marker, followed by a circumstantial focus, as in the examples listed by Shisha-Halevy (1978: 52 ff.): # [*ἰr* (theme marker) + *ḏr* (preposition) + *sḏm*.N (that-form)]$_{\text{circumstantial theme}}$ [*ἰw*.N + *ḥr sḏm*]$_{\text{adverbial rheme}}$ #, although none of the examples quoted by Shisha-Halevy are of the # [*ἰr ḏr ἰṯ3*. N] $_{\text{theme}}$ [*ἰw*.N + *ḥr sḏm*] $_{\text{focus}}$ # type. For *LEG* § 38.1, Satzinger (1976 : 21) and Junge (1986: 125 and 1996 : 268), the construction is a protasis-apodosis complex ('closed complex' for Junge, *op.cit*., p.276). The full-fledged 20th dynasty degree 3 Neo-Egyptian construction is *ἰr m-ḏr/m-dἰ sḏm.f* (*ἰr* when in initial position for *LEG* § 32.3; Groll 1970: 145; Frandsen 1974: 26 (8)); on *ḏr* and *m-ḏr*, see Winand (1992: 248-249). The direct speech texteme uses a degree 2 form; it is perhaps not the spoken 19th dynasty 'low class' sociolect that would be expected of a simple herdsman under *Stḫy* I (although we have no clue as to the expected form) or the construction does not really 'disguise' itself (see also the use of *p3 mnἰ*). See also Hintze (1952: 299) on the use of *m-ḏr* in direct speech (to convince the speech addressee).

- *p3y:* Neo-Egyptian deictic or possessive determinator.

* 'Classical' degree 0 forms used:

- *ἰr nty nb r tht:* topicalized relative clause with adverbial rheme (preposition + infinitive). Note the absence of *p3* before *nty* (compare line 44), of *ἰw.f* before *r tht* (see line 43, for instance, and Lorton 1977: 55 'transition from the employment of the *sḏm.ty.fy* form'), and the colon-enclitic placement of the distributive *nb*, junctural openness, see Shisha-Halevy (1981: 318), which may be a mark of the substantivization of *nty* or *nb*. Compare 13th dynasty *Abydos decree* of *Ḫwt3wyrʿ Wgf* (*ἰr rf nty ṯw* [=*tw*] *nb r gmt.f*) and 17th dynasty *Stèle juridique de Karnak*, line 7 (*ἰr nty nb r ἰἰt*). Note the valence of *thἰ* with object *w{3}ḏ*, as in *Ḥrmḥb*'s *Karnak decree*, line 34, *rmṯ ἰr thἰ wḏwt*), unlike the previous examples with the preposition *r* (see also the *Kanais decree*, lines 16 & 17, with *rmṯ*, 'to lead people astray').
- *w{3}ḏ tn*: use of the classical feminine proximal deictic determinator, although the substantive has lost its feminine ending.
- (*m*) *r-pw:* as Gardiner (1952: 27) and Kitchen (1979: 456) put it: 'requisition and (transfer) from a district to (another) district are here expressily distinguished' by an 'explicit disjunctive construction' (the connectedness marker is placed between two adverbial adjuncts). The presence of *m* before *r-pw* is considered by the *Wb* II, 397. 1 & 2 as Neo-Egyptian (*pAnastasi* III 6, 12 and V 21, 2; *Rʿmss* II's *Hittite Treaty*, line 21, etc.). In lines 69-70 (which could have passed for a more colloquial direct speech), the classical *r-pw* is placed in each case

('Polysyndeton', see Hintze 1950: 109) before the quantifiers following the first option.

- *iw 3ḳw ḥr ḫpr:* adverbial nexus following *ir ḏr iṯ3*.N in the direct speech. Formally, it can be either the Middle Egyptian independent or circumstantial actual present with *ḥr ḫpr* as converb, the Neo-Egyptian circumstantial present (although for Shisha-Halevy (1978: 60-61 and note 31) 'L'hypothèse d'une forme-modèle indépendante *iw.f* + adverbe en néo-égyptien ne peut être écartée (...) continuant le *iw-* superordinateur du moyen-égyptien' and for Junge (1996: 288) '*jw.f ḥr sḏm* sich in jenen Konstruktionen in Austauschbeziehung zu den Satzkonjugationen und Nominalsätzen befindet und daher als Relikt des selbständigen *jw*-Satzes des Mittelägyptischen zu verstehen ist.'), or the Neo-Egyptian narrative non durative sequential 'successive past' *iw.f ḥr sḏm*, a 'non-initial main clause'. The option of the sequential is adopted by *LEG* § 38.1; Frandsen (1974: 98-99); Satzinger (1976: 33-35 for a report, but the descriptive 'progressiv' uses in the 'Stories' and in 'nichtliterarischen Texte'[106] *iw* + first present, in 'kontinuativ gebraucht'); Loprieno (1995: 230). For Junge (1996: 242, 265, 276), we have an 'Umstandssatz des Präsens' in 'non-initial main sentence' function, 'offenbar inhaltlich selbständigen, aber formal abhängigen Satz'.We believe that *iw 3ḳw ḥr ḫpr* represents the focus of the protasis-apodosis complex, a circumstantial present with durative or progressive aspect and perhaps an 'as soon as' effect as we have discussed for the complex *wp-ḥr wnn.sn ḫwy mky iw*.N *ḥr irt*. On the value of *ḫpr,* see Hintze (1950: 103-104) 'ingressive Bedeutung' in narrative Neo-Egyptian context; Satzinger (1976: 147-148) 'progressive Aspekt' or 'dynamischer Gebrauch' of verbs like *ḫpr* that have a double semantics, the statal 'to be' and the *ḥr* + infinitive dynamic 'to become, to result'.
- *wꜥ*: used as quantifier (one unit) of an expanded noun and written out in full (not with a simple stroke), unlike the other non-expanded quantifiers of the disjunctive construction (a common usage, see EG § 260). *m wꜥ tp n i3t* relates to *3kw* (it typifies the loss).

* General dialectal features: degree 2.

* Legal terms:

thi w{3}ḏ - classifier: 𓂾 (to transgress/violate a decree, to infringe); see *CLEM*, 274 in the sense of disobey. The basic level [LEG] category 𓂾 classifier (it relates metaphorically to the lexeme, when 'violating a decree is like trampling on it', in the sense of being superior, above the law) is used in an expression that has parallels in English and Hebrew, for instance, לעבור את החוק (to transgress the law).

w{3}ḏ - classifier: 𓄛 (the papyrus/leather decree).

iṯ3 – classifiers: 𓂡 𓂝 (to seize, appropriate).

kfꜥw - classifier: 𓂡 (coercion).

106 Although Satzinger notes 'Nicht belegt' in this case (note 4, p. 270).

ꜣḳw - classifier: (loss of material property). For the multiple implications of the 'bad bird' classifier, see David 2000 (metaphoric relation with the superordinate [INFERIORITY-PERTURBATION] category). See also *ꜣḳy m ḫt* (line 103).

* Legal formula: *ỉr nty nb* (offender) + *r tht w{ꜣ}ḏ* + conjunctives (object of the crime) + *m* (method) + illustrative constructed speech (*m[tw]*.N *ḏd ỉr ḏr ỉṯꜣ*.N).

I.2.19 Operative part: the penalties (part 6)

(70) (…) *ỉr.tw hpw r.f m ḥwitw.f m sẖ* 200 *m-di šd pꜣ tp n ỉꜣwt* (71) *n tꜣ ḥwt Mnmꜣꜥtrꜥ ỉb hrw m ꜣbdt m-di*[*.f*] *ṯꜣ ỉw* 100 *m-sꜣ wꜥ* (70) (…) (the) rule will have to be enforced against him by beating him with 200 blows and confiscating the head/kind of livestock (71) of the temple '*Mnmꜣꜥtrꜥ*'s heart is contented in Abydos' in [his] possession, fined when 100 (is) after 1 (= of 100 to 1);

* Neo-Egyptian characteristics:

- *m ḥwitw.f*
- *pꜣ tp:* anaphoric and cataphoric reference of the articloid.
- *tꜣ ḥwt*
- *m ḥwitw.f... m-di šd:* 'embryo-conjunctive' with *šd* instead of *šdit.*
- *m-di.f*

* 'Classical' degree 0 forms used:

- *ỉr.tw hpw*
- ø *ṯꜣ ỉw* 100 *m-sꜣ wꜥ:* slightly different from the preceding formula in line 55 (*m ṯꜣwt*), *ṯꜣ* probably a passive participle whose antecedent is *.f*; it could also be a case of prepositional omission and minimalistic spelling of the lexeme.

* General dialectal features: degree 2.

* Legal terms:

ỉr – classifier: ø (to enforce).

hpw – classifier: (rule, legal norm). Note here the substitution of the [ABSTRACT] superordinate category classifier to the string of the basic level [BINDING] category previously used in our text.

šd – classifier*:* ø (to confiscate).

ṯꜣ – classifier*:* (to seize, fine).

* Legal formulas: - law enforcement: *ỉr.tw hpw r.f m* + infinitive (types of penalties coordinated by *m-dỉ*)

- fine: *ṯꜣ ỉw* 100 *m-sꜣ wꜥ* (basis of computation).

I.2.20 Operative part: the crimes (part 7 – requisition of livestock)

(71) (…) *m-mitt pꜣ nty* (72) *iw.tw r gmit.f ḥr iṯꜣ tp n iꜣt nb n tꜣ ḥwt Mnmꜣꜥtrꜥ ib hrw m ꜣbdt*
(71) (…) likewise, the one who (72) will be caught seizing any head/kind of livestock of the temple '*Mnmꜣꜥtrꜥ*'s heart is contented in Abydos',

* Neo-Egyptian characteristics:
- *pꜣ nty iw.tw r gmit.f*
- *tꜣ ḥwt*

* 'Classical' degree 0 forms used:
- *m-mitt:* used instead of the topicalizer *ir*
- *gmit.f ḥr iṯꜣ:* 'verb of incomplete predication' + rhematic converb expressing the fact that the offender is caught in the act (see *supra* lines 53-54).

* General dialectal features: degree 2.

* Legal terms: *gmi ḥr* + infinitive – classifier: ø (to catch in the act).
iṯꜣ – classifier:  (seize, appropriate).

* Legal formula: *m-mitt* + *pꜣ* (offender) + *nty iw.tw r gmit.f* + *ḥr* + infinitive (object of the crime).

I.2.21 Operative part: the penalties (part 7)

(72) (…) *ir.tw* (73) *hpw r.f m swꜣ fnd.f msḏrwy.f diw r ꜥḥwty m tꜣ ḥwt Mnmꜣꜥtrꜥ ib hrw m ꜣbdt* (74) *r sṯꜣ/swꜣ? [hb].f ḥnꜥ dit ḥmt.f ẖrdw.f r nḏwt imy-r pr pn*
(72) (…) (the) rule will have to be enforced (73) against him by cutting off his nose (and) ears, (when) reduced to a cultivator in the temple '*Mnmꜣꜥtrꜥ*'s heart is contented in Abydos' (74), to drag?[107] his [plough] and reducing his wife (and) his children to (the) servitude of (the) overseer of the aforementioned temple;

* Neo-Egyptian characteristics:
- *tꜣ ḥwt*
- *m swꜣ… ḥnꜥ dit*

* 'Classical' degree 0 forms used:
- *ir.tw hpw*
- *diw:* see *didiw*, lines 47, 50, 52.
- *r sṯꜣ? [hb].f:* preposition + infinitive expressing purpose.
- *pr pn*

* General dialectal features: degree 2.

107 Griffith (1927: 203) 'in exchange (?) for his crime (?)' or 'to drive (?) his plough (?)'; *RITANC* I, 54.

* Legal terms: *ir* – classifier: ø (to enforce).
hpw – classifier: ø (rule, legal norm).
rdi r – classifier: ø (to reduce someone to an inferior position).

* Legal formula: law enforcement: *ir.tw hpw r.f m* + infinitive (types of penalties coordinated by *ḥnꜤ*).

I.2.22 Operative part: the crimes (part 8 – 'rerouting' of livestock)

(74) (…) *ḫr ir imy-r*  *nb imy-r Ꜥ3 nb mniw* (75) *nb n t3 ḥwt Mnm3Ꜥtr*Ꜥ *ib hrw m 3bdt nty iw.f r dit tp n i3t nb n t3 ḥwt Mnm3Ꜥtr*Ꜥ (76) *ib hrw m 3bdt m šb n ky*
mi p3 nty iw.f r dit m3Ꜥ.f ḥr ky mtnw iw bn m3Ꜥ.f (77) *n Wsir p3.f nb m t3 ḥwt Mnm3Ꜥtr*Ꜥ *ib hrw m 3bdt*

(74) (…) And as for any overseer of cattle, any superintendent of donkey(s), any herdsman (75) of the temple '*Mnm3Ꜥtr*Ꜥ's heart is contented in Abydos' who will put any head/kind of livestock of the temple '*Mnm3Ꜥtr*Ꜥ's (76) heart is contented in Abydos' in exchange to/for another,
as the one who will cause its offering (that it will be offered) by another document[108], but not offering it (77) to Osiris, his Lord, in the temple '*Mnm3Ꜥtr*Ꜥ's heart is contented in Abydos';

* Neo-Egyptian characteristics:
- *t3 ḥwt*
- *p3 nty iw.f r dit*
- # ø nouns + *nb* + *nty iw.f r dit* #: list [singular hyponyms + distributive *nb*] and adnominal relative clause with singular reference (*iw.f*).
- *iw bn m3Ꜥ.f:* see above, lines 60-61, the direct parallel.
- *p3.f*
- *dit m šb n:* Neo-Egyptian expression (*Wb* IV, 436, n. 16).
- *mtnw*: Neo-Egyptian (*Wb* II, 170-171).

* 'Classical' degree 0 forms used:
- *mi*: used as *m-mitt* instead of the topicalizer *ir*.
- *dit m3Ꜥ.f: m3Ꜥ.f* is a dependent prospective, object of *dit*.

* General dialectal features: degree 2.

* Legal terms: *dit m šb n ky* – classifier: × (to give/put in exchange to/for another). Without the papyrus roll (see above).

* Legal formulas: - *ḫr ir* + offenders *nb* + *nty iw.f r sḏm* (object of the crime).
- *mi* + *p3* (offender) + *nty iw.f r sḏm* (object of the crime).

108 Griffith (1927: 203) 'on another direction (?)'.

I.2.23 Operative part: the penalties (part 8)

(77) (…) *ir.tw hpw r.f m sẖr.f diw ḥr* (78) *tp ẖt ḥnꜥ m-ꜥ ṯꜣw ḥmt[.f] ẖrdw.f ẖt.f nb r tꜣ ḥwt Mnmꜣꜥtrꜥ ib hrw m ꜣbd* (79) *ḥnꜥ šd pꜣ tp n iꜣt m-di pꜣ nty iw.f [di]tw.f n.f m ṯꜣ tꜣ ḥwt nt ḥḥw m rnpwt* (80) *n ni-swt bity Mnmꜣꜥtrꜥ ib hr[w m ꜣb]dt iw* 100 *m-sꜣ wꜥ*

(77) (…) (the) rule will have to be enforced against him by throwing him down placed on (78) (the) tip of a staff (= impaled)[109], and by committing [his] wife, his children, all his material property to the temple '*Mnmꜣꜥtrꜥ*'s heart is contented in Abydos' (79), and confiscating this head/kind of livestock in the possession of the one whom he will [giv]e it to, with a fine of/to the temple of millions of years (80) of (the) king of Upper and Lower Egypt '*Mnmꜣꜥtrꜥ*'s heart is content[ed in Ab]ydos', when 100 (is) to 1;

* Neo-Egyptian characteristics:
- *tꜣ ḥwt*
- *pꜣ tp n iꜣt*
- *m sẖr.f... ḥnꜥ m-ꜥ ṯꜣw:* either double coordination (binomial; sole occurrence of *m-ꜥ* instead of *m-di* in the legal register of the decree; error or insisting 'and also/even'), unusual orthography/error for *ḥnꜥ m ṯꜣw* (but then the presence of *m* is inconsistent with the other 'embryo-conjunctive' examples in the text), or a verbal lexeme *mṯꜣw* (+ *r*…), perhaps connected to *Wb* II, 175.6 *mṯꜣt* (a possession devolved ?), as for Griffith (1927: 203 'forfeiting (?)') and Edgerton (1947: 223 and n. 47 'dedicating').
- *m-di*.N
- *pꜣ nty iw.f [di]tw.f n.f:* see above, and note the omission of the preposition (a Neo-Egyptian feature) and the intrusive *w* in the infinitive *[di]tw.f*.
- *m sẖr.f... ḥnꜥ šd*

* 'Classical' degree 0 forms used:
- *ir.tw hpw*
- *diw:* adnominal participle (relating to *.f*) or rhematic stative (with a verb of incomplete predication?).
- *m ṯꜣ* (...) *iw* 100 *m-sꜣ wꜥ*

* General dialectal features: degree 2.

109 See Youssef (1964: 274), line 5 of the *Amada text*: 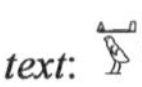. Concerning the death penalty for robbery and sale of the stolen goods, see Lorton (1977: 26-27, esp. n. 112; 1995: 358). We may have here a case of appropriation that is not for the personal benefit of the offender, a reorientation to another temple (Spalinger 1991: 34 'As these offerings were eventually recirculated within the temple as payments, such a misdirection of resources entailed the theft of salaries.'). See also *pMayer* A, 8, 13; Lurje (1971: 146, n.31); Bedell (1973: 153-159); Allam (1973: 218-219, note 20 and 278-279, note 12 in oaths); Morschauser (1991: 185); Tyldesley (2000: 29, 64-66). This crime is the only one punished by death in the *Nauri decree*; the offender is an employee of the temple and the object is a *res sacra*; furthermore, as death penalty must be decided by the king, he must know of this type of crime.

* Legal terms: *ỉr* – classifier: ø (to enforce).
hpw – classifier: ø (rule, legal norm).
ṯꜣw r – classifier: (to commit to). [COERCION] again marked by the 'strong arm'.
ḫt – classifier: ø (material property).
šd – classifier: ø (to confiscate).
ṯꜣ – classifier: (fine).
* Legal formula: - law enforcement: *ỉr.tw hpw r.f m* + infinitive (types of penalties coordinated by *ḥnꜥ* (*m-ꜥ*)).
- fine: *m ṯꜣ* (...) *ỉw* 100 *m-sꜣ wꜥ* (basis of computation).

I.2.24 Operative part: the crimes (part 9 – disturbing of herdsmen in their work)

(80) (…) *ḫr ỉr rmṯ nb nty m tꜣ* (81) *r ḏr.f nty ỉw.f r hd mnỉ*[*w*] *n tꜣ ḥwt Mnmꜣꜥ*⌈*rꜥ*⌉ *ỉb hr(w)*[110] *m ꜣbdt ḥr pꜣ.f symw* (82) *n*
(80) (…) and as for anybody who (is anywhere) in (the) entire land (81) who will assault a herdsma[n] of the temple '*Mnmꜣꜥ*⌈*rꜥ*⌉'s heart is contented in Abydos' on his (82) cattle pastures

* Neo-Egyptian characteristics:
- *ḫr ỉr rmṯ nb* (…) + *nty ỉw.f r hd*
- *tꜣ ḥwt*
- *pꜣ.f*
- *symw:* spelling variation (compare in another register, line 22, and in the same, line 64: *smw*).

* 'Classical' degree 0 forms used:
- *rmṯ nb nty m tꜣ r ḏr.f:* relative clause with adverbial rheme and augens.

* General dialectal features: degree 2.
* Legal terms: *hd* – classifier: (to assault).
* Legal formula: *ḫr ỉr* + offender + *nty ỉw.f r sḏm* (the crime) + victim + *ḥr* (crime's location).

110 Note the variations in spelling of *hrw*: in the beginning, full spelling, with classifier ( ), from line 30 to 67 (a few times only with instead of the fledgling: lines 35 and 51); then the classifier disappears (lines 71 to 80), followed by the fledgling/rope (lines 81 to 118:) with remarkable consistency. The internal organization of the text follows a simplificating line or 'economizing script'.

I.2.25 Operative part: the penalties (part 9)

(82) (…) *ir.tw hpw r.f m ḥwitw.f m sḫ* 100 *wbnw sd* 5

(82) (…) (the) rule will have to be enforced against him by beating him with 100 blows, 5 open wounds;

* Neo-Egyptian characteristics:
    - *m ḥwit(w).f*
* 'Classical' degree 0 forms used:
    - *ir.tw hpw*
* General dialectal features: degree 1.
* Legal terms: *ir* – classifier: ø (to enforce).
  hpw – classifier: ø (rule, legal norm).
* Legal formulas: *ir.tw hpw r.f m* + the type of penalty

I.2.26 Third enacting clause (authority, object, beneficiary - protection of the fleet)

(82) (…) *m-mitt iw w{ꜣ}ḏ.n ḥm.f* (83) *rdit ḥn.tw nꜣ ꜥḥꜥw n inw n Kš n tꜣ ḥwt Mnmꜣꜥtrꜥ ib hr(w) m ꜣbdt*

(82) (…) Likewise, his Majesty has decreed (83) to cause that be attached the fleet of Kush tributes/income[111] to the service of the temple '*Mnmꜣꜥtrꜥ*'s heart is contented in Abydos',

* Neo-Egyptian characteristics:
    - *m-mitt:* textemic transition-continuation.
    - *w{ꜣ}ḏ*
    - *tꜣ ḥwt*
    - *nꜣ ꜥḥꜥw n inw:* cataphoric function of the prenominal articloid (*inw* is non-specific).
* 'Classical' degree 0 forms used:
    - *iw w{ꜣ}ḏ.n ḥm.f*
    - *ḥn.tw nꜣ ꜥḥꜥw:* dependent passive or impersonal prospective, nominal object of *rdit*.
* General dialectal features: degree 1.
* Legal terms: *w{ꜣ}ḏ* - classifier: ø (to decree, command).
  ḥn.tw - classifier: ø (to be attached to the service of).

111 Haring (1997: 51) 'occasional/external' temple revenue, opposed to *bꜣkw* (*supra*).

* Legal formula: *m-mitt iw w{ꜣ}ḏ.n ḥm.f* (source of the decree) + *rdit* (the executive power's implementation) + *ḥn.tw* (nature of the measure: allocation) + object + *n* (beneficiary).

I.2.27 Preamble *sensu stricto* (negative intents) – part 3

(83) (…) *r* (84) *tm dit iṯꜣ imy-r ḫtm nb ḫpr.ty.f(y) ḥr pꜣ ḫtm n Stḫymrnptḥ nty m Sḫmt ḫt* (85) *nbt im.sn m nbw m šdw m in[w n]b n ḫtm m ḫt nbt n w[ꜥ]w m sḫr n wstnw* (86) *r nḥḥ ḥnꜥ ḏt* *m-mitt r tm [dit iṯꜣ.]tw wꜥw nb n wsḫ n pꜣ inw n tꜣ* (87) *ḥwt Mnmꜣꜥtrꜥ ib hr(w) m ꜣbdt r ditw.f [irt w]pt ḥr kt*[112] *mit* *m-mitt r tm dit thi sꜣ ni-swt nb* (88) *ḥry pḏt nb ḥry Nḥsyw nb n pꜣ tꜣ n Kš r* boat *n tꜣ ḥwt Mnmꜣꜥtrꜥ ib [hrw m ꜣbdt] ḥn[ꜥ] nꜣy.sn* (89) *iswt*
(83) (…) to (84) prevent that any fort superintendent who will be from the fort of *Stḫymrnptḥ* that (is) in *Sḫmt* shall seize any material property (85) from them, consisting of gold, of pelts, of [an]y produces/income/tribut[es] of[113] a fort, of any material property of a s[ai]lor in an arbitrary plan (86), eternally and forever; likewise, to prevent [that be seized] any sailor of a barge of the produces/income/tributes of the (87) temple '*Mnmꜣꜥtrꜥ*'s heart is contented in Abydos' to make him [accomplish a tas]k on another route; likewise, to prevent any Viceroy, (88) any troop(s) commandant, any Nubians commandant of the land of Kush's transgression against a boat of the temple '*Mnmꜣꜥtrꜥ*'s heart is cont[ented in Abydos'], an[d] their (89) crews.

* Neo-Egyptian characteristics:
  - *tꜣ ḥwt*
  - *pꜣ ḫtm n Stḫymrnptḥ nty m Sḫmt:* cataphoric use of the articloid.
  - *pꜣ inw n tꜣ ḥwt:* cataphoric use of the articloid.
  - *pꜣ tꜣ n Kš*
  - *r ditw.f: r* + infinitive (purpose), with an intrusive *w* after the infinitive feminine ending.
  - *nꜣy.sn*: the determinator is not coreferent to a singular lexeme (*wsḫ*). *ḥnꜥ* is the coordination used between the whole (*wsḫ*) and one of its components (*nꜣy.sn iswt*).
  - *mit*: Neo-Egyptian (*Wb* II, 41).
* 'Classical' degree 0 forms used:
  - *r tm*
  - *iṯꜣ*.N: dependent prospective, object of *(r)dit*.

112 Note the concord with its nominal expansion.
113 *RITANC* I, 55: 'in transit in'?

- *ḫpr.ty.f(y)*: future participle (antecedent: *imy-r*). It is the only occurence in our decree of this classic synthetic form belonging to a formal register. The verbal lexeme constituency (*ḫpr*) may be connected to the choice of this form expressing provenience or appurtenance.
- *nty m Sḫmt*: relative clause with adverbial rheme.
- *iṯ3.tw*.N: dependent passive or impersonal prospective, object of *dit*.
- *thi*.N: dependent prospective, object of *dit*.

* General dialectal features: degree 1.

* Legal terms: *r tm dit* – classifier: ø (to prevent).
iṯ3 – classifiers: [classifiers] (to seize).
ḫt - classifier: ø (material property).
m sḫr n wstnw – classifier: ø (in arbitrary, premeditated manner).
thi r - classifier: [classifier] (to transgress).

* Legal formula: *r tm dit* + [*sḏm.tw* (offense) + victim + *r* (purpose)] or [*sḏm*.N (offender) + ø/*r* (object)].

I.2.28 Operative part: the crimes (part 10 – requisition of cargo)

(89) (...) *ir imy-r ḫtm nb sš nb n p3 ḫtm rwḏ nb n p3* [*ḫtm nty*] (90) *r hy* (= *h3i*) *r* boat *n t3 ḥwt Mnm3ʿtrʿ ib hr(w) m 3bdt ḥnʿ ntf iṯ3 nbw* [*3bw hbny*] (91) *ḫnt 3by ḫnt ḥwt*/*šwt sd n mmy dḥrit n mmy sty* [...*ḫ3w*] (92) *ḫt nb n Kš nty tw.tw ḥr int.f m inw r t3 ḥwt Mnm3ʿtrʿ ib hr(w) m 3bd*[*t*]

(89) (...) Concerning any fortress commandant, any scribe of this fortress, any agent of this [fortress who] (90) shall have access to a boat of the temple '*Mnm3ʿtrʿ*'s heart is contented in Abydos' and take gold, [ivory, ebony] (91), leopard skin, (another animal) skin[114], giraffe tail, giraffe hide, ochre[115], [...plants] (92), any product of Kush that one usually brings as tribute/income to the temple '*Mnm3ʿtrʿ*'s heart is contented in Abydos',

* Neo-Egyptian characteristics:

- *t3 ḥwt*
- *p3 ḫtm*: anaphoric use of the specific determinator.
- [*nty*] *r hy*... *ḥnʿ ntf iṯ3*: conjunctive nexus following a relative future protasis; see Gardiner (1928: 86-96) and above; Goldwasser (2001: 129). The same form of conjunctive appears in the *Kanais decree*, line 11, and before it in *Ḥrmḥb*'s decree, line 17 ([*ir*...] *ḥnʿ ntf nḥm*). The protasis expresses the background that enables the offence (the fact of having access to the boat), the apodosis giving the rhematic expression of the crime (the seizing of the goods).

114 See Griffith (1927: 204).
115 *RITA* I: 49.

- # singular nouns + *ḫt nb* + *nty tw.tw ḥr int.f #:* diminishing progression list (from gold to plants) followed by an impersonal relative 'first present' with Neo-Egyptian 'preformative pronoun', retaining the preposition. The list comprises a series of singular hyponyms representing types of goods (without *nb*), followed by the summarizing hyperonym *ḫt* + distributive *nb* (absence of concord, a constant feature from this line on) and the relative clause with resumptive object *.f* referring to any item of the list. For the relative first present, see *LEG* § 53.9.2; Frandsen (1974: 57-59); Winand (1992: 406-408); Junge (1996: 214-216). The first present expresses the progressive aspect of a durative or habitual background circumstance (the *ḥr int.f* converb, see Satzinger 1976: 124).

* 'Classical' degree 0 forms used:
  - # singular nouns *nb* [*nty*] *r hy #:* relative sentence with adverbial rheme (note the absence of *iw.f*). The list is expressed by [singular lexemes + distributive *nb*] + [relative clause].
* General dialectal features: degree 2.
* Legal terms: *iṯ3* – classifiers: (to seize).
* Legal formula: *ir* + offender *nb* + *nty r sḏm... ḥnʿ ntf iṯ3* (the crime).

I.2.29 Operative part: the penalties (part 10)

(92) (…) [*ir*].*tw* [*h*]*p*[*w r.f*] *m* [*ḥ*]*witw.f* (93) *m sḫ* 100 *m-di šditw p3* [*n*]*kt m-di.f m ṯ3 t3 ḥwt Mnm3ʿtrʿ ib hr*(*w*) *m 3bdt iw* 80 *m-s3 wʿ* (94)

(92) (…) (the) [r]ule will have to be [enforced against him] by [b]eating him (93) with 100 blows and confiscating those [val]uables in his possession, with a fine for the temple '*Mnm3ʿtrʿ*'s heart is contented in Abydos', when 80 (is) after 1 (= of/at 80 to 1)[116] (94);

* Neo-Egyptian characteristics:
  - *m* [*ḥ*]*witw.f*
  - *m* [*ḥ*]*witw.f... m-di šditw*
  - *p3* [*n*]*kt:* anaphoric function of the determinator (with probably a cataphoric allusion to *m-di.f*).
  - *m-di.f*
  - *t3 ḥwt*
* 'Classical' degree 0 forms used:
  - *ir.tw hpw*
  - *m ø ṯ3* (...) *iw* 80 *m-s3 wʿ*
* General dialectal features: degree 2.
* Legal terms: *ir* – classifier: ø (to enforce).

116 Kemp (1989: 238) 'and he shall be fined on behalf of the Temple in terms of the value of the goods at the rate of eighty to one'.

hpw – classifier: ø (legal norm, rule).
šdi – classifier: ø (to confiscate).
ṯꜣ – classifier: 𓂝 𓂡 (fine).

* Legal formulas: - law enforcement: *ir.tw hpw r.f m* + infinitive (types of penalties coordinated by *m-di*)
- fine: *m ṯꜣ iw* 80 *m-sꜣ wꜥ* (basis of computation).

I.2.30 Operative part: the crimes (part 11 – requisition of cargo and crew)

(94) *ḫr ir sꜣ ni-swt nb imy-r iwꜥ nb rwḏ nb sš nb n pꜣ tꜣ n Kš nty iw.f r wstnw* (*m*) boat *n tꜣ ḥwt Mnmꜣꜥtrꜥ ib hr(w) m ꜣbdt mtw.f* (95) [*iṯꜣ*] *ḫt nb im.f*
m-mitt pꜣ [*n*]*ty iw.f* [*i*]*ṯꜣ wꜥ(w) nb n wsḫ n tꜣ ḥwt Mnmꜣꜥtrꜥ ib hr(w) m ꜣbdt r h(ꜣ)b.f* (96) *m wpt* [*r Kš*]

(94) And as for any Viceroy, any garrison commander[117], any agent, any scribe of the land of Kush who will deal arbitrarily with a boat of the temple '*Mnmꜣꜥtrꜥ*'s heart is contented in Abydos', and will (95) [seize] any material property in it,
likewise, the one [w]ho will [s]eize any sailor of a barge of the temple '*Mnmꜣꜥtrꜥ*'s heart is contented in Abydos' to send him (96) on a mission [to Kush],

* Neo-Egyptian characteristics:
- *tꜣ ḥwt*
- *pꜣ tꜣ n Kš*
- # [singular nouns + *nb*] + *nty iw.f r wstnw* #
- *nty iw.f r wstnw... mtw.f* [*iṯꜣ*]*:* the apodosis conjunctive expresses again the main aspect of the crime, the protasis giving the general frame of it.
- *pꜣ* [*n*]*ty iw.f* [*i*]*ṯꜣ:* substantivized relative clause, with omission of the future preposition (see above).
- *h(ꜣ)b.f:* for the spelling, see above.

* 'Classical' degree 0 forms used:
- *r h(ꜣ)b.f:* purpose.
- *m-mitt*: instead of topicalizer *ir*.

* General dialectal features: degree 2.

* Legal terms: *wstnw* - classifier: ø (to deal arbitrarily).
iṯꜣ - classifier: 𓂝 𓂡 (to seize).
ḫt - classifier: ø (material property).

* Legal formulas: - *ḫr ir* + offenders *nb* + *nty iw.f r sḏm... mtw.f sḏm* (the crimes).
- *m-mitt pꜣ nty iw.f sḏm* (the offender + his crime) + *r* (purpose)

117 Gardiner (1952: 31) for *iwꜥyt*.

I.2.31 Operative part: the penalties (part 11)

(96) (…) *ir.tw hpw r.f m-di š[d] p3 [nk]t m<-di>.f m t3 ṯ3 t3 ḥwt Mnm3ˁtrˁ* (97) *ib hr(w) m 3bdt m-di šd b3[kw n wˁw n t3 ḥwt Mnm3ˁtrˁ ib hr(w) m 3bdt m-di.f m hrw] nb [n]ty [i]w.[f] r ir.f m-di.f*

(96) (…) (the) rule will have to be enforced against him and will be confi[scated]/with confi[scation] of those [valuabl]es in his (possession) as the fine of/for the temple '*Mnm3ˁtrˁ*'s (97) heart is contented in Abydos', and will be confiscated/confiscation of (the) reve[nues/work's product of (the) sailor of the temple '*Mnm3ˁtrˁ*'s heart is contented in Abydos' in his possession for] each [day th]at [he w]ill spend in his realm.

* Neo-Egyptian characteristics:

- *ir.tw hpw... m-di š[d]*.N… *m-di šd*.N*:* change in the construction of the penalty after the prospective (absence of the beating *m ḥwitw.f*), *m-di šd*.N being passive *sḏm.w*.N prospectives (apodetic nexuses, conjunctives in a syndetic form) or two nouns in loose composition used as embryo-conjunctives (the penalties) after the framing *ir.tw hpw*. Apodotic conjunctives were up to now used only in the crimes segments, and in a *ḥnˁ ntf sḏm* or *mtw.f sḏm* form; in the penalties segments, only embryo-conjunctives were used, in the form *ḥnˁ sḏm, m-ˁ sḏm, m-di sḏm* or *ḥnˁ m-ˁ sḏm*. For this reason, it may be more appropriate to view the construction as the coordination of nouns with an independent prospective.
- *m-di.f*
- *t3 ḥwt*
- *p3 [nk]t:* see line 93.
- *t3 ṯ3:* cataphoric use of the specific determinator.
- # singular noun *nb* + *[n]ty [i]w.[f] r ir.f* #

* 'Classical' degree 0 forms used: *ir.tw hpw*

* General dialectal features: degree 2.

* Legal terms: *ir* – classifier: ø (to enforce).
hpw – classifier: ø (legal norm, rule).
šdi – classifier: ø (to confiscate).
ṯ3 – classifier: (fine).

* Legal formulas: - *ir.tw hpw r.f* + *m-di šd*.N (types of penalties).

I.2.32 Fourth enacting clause (authority, object, beneficiary - protection of specific temple staff)

(97) (...) *m-mitt iw w{ꜣ}ḏ.n ḥm.f* (98) *rdit ḥn.*[*tw* (...) *ḥm*].*w*-[*nṯr*] *wꜥbw ẖry-ḥbwt*[118] *kꜣwt(yw) sꜣ*[*w... n tꜣ ḥwt Mnmꜣꜥtrꜥ ib hr(w) m ꜣbdt*] (99) *mi ḳd.sn*
(97) (...) Likewise, his Majesty has decreed (98) to cause that [be] attached [...prophet]s, priests, lectors, workmen/porters[119], [door-]keeper[s[120]... to the service of the temple '*Mnmꜣꜥtrꜥ*'s heart is contented in Abydos'] (99) in all their kinds;

* Neo-Egyptian characteristics:
- *w{ꜣ}ḏ*

* 'Classical' degree 0 forms used:
- *m-mitt:* textemic transition-continuation.
- *iw w{ꜣ}ḏ.n ḥm.f*
- *ḥn.*[*tw*] + list of plural nouns*:* dependent passive or impersonal prospective, nominal object of *rdit.*

* General dialectal features: degree 1.

* Legal terms: *w{ꜣ}ḏ* - classifier: ø (to decree, command).
ḥn - classifier: ø (to allocate).

* Legal formula: *m-mitt iw w{ꜣ}ḏ.n ḥm.f* (source of the decree) + *rdit* (the executive power's implementation) + *ḥn.tw* (nature of the measure: allocation) + object + *n* (beneficiary).

I.2.33 Preamble *sensu stricto* (negative intents) – part 4

(99) (...) *r tm dit thi.tw* (100) [*r.sn r rmṯ.sn nb r ẖt.sn nb* *r tm dit iṯꜣ.tw*] *nꜣy.sn ḥmwt nꜣy.sn bꜣk*[*w* (101) *m w n w m bꜣrti m bḥw n skꜣ m bḥw n*] *ꜥwꜣyw in sr nb ḥꜣty-ꜥ nb rmṯ nb nty* (102) [*m tꜣ r ḏr.f*]
(99) (...) to prevent that one shall commit a transgression (100) [against them, against any of their people, against any of their material property; to prevent that be seized] their wives, their servant[s (101) from a district to another(,) by (submission?) contract, by/as a forced labour of ploughing, by/as a corvée of] harvesting by any civil servant, any mayor, anybody who (102) [(is) in (the) entire land];

* Neo-Egyptian characteristics:
- *nꜣy.sn* ; *bꜣrti*

---

118 Compound with plural mark appended by the end of the compound.
119 Gardiner (1952: 31).
120 Jelínková-Reymond (1953: 47 & 48, n. 8); Meeks (1979: 647) 'service d'ordre'.

* 'Classical' degree 0 forms used:

- *r tm dit* + object (dependent prospective): see above. Concerning the restoration of line 100, *dit* being followed by a dependent prospective form (and not an infinitive + suffixed object), the proposed reconstruction of *KRI* I: 57 (*iṯ3.sn*), following Griffith (1927: 204) and Edgerton (1947: 226), is problematic: the agent being expressed by *in sr nb ḥ3ty-ʿ nb rmṯ nb*, *iṯ3*'s diathesis must be passive. In all but three instances in the decree, it is a passive or impersonal prospective that follows *r tm dit* in the preambles *sensu stricto*, the exceptions being active prospective forms in lines 58, 83-84 and 87, but each time with a nominal actor, never a suffixed pronoun, and of course without an agent introduced by *in*. A similar disposition in lines 65-66 is also expressed by a passive prospective: [*r*] *tm dit iṯ3.tw n3y.sn ḥmwt n3.sn b3kw* (…).
- # (singular hyponyms+ *nb*) + hyperonym *rmṯ nb nty* [*m t3 r ḏr.f*] #: see above. Another objection to Kitchen's restoration (*m p3 t3 r ḏr.f*): the determinator *p3* never appears in this syntagm in the decree.

* General dialectal features: degree 1.

* Legal terms: *r tm dit* – classifier: ø (to prevent).
thi [*r*] - classifier: 𓌙 𓂻 (to transgress).

* Legal formula: *r tm dit* + [*sḏm.tw* (offense) + *r* (victim)] or [*sḏm.tw*.N (victims) + *m* (method) + *in* (offenders)].

I.2.34 Operative part: the crimes (part 12 – transgression against specific temple staff)

(102) [(…) *ir sr nb ḥ3ty-ʿ nb rmṯ nb nty m t3 r-ḏr.f nty iw.f r thi*][121] *r.sn r rmṯ.sn nb r ḫt.sn nb* (103)

(102) [(…) As for any high rank official, any mayor, anybody who (is) in (the) entire land who will commit a transgression] against them, against any of their people, against any of their material property (103),

* Neo-Egyptian characteristics: reconstruction.

* 'Classical' degree 0 forms used: reconstruction.

* General dialectal features: ?

* Legal terms: [*thi*] *r* - classifier: [𓌙] 𓂻 (to transgress).
ḫt - classifier: ø (material property).

* Legal formula: reconstruction.

121 Kitchen's restoration [*ir sr nb ḥ3ty-ʿ nb rmṯ nb m p3 t3 r-ḏr.f p3 nty nb iw.f r thi*] may be adapted to correspond more closely to a disposition of our document, as in line 52: *m-mitt rmṯ nb nty m t3 r-ḏr.f nty iw.f r hd* (…) (*nty* inserted before *m t3 r-ḏr.f* without the determinator *p3*, and *nty* instead of *p3 nty nb* before the future).

I.2.35 *Missing operative part*: the penalty (part 12)

(103) [*ir.tw hpw r.f m...*]   (103) [(the) rule will have to be enforced against him by...]

I.2.36 Operative part: crime resulting in loss of material property (part 13)[122]

(103) (...) *ḫr swt ir ḫpr ꜣḳy m ḫt nb n tꜣ ḥwt* (104) [*Mnmꜣʿtrʿ ib hr(w) m ꜣbdt* (...) *rm*]*ṯ nb n tꜣ ḥwt Mnmꜣʿtrʿ ib hr(w) m ꜣbdt* (105) [*nty iw.tw r tht r.f mtw.f ḏd in/m*][123] [*r*]*w*[*ḏ*] *mn kꜣḏn mn ḥry-iḥw mn wʿ(w)* (106) [*mn thi r.i...*][124]   (103) (...) But if will result/as for (the) resulting of a loss of any material property of the temple (104) ['*Mnmꜣʿtrʿ*'s heart is contented in Abydos' (...) for] any[bod]y of the temple '*Mnmꜣʿtrʿ*'s heart is contented in Abydos' (105) [against whom one will commit a transgression, and he will say 'it is] an [age]nt so-and-so, an officer so-and-so, a stable-master so-and-so, a soldier (106) [so-and-so who commited a transgression against me ...']

* Neo-Egyptian characteristics:
  - *tꜣ ḥwt*
  - # [*rm*]*ṯ nb* [*nty iw.tw r tht*] #
* 'Classical' degree 0 forms used:
  - *ḫr swt ir ḫpr ꜣḳy:* particles *ḫr swt* (*swt* expressing contrast; see *Ḥrmḥb*'s *Karnak decree*, line 30; Kruchten 1981: 108; Neveu 1985: 131) + *ir sḏm*.N in a conditional protasis or a topicalization of the noun *ḫpr* expanded ('loose composition' or zero-relator). In the case of a conditional protasis, the *sḏm*.N form is a prospective (whose nominal or adverbial nature is controversial, see Polotsky (1965: § 11, note 9); for Old and Middle Egyptian, Malaise (1985: 152-167) proposes a substantival prospective expressing eventuality; for Shisha-Halevy (1974: 381, note 48) the '*casus adverbialis* function of a substantive-clause form.'; see also Junge (1996: 280). For the first time in the crimes exposition casuistic-logic texteme, instead of the topicalization of the offender, the damage is topicalized and nominalized (it appears again with *ḫpr,* as in lines 68-19 *iw ꜣḳw ḥr ḫpr*). If the restoration is correct, the apodosis consists of the

122 The question of this entire last segment connection (court competence, denial of justice, slowness to proceed) to the temple's staff provisions (lines 97-102, as Spalinger 1991: 36-37 understands it) or its independent character (see the general *rmṯ nb* used, without reference to specific staff) remains open.

123 Possible restoration on the basis of *Elephantine Rʿmss* III's *decree*, line 7: N *nty iw.tw r thtw r.f ntf ḏd m rwḏ mn* (...) *thi r.i* and the introduction of the direct speech in the *Nauri decree*, line 68. Following Griffith (1927: 204) and Gardiner (1952: 31), one should perhaps add the verb 'complain' (*smi.f*) before *ḏd*, but this seems less relevant than the conjunctive.

124 See previous note.

following 106-107 lines with prospective *ir.tw hpw*. For the affinity of *ir* topicalizer and *ir* conditional, see Haiman (1978); Satzinger (1976); Lorton (1977: 54-59), and previous references. For the use of the condition in the same environment of a New Kingdom decree, see *Ḥrmḥb*'s *Karnak decree*, line 13, with *ir iry n.f p3 nmḥy* (…) and *Rʿmss* II's *Hittite Treaty*, line 15 (*ir sḏm*.N).

- N *mn*: see *p3 mn supra*, probably here also in a tagged direct speech (illustrative constructed quotation texteme).

* General dialectal features: probably degree 2.
* Legal terms: *3ky m ḫt* – classifier:  for *3ky* and ø for *ḫt* (loss of material property).
* Legal formula: *ḫr swt* (contrast) + *ir sḏm*.N or noun expanded (damage) + probably illustrative direct speech.

I.2.37 Operative part: penalty and courts competence (part 13)

(106) (…) [*ir.tw hpw r.f m šdit*] *p3 <n>kt nty iw.*[*f*] *r 3kw m-di.f* (107) [*m t3 ṯ3 rmṯ nty iw.f r*?] *tht r r.f*

ḫr swt ir.n ḥm.f tm di (108) [*sḫr.tw.f?…*][125] *diw ḥr tp ḫt n-mr(wt) dit hd.t(w).f m ḳnbt* (109) *nb n niwt nb spr.sn r r.sn*

(106) (…) [(the) rule will have to be enforced against him by confiscating] the valuables in his possession that [he = the victim] will lose (107) [as the fine of/for (the) person?] against [whom he will?] commit a transgression[126];

But it was in order to cause that he shall be attacked/convicted in any court (109) of any city to which they will go that his Majesty did not cause (108) [that he be thrown down?...] put on (the) tip of a staff[127];

* Neo-Egyptian characteristics:
  - *p3 <n>kt:* cataphoric use of the specific determinator.
  - # determined noun + *nty iw.*[*f*] *r 3kw #:* note that *3kw* is an infinitive here.
  - *m-di.f*
  - *r r.f:* first instance of preposition isotopy, a Neo-Egyptian feature; see *LEG* § 7.1.2.iii (restricting the phenomenon to *r* + plural pronominal suffixes); Junge (1996: 34).
  - *ḫr swt ir.n ḥm.f tm di: ir.n.*N *tm sḏm* is for Polotsky (1957: 117) a pseudo-archaism for Neo-Egyptian *i.ir.f tm sḏm* ('emphatic'), *tm* being the negator of the that-form (note the absence of feminine ending of the infinitive *di*). See also Winand (1992: 281) who notes that it negates the 'action verbale', which means

125 See line 77.

126 For Griffith (1927: 204), line 107 must be restored as '[and he shall recover the goods from the man who has] interfered with him.' Our restoration is based on line 96 (*š*[*d*] *p3* [*nk*]*t m<-di>.f m t3 ṯ3 t3 ḥwt* (…)).

127 See Bedell (1973: 23). This provision must be paralleled to lines 77-78 (death penalty).

the theme, not the nexus; Groll (1987: 157-158) sees an analytic 'emphatic formation with reference to past time: negation of the subject', *swt* being 'a tense marker'). The cleft sentence theme *ỉr.n ḥm.f tm dỉ(t)* is an analytic verbal nexus in nominal function with relative anteriority value, the focused rheme being *n-mr(wt) dỉt hd.t(w).f* (...). The function of the cleft sentence is contrastive (the 'independence' markers *ḫr swt* reinforcing the contrast; see Cassonnet (2000: 70, n. 253) for *ḫr* as an 'auxiliaire de cohérence transphrastique' expressing 'coordination et démarcation' and *swt* as a 'particule adversative'), the rheme exposing the prominent actor's (*ḥm.f*) motivation and the theme his abstention concerning the death penalty.

- *r r.sn:* preposition isotopy. The plural resumption (reference to *ḳnbt nb n nỉwt nb*) is surprising, the evident distributive character of *nb* excluding plural reference.

* 'Classical' degree 0 forms used:
  - *dỉw:* see above, line 77.
  - *n-mr(wt)* + infinitive: see *EG* § 181.
  - *hd.t(w).f:* dependent passive prospective, object of *dỉt.*
  - *spr.sn:* relative prospective form with pronominal plural actor, referring to the offender (*hd.t(w).f*) and probably to his victim/plaintiff. *spr* being a motion verb, the reference of the relative form to its antecedent (*m ḳnbt nb n nỉwt nb*) is 'indirect' and a resumptive pronoun is supplied to the preposition following the relative form (*r r.sn*); see Polotsky (1976: 10-12 [IIBb]).
* General dialectal features: degree 2.
* Legal terms:

  <*n*>*kt* – classifier: × (valuables). The superordinate [UNION/DIVISION] category classifier is used here instead of the papyrus roll classifier, perhaps focusing upon the mathematical operations applied to *genera* as computable units.

  ꜣḳw – classifier: 𓅪 (to conjure away/disappear/lose).

  hd m ḳnbt – classifier: 𓂣 (to attack in a law-court/to be convicted/found responsible for). See Malinine (1947: 120-121) 'litt. "repousser un plaignant", which means lose the case; Allam (1973b: 66); McDowell (1990: 28) *hꜣd*. For the classifier, see *hd* above.
* Legal formulas: [*ỉr.tw hpw r.f m sḏm*] + *ḫr swt ỉr.n*.N *tm sḏm... n-mr(wt) dỉt* (contrastive motivated abstention)

I.2.38 Operative part: the crimes (part 14 - administration/individuals (?) slowness/omission to proceed[128] or report a crime)

(109) (…) [*ḫr ir rmṯ/srw/rwḏw? nb n*]*ty m tꜣ r-ḏr.f nty r rmṯ nb n tꜣ ḥwt Mnmꜣʿtrʿ ib hr(w)* (110) *m ꜣbdt tht* (= *spr?*)[129] *r r.sn r-ḏd tht* [*pꜣ mn r.i*] *iṯꜣ.f pꜣy.i*  *iṯꜣ.f pꜣ ʿꜣ iṯꜣ.f* (111) *pꜣy.i ʿnḫ ḫt nb nty iw.tw r iṯt.f m-di rmṯ r-pw iṯꜣ pꜣ mn pꜣ rwḏ pꜣy.i rmṯ* (112) *m kfwʿ*(= *kfʿw*) *r irt wpt nb mtw.sn tm pꜣy ḥr ḫrw.f r dit in.tw pꜣ.f iry n wp ꜣs r wptw.f* (113)

(109) (…) [and as for all (the) persons/officials/agents? w]ho are in (the) entire land, to whom anybody of the temple '*Mnmꜣʿtrʿ*'s heart is contented (110) in Abydos' will come, saying: '[this so-and-so] has committed a transgression [against me], (since) he took my ox (/since) he took this/my ass (/since) he took (111) my goat', (or) any material property that one would take from a man, or 'this so-and-so, this agent, took my people (112) by coercion, to execute any mission', and they will not fly at his voice to cause that his opponent be brought diligently in order to try him (113),

* Neo-Egyptian characteristics:

- *nty r*.N (*r*) *tht:* future (with preposition omission) in a relative clause, the nominal actor explaining the presence of *r* (for *ir?*) instead of *iw*. The reading *r*.N has hereby been adopted because it probably suits better the traces left in the text (see Gardiner 1946: 101) and also corresponds to the form in line 115 (see *infra*). Concerning this construction, see Kuentz (1929: 103); Gardiner (1930: 222-224 and 1946: 101); *LEG* § 17.1.2; Frandsen (1974: 44); Satzinger (1976: 205); Junge (1996: 130) 'graphophonematische Variente'; Winand (1992: 495-504) who proposes to see, at the origin of *ir*.N's use, a 'periphrastic' form of the prospective *sḏm.f*. Kitchen (*RITA* I: 50 'against whom anyone (…) has acted'), probably views the construction as a case of auxiliary *iri* + 'intransitive' infinitive (*spr* could be a good candidate for a case of 'scribal error'), an *ir*.N *sḏm* perfect analytic form (past analytic forms are already in use in Middle Egyptian, see *EG* § 485.2 & 455, last example on p. 375 from *Ḏḥwtyms* III's *Annals n ir*.N *sḏm*; Kroeber (1970: 181); for Neo-Egyptian examples, see Winand (1992: 197-198) who adds that the analytic perfect appears during the reign of *Rʿmss* II); but in *LEG* § 14.4.2, Groll notes that 'the perfect active *stp.f* and *nty* are mutually exclusive'. Thc construction of the crimes texteme in our decree enables us to choose the first solution, the relative future, maintaining

128 Abstention from exercising ones duty. *RITA* I, 51: 'dereliction of duty'. In the case of an administrative service prolonged silence towards a citizen's claim, today's courts may qualify the public service inertia as a 'silence circonstancié' equivalent 'au refus ou surséance à statuer' (decision of the Belgian Cour de Cassation in 1942, i.e.) and its responsibility implied in case of excessive delay.

129 Griffith (1927: 205 and n. 1) corrects it in *spr r r.sn* ('scribal error'), Gardiner (1952: 32) also proposes *smi n.sn*.

also its opposition with the modal prospective (for a sure instance of relative prospective in the same texteme in our corpus, see *infra Rˁmss* II *Armant decree*). Note that we have again two relative clauses expanding a topicalized element, as in line 52 (see above).

- *r r.sn*
- *tꜣ ḥwt*
- *tht* [*pꜣ mn*]*: sḏm*.N after the tagged speech marker *r-ḏd,* Neo-Egyptian 'perfect' report tense with nominal actor in a locutive illustrative texteme (constructed quotation) exposing the plaintiff's argument, in the general context of the topicalized object of the divine punishment of line 113. The ending of *tht* is rather unusual for a perfect form. The pseudo-quotation emphasizes the fact that there is an actual complaint from the victim that is not answered.
- *iṯꜣ.f:* iterative use of a Neo-Egyptian perfect report tense or a circumstantial *sḏm.f* in the illustrative texteme, to constitute three separate speech options (the victim says either 'since he took my ox' or 'since he took my ass', or even 'since he took my goat').
- *pꜣy.i, pꜣ.f*
- *pꜣ ˁꜣ:* deictic or possessive determinator.
- *nty iw.tw r iṯt.f:* impersonal relative future.
- *m-di*.N
- *r-pw iṯꜣ pꜣ mn:* perfect report tense, disjunctive to *tht* [*pꜣ mn*]. It also constitutes an alternative to direct speech, without paraphrase. Note the distinction between speeches concerned with material/animal seizure as against human seizure.
- *pꜣ mn:* see above, line 69.
- *pꜣ rwḏ:* deictic determinator.
- *mtw.sn tm pꜣy:* negation of conjunctive (*tm* and *pꜣy* are probably infinitives) after relative future protasis *nty ir*.N *tht r r.sn* (see *LEG* § 43 and above). Again, the apodosis contains the expression of the crime of which the protasis constitutes the background (the complaint about a prior crime). See also Lorton (1977: 57); Morschauser (1991: 61).
- *r wptw.f:* for the spelling of the infinitive, see above.

* 'Classical' degree 0 forms used:

- [N *n*]*ty m tꜣ r-ḏr.f*
- *r irt: r* + infinitive (purpose).
- *r dit in.tw*.N: *r* + infinitive (purpose) + object (dependent impersonal/passive prospective).

* General dialectal features: degree 2.

* Legal terms:

tht r – classifier: 𓂾 𓂻 (to transgress).
iṯꜣ – classifiers: 𓂡 𓂢 (to seize).
ẖt - classifier: ø (material property).
iṯi - classifier: 𓂡 (to take possession, seize, abduct).
m kfˁw - classifier: ø (by coercion).

iry n wp – classifier: × (related to the trial, party, litigant). Again, the crossed sticks classifier implies a two-sided (conflictual) relationship, as in the exchange previously examined, and represents the superordinate [UNION/DIVISION] category.

wpi – classifier: × (to judge). The function of the judge is to settle a conflict between (at least) two opponents (metaphoric use of the crossed sticks icon); the lexeme belongs to the [UNION/DIVISION] category.

* Legal formula: [*ir* + offender] + illustrative constructed direct speech + *mtw.f tm sḏm* conjunctive (crime of omission)

I.2.39 Operative part: penalty (curse, divine punishment) (part 14)

(113) *ir Wsir ḫnty imntt p3 nb n3 n rmṯ p3 nb n3 n ḫt m-s3.f m-s3 ḥmt.f m-s3 ẖrdw.f* (114) *r sswn rn.f r sḥtm b3.f r tm dit ḥtp ḫ3t.f m ẖrt-nṯr*

(113) Osiris, foremost of (the) West, the lord of Mankind, the lord of Property, is/will be after him, after his wife, after his children (114) to destroy his name, to annihilate his soul, to prevent that his corpse will rest in (the) necropolis[130].

* Neo-Egyptian characteristics:

- *Wsir (...) p3 nb n n3 n rmṯ/ḫt:* the first *p3* determinator in this theological titulary apposition to the proper name *Wsir* (theme) is cataphoric, with *nota relationis* expansions; *n3 n* is not phoric and determines two generic (collective, unquantified, conceptual) prominent notion names and hyperonyms *rmṯ* and *ḫt,* representing the fundamental categories of the human and material worlds (see Shisha-Halevy 1989d: notes 51 and 127 for Bohairic). Our English translation (without articles and with capital letters) reflects notion name markers in a linguistic system where the article is omnipresent, as opposed to the Egyptian state of language represented by our text.
- *ir*.PN *m-s3.f:* for Gardiner (1930: 224-225), *ir* alternates with *iw* before a nominal actor as in *Stḫy* I's *Kanais decree*, line 19 (*ir Wsir m-s3.f iw 3st m-s3 ḥmt.f iw Ḥr m-s3 ẖrdw.f*) and other examples of curses against infringers of decrees, with 'an inherent future force'. In this case, the introduction of a divine actor after 'secular' dispositions is accompanied by a textemic change, the abandonment of modal prospective *ir.tw hpw* in favour of an adverbial nexus, usually translated as a future expression (see Satzinger 1976: 198-200 'Adverbialsatz des Futurums'). The contextual future value of the nexus was inferred by Gardiner's (1930) parallel with the 'third future' 'transformation' cases of *iw* in *iri* before a nominal actor (see *supra*, line 109), although the

130 Does it mean that the offender is refused burial (a concrete measure with metaphysical implications) as Morschauser (1991: 186) regards it? Note also his comparison (p. 188) between the offender's family and the divine trinity.

phenomenon might not necessarily be related to the present construction. If one adopts the adverbial nexus option and as uttering a curse is already performing its execution (the magic word that kills), it has rather to be viewed as a performative with a divine actor, as Assmann (1992: 159) proposed it. Gardiner's (1930: 225) objections to Spiegelberg's proposal (1896: 17) of an idiomatic *ỉrt m-sꜣ* "to be after someone" were not absolutely conclusive (see Coptic **ⲉⲓⲣⲉ** + adverb, Polotsky 1959: 459 and n.3), a doubt thus remaining as to the adverbial nature of the nexus (possibility of a modal prospective *ỉri*.N). More generally, the earliest example in our possession of a curse in a criminal law decree belongs to *Nbḫprwrꜥ Ỉntf Coptos decree* (17th dynasty), directed against future kings and empowered high civil servants who would not take the described measures against an offender. The curse is expressed by negative modal prospectives (*nn sḏm.f*) among which the final *nn ḥtp n.f nbty m mrrw.sn* ("the Two Ladies shall not pardon him as their beloved") is directly related to divine beings. The 21st dynasty *Medinet Habu* copy of *Ỉmnḥtp* III's *decree* to *Ỉmḥtp* son of *Ḥp* also uses prospective forms as well as adverbial nexi, but due to its being a late version it will not be detailed here. For curses of the type *ir* God *m-sꜣ*, see *Anîbeh inscription*, line 19 (probably also *KRI* III, 130 n.80, 3, *Sbꜣwḫꜥ*'s Anîbeh tomb); *Mrnptḥ*'s *victory hymn*, line 9; Gardiner (1930), esp. *pSallier* IV example and Morschauser (1991: 24). Religious curses are also used in *Rꜥmss* II's *Hittite Treaty* (line 31), followed by the example of a positive behaviour entitling to a divine blessing. Concerning affinities between modern legal and religious discourses, see Charrow, Crandall & Charrow (1982: 181); Danet (1980: 543) for whom the legal discourse poeticization is rooted in 'the magic power of words'; Goodrich (1987: 126). Because of the difficulty of proving the official's knowledge of the crime, a curse is used, as Wilson proposes (1969: 327); for Morschauser (1991: 185-186), (private) 'persons merely refusing *to report* a crime,' (abstention) 'an individual maintaining silence was beyond the reach of the law per se' and p. 182: increase of divine intervention in mundane affairs typical of the Ramesside Period. On the functions of curses, see Assmann (1992: 149-162, esp. 153) 'the curse protects the law' for instance when institutions fail to act. As for the administration crime of non-compliance with a decree in the Old Kingdom, see Harari (1950: 19-20); *Nfrirkꜣrꜥ Abydos* and *Ppy* II *Coptos B/C/D decrees* (the offender is brought to court); for 9th dynasty, see *Dmḏibtꜣwy Coptos R decree* (the offender loses the right to exert his office).

* 'Classical' degree 0 forms used:

- *r sswn/sḥtm/tm dit*: *r* + infinitive (purpose). On the negative *r tm dit*, see above.
- *ḥtp*.N: dependent prospective, object of *dit*.

* General dialectal features: degree 2.

* Legal/curse terms: *ỉr m-sꜣ* - classifier: ø (to pursue, of a god).
ḫt - classifier: ø (material property).

* Curse formula: *ỉr* + god + *m-sꜣ.f* (religious curse, a divine punishment) + *r* + infinitive (purpose)

I.2.40 Operative part: the crimes (part 15 – miscarriage of justice)[131]

(114) (…) *ỉw swt ỉr* [*sr n*] *ḳnbt* (115) *nb nty m niwt nb nty r rmṯ nb n tꜣ ḥwt Mnmꜣʿtrʿ ib hr(w) m ꜣbdt spr r.f* (116) *r smi n.f mtw.f sẖ-ḥr r r.f r tm pꜣy ḥr ḫrw r ỉrt* (117) *tꜣy.f wpt ꜣs*
(114) (…) But as for any [magistrate of] a court (115) who (is) in any city, to whom anybody of the temple '*Mnmꜣʿtrʿ*'s heart is contented in Abydos' will come (116) to complain to him and he will not respond to him, so as not to fly at (his) voice to exert (117) his judgment diligently,

* Neo-Egyptian characteristics:
  - *tꜣ ḥwt*
  - *ỉw swt*: for Kruchten (1981: 170), '*ỉw* de subordination renforcé par la particule enclitique *swt*', a dubious solution, as the topicalized crime is never circumstantially converted in our corpus. We are left with a mysterious alternative to *ḫr swt* (coordination + contrast) or a scribal error.
  - *nty r*.N (*r*) *spr:* relative future (with preposition omission), the nominal actor explaining the presence of *r* instead of *ỉw;* see above and Griffith (1927: 205, n. 3); Gardiner (1930: 222 (18)). Note that in line 109, the hesitation between a *ỉr* or *r* reading of the damaged sign may be resolved in the light of the indisputable instance of *r* in line 115.
  - N *nty r*.N *spr... mtw.f sẖ-ḥr:* conjunctive apodosis expressing the crime after relative future background protasis.
  - *r r.f*
  - *tꜣy.f*
* 'Classical' degree 0 forms used:
  - [N] *nty m niwt nb:* relative clause with adverbial rheme.
  - *r smi, r tm pꜣy, r ỉrt: r* + infinitive (purpose).
* General dialectal features: degree 2.
* Legal terms:

131 Wilful refusal/default of the courts to take cognizance, to exercise their powers. In this case, it is explicitly the courts that would not fulfill their duty (crime of omission), but no curse is evoked as in line 109. For further cases of administrative default, see *The Eloquent Peasant* and *The Installation of the Vizier*, esp. lines 13-14. See Labib (1948: 477); Bedell (1973: 31) 'judges who were derelict in their duty.' Apparently, for Lorton (1995: 358), this disposition concerns the same crime as in line 109. But the crucial lexeme in line 109 is destroyed (the offender's identity) and it is not possible to explain a difference of treatment in those provisions (divine curse versus beating and removing from office) on the basis of a missing word as Morschauser (1991: 185-186) tries to.

smi – classifier: 𓀁 (to complain, report). Gardiner (1964: 14, note 18) views it as a 'technical term for the preliminary plaint which had to be made, before permission was granted to bring a suit before the court'. Of course the lexeme is not always used with this restricted meaning and belongs primarily to the non technical lexicon.

sḫ-ḥr r – classifier: 𓂻 for 𓏛? ('face-deaf', to be deaf to, ignore, not respond/react, refuse to take cognizance; demurrer): 'adjectival verb' + inalienable bodypart noun forming an exocentric compound[132] (the hypallage 'face-deaf' man) functioning here as the rheme of the conjunctive apodosis. On exocentric compound attributes, see Rosén (1984: 121-125) for Hebrew, Jansen-Winkeln (1994: 51-75, esp. 56 and 65) for Egyptian; the *Bilgai stela*, line 4 and *Kanais decree*, line 19, both in curse contexts. But none of them reveals the *raison d'être* of those compounds; for us, it is in the syntactic/stylistic way they express something more than a woman with a beautiful face (*nfrt-ḥr*), a man with big favors (*wr-ḥswt*) or a sharp face (*spd-ḥr*), which would have been written *ḥr nfr, ḥswt wrwt* and *ḥr spd.* The sequence has been inverted and the adjective qualifies the preceding character (woman/man). The compound creates a new entity that must be understood on a different level, forcing us to leave the 'literal sense' and to enter the 'figurative meaning'. Hypallage ('Hippolyte soulevait une noble poussière') is the key to understanding these syntactic constructions: '*déplacer* un mot dans la phrase, de manière à lui faire remplir une fonction grammaticale différente de celle que le sens exigerait. Ce déplacement touche souvent l'adjectif épithète' and creates a 'flou sémantique, résultant de la diffusion et même de la diffraction du sens', representing '[des] jeux complexes de la syntaxe et du sens' (Bacry 1992: 143-145). The adjective, although qualifying the following noun, is linked on the semantical level with the preceding one, and the syntax (the adjective is in concord with the noun preceding it) and stylistics convey this link (see Rosén (1984: 123, note 1 '[ils] supposent une liaison intime entre le 'possesseur' et le deuxième membre du composé pour que l'élément adjectival puisse se trouver en accord grammatical avec le 'possesseur' et néanmoins décrire l'objet possédé désigné par le deuxième membre'). For instance, the compound (a man) *ḫpn k3w* 'fat of bulls' is a nice way to present a rich man whose cattle are well fed; it corresponds precisely to the description in Egyptian visual arts of the wealthy, successful man as a fat, middle-aged person (e.g. the famous 'Sheikh al-Balad' statue, Cairo *CG 34*), his fat cattle enabling him to lead a 'fat' existence. The compound *ꜥš3 ḫrw* 'noisy' is to be understood as a man so loud that he seems multiplied, as if several people were talking through his lips; some cases (see

132 Rosén (1984: 123): adjectival compounds 'Exocentriques (possessifs du type indo-européen bahuwrīhi) sans restriction du premier membre, et dont le deuxième membre est un substantif désignant un objet inaliénablement possédé (…) par un possesseur dont le substantif désignateur motive par accord grammatical le genre et le nombre de l'adjectif, premier membre du syntagme'.

ȝw-ib 'long of heart', 'joyful') appear to be problematic only because we have limited knowledge of the Egyptian metaphoric world at play in those compounds (length is here understood in a positive way, as in *ȝw-ḏrt* 'generous', perhaps with the meaning of far reaching, capable to go and see beyond immediate reality). Even in the case of a compound of the type 'a green-eyed goddess', though only the eyes are green, the goddess is reduced to a green vision, to those eyes and their color, a 'thumbnail' image where green prevails and consumes her other features. See David (2004b). The classifier meant is probably *EG*'s listed F21 𓄔 'ear of ox?', used to represent the 'missing quality' (Goldwasser 1995: 92-93), in a reversed schematic relation with the [HEARING] category (the organ for the missing sense) and a metaphoric relation with the lexeme ('not to respond is like being face-deaf'). Interestingly, one example of anti-Maat behaviour consists of being deaf to instructions, to justice, to the law, as highlighted in *The Instruction of Ptahhotep* (Lichtheim 1973: 73-75); see also Nordh (1996: 41-42) which deals with it in a curse context, as in the *Kanais decree*. The lexeme is not exclusively related to the legal register but it properly defines the administrative apathy constitutive of a crime.

iri wpt – classifier: × (to exert a judgment).

* Legal formula: *iw (?) swt ir* + offender + *nty r*.N + infinitive (the victim's complaint) + *mtw.f sḫ-ḥr* (criminal apathy)

I.2.41 Operative part: the penalties (part 15)

(117) (...) *ir.tw hpw r.f m ḥwitw.f m s[ḫ]* (118) 100 *dr m iȝt.f diw r ʿḥwty m [tȝ ḥwt] Mnmȝʿtrʿ ib hr(w)* (119) *m ȝbdt*
(117) (...) (the) rule will have to be enforced against him by beating him with 100 blo[ws] (118), expelling (him) from his office, reduced to a cultivator in [the temple] '*Mnmȝʿtrʿ*'s heart is contented (119) in Abydos.'

* Neo-Egyptian characteristics:
- [*tȝ ḥwt*]
- *m ḥwitw.f*

* 'Classical' degree 0 forms used:
- *ir.tw hpw*
- *dr:* participle if it is an adnominal expansion to the determined *.f*, infinitive (but without coordination or object) if it is another adverbial punishment method.
- *diw*

* General dialectal features: degree 1.

* Legal terms:

ir – classifier: ø (to enforce).

hpw – classifier: ø (norm, rule).

dr m i3t - classifiers: × ⌴ (to expel from an office, dismiss). [COERCION] (⌴ classifier) exerted in a division and conflictual situation ([UNION/DIVISION] × classifier).

rdi r – classifier: ø (to reduce someone to an inferior position).

* Legal formula: *ir.tw hpw r.f m* (method) + infinitive (type of penalty).

II. *Hermopolis decree*

What remains of *Stẖy* I's *Hermopolis decree* stela (*KRI* I, 125 n. 67 and VII, 428 n. 3-7, following Helck 1975: 18[1]) is the bottom right fragment containing the following provisions about the personnel and material property of the temple, the closing exordium (which does not concern legal matters) and the colophon. The other textemes have been lost, but were most certainly comparable with the *Nauri decree* ones. The decree fragment was found to the North of the Hermopolis temple of *Stẖy* II (Brunner 1939: 161).

1. Preamble *sensu stricto*? Operative part?

(1) [*n*]*ꜣ n ꜣḥw*[*t n pr pn*...]
(1) [tho]se fiel[ds of the said temple...]

The first passage is too fragmentary to be of much help, although fields are also affected by the protective measures taken against encroachment by *Stẖy* I in the *Nauri decree* (lines 33, 50-51). Kitchen's reconstruction is far from being certain (*RITA* I, 106). It is probably a fragment of an operative part, due to the fact that the following crime disposition begins with [*ẖ*]*r*, which means that it is not the first one.

2. Operative part: the crimes (confiscation of material property)

(1) (...) [*ẖ*]*r ỉr ḥmw-nṯr*[2] *nb wꜥbw* [*nb n*] *ḥwt-nṯr n nỉwt*[3] *nty ỉw.f r šd ẖt nb*[4] (2) [*rmṯ*] *nb*
(1) (...) [A]nd as for any prophets, [any] priests [of] a temple of (the) town who will exact any material property, (2) any [people],

* Neo-Egyptian characteristics: # [*ẖ*]*r ỉr* + [ø plural hyponyms + *nb*] + *nty ỉw.f r šd* #: relative future, expansion of the topicalized theme (singular reference of the suffix pronoun *.f* although the antecedents are each marked for plural number; distributive quantifier value of *nb*). Typical construction of offender lists in the crimes texteme (hierarchical diminishing progression, less cohesion than in the case of a # nouns + unique final *nb* # list), except for the tendency observed in the *Nauri decree* to list singular lexemes. The offenders do not belong to the civilian administration, but it is not clear if they belong to the temple of Hermopolis (in which case we have a

1 Prior text edition: Brunner (1939: 161-164).
2 Gardiner (1947: 30*).
3 See *RITA* I, 106: 'temple of the City'?
4 Note the absence of concord.

disposition of a different type from that of the *Nauri decree),* or more probably to another temple in the same town (note that in the *Nauri* and *Elephantine decrees*, *šd* is used exclusively in the penalties, about personnel or property or the revenues they produce, and that *iṯt* is used in the penalty instead of *šd*).

* 'Classical' degree 0 forms used: -
* General dialectal features: degree 2.
* Legal terms: *ẖt* – classifier: 𓏛 (material property).
  šd – classifier: ø (to confiscate, exact).
* Legal formula: *ḫr ir* + offenders + *nty iw.f r sḏm* (object of the crime).

3. Operative part: the penalty

(2) (…) *ir.tw hp r.f m sḫr.f diw ḥr tp ẖt r-gs t3 ḥwt-nṯr nty iw.f r iṯt ẖt nb rmṯ nb im.s*
(2) (…) (the) rule will have to be enforced against him by throwing him down (when) placed on (the) tip of a staff (= impaled)[5] beside the temple of which he will seize any material property (or) any people.

* Neo-Egyptian characteristics:
  - *t3 ḥwt-nṯr:* cataphoric use of the determinator.
  - *nty iw.f r iṯt:* relative future expansion of *t3 ḥwt-nṯr* (see above). See the parallel *nty iw.f r iṯi ẖt nb rmṯ nb* subsisting in *Rˁmss* II's *Armant decree* (line 7). The object is typically summed up by two hyperonyms representing the fundamental human and material categories (see above Osiris' title in line 113 of the *Nauri decree*).
* 'Classical' degree 0 forms used:
  - *ir.tw hp*: see above. Note the spelling of *hp*.
  - *diw:* stative or passive participle (see *Nauri decree*, line 77).
* General dialectal features: degree 2.
* Legal terms: *ir* – classifier: ø (to enforce).
  hp - classifier: 𓏛 (rule, legal norm).
  ẖt – classifier: 𓏛 (material property).
* Legal formula: law enforcement *ir.tw hpw r.f m* (method) + infinitive (type of penalty).

Closing exordium.

5 For Lorton (1977: 27-28), it is another case of a capital sentence due to the alienation of stolen property, a fact that cannot be assessed.

4. Colophon (delivery and copy for archiving)

(8) *ỉy ḥr.s sš ni-swt ḥry-tp Ḥ3tyꜥỉ3y n wḥm ni-swt Nḏm wḥm ni-swt Rꜥms r ỉrt m[-mitt...] n sšw m t3 st [mḏ3wt/sšw*[6]]
(8) It is about it (= the decree) that (the) royal scribe in chief, *Ḥ3tyꜥỉ3y*, has come to (the) royal herald *Nḏm* (and the) royal herald *Rꜥms*, to do like[wise (= a copy)[7]...] of writings in the bureau [of (the) scrolls/writings]

* Neo-Egyptian characteristics:

- *ỉy... sš:* focalization pattern in a new delocutive texteme. The colophon is of technical-legal importance, has an extra-textual relevance, the recording of the proper execution of formalities by the chancery (descriptive bureaucratic statement, non prescriptive); but it is also of intra-textual interest, because it signals the end of the document and enriches it with an 'authentic' flavor. It is a nominal that-form ('emphatic') marking the textemic change, referring to the present (literal copy of the original papyrus, the colophon's redaction being simultaneous with the execution of the formality) or the past (see Winand 1991: 367 and 1992: 261-264), the adverbial focus being *ḥr.s* or *n*.N or *r ỉrt,* or even an adverbial complement of the erased section (see Satzinger 1976: 133-134). See Groll (1975: 239, 244-245) on the 'emphatic' *sḏm.n.f* in Neo-Egyptian 'a mid-position *n* was dropped from pronunciation'; Winand (1992: 261). Note that Polotsky (1965: n. 11) and Doret (1980: 39) have signaled that the Middle Egyptian emphatic *sḏm.f* is rendered by the *ỉw* and not the *ỉy* verb. For Neo-Egyptian, Winand (1991: 367) remarks that the 'emphatique du passé' is expressed by *ỉy.f* during the 19th dynasty. Of course, an infinitive must also be considered (see Winand 1991: 363, note 20 for the Neo-Egyptian, and p. 377 for the Coffin Texts), of which the spelling in Neo-Egyptian is often *ỉy* (although the presence of *ḥr.s* before the nominal expansion *sš* of the infinitive, open juncture of the syntagm constructed without relator, could invalidate this option[8]). Nominalizations are frequent in modern bureaucratic language (Charrow 1982: 183) 'making concrete acts into static abstract concepts.' The form cannot be a Neo-Egyptian 'perfect', because its use with verbs of movement is excluded, see Groll (1969: 185) for 20th dynasty 'non-literary' texts; *LEG* § 14.2; Satzinger (1976: 133); Winand (1992: 192). The option of a

---

6 As the *t3 st nt sšw:* 'bureau des écrits' mentioned by Vernus (1990: 245 and note 43); see also Newberry (1900: 104-105); *LÄ* I, 422 (Archive); Kruchten (1981: 218); Hafemann (1985: 9-10) for the Old Kingdom; *pHarris* I 26, 9 (*ỉry.ỉ n.k wḏwt ꜥ3yw r ḥnw r-pr.k smn m ḫ3 n sšw n t3 mrỉ*); *ibidem* 47, 8 & 60, 9 (*ḫ3 n sšw*); Grandet (1994 II: 116 (478)).

7 See Spiegelberg (1928: 113) for the same expression in *pMunich* ÄS 809 (*Ḏḥwtyms* IV), and also *pBerlin* 3047, line 36 (*Rꜥmss* II; Helck 1963: 70 & 73), *pTurin* 2021/271 (20th dynasty, *iw.tw iry m-mitt*); Helck (1974: 126 (e)); see also *The Inscription of Mes*, S8 (19th dynasty).

8 For Middle Egyptian, see *EG* § 85 'Examples where the direct genitive is separated from its noun are of extreme rarity.'

prospective form must also be excluded not merely for semantic reasons (this kind of texteme does not express a formality that remains to be executed, the decree has already been registered when its monumental copy is engraved; see also *infra* earlier decrees), but because in Middle and Neo-Egyptian, the verb used would be *iw* (Doret 1980: 39; Winand 1991: 369 & 375). See *infra Rꜥmss* II *Deir el-Medineh decree* for a partially erased, similar formula upon a statue. The same formula as in our decree is used in *Ḏḥwtyms* IV's *decree* for *Nbimn* (*iy ḥr.s sš ni-swt* + proper noun), as on private statues of *Ḏḥwtyms* III's (*Urk.* IV, 1021) and *Ỉmnḥtp* III's times (*Urk.* IV 1885, 14 and Helck (1961: 301)). In fact, the only royal decree preserved with its colophon from Middle Kingdom to 18th dynasty is *Ḏḥwtyms* IV's decree for *Nbimn*. For Sethe (*Urk.* IV, 81, note a) a reconstructed recording colophon ([*spẖr.s m*] + date) closes *Ḏḥwtyms* I's *Wadi Halfa/Kuban/Buhen decree*, on the basis of an 'Ergänzung nach Pap. Turin 67 (Pleyte-Rossi)', which is *pTurin* 1896 (see *infra)*, although this text belongs to the reign of *Rꜥmss* IX, it is of a very distant period and does not exhibit such a formula. Note that a delivery colophon is already used in Old Kingdom decrees: see *Ppy* II's *Dakhla* and *Coptos D* (6th dynasty), *Nfrkꜣwḥr Coptos J, K, L, M, N, Q* (8th dynasty) and *Dmḏibtꜣwy Coptos R* (9th dynasty?) *decrees,* with *iw rdiw iwt* N *r.s* 'the coming of N has been caused for it', clearly an Old Egyptian delocutive passive *iw sḏm.w*.N report tense (historical record); see also Goedicke (1964: 36); Helck (1974: 108-116, 126 (f)). On the copy process during the Old Kingdom, see Goedicke (1964: 37). Compare also with the formula in the *Stèle juridique de Karnak*, lines 11-13 (17th dynasty) *ir in ẖꜣ* (done by the office, with participle) (...) *ir.n.ṯw n.f mi ntt r hp* (it is in conformity with (the) legal norm that one has acted, with a nominal *sḏm.n.f* that-form) (...). It seems that focalization patterns are used in colophons in Demotic (*isẖ-*) and Coptic (Prof. Shisha-Halevy's personal communication). As with modern legalese that uses conventionalized methods of recording facts and repeats formulas *ad nauseam* in similar contexts, our decree uses a disposition created at least 150 years earlier by the royal chancery.

* 'Classical' degree 0 forms used: *r irt:* preposition + infinitive (purpose)

* General dialectal features: degree 1.

* Legal terms: *st* [*mḏꜣwt*/*sšw*] – classifier: [?] (archive bureau).

* Legal formula: *iy ḥr.s* + title and proper name (delivery responsible) + *n* + title and proper name (registration scribes) + *r irt m-*[*mitt*] (purpose: registration and filing) + *m tꜣ st* [*mḏꜣwt*/*sšw*] (archive location)

III. *Kanais/Wadi Abbad* or *Mia/Redesieh decree*

The three Kanais/Wadi Abbad or Mia/Redesieh inscriptions (*Stẖy* I, Year 9, *KRI* I, 65 n. 32[9]) relate the organisation of water supplies and settlement for gold mining and transporting activities in the region, as well as the dedication of the local sanctuary, as part of the gold supply infrastructure, to *Stẖy* I's new funerary temple of Abydos (see *Nauri decree* and Vercoutter 1959: esp. 133).

Although the enacting clause *ỉw wḏ.n ḥm.f* or its variants is not used in the inscriptions (to be distinguished from the narrative *ʿḥʿ.n wḏ.n ḥm.f* in lines 9-10), the third part of the inscriptions on the North wall ('Text C', line 19) mentions *wḏ(t) tn* ('this decree') uses the familiar *ḥn, ẖwi/mki* lexemes as well as curses against eventual offenders against the royal provisions already observed in the previously studied *Nauri decree,* and has a structure reminiscent of the previous decrees. It is considered a decree by Otto (1956: 154), Lichtheim (1976: 52) and Trapani (1993: 539); *contra:* Lorton (1977: 27) because it 'omits mention of criminal penalties inflicted during life and states only the religious consequences for royalty and commoners' (...) 'the text is not a decree (...) but this section of the text presupposes such a decree'; *LÄ* VI: 380 (*Königsnovelle* genre). For Morschauser (1991: 37), 'codified law and its use of defined legal statutes served as the conceptual basis for the formation of the threat in ancient Egypt.' The enacting clause is an essential part of a legal text, and its presence is attested in all the documents included in our corpus, or at least there must be a strong presumption that there was such a clause in the complete form of a damaged text. Nevertheless, the *Kanais decree* contains too many other elements belonging to the legal register to be ignored and omitted from the corpus. As for the threefold inscriptions structure, text A represents 'the formal building-dedication' (*RITANC* I, 61) in commemoration of the well excavation and the ensuing benefit for gold transportation; it does not show elements of legal register. Text B begins with the pre-material and covers the narrative background (the project's genesis and execution); text C deals with the issue of the foundation/endowment[10] maintain and divine punishment of eventual offenders. Texts B and C both belong to the decree.

Text B

Pre-material (identificative and backgrounding aetiologic texteme):

1. **date** (line 1);
2. **authority** (line 1): # *ḥr ḥm n* + king's titulary #;

---

9 For earlier editions of the text, see, for instance, Reinisch (1873: Taf. 9); Sottas (1913: 128-132); Gunn & Gardiner (1917: 250); Sander-Hansen (1933: 25-29); Schott (1961: pl. 12-17, 19).

10 See Harari (1987b: 87) 'personnes morales autonomes que nous pouvons qualifier de Fondations'. An endowment is 'a permanent fund of property or money bestowed upon an institution or a person, the income from which is used to serve the specific purpose for which the "endowment" was intended.' (Gifis 1984: 155)

3. **eulogizing aetiologic/narrative background** (lines 1-14) that constitutes the general preamble of the decree;

The text closes with a pictorial scene.

Text C

1. The decree's proclamation to the kings[11] and introduction of the content

(1) *ni-swt bity Mnmꜣꜥtrꜥ sꜣ Rꜥ Stẖymrnptḥ ḏd.f ẖr itw.f ni-swtyw nbw bityw ḥkꜣw rḫyt*
(1) (The) king of Upper (and) Lower Egypt *Mnmꜣꜥtrꜥ* son of *Rꜥ Stẖymrnptḥ*, he says to his fathers, all Upper-Egyptian kings, Lower-Egyptian kings, rulers of (the) people:

* Neo-Egyptian characteristics: -
* 'Classical' degree 0 forms used: PN *ḏd.f*: the proclamation/introduction of the content is a personal, verbal address by the king to previous (dead) sovereigns; it is quite different from the proclamation and introduction observed in the *Nauri decree* (public reading of the content of a written decree introduced by a tag clause whose theme is the document itself), the royal speech act being central on this occasion. Consecutively, the construction used is a Middle Egyptian PN *ḏd.f*, the extraposed actor preceding a temporal (present) delocutive *sḏm.f* of the *verbum dicendi* opening the direct speech, proclamatory; among abundant literature, see Westendorf (1953) for an adverbial nexus expressing duration; Doret (1980 and his references) who does not distinguish cases of N *ḏd.f* from other topicalized N + *sḏm.f*, and considers that N *sḏm.f* constructions are either prospectives with extraposed actor, or adverbial nexuses with circumstantial *sḏm.f*; Junge (1989: 69) who notes that PN *ḏd.f* is not a contrastive or specifying focus but a 'topic shifting construction'; Shisha-Halevy (1989c: 252) for whom *ḏd.f* in Middle Egyptian signals 'the narrative/dialogue seam'. Note that the addressees are preceded by the preposition *ẖr*, frequently used when the speech is addressed to the divine (*Wb* V, 620).
* General dialectal features: degree 0.
* Legal terms: -
* Legal formula: king + proper noun + *ḏd.f* + *ẖr* (divine addressees).

The address begins with Stẖy asking for the kings' attention (material having no legal bearing has been omitted; see *supra* the discussion of the ambiguous nature of the document).

11 See Théodoridès (1972: 189) on the religious menace used against future kings who will have complete sovereignty concerning public law measures. Compare with the first imprecatory royal decree that has been preserved: 17th dynasty *Nbḫprwrꜥ Ꞽntf Coptos decree* (the curse interrupting 'secular' penalties concerns kings who will pardon the offender).

2. Preamble *sensu stricto* (authority, object, beneficiary, inner motivation, warnings)

(2) (…) *ḏd.n.i nn ḥr ḥn n3yw.i ḳ3rw n iʿw nbw r ḥwt-nṯr.i r dit.w ḥr sṯ3t* (3) *n ḥwt.i* [*m 3bdt r ḫrp nbw ? r*]*-pr.i*[12] (...)

(2) (…) It is concerning the affectation of/while posting my staff[13] of mine-water transporters[14] for gold-washers to my temple[15], to place them for (the) supply (3) to my house[16] [in Abydos, for the delivery of gold ? to[17]] my [ch]apel, that I have said the following:

… *then follows a warning (s3w) against misuse of gold and interference (tḫny and thh) with people appointed to the service of the gods* (instead of a decree negative intents)

(6) (…) *ir.n.i ḳ3wrw m iʿw nbw m š3w* (7) *ḥr rn*[*.i … ni-sw*]*t ḥr ḫw.i ir.n.i sn m ḳ3wrw m m3w n-mrwt mn.sn ḫr.i bw in.i m ky*[18] *ḳ3wrw* (8) *r* [*irt ḥnwt.sn ?… ḫwit.w m*]*kt.w*[19] *m msw n ḥwt.i m wnḏwt n r-pr.i*

(6) (…) It is in proper fashion that I have appointed mine-water transporters for (the) gold-washing (7) in [my] name [… k]ing beside me[20]; it is for the sake of remaining subjected to me that I appointed them newly as transporters. It is not in my nature to have recourse[21] to other transporters (8) to [carry their service… to retain (and) pr]eserve them as children of my house, as subjects of my chapel.

* Neo-Egyptian characteristics:

- *ḥr ḥn:* Neo-Egyptian absence of feminine ending of the infinitive *ḥn.*
- *n3yw.i:* Neo-Egyptian possessive determinator, its spelling being the same as in line 8 of the *Elephantine decree.*
- *ḳ3rw/ḳ3wrw/ḳwrw:* 19th dynasty spellings of a New Kingdom lexeme (see *Wb* V, 21; Gunn & Gardiner 1917: 247, n. 3). For *ḳ3rw/ḳ3wrw/ḳwrw n iʿ nbw,* see *Nauri*

12 *r(3)-pr*: chapel or secondary/provincial temple for Gardiner (1941: 70), Grandet (1994 II: 31 (131)); *contra*: Spencer (1984: 37-42, 54-55) 'offering place' and by extension 'temple'; Moreno Garcia (1999: 55) 'il est impossible de cerner la différence existant entre *ḥwt-nṯr* et *r3-pr*.'

13 Gunn & Gardiner (1917: 247 and n. 3); Schott (1961: 149, n. 3 and 176-177).

14 *RITA* I, 59: transport contingents.

15 Kanais temple.

16 Abydos funerary temple.

17 Schott's restitution (1961: 149).

18 Note the absence of concord.

19 The reading is quite problematic. Schott (1961: 151, e) notes 'Über Buchrolle mit Pluralstrichen undeutliche Spuren von *t* unter *k* (?)'; if it is the right reading, then it cannot be a stative as in line 17 or in the *Nauri decree*, lines 26 and 41 and Schott, Kitchen (*RITA* I, 58) and Davies (1997: 215) translations are not justified.

20 Gunn & Gardiner (1917: 247) '[for] me alone' (on the basis of *wʿ ḥr-ḫw.f*); Schott (1961: 151) '[(…) wie es sich ziemt für] einen König meinesgleichen.' (see *Wb* III,216 in expressions where *ḫw* is translated as 'Art').

21 *CD*, 22 (7). For Schott (1961: 151) 'Ich habe (sie) nicht von einer anderen Transporttruppe geholt'.

decree, line 40 and *Rʿmss* II's *Kuban stela*, line 10. On the translation and classifiers of *ḳꜣrw/ḳꜣwrw/ḳwrw*, see *ARE* III § 175 'caravaneers of the gold-washers' and Vercoutter (1959: esp. 142-144) for water transporters to the mines for the purpose of gold washing.

- *r dỉt.w:* either purpose expressed by the preposition + infinitive + 3rd plural suffixed object in its Neo-Egyptian form (see Gunn & Gardiner 1917: 247; Kruchten 1981: 54 'pour leur faire payer régulièrement redevance à mon temple'; for the infinitive of *rdỉ*, see Winand 1992 : 89), or independent (or dependent, apparently, for Davies 1997: 212-213) passive prospective *rdỉ.tw.w* (an impersonal *rdỉ.tw* is less probable because of the ending ), with Neo-Egyptian 3rd plural suffixed actor. The independent passive prospective is mentioned in Neo-Egyptian by Junge (1996: 148); in *LEG* § 10.12.1.I.d.8 and 10.12.2.V.a.ii there is mention of an 'initial' passive prospective (optative) *stp.w st* or *stp.tw st* and a 'non-initial prospective *stp.f* with *.tw* as actor expression (?)', also in § 47; for Winand (1992: 213), the prospective of *rdỉ* is always written *dỉ*, and the dependent passive prospective *dỉ.tw.f* (p. 325) is the form used during the 19th dynasty (with a first example of geminated *dỉdỉ.tw* by the time of *Stẖy* II). A passive emphatic form ('it is for the supply… that they have been placed') could theoretically be postulated, although Winand (1992: 320) again notes that *dỉ* is used during the 19th dynasty (*dỉ.tw.w* for 'emphatique prospectif' and 'emphatique perfectif'). Finally, *rdỉ.tw.w* is translated by Schott (1961: 149) as 'Sie sind bestimmt' and by Kitchen as 'They are committed ("given") to delivering (…)' (atemporal?). The purpose (*r dỉt.w*) is well suited to the focus on the king's motivation as well as the morphological analysis.
- *ḥr sṯꜣt:* preposition + noun or infinitive with intrusive Neo-Egyptian feminine mark before its classifier (the *3-lit.* with *ult.- ꜣ* are masculine infinitives but may acquire a feminine ending during the 19th/20th dynasties if assimilated to feminine nouns or to *2-lit.* – see Winand 1992: 91-92).
- *m mꜣw*: 19th dynasty spelling (without final *t*).
- *bw ỉn.ỉ:* Neo-Egyptian negative aorist (atemporal, generic, action not in the nature of the actor), in past locutive context, with *bw,* preverbal negation, for a general expression of the king's resolution (not limited in time) not to use other transporters (taken from other contingents) than the ones he appointed for the service, as if he justifies himself and declares again that he has appointed his staff 'in proper fashion'. See on the sequence *n sḏm.n.f – bw sḏm.n.f – bw sḏm.f – bw ỉr.f sḏm* and the aorist in general Davis (1973: 23-33, esp. 27); Frandsen (1974: 31-38); Groll (1975: 242-243); Kruchten (1981: 89), on *Ḥrmḥb*'s decree, line 26: *ẖr ỉw bw gm.n.tw*; Winand (1992: 238); Junge (1996: 104-105); Goldwasser (1999: 13, n. 49).

* 'Classical' degree 0 forms used:

- *ḏd.n.ỉ:* independent thematic abstract that-form *sḏm.n.f*, with locutive actor. The form expresses a change of texteme (explicative), not a polemic contrast. The focus is on the adverbial expression of the king's motivation (the permanent appointment of a staff dedicated to a specific service). It opens a speech into a speech (see above *ḏd.f*) and appears in our text instead of the enacting clause, expressing in a simple locutive the authority source of the measures, their object and beneficiary, but also instead of the negative and positive intents in the form of a more personal, inner motivation. Formally, it could also be an intermediate 19th dynasty form of report (see Winand 1992: 184-185), but the textemic change and the adverbial focus argue in favor of the first alternative.

- *nn:* Middle Egyptian demonstrative with proximal cataphoric referentiality to the entire subsequent speech and dispositions.
- *ir.n.i:* see *ḏd.n.i*. Note the verbal constituency of the that-forms (to say, to do) and the second *ir.n.i* adverbial focus (*n-mrwt mn.sn*); see Polotsky (1944: 189) *n-mrwt* + *sḏm.f* referring to the future, and (1976: 18-19, esp. 22) 'La forme substantive du *sḏm.n.f* figure dans certains clichés où elle sert à résumer en termes généraux (verbe « faire », complément « cela ») les actions racontées dans les phrases précédentes pour leur ajouter, comme prédicat (...), l'expression de leur motif.'). See *supra*, *Nauri decree,* lines 107-108.

* General dialectal features: degree 2.

* Legal terms:

ḥn – classifier: (to allocate personnel/property, appoint). See Harari (1987b: 89). Instead of the classifier (see *Nauri decree*), the papyrus roll appears as the superordinate [ABSTRACT] category classifier of *ḥn* (as in the *Elephantine decree*), perhaps because it involves the recording of the personnel's management and other documents. Furthermore, the classifier is more widely used than because it represents a larger category.

[*ḫwit/m*]*kt*? – classifier: (to retain (and) preserve).

wnḏwt – classifier: (subjects, dependents). The triple classifier (man, woman and plural marker) gives information pertaining to the nature ([BOTH SEXES HUMANS] superordinate taxonomic category) and number or collective quality (superordinate [PLURAL/ABSTRACTION] category) of the object represented by the lexeme. Although the plural grapheme is far too widely used to require special attention in the analysis of legal register classifiers, we might add that it works on the semantic level as Gombrich's 'etc. principle' (1986: 184-185) in visual art, 'the assumption we tend to make that to see a few members of a series is to see them all'. Three small strokes (where in fact the sub-decimal cardinal unit is used in an unspecific way) are read as representing an indeterminate number of elements (extrapolation), and the way those elements are very cursorily represented (abstraction) permits their identification with any given object. On the summarizing ('raccourci') value of the number three in Egyptian script, see Lacau (1954: 24-54). Note that the category represented by the classifier covers also abstractions and nominalizations for which the 'plural' notion is not pertinent, the three strokes marking the lexemes as abstract notions.

* Legal formula: *ḏd.n.i/ir.n.i* (source of measures and speech) + adverbial focus (motivation)

Follows the blessing that a respectful king will enjoy (positive behavior)[22].

2. Operative part: the crime (part 1 – later king's cancellation of *Sthy* I's dispositions)

(11) (...) *hr ir ni-swt nb nty r hpr shnn.t.f shrw.i nb hnᶜ ntf dd t3w r ht.i ink sn mi wn.sn* (12) *hr.f sp ksn hr ibw ntrw* (11) (...) And as for any king who is yet to be who will destroy[23] any of my plans and say: 'lands are under my authority, mine they are as they were (12) under him (= his)[24]', a troublesome case for (the) gods' hearts,

* Neo-Egyptian characteristics:

- *nty r hpr... hnᶜ ntf dd:* delocutive conjunctive joining a rhematic apodose to a relative future protase (from a diachronic perspective, we have seen that our form represents the 'third link' in the evolution of the form: *hnᶜ sdm – hnᶜ sdm ntf – hnᶜ ntf sdm – ntf sdm – mtw.f sdm*). It is this conjunctive form that also appears twice in our text in the blessing segments. See above, esp. Gardiner (1928: 86, 88); Morschauser (1991: 13). As in the *Nauri decree*, conjunctives appear especially in the casuistic-logic texteme of crime and penalty. The apodosis *hnᶜ ntf dd* opens a direct speech, a locutive illustrative constructed quotation that indicates the future king's pretence and self-justification (interior monologue or defense in front of divine authorities?), its sovereignty, which is precisely the 'raison d'être' of the curse, the legitimacy of the act but its discordance with *Sthy* I's will. The apodosis again presents the main interest in the enunciation of the crime, whereas the protasis provides its general background.
- *mi wn.sn:* preposition + nominal relatively past that-form, adverbial adjunct to the preceding nominal nexus. See Polotsky (1944: 186); Frandsen (1974: 165-166) on the restricted use of that-forms after prepositions in Neo-Egyptian ('In fact, it is only in literary and religious set phrases that we find the syntagm prep. + that-form'); Winand (1992: 261-264) 'perfective'. The form appears in the constructed quotation texteme; the Middle Egyptian *sdm.n.f* relatively past that-form has been modified to suit the way a 19th dynasty king would be expected to speak in an Egyptian highly ideological oriented text.

* 'Classical' degree 0 forms used:

---

22 See Assmann (1992: 151): legal texts *sensu stricto* never reward positive behavior, but imprecation texts juxtapose curses for the offender and blessings for the righteous. The same situation is to be found in *Imnhtp* III (21st dynasty copy) *Medinet Habu decree* with its curses and contrastive formula of positive behavior (*hr wnn.f* (*hr*) *sdm*) and in *Rᶜmss* II's *Hittite Treaty*. See also Nordh (1996).

23 Morschauser (1991: 55) ' "to tear down", i.e. "interfere, upset, violate."'

24 For Gunn & Gardiner (1917: 247), *hr.f* closes the direct speech (text-final subdividing signal).

- *# ḫr ỉr* + noun + *nb* + *nty r ḫpr #:* topicalized category of offenders expanded by a relative clause with adverbial rheme (note the absence of *ỉw.f* as in *Nauri decree*, line 66). Note the use of *ḫr* introducing the first crimes category, the preceding positive behaviour having been topicalized by *ỉr*. Compare with Morschauser (1991: 10-11, 16) for threat formulas with # *ỉr* + *nty* (*n*) + infinitive # in protasis; *Ỉntf Nbḫprwrᶜ Coptos decree* (17th dynasty) *ỉr ni-swt nb sḫm-ỉr.f nb nty r ḥtp*.
- *sḫnn.t.f:* archaism with future *sḏm.ty.fy* geminated participle, as in Old Kingdom decrees; see *EG* § 364; Gunn (1924: 43); Lorton (1977: 53); Morschauser (1991: 8) who notes that the most common threat formula protasis up to and including New Kingdom uses the *sḏm.ty.fy* form. The archaism probably adds the magical touch of an age-old formula pertaining to a mythical time.
- *ỉnk sn:* nominal ('adjectival') nexus expressing rhematic possession ('independent' pronoun, rheme + possessum, theme) in a locutive constructed quotation. See Gardiner (1904: 135); *NÄG* §107-108 ('Pronomina absoluta als Possessivausdruck'); Groll (1967: 37 n. 128) 'adjectival sentence'; Junge (1996: 182); Shisha-Halevy (1998b: 596). On a diachronic level, it is a productive pattern (see for instance *EG* § 114.3 examples and *Wenamun* 2, 24).

* General dialectal features: degree 2.

* Legal terms: -

* Legal formula: *ḫr ỉr* + offender *nb* + *nty r sḏm... ḥnᶜ ntf sḏm* (crime) + illustrative constructed direct speech.

3. Operative part: the curse penalty (part 1)

(12) (...) *m.k tw.*[*t*]*w r wšbw.f m Ỉwnw mntsn ḏ3ḏ3t*[...] *ỉr.sn wšb ḥr ḫt.w dšr.sn mi bsi n sḏt n snwḫ.sn ḥᶜw.sn tmw* (13) *sḏm n.ỉ st r sswn ḥḏ sḫrw.ỉ r rditw.f r ḫbt dw3t*

(12) (...) See o[n]e about to arraign him (= royal offender) in Heliopolis: they are (the) judges [...]; may they make answer for (= defend) their material property; may they redden as firebrand because they boil[25] the(ir) flesh[26] of those who do not (13) listen (obey) to me; they will destroy the one who disturbs my plans (and) will hand him over to (the) Netherworld execution chamber[27].

* Neo-Egyptian characteristics:

- *m.k tw.*[*t*]*w r wšbw.f:* independent modal prospective *m.k* (exhortation) + Neo-Egyptian impersonal pronominal object + adverbial adjunct; for the value of *m.k*, see David (2000b: 113-123). It would be classical Middle Egyptian if it were not for the pronoun *tw.tw* (degree 1 form of Neo-Egyptian). *m.k tw.tw r sḏm* is not

25 On 'Crime, Cult and Capital Punishment', see Willems (1990: 27-53).
26 For Schott (1961: 154 and note 9) '*.sn ḥᶜw.sn* "sie selbst"'.
27 See Moret (1917: 373-374); Morschauser (1991: 187).

equivalent to *tw.i r sḏm* ('frühneuägyptische Futur' as Kroeber 1970: 93-97 calls it), an adverbial nexus found in a few examples from the 17th to the 20th dynasty. The construction is rare and is not mentioned in grammars of Neo-Egyptian. On the other hand, the existence of the pattern *ptr tw.i* + stative/*ḥr sḏm* in Neo-Egyptian (*Naunakhte* 1, II, 4-5: 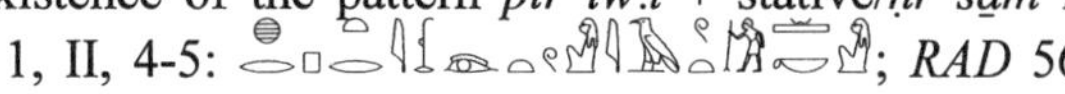; *RAD* 56, 9-10: ) may confirm the logic behind our pattern. On the evolution of *m.k* in Neo-Egyptian, see *LEG* § 9.5.4; Winand (1992: 403, note 9 and 481, note 2 'Le futur III est la seule construction qui survit en néo-égyptien parmi toutes celles de l'égyptien classique ayant pour prédicat *r* + infinitif.', following the traditional view of the constructions like *m.k sw r sḏm* as adverbial nexi); Junge (1996: 116) for whom *m.k sw r sḏm* belongs to 'futurischen Adverbialsatzes' whose 'Spätmittelägyptischen Variante' is *tw.i r sḏm*, although they belong to different paradigms; Goldwasser (2001: 125-128) for the use of *m.k* in various 19th and 20th dynasty registers.

- *mntsn ḏ3ḏ3t:* thematic plural delocutive pronoun used in a nominal nexus (see Groll 1967: 30-33), its spelling being an odd compromise between Middle Egyptian *ntsn* and Neo-Egyptian *mntw*. Davies (1997: 216-217) transcripts *m ntsn* and translates 'for they are the magistrates'.
- *ir.sn wšb:* analytic independent prospective with optative curse value, the curse function being 'to deal with a ruler who invalidates the law itself, either by changing or by failing to enforce existing law' (Assmann 1992: 153; see Morschauser 1991: 21, also for Middle Kingdom, and p. 187). The imprecation aims at the physical destruction of the offender, but as Tyldesley (2000: 30) puts it 'the offender is destined to enjoy the flames of hell rather than to be burned alive'. The punishment in a curse may thus be realized by the same form (analytic or synthetic, see *infra*) as in the 'actual' penalties of decrees (prospective *ir.tw hpw* as previously observed); see Morschauser (1991: 21-25).
- *ḫt.w:* Neo-Egyptian third plural suffix expressing possession ().
- *st r sswn:* Neo-Egyptian form of the delocutive plural dependent pronoun (theme) in an 'early' (degree 1) Neo-Egyptian independent adverbial nexus (Kroeber 1970: 93-97; *EG* § 43, Obs. 1 & § 124). The value of the adverbial syntagm has to be opposed to the earlier imprecatory prospective: it is not modal, but underlines the inevitable character of the punishment and summarizes its principle. See Junge (1996: 134) 'Offensichtlichkeit oder notwendige Folge'.
- *r rditw.f:* preposition + infinitive (Neo-Egyptian spelling) + object, second rheme of *st r sswn*. Note here the use of *rdit* as infinitive (compare line 2 *dit*).

* 'Classical' degree 0 forms used:

- *dšr.sn:* independent imprecatory synthetic prospective (compare with *ir.sn wšb*).
- *n snwḫ.sn:* preposition *n* + nominal 'that-form' expressing a motive; see *EG* § 164.9 and the example p. 120 *in fine*. Gunn & Gardiner (1917: 247) translate the form as an independent prospective, ignoring the presence of *n*; Davies (1997: 216-217) sees *nwḫ.sn* ignoring anything preceding it; Schott (1961: 154 and n.

9) and Kitchen (*RITA* I, 59 'so that they may burn up') view the construction as a purpose expressed apparently by *r sḏm.f.*

- *tmw sḏm:* active participle + infinitive (see Gilula 1970: 212). The participle is translated as a prospective form by Gunn & Gardiner (1917: 247), a present one by Kitchen (*RITA* I, 59), and a 'perfective' one for Winand (1992: 345, 355). There is evidently an atemporal value attached to this participle used as a nominal expansion of *ḥꜥw.sn,* 'the non-listeners'.
- *ḥḏ:* active participle, object of the infinitive *sswn.*

* General dialectal features: degree 1.

* Legal terms:

wšb – classifiers: (to answer, to prosecute). Morschauser (1991: 72) 'formal arraignment or "prosecution" of a criminal.' The double classifier of the metaphoric superordinate [UNION/DIVISION] category crossed sticks classifier and the man with a hand close to the mouth of the [MOUTH LINKED ACTIVITIES] category (taxonomic relation with the lexeme) refer respectively to the two parties and verbal prosecution, the two icons representing the 'contradictoire' principle of criminal procedure (the judgment is given after due hearing of the parties).

ỉr wšb ḥr – classifier: (to answer for; to defend/protect someone). See Vernus (1980: 225); Green (1980: 43-45); Grandet (1994 II: 32 (131)) '"garantir (juridiquement)" l'existence d'une institution, l'observance d'une réglementation'. The relation between the classifier of the [MOUTH LINKED ACTIVITIES] category and the lexeme is of a taxonomic nature, as observed for *wšb* above.

ḏꜣḏꜣt – classifier: (judges, court, counsel). See Harari (1950: 15-22); Otto (1956: 157); Lurje (1971: 63-67) 'in Wirklichkeit gar nicht mehr existierte' during the New Kingdom, only as a divine court, its usual classifier being 'die Form eines Kreises' (again the [UNION/DIVISION] category); Bedell (1973: 276-278, n. 12) 'to designate the court of the gods as well as the earthly court'. The *EG*'s list A40 'seated god' superordinate classifier, anthropomorphic, male, bearded and seated replaces the seated man here to classify the court composed of divine judges in the superordinate [DIVINE] category. See Shalomi-Hen (2000: 61) about the divine classifier in *CT* 335 and *BD* 17; Goldwasser (2002: chapters 1 and 6). The lexeme is already used in *Ppy* II *Coptos G decree* (*ḏꜣḏꜣt nt ꜣḥt*, with the classifier).

ḫt – classifier: (material property).

* Curse formula: [*m.k tw.tw r wšb* (procedure) + *m* (location) + *mntsn ḏꜣḏꜣt* (judges identity)] background + *ỉr.f sḏm/sḏm.f* (curse penalty) + *st r sḏm* (principle of inevitable penalty).

4. Preamble (continued - inner motivation and general outcome of positive/negative behavior)

(13) (…) *ḏ*[*d.n*].*i* [*nn nḏ.i*] *ḫr.tn imi nḥm sw šw m bt3.f ḫy rʿ ky sbn*-(14) *ḥ3ty m* (=*in*) *psḏt sḫn.sn ḥnʿ.f*   (13) (…) It is [because I/in order to protect] you that I s[aid this]. Let save himself one who is void of (his) crime; but as for (?) another one straying of (14) heart (= with a straying heart), it is (the) Ennead who will arraign him.

* Neo-Egyptian characteristics:

- *ḫy rʿ*: for Gunn & Gardiner (1917: 248, n. 1) 'a crux that occurs again in *pAnastasi* IV, 10, 10' translated 'why then (?)'(but translated in *CLEM*, 176 and 178: 'meanwhile'); in the *Wb* III, 238, esp. n. 15, *ḫy* is 'belegt Nä. als Schreibung für *ḫr*.' and occurs 'in der Verbindung: [*ḫy rʿ*]'; Spiegelberg (1967: 42-43) views *ḫr rʿ* as a conjunction of time 'zur der Zeit' or 'wenn' as in *pOrbiney* 8,6; Kitchen (*RITA* I, 59) translates the compound 'but indeed, (as for)'; see also *oGardiner* 309, l. 3. Note that there is also an 'interjectional' *ḫy* 'Only one ex. noted before Dyn. XIX.' (*EG* § 258 A. on p. 427). The expression is probably parallel to *ḫr ir* used, as we have seen, in similar circumstances, as coordinator + topic marker.
- *ky sbn-ḥ3ty*: # definite quantifier *ky* + participial attribute (19th dynasty spelling of *sbn*, see *Wb* III, 433 + inalienable (body part) # in an exocentric attributive compound constituting an hypallage.
- *m* (=*in*) *psḏt sḫn.sn*: nominal focus initial cleft-sentence (participial statement) with # focus marker + proper noun + relative thematic prospective *sḏm.f* #. Compare with line 19. The substitution of *m* and *in* as the focus marker is Neo-Egyptian; see Gunn & Gardiner (1917: 248, n. 1); Kroeber (1970: 41-45); *RITANC* I, 62; Junge (1996: 189-190). For another example of the same phenomenon, see the *Elephantine decree*.

* 'Classical' degree 0 forms used:

- *ḏ*[*d.n*].*i* [*nn nḏ.i*]: as in line 2, cleft sentence with locutive topical 'emphatic' *sḏm.n.f* (marking the change of texteme) + anaphoric proximal demonstrative (object) and circumstantial *sḏm.f* (converb with an identical actor) as rhematic focus (the king's motivation). This construction is used to close the reported direct speech opened in line 2.
- *imi nḥm sw* N: iussive/3rd person grammatical causative imperative formed of # causative exponent, the imperative of *rdi* (see *LEG* § 24.5.2 and Winand (1992: 173-174) for usual Ramesside spelling in monumental inscriptions, without prothetic *yod*) + causated lexeme, dependent prospective + delocutive dependent pronoun (reflexive object) + nominal (participial) actor #. On causative imperatives, see *EG* § 338.2 for Middle Egyptian; Frandsen (1974: 80 ff.) and Junge (1996; 153-154) for Neo-Egyptian.

* General dialectal features: degree 1.
* Legal terms:

bt3 – classifier:  (crime). See David (2000: 50-58 & 102) for the superordinate category of [INFERIORITY-PERTURBATION].

sḫn ḥnʿ – classifier:  (to go to law with, plead against, arraign). See Gardiner (1964: 14) for *The Inscription of Mes,* lines N13, 32 & 33. The lexeme belongs to the [MOUTH LINKED ACTIVITIES] category, due to the verbal nature of the pleading.

* Legal formula: *ḏd.n.ỉ* (source of the preceding speech) + adverbial focus (motivation)

Follows the blessing that a respectful official will enjoy (positive behavior).

5. Operative part: the crimes (part 2 – advising personnel displacement)

(15) (…) *ḫr ỉr sr nb nty sw r stkn ỉb pn nb.f r nḥm ḥsbw r dỉtw.w ḥr ky sdf m sḫr n mty bỉn*
(15) (…) And as for any official who will induce this desire of (= suggest, influence)[28] his lord to take away personnel[29] members to place them in another service as a plan of (= premeditated) evil advice,

* Neo-Egyptian characteristics:

- *r dỉtw.w:* purpose expressed by # preposition + infinitive + Neo-Egyptian 3rd plural suffixed object # (see above). For Winand (1992: 87, ex. 212) we have here a rare 19th dynasty spelling of the infinitive with 'thème plein' *rdỉ*. A formulation close to the one used in the *Bilgai stela* (which is not a decree) from *S3ptḥ* (Siptah)'s reign, 19th dynasty, in the exposé of the crime that it curses (line 6): [*ỉr…*] (…) *nty ỉw.f r ḫpr* (…) *mtw.f* [*ỉṯ3*] *rmṯ ỉm.s r dỉtw.f r ky h3w* (…). The curse is also followed here by the benediction on the state agent who behaves properly. See Théodoridès (1972: 189).
- *sdf:* Neo-Egyptian lexeme (*Wb* IV, 370).

* 'Classical' degree 0 forms used:

- *# ỉr sr nb nty sw r stkn #:* topic marker + singular noun + distributive *nb* + relative expansion with adverbial rheme. Note the redundancy of the theme *sw* in the adverbial nexus (identical to its antecedent), although usually not expressed in these circumstances in Middle Egyptian (see *EG* § 200.1), a probable sign of *nty* becoming a converter. See also Schott (1961: 155-156) for the distinction between positive behavior expressed by the 'Present 2' (custom), and its negative counterpart expressed by the 'Present 1' (isolated case).

---

28 The counselor activity; see Théodoridès (1981: 630-631 and n. 16).

29 See Schott (1961: 156) for *ḥsbw*.

- *ỉb pn:* cataphoric use of the proximal classical demonstrative, a function that it does not possess in its limited uses in degree 3 Neo-Egyptian (always anaphoric, see *LEG* § 3.1.1).
- *r nḥm:* preposition + infinitive (purpose).

* General dialectal features: degree 1.

* Legal terms:

nḥm – classifier: (to take away, divert).

sdf – classifier: (service, foundation, dependency). See *RITA* I, 59; for Gunn & Gardiner (1917: 248, n.2), 'endowment'; Helck (1960b: 790-791) *sdf* (old *sḏfꜣ*) 'Wirtschaftseinheit'; Schott (1961: 156); Théodoridès (1972: 192, n. 4); Haring (1997: 169-173, 208) '(material) provision' originally, then 'administrative (and perhaps also economic) responsibility of one institution for another'. The classifier of the superordinate [ABSTRACT] category is in a complex relation with the lexeme (the medium for the writing; a legal right is an abstract notion usually translated in a document and involving lists and counts).

sḫr – classifier: (plan, premeditation). See above, *Nauri decree*, lines 35 and 85.

mty bin – classifier: and (evil witness/advice). See Schott (1961: 156). The witness/advising procedures are characterized by verbal statements ([MOUTH LINKED ACTIVITIES] category classifier – taxonomic relation with the lexeme) and their negative nature is represented by the [INFERIORITY-PERTURBATION] category classifier.

* Legal formula: *ḫr ỉr* + offender *nb* + *nty* + *sw r sḏm* (the crime) + *r* (purpose) + *m* (qualification of the crime).

6. Operative part: curse as penalty (part 2)

(15) (…) *ỉw.f n nsrt tkꜣ.s ḥꜥw.f n ꜣḫt* (16) *wnmw.s ꜥwt.f ḥr-nty ỉr.n ḥm.f nn r-ḏr.sn n kꜣ.sn nꜣ nbw ḥwt.ỉ bw n nṯr th rmṯ.f bw tm.n.f ꜥn ḏrt ḥḏ*

(15) (…) he belongs to a flame, may it burn his body, to a fire (16), may it devour his limbs, because it is for the(ir) *kꜣ* of the lords of my house that his Majesty has done all this. An abomination to (the) divine is the fact of (or one) leading astray his people; he never fails to avert a disobeying hand[30].

* Neo-Egyptian characteristics:

- *nꜣ nbw ḥwt.ỉ:* cataphoric use of the determinator. As in line 12 (*ḥꜥw.sn tmw sḏm*), note in *kꜣ.sn nꜣ nbw ḥwt.ỉ* the expression of possession (suffixed *.sn*) with an expanded noun for cataphoric reference, instead a cataphoric articloid.

30 For Davies (1997: 217) 'He does not turn his hand from the destroyer' (?); Groll (1987: 157) translates 'It does not happen that he cannot repel the destroying hand'.

- *bw tm.n.f ꜥn:* negative aorist, degree 2 of Neo-Egyptian; see Davis (1973: 86); Frandsen (1974: 31-38); Satzinger (1976: 180); Winand (1992: 236-238); Junge (1996: 104-105). The negative aorist has taken the forms *n sḏm.n.f* (Middle Egyptian) – *bw sḏm.n.f* (Neo-Egyptian degree 2) – *bw sḏm.f* (Neo-Egyptian degree 2) – *bw iri.f sḏm* (Neo-Egyptian degree 3). The 'double negative' litote (*EG* § 346.3) # *bw/n* (preverbal nuclear negator) + *tm.n.f* (verb of negative semantics) + negated lexeme # appears in *Urk.* IV, 519 with same lexeme constituency (*n tm.n.f ꜥnw*). For Groll (1987: 157, 166), *bw tm.n.f sḏm* + object expresses inability in an independent clause and is equivalent to a nominal theme (*iw tm.f*) + adverbial rheme in the simple present tense. Note also the prosodic value in legal and religious contexts of the possible alliteration of ***bw** n nṯr th rmṯ.f **bw** tm.n.f ꜥn ḏrt ḥḏ*. As in line 13 (with the same lexeme *ḥḏ* used for the offender but in another type of construction), it is the inevitability of the punishment that is emphasized here.

* 'Classical' degree 0 forms used:
  - *iw.f n nsrt:* adverbial nexus composed of # deictic thematic exponent *iw* + suffixed possessed theme + *n* (*EG* § 114.1) + nominal possessor #. Common in curses and testaments (see Satzinger (1976: 198-199); Nordh (1996: 82)), and already during the First Intermediate Period (Morschauser 1991: 31), this possession formula is translated by Satzinger as 'er soll der Flamme gehören damit sein Leib verbrenne, und der Lohe, damit sie seine Glieder verzehre', an 'Adverbialsatz des Furturums'. But we believe that it is a generic, atemporal construction, with performative value, as proposed for the curse *ir Wsir m-sꜣ.f* of the *Nauri decree*, line 113; see Assmann (1992: 159) about the distinction between prescriptive (legal dispositions) and performative sentences (curses); Moschauser (1991: 31) '*iw.f* + *n* noun (…) seems to have expressed a more concrete result of "actually" being under punishment' than a future *iw.f r* + noun. As for the use of a curse in the case of the kings' exercise of their sovereign right of decision (previous crime), a curse may only be applied against a counselor who executes his mandate in following the interests of his master rather than *Stḫy*'s. On motives for curses, see Grimal (1986: 647) 'les « sanctions sacrées » du décret de Nauri, comme celles de Kanaïs, complètent les peines civiles en infligeant des variantes de ce châtiment', to be understood as a 'vengeance divine', 'l'expression de la solidarité face à l'équilibre, une transposition transcendante du talion'; Moschauser (1991: 182, 187); Assmann (1992: 155) who attributes the increased use of curses to 'a profound transformation of Egyptian beliefs concerning divine intervention in human life'; Nordh (1996: 98-99). On death by fire, see Leahy (1984: 199-206).
  - *tkꜣ.s/wnmw.s:* independent prospective forms with feminine pronominal actor and optative imprecatory value.
  - *ḥr-nty ir.n ḥm.f:* instead of the more classical *ḥr-ntt* (*NÄG* § 680, Anm.), the prepositional-relative converter is followed by a nominal abstract that-form *sḏm.n.*N (observe the verbal constituency). See Polotsky (1944: 82) 'Il semble

qu'une phrase (apparemment) verbale n'est introduite par la conjonction *ntt* (...) que lorsqu'il y a insistance sur un complement adverbial. Il s'agit donc des phrases coupées, et la forme verbale doit être "emphatique", bien que des exemples avec des verbes faibles nous fassent défaut'. The curse is motivated.

- *ḥm.f:* the king uses for himself the delocutive suffix in the middle of his locutive monologue (see *ḥwt.i*), in our opinion in a way similar to a 'pluriel de majesté' ('Nous, Anne, par la grace de Dieu royne de France et de Navarre'; or 'Elizabeth R. (...) We appointed X (...) By Her Majesty's Command' quoted by Crystal & Davy (1969: 216) from a 1966 royal English warrant) that uses the locutive plural instead of singular, or the delocutive singular instead of the second person polite form to address the king ('Sa Majesté daignera-t-Elle...' instead of 'Votre Majesté'). This sudden change of person (*enallage*) is not uncommon in Neo-Egyptian texts (Schott 1961: 156 for other examples), and it may be too easily dismissed as an error by many authors as Gunn & Gardiner (1917: 248, n. 3); Schott (1961: 160); Lichtheim (1976: 57, n. 17). The use of the delocutive suffix with the prominent lexeme *ḥm* reinforces distance, bringing the king to a superior level of untouchability. Note that in the case of *The Tale of Two Brothers* 19,4, Peust (1996: 50 n. 184 and p. 51) proposes to see *ḏd imi ini.tw n.i nꜣy.i srw ꜥꜣyw n* ***ḥm.f*** as a 'Hinweis auf indirekte Rede'.
- *nn r-ḏr.sn:* see *NÄG* § 117 and his example with Neo-Egyptian delocutive plural suffix from *pAnastasi* IV 3, 2 (*nn r-ḏrw.w*); *EG* § 100.I for a more 'Middle Egyptian' formula from *Siut* I, 269 (*nn n ḫt r ḏr*) with the relator after the anaphoric proximal *nn*.
- *bw n nṯr th rmṯ.f:* nominal nexus # *bw n*.N (rheme) + N expanded in loose composition (theme) # expressing an aphorism. Gunn & Gardiner (1917: 248), Schott (1961: 156), Kitchen (*RITA* I, 59) and Davies (1997: 217) translate the sentence as if it was an aorist ('God abominates'), but *bw sḏm.n*.N does not have this value. Only Breasted (*ARE* III, § 192) translates the sentence as a nominal nexus 'An abomination of the god is the transgression against his people.' This type of nominal nexus is quite common, see the pattern # *bwt.f* + N # in the examples brought by Groll (1967: 23-24, n. 72, 74, 75) from *Amenemope*, *pAnastasi* I and *pTurin* 1882. For Groll (p. 28), it is the definition of one of the nouns 'that determines which of the members is the subject and which the predicate'. But in our case, the two nouns being expanded, and the theme being the offender who commits the crime (the topic of the disposition), the rhematic qualification of the crime is *bw n nṯr*.

* General dialectal features: degree 2.

* Legal terms: *thi rmṯ* – classifier: (to lead people astray). Used without preposition. See Parant (1982: 155) 'dévoyer'. For the classifiers, see *thi r*.

* Curse formula: *iw.f n* + noun + *sḏm.f* (curse penalty) + *ḥr-nty ir.n ḥm.f* (motivation) + *bw n*.N (aphorism) + *bw tm.n.f sḏm* (inevitable character of the penalty).

7. Preamble *sensu stricto* (positive intent)

(16) (...) *wpw-ḥr wnn p3 ḳ3wrw* (17) *n iʿw nbw ir.n.i r t3 ḥwt Mnm3ʿtrʿ ḫw mkw nn ḫʿmtw n.f in rmṯ nb nty m t3 r-ḏr.f in ḥry pḏt nb n p3 nbw in rwḏ nb n ḫ3st* (16) (...) In contrast, it is retained (and) preserved that will be the mine-water transporters (17) for gold washing that I have established for the temple of *Mnm3ʿtrʿ* without him being approached/threatened[31] by anybody who is in (the) entire land, by any troop commander of this gold[32], (or) by any agent of the high land.

* Neo-Egyptian characteristics:
- *p3 ḳ3wrw:* cataphoric use of the determinator.
- *t3 ḥwt Mnm3ʿtrʿ:* anaphoric and cataphoric determinator (*ḥwt* is expanded by a proper noun with appurtenance relation to it).
- *p3 nbw:* anaphoric determinator (see *iʿw nbw*) used in an adnominal expansion (*nota relationis*) of *ḥry pḏt nb.*
- *ḫʿmtw:* Neo-Egyptian spelling of the infinitive.

* 'Classical' degree 0 forms used:
- *wpw-ḥr wnn*.N *ḫw mkw:* # contrast proclitic particle + adverbial nexus composed of [*sḏm*.N nominal that-form + adverbial binomial focus] #. See above, *Nauri decree* lines 40-41, although in the *Kanais decree* there is no *iw*.N *ḥr sḏm* circumstantial nexus following *wpw-ḥr wnn*.N *ḫw mkw* (the reason that we saw the focus upon the statives in the *Nauri decree*). The contrastive function of this construction opposes the king's safeguarded staff to the previously addressed potential transgressor, the divine imprecatory penalties to the royal protection (it is not a question of specification of the curse, as *RITA* I, 59 suggests it by 'Specifically:', the royal protection being already extended to his staff by the decree, and it is not a measure that should be taken in the event of a crime). For Schott (1961: 175), the articles introduced by *wpw-ḥr* are not punished by criminal penalties because 'in der Wüste, abseits der Gerichtshöfe im Lande, der Hinweis auf rächende Götter wirksamer scheint als eine Drohung mit verhängten Strafen wie etwa im Nauridekret'. Only a comparison of the inner structure of the protection/criminal decrees permits an understanding of the exact function of this texteme: to establish the protected status of the temples personnel by contrast with the crimes the decree tends to prevent (it is the function of the preamble *sensu stricto).*
- *ir.n.i: sḏm.n.f* relative synthetic form (anteriority) with locutive actor (note again the verbal constituency). It expands the adverbial nexus theme.
- *nn ḫʿmtw n.f* (...) *in rmṯ nb* (...)*:* # negator of existence + infinitive of a motion verb + *n* (prepositional object) + *in* (agent or instrumental actor) #. Winand's

31 Spiegelberg (1907: 56) 'angetastet (?).'

32 See Vercoutter (1959: 147-148) 'military official (...) responsible for the supervision of the gold work'.

view (1992: 337, ex. 826) of an 'active' prospective with impersonal actor is problematic due to the presence of the instrumental actor. Obviously, the traditional approach to this issue (transitive/intransitive – direct/indirect object) is not appropriate (see Shisha-Halevy (1986: 106-109) for Coptic), one of its ground rules being that an intransitive verb cannot have a passive diathesis. Following *Wb* III, 364, *ẖꜥm* or *ḫꜥm* covers homonyms with diverse rectional expansions: the bivalent 'to approach' + immediate object expansion (a person), which is a 'transitive' motion verb, and several lexemes expanded by different prepositions that change their overall meaning: 'to threaten' (+ *n*), 'Böses trifft jem.' (+ *r*), or even 'to plumb the depths of' (+ *m*). In our case, *ḫꜥm* has a lesser motion quality (metaphorical 'to march against'), is constructed with a prepositional object and has a passive diathesis. The construction consists, therefore, of a circumstantial non-existence (Gilula 1970: 210, note 4, and 212) equivalent to the *Nauri decree ỉw nn rdỉt* (line 41), to be compared with *ỉw bn sḏm* (lines 60-61), but in *Kanais decree* without circumstantial *ỉw* (an anterior stage of development of the circumstantial phrase negation for Gilula (1970; 210, note 4)).

- # *ỉn* + *rmṯ nb* + *nty m tꜣ r-ḏr.f* + [singular hyponyms + *nb* + *nota relationis]* #: list beginning atypically with the most general, all-encompassing expression, followed by the more precisely circumscribed hyponym and closed by an hyponym covering a larger semantic field, each one with the same preposition (isotopy). It is the first administrative hierarchy list that does not follow a strict diminishing progression in our corpus (see *supra*, concerning lines 29-30 of the *Nauri decree*). Note also that as in the *Nauri decree*, *pꜣ* never determines *tꜣ* in the syntagm *nty m tꜣ r-ḏr.f*.

* General dialectal features: degree 1.
* Legal terms: *ḫw mkw* – classifier: (to retain (and) preserve).
* Legal formula: contrast proclitic particle *wpw-ḥr* + *wnn*.N (protected group) + *ḫw-mkw* (protection) + *nn sḏm ỉn* N (specific criminal behaviour)

8. Operative part: the crimes (part 3 – requisition of staff)

(17) (…) *ỉr pꜣ nty nb ỉw.f r thỉ rmṯ ỉm.sn* (18) *dỉdỉ r kt st*
(17) (…) As for anyone who will lead astray people among them (18), reduced to another position[33]

* Neo-Egyptian characteristics:

- # *ỉr pꜣ nty nb* + *ỉw.f r th* #: topicalized relative future. The colon-enclitic placement of the quantifier *nb* (singular resumption of *pꜣ nty nb* in *ỉw.f;* the

33 Compare with line 15 *r dỉtw.w ḥr ky sdf*, where *sdf* is used instead of *st*.

pronominal delocutive actant is coreferent to *pꜣ*) points to the open juncture of the relative syntagm and the substantivation of the relative clause (see *Nauri decree*, line 66 without *pꜣ* determinator and *ỉw.f*). Note the absence of the infinitive feminine mark. An interesting parallel may be drawn with the *Bilgai stela*, line 6: [*ỉṯꜣ r*]*mṯ ỉm.st r dỉtw.f r ky hꜣw*.

- *didi:* geminating form, adnominal imperfect passive participle referring to undetermined *rmṯ*, or rhematic stative (see above *diw* and *didiw*). See also Winand's table (1992: 370) of passive participles, where he does not note this form for the 19th dynasty, but refers to it as a stative in the table on page 149.

* 'Classical' degree 0 forms used: -

* General dialectal features: degree 2.

* Legal terms: *thi rmṯ* – classifier:  (to lead people astray).
rdi r – classifier: ø (to reduce to).

* Legal formula: *ỉr pꜣ nty nb* (offender) + *ỉw.f r sḏm* (crime) + *rmṯ* (victim) + *didi r* (method)

9. Operative part: the curse penalty (part 3)

(18) (…) *ỉr n.f nꜣ nṯrw nṯrywt nbw ḥwt.i r ỉry n ꜥḥꜣ pꜣ-wn ẖt.i nb m ỉmy-pr ẖr rdwy.sn r nḥḥ ḥnꜥ ḏt* (18) (…) may those gods (and) goddesses, Lords of my house, act for him as adversary, because all my material property is a disposition act under their feet, forever and ever (= in their everlasting use).

* Neo-Egyptian characteristics:

- *nꜣ nṯrw nṯrywt:* anaphoric (see line 16) use of the articloid. Note the masculine apposition *nbw,* referring to masculine and feminine divine entities. *nṯrw nṯrywt* is a binomial expression.
- *pꜣ-wn ẖt.i nb m ỉmy-pr:* 19th dynasty (with rare occurrences during the 20th dynasty) 'particle' (Goldwasser 1985: 51 and 2001: 124; Junge 1996: 91) or 'conjonction' (Hintze 1952: 301-302, after optative 'explicative'; Winand 1995: 197 and n. 35) + adverbial nexus (N *m* N). For Théodoridès (1972: 192, n. 6), the verb *wn* is missing for haplographic reasons; but *pꜣ-wn* may precede an adverbial nexus without the intervention of *wn* (see example 513 in *LEG* § 11.1, *oDelM* 251, 2-3). Again, the motivation follows the curse, as in lines 15-16.
- *r nḥḥ ḥnꜥ ḏt:* binomial expression; following the *Wb* II, 301 n.17, the presence of the preposition *r* is noted in this formula since the 18th dynasty; on the other hand, the connector *ḥnꜥ* is already used during the Middle Kingdom (see *Hammamat* 110, 9 & 191, 10).

* 'Classical' degree 0 forms used: *ỉr*.N*:* independent prospective with nominal actors (imprecatory optative value).

* General dialectal features: degree 1.

* Legal terms:

iry n ꜥḥꜣ – classifier: *iry* classified with for Schott (1961) and *KRI* I, 69 *in fine* but for Gardiner 1930: 224) for the *nisbe*, and *ꜥḥꜣ* with (legal opponent, litigant). See Piehl (1891: 49-52) 'compagnon de querelle', 'adversaire'; Morschauser (1991: 70-71) 'The use of the term in threats is confined to the Ramesside Period, and is applied to divine, rather than human parties.' The 'strong arm' implies the use of constraint (superordinate [COERCION] category); the quality of the-one-in-relation-with the fight is expressed here by a seated male figure with a long garment holding a flagellum or the shepherd stick (*EG*'s list A47), which appears 'Sometimes inaccurately for A48 in *iry* 'relating to'' (*EG*, 447). The *nisbe* is used in several locutions related to the function of guardian, keeper, responsible for (as in *iry-iḫt, iry-ꜥt, iry-ꜥꜣ, iry-pḏt, iry-mḫꜣt, iry-nfr-ḥꜣt, iry-rdwy, iry-hp, iry-ḥꜣt, iry-ḥmw, iry-ḫt, iry-sꜣ, iry-sšm*) which could explain the presence of the knife or stick in the hand of the seated man (basic level [GUARDING] category). Moreover, the papyrus roll refers to the [ABSTRACT] category suiting the written legal procedure and abstract quality.

ḫt – classifier: (material property).

imy-pr ḫr rdwy.sn r nḥḥ ḥnꜥ ḏt – classifier: (*sub modo* disposition act[34] for everlasting use, literally 'what is in the house under their feet for ever and ever'). See Lacau (1949: 7-9) 'transfert écrit de propriété'; Théodoridès (1971: 298) 'certified deed of conveyance', (1972: 188-192) 'expression prise au figuré' ; 'la préposition *ḫr* sert donc à caractériser un droit de propriété incomplet, démembré par des clauses restrictives', and (1993: 105, note 52); Grimal (1986: 640) 'état descriptif de la propriété (…) qui rend possible son transfert'; Grandet (1994 II: 31 (131)) and his references. The presence of the [BINDING] category classifier probably implies that the legal title is registered and archived (schematic relation between the classifier and the lexeme).

* Legal formula: imprecatory *sḏm*.N + *pꜣ-wn* N *m* N (motive).

10. Second preamble *sensu stricto* (positive intent)

(18) (…) *wpw-ḥr wnn pꜣ ḥry pḏt n pꜣ kꜣwrw n iꜥw nbw n tꜣ ḥwt* (19) *Mnmꜣꜥtrꜥ ḥr ḏrt.f ḥr ḫrp bꜣkw.sn m nbw r tꜣ ḥwt Mnmꜣꜥtrꜥ*

(18) (…) In contrast, it is by his hand(ling) that will be (= proceed) the troop/bowmen commandant of the mine-water transporters for gold-washers of the temple (19) of *Mnmꜣꜥtrꜥ* when providing their product of gold to the temple of *Mnmꜣꜥtrꜥ*.

34 Transfer of property 'Under some restriction, modification or qualification' (Curzon 1988: 421).

* Neo-Egyptian characteristics:
    - *p3 ḥry pḏt:* cataphoric use of the determinator.
    - *p3 ḳ3wrw:* anaphoric and cataphoric uses of the determinator.
    - *t3 ḥwt*
* 'Classical' degree 0 forms used:
    - *wpw-ḥr wnn*.N... *ḥr ḏrt.f ḥr ẖrp:* # contrast proclitic particle + adverbial nexus composed of [*sḏm*.N nominal geminated that-form + adverbial focus] #. Up to now, the construction has appeared in our corpus with a stative binomial focus (*ẖwy mky*). The focus may lie on *ḥr ḏrt.f* or *ḥr ẖrp;* for Schott (1961: 158) *wnn ḥr ḏr.t.f* means '"selbständig sein" WB V 583[19]', and he translates the sentence 'Es soll der Oberst der Transporttruppe (...) selbständig sein und ihre Lieferungen an Gold zum 'Haus des Men-Maat-Rê' leiten.'). In this case *ḥr ẖrp* is an adverbial adjunct.
* General dialectal features: degree 1.
* Legal terms:
    ḥr ḏrt.f – classifier: ø (by his (proper, free, own) hand(ling); independently). See *pHarris* I 59, 11 (*diw.i ḥmw-nṯr rwḏw n pr.f ḥr ḏrt.w*); Gunn & Gardiner (1917: 248, n. 4); Kruchten (1979b: 43-45) 'par sa (propre main) (...) valeur instrumentale'. Compare with *m ḏrt* (under the responsibility of) in Haring (1997: 286-287 & 337).
    b3kw – classifier: (work yield/product).
* Legal formula: proclitic contrast particle *wpw-ḥr* + *wnn*.N *ḥr ḏrt.f* (independent official) + *ḥr* + infinitive (circumstances).

11. Operative part: the crime (part 4 –non compliance with the decree)

(19) (...) *ir p3 nty nb iw.f r sẖ-ḥr r wḏ(t)*[35] *tn*

(19) (...) As for anyone who will be deaf to this decree,

* Neo-Egyptian characteristics: # *ir p3 nty nb* + *iw.f r sẖ-ḥr* #. Note that *sẖ-ḥr* is treated as an infinitive.
* 'Classical' degree 0 forms used:
    - *sẖ-ḥr:* see *Nauri decree*, line 116. Note that the *Kanais decree* disposition has a much wider scope than the corresponding *Nauri decree* definition of the crime.
    - *wḏ(t) tn:* proximal classical demonstrative (anaphoric to the text itself). See Schott (1961: 158) ' "dieser Befehl" schließt an die letzte Bestimmung der Stiftung (Abschnitt 29) an, bezieht sich aber auch auf den vorangehenden, gleichfalls juristisch formulierten Paragraphen über die Truppe der Goldwäsher (Abschnitt 27)'.

35 Probable haplography.

* General dialectal features: degree 2.

* Legal terms:

sḫ-ḥr – classifier: (to be deaf to, refuse to comply with, ignore). See *ARE* III, 80 'disregard ("*avert the face from*")'; Morschauser (1991: 60).

wḏ(t) – classifier: [?] (decree).

* Legal formula: *ỉr p3 nty nb* (offender) + *ỉw.f r sḫ-ḥr* (crime).

12. Operative part: the penalty (part 4)

(19) (...) *ỉr Wsir m-s3.f ỉw 3st m-s3 ḥmt.f ỉw Ḥr m-s3 ẖrdw.f m (=in) n3 wrw*[36] *nbw t3 ḏsr ỉr.s[n] wpw.sn ḥnꜥ.f*

(19) (...) Osiris is after him, while Isis is after his wife, while Horus is after his children. It is those Great Ones, Lords of (the) necropolis, wh[o] will execute their verdict against him.

* Neo-Egyptian characteristics:

- *ỉr*.PN *m-s3.f:* see *Nauri decree*, line 113), but here followed by classical degree 0 *ỉw*.PN *m-s3*.N with other gods dealing with the offender's wife and children. From the examples offered by Gardiner (1930: 224-225), only in two cases more than one god is charged with the persecution: in our text and in the *Anîbeh inscription* (but only the *Kanais decree* exhibits the alternation *ỉr*/*ỉw*). As for the inscription in the Anîbeh (Memphis) tomb of *Pnnwt* (20th dynasty), we may have two independent syntagms and one circumstantial: *ỉr Ỉmn Rꜥ ni-swt nṯrw m-s3 r s3{s3?}.f ỉr Mwt m-s3 ḥmt.f Ḫnsw m-s3 ẖrdw.f*
- *n3 wrw:* anaphoric/cataphoric uses of the determinator.
- *m (=in)* + proper noun + *ỉr.s[n] wpw.sn ḥnꜥ.f:* nominal focus initial cleft-sentence (participial statement), see Gunn (1924: 57, n. 99), composed of # focus marker + determined proper noun (focus) + relative thematic and analytic prospective #. For Winand (1992: 267), *ỉr.s[n]* is an 'emphatic' prospective form; in fact, *ỉr.sn wpw.sn* is a prospective that-form, be it a nominalization of the verb *wpi* with *ỉri* prospective that-form, or an analytic prospective Neo-Egyptian form of *wpi*. Comparing the use of the participial statement in line 14 *m (=in) psḏt sḫn.sn ḥnꜥ.f,* we may see that once again the focus (and contrast with the preceding sentence) is on the actors; if the divine Triad pronounces the verdict, the executants are the gods of necropolis gods. The use of the preposition *ḥnꜥ* is Neo-Egyptian (*Wb* I, 299). For Schott (1961: 159) 'vulgär für gewählt - im Schlußwort an Künftige Könige - *sḫn.sn ḥnꜥ.f* oben', but the two expressions are perhaps not precise synonyms (see above, line 14).

36 *srw* for Morschauser (1991: 188).

* 'Classical' degree 0 forms used: *ỉw*.N *m-sꜣ*.N: adverbial circumstantial nexuses, performative. See Satzinger (1976: 200, 278); Morschauser (1991: 24, 35). Prosodic isotopy suits imprecatory texts extremely well.
* General dialectal features: degree 2.
* Curse/legal terms:
  ỉr wpw ḥnʿ – classifier: × (to execute a verdict against, to exert a judgment against). See McDowell (1990: 39) underlining the nuance of hostility of *ḥnʿ* with verbs of litigation (with examples from Deir el-Medineh); *Nauri decree* lines 116-117 (without *ḥnʿ*); *pOrbiney* 19, 5 (with × and  classifiers).
  ỉr/ỉw m-sꜣ – classifier: ø (to be after, pursue, of a god). See Morschauser (1991: 79) 'divine pursuit'.
* Curse formula: *ỉr/ỉw* + god proper name + *m-sꜣ.f* (religious curse = verdict); *m* (=*in*) + gods + *ỉr.s*[*n*] *wpw.sn* (execution of the verdict) + *ḥnʿ* (victim).

IV. *Armant decree*

Rꜥmss II's *Armant decree* (*KRI* II, 712 n. 261 D; previously Mond & Myers 1940: pl. CII, 7) belongs to the pylon's North face of the Armant Temple. Very few lines remain of what is certainly a long text that resembles the *Nauri* and *Hermopolis decrees*. Despite its lacunary state, it provides a further insight in the linguistic structure royal decrees represent.

1. Part of an enacting clause?

(1) [...] *r nꜣ n.sn wpwt* *m-mitt* [*iṯꜣ.tw nb?*][37] *m-di.sn* (1) [...] from their missions. Likewise [everything will be seized?] from them.

Too fragmentary to be usefully analyzed.

2. Preamble *sensu stricto* (positive intent)

(1) (...) *wpt-ḥr wnn rmṯ* (2) [*n ḥwt... ḫw mkw? pꜣ iry sꜣw*] *m iry sꜣw pꜣ wpwty m wpty* (3) *pꜣ bity m bity pꜣ wḥꜥ* [*m wḥꜥ... m sꜣ n sꜣ smn ḥr ḥn.f*[38] *ḥr?*] *m*[*t*]*n*[39] *r nḥḥ ḥnꜥ ḏt* (1) (...) In contrast, it is [retained (and) preserved?] that people [of the temple of...?] will (2) be, [the gatekeeper] as a gatekeeper, the messenger as a messenger (3), the beekeeper as a beekeeper, the fisherman [as a fisherman... from son to son, confirmed in his service by?] a documen[t] forever and ever.

* Neo-Egyptian characteristics:

- [*pꜣ iry sꜣw*]/*pꜣ wpwty*/*pꜣ bity*/*pꜣ wḥꜥ*: because the previous part is missing, it is not easy to evaluate the determinator in this series of homo-structured syntagms. It is tempting to see in these binary units the # [articloid (non-phoric) + definite but non-specific noun of profession-member] + ['assimilation' preposition ('*m* of predication') + ø same noun (indefinite function name, professional status)] # construction, each member of a profession being retained-preserved as such, so as to exclude his transfer to another service where he would not practise his

---

37 See the *Elephantine decree*, line 10, but Mond & Myers (1940: 161) restore '[their occupations shall not be taken?] from them'.

38 As in the *Nauri decree*, line 27.

39 *RITA* II, 469: 'way'. The lexeme proposed here is also found in the *Nauri decree*, line 76, although in another context and despite the fact that the spelling is atypical.

profession anymore. Of course, the determinator may also be deictic, referring to an exemplary member of the profession. The non-phoric use of the *pꜣ, tꜣ, nꜣ* determinator was actually the final clear step towards the notion of 'article' (which may only qualify its systematic use; see Kroeber 1970: 3, 24). In our register, the 'grammaticalization' of the article was not attained during the Ramesside Period.

- *r nḥḥ ḥnꜥ ḏt:* see *supra*, probably in relation with an everlasting protection granted to the staff.

* 'Classical' degree 0 forms used:

- *wpt-ḥr wnn rmṯ...[ḫw mkw]:* restitutions from Mond & Myers (1940: 161) 'but the people shall [remain in their own posts?]' and from Kitchen (*RITA* II, 469) 'but men of [.......] shall (remain) [men of (...)]' do not take into account similar sentences in *Nauri* (lines 40-41) and *Kanais* (lines 16-17) *decrees*, pertaining also to the preamble *sensu stricto* where *wpt-ḥr wnn*.N is followed by the binomial stative *ḫwy mky*. Of course, in a third instance (lines 18-19 of the *Kanais decree*), the focus is not of the type *ḫwy mky* but *ḥr ḏrt.f*.

* General dialectal features: degree 1.

* Legal terms: ?

* Legal formula: contrast proclitic particle *wpt-ḥr* + *wnn*.N (protected group) [+ *ḫw-mkw?* (protection)].

3. Operative part: the crime (part 1 - ?)

(4) *i͗r pꜣ nty i͗r pꜣ [ḥm-n]ṯr r[.f nty i͗w.f r nis ḫt nb?] ḥr ḥm-nṯr nb n nṯr nb n nṯrywt nb* (5) *mtw.f di͗t ḥny sš sꜣwy (n?) i͗my- r gs [-pr?...] n nṯrywt nb myn[t]* (6) *ḥr ꜣḥt n nꜣ i͗tw nṯrw*

(4) As for the one against [whom?] this [proph]et will act [who will request any material property] from any prophet of any god (or) of any goddesses (5) and cause a scribe of his to go (to?) an Adm[inistration?] overseer [...] of any goddesses of (the) estat[e] (6) upon (the) land of those fathers of gods,

* Neo-Egyptian characteristics:

- *i͗r pꜣ nty i͗r*.N *r[.f]*: # topic marker + *pꜣ* substantivizer + relative expansion with prospective *sḏm*.N + *r.f* (coreferent to *pꜣ*) #. In Old Kingdom decrees, a (future) participle would have been used; we have seen in preceding decrees the relative future instead of this participle; but here we observe a prospective form after the relative adjective without any modal value. Compare the *Elephantine decree*, lines 9 and 11, on the basis of which we propose the restoration. Note that as in Old Egyptian, a relative sentence with *sḏm.f* nexus is rare in Middle Egyptian; see *EG* § 201, where Gardiner does not offer any example of future relative tense; Polotsky (1944: 173, note 2).

- *ir*.N… *mtw.f dit:* the prospective is followed by a full-fledged conjunctive, again in the context of the exposition of the crime.
- *s3wy:* Neo-Egyptian *sw* (*Wb* IV, 13.16 'ihm gehörig'/'gehört').
- *imy- r:* our reconstruction. See *Wb* II, 94 (18th dynasty spelling).
- *myn*[*t*]*:* Neo-Egyptian (*Wb* II, 43), see Helck (1958: 129 & 133).
- *n3 it nṯrw:* anaphoric use of the articloid?

* 'Classical' degree 0 forms used:
- *ḥm-nṯr nb n nṯr nb n nṯrywt nb:* note that *nb* is not gender/number marked, and that, although distributive, it may follow both a singular (*nṯr*) and plural/ abstract notion name (*nṯrywt*).
- *ḥny sš:* dependent prospective object of *dit.*

* General dialectal features: degree 2.

* Legal terms: -

* Legal formula: *ir p3 nty sḏm*.N… *mtw.f sḏm* (crime).

3. Operative part: the penalty (part 1)

(6) (…) *ir.tw* [*hpw r.f m sḫr.f diw ḥr tp ḫt r-gs t3 ḥwt-nṯr nty*] (7) *iw.f r iṯ3 ḫt nb*[40] *rmṯ nb* [*im.s*...] (8) *ḥn ḫt.sn m t3 r ? nb* [...]
(6) (…) [(the) rule] will have to be enforced [against him by throwing him down placed on (the) tip of a staff beside the temple of which] (7) he will seize any material property (or) any people […] (8) allocating their material property from a land to any ? […]

* Neo-Egyptian characteristics:
- *iw.f r iṯ3:* (probably relative) future. Consistent with the penalty formula of the other decrees, especially with *Hermopolis decree* line 2 (although neither Mond & Myers (1940: 161), nor Kitchen (*RITA* II, 469) recognize it as such).

* 'Classical' degree 0 forms used: -

* General dialectal features: degree 2.

* Legal terms: *ir r* - classifier: ø (to enforce)
iṯ3 - classifier: 𓂡 (to seize).
ḫt - classifier: 𓏴 (material property).
ḥn - classifier: ø (to allocate personnel/property).

* Legal formula: *ir.tw* [*hpw r.f m*] (type of penalty)

40 Absence of concord (see *Nauri decree*).

V. *Karnak decree*

Sṯḥy II's Karnak stela fragmentary decree (Helck (1956: 82-86), (1958b: 145-146) and (1963b: 37-38); *KRI* IV, 263-266 n.18) consists of perhaps six blocks found in the 'cachette' court between the main axis constructions of the Amun temple and its seventh pylon (the first amongst the fallen blocks of the court's West wall, the others in the South-West, outside the court). Under a scene presenting a series of divine protectors of the king, the date, the royal titulary (pre-material) are followed by the eulogy; what is left of the decree has been completed by Helck and Kitchen[41]. Helck's restorations convinced him and Kruchten (1981:159 & 220) that the purpose of this decree was to forbid the selling of priestly functions (or bribing in this context); in this case, we do not have a text protecting temple resources against administrative requisitions as in the *Nauri decree*. The last line seems to belong to an epilogue (the line numbering adopted here follows *KRI* IV, 263-266).

1. Enacting clause (authority, object, beneficiary?)

(15) [... *iw wḏ.n ḥm.f*] *rdit ḥnt.tw tꜣ* (16) *fꜣyw n Ỉmn M*[*w*]*t* [*Ḫnsw m Wꜣst Nfrḥtp nṯrw nṯ*]*rywt nbw* [*šmꜥw mḥw itw-nṯr*] *wꜥbw ẖryw-ḥbt*

(15) [... His Majesty has decreed] to cause that be allocated the (16) porters of/to Amun, M[u]t, [Khons-in-Thebae-*Nfrḥtp,* gods (and) godde]sses, lords of [Upper (and) Lower Egypt, (and also?) god's fathers,] *wꜥb* priests (and) lectors;

* Neo-Egyptian characteristics:

- *ḥnt.tw:* dependent prospective object of *rdit* (*sḏm.f* impersonal or *sḏm.tw*.N passive), with unusual spelling (see spelling variations of this lexeme used in the same texteme of the *Nauri decree*, lines 30 and 83, *ḥn.tw*, and line 55 *ḥny.tw*).
- *tꜣ fꜣyw:* see *Wb* I, 574, n. 13 'belegt Nä., mit Artikel *tꜣ*.' As for the value of the determinator, it depends on the way we understand *n Ỉmn M*[*w*]*t* [*Ḫnsw m Wꜣst Nfrḥtp nṯrw nṯ*]*rywt nbw* [*šmꜥw mḥw*]: if it represents an adnominal expansion (*nota relationis*) of *fꜣyw*, the determinator is used cataphorically (but then the beneficiary temple (* *n tꜣ ḥwt*) or institution remains unknown to us, it does not indicate where the priesthood is posted, as in *Nauri's decree*, lines 25-26, 30, 97-98); on the other hand, if it represents the beneficiaries of the allocation, the determinator must have either an anaphoric (to a previous missing part of the decree) or an exophoric value. For *LÄ* VI: 383-384, n. 8 and Kruchten (1981: 220), this decree may be an exception to the limited applicability of temple decrees to a specific institution due to the formulation 'all gods of Upper and

41 See also Gaballa & Kitchen (1968: 270).

Lower Egypt'; the basis for such an argument is meager due to the fragmentary state of the decree.

* 'Classical' degree 0 forms used: [*iw wḏ.n ḥm.f*] *rdit*
* General dialectal features: degree 1.
* Legal terms: *ḥn* - classifier: ø (to allocate/attach personnel/property to a service).
* Legal formula: [*iw wḏ.n ḥm.f*] (source of the decree) + *rdit* (executive power implementing the royal order) + *ḥnt.tw* N (the measure) + the beneficiary?

2. Preamble *sensu stricto* (negative intent)

(16) (...) *r tm di wḫ3.tw* [*n*]*kt m-di.sn*[42] *in ḥm-nṯr*[43] *nb ḫpr m r*[*k ḥm.f*]

(16) (...) to prevent that [val]uables be requested from them by any prophet existing in (the) tim[e of his Majesty];

* Neo-Egyptian characteristics: *m-di.sn*
* 'Classical' degree 0 forms used:
    - *r tm di:* preposition + infinitive (purpose) + the 'classical' Egyptian *di* that is called a 'negatival complement' by Gardiner (*EG* § 341 & 348) who considers it adverbial, although it is nominal (Gilula 1970: 212); it is replaced by the infinitive *rdit* in the *Nauri* and *Elephantine decrees* (except for one instance in the last, line 8).
    - *wḫ3.tw* [*n*]*kt:* dependent prospective *sḏm.tw*.N, object of di.
* General dialectal features: degree 1.
* Legal terms:

    r tm di – classifier: ø (to prevent).

    [*n*]*kt* – classifier: [×] (share, valuables). For the expression *wḫ3 nkt*, see *Ḥrmḥb*'s *Karnak decree*, line 28, translated by Kruchten (1981: 102) as 'to perceive a contribution' (here in exchange of a priestly office). Kruchten (*ibidem*, p. 159 and note 534) translates *nkt* by 'un petit quelque chose', an 'euphémisme' for 'un profit situé à la limite de ce qui était toléré' in the context of the *Karnak decree*.
* Legal formula: *r tm di* + *sḏm.tw* (offense) + noun (object) + *m-di.sn* (victim) + *in* (offender).

Note that the text does not include here the expression of the positive intents.

42 The inferior priests.

43 The *ḥm-nṯr* belongs to the high caste of priests, and the *it-nṯr*, *wʿb* and *ḫry-ḥbt* to inferior ones.

3. Operative part: the crime (part 1 – asking for a bribe)

(16) (…) [*ir ḥm-nṯr nb nty iw.f r*][44] *wḫ*[*ȝ*] *nkt m-di.sn*
(16) (…) [As for any prophet who will] re[qu]ire valuables from them,

* Neo-Egyptian characteristics:
- [*nty iw.f r*] *wḫȝ:* relative future.
- *m-di.sn*

* 'Classical' degree 0 forms used: -
* General dialectal features: degree 2.
* Legal terms: *nkt* – classifier: × (share, valuables).
* Legal formula: [*ir* + offender + *nb* + *nty iw.f r*] *sḏm* (the crime) + *m-di.sn* (victim).

4. Operative part: the penalty (part 1)

(16) (…) *iw.tw* (17) *rwi.f m iȝt.f didi r iḥwty*
(16) (…) one will (17) expel him from his office, reduced to (the status of) a cultivator.

* Neo-Egyptian characteristics:
- *iw.tw rwi.f:* future with omission of the preposition in the expression of the punishment, instead of a modal prospective (*ir.tw hpw*). The usually non-modal future is also present in the *Elephantine decree* (line 9), and it corresponds with the progressive disappearance of the independent prospective in Ramesside Neo-Egyptian (see Frandsen (1974: 41-42); Satzinger (1976: 192-194) who remarks that the 'sogenannten Futurum III' is not opposed to another future form in 'administrative' texts, and in page 13, that the future apodosis following a topicalized theme usually contains a 'Futurum III' in Neo-Egyptian; Winand (1992: 214-217); Loprieno (1995: 91, 94-95) who describes a process in Coptic already perceptible in Ramesside texts; Junge (1996: 147) who notes that it is a question of 'Registerstruktur der Texte' and 'Schichtung ihrer Normhierarchie', 'In den Textsorten der sozialideologischen Kundgabe (Staats- und Königstexte) und denen von Unterricht, Hymnik und Liturgie bleiben die Gebrauchsweisen aller Formen des mittelägyptischen *sḏm.f* einerseits weiter im Gebrauch'). Lorton (1977: 57) notes the presence in the Demotic *Hermopolis Code* of the

44 Helck's second restoration [*ir ḥm-nṯr nb iw.tw r sḏm r-ḏd*] (adopted in *KRI* IV, 266) seems problematic as it omits *nty* in front of *iw.tw* (as in line 17 in *KRI* IV, 266 upon which it is based) and shows discrepancies between his reconstruction of the line (*iw.tw r sḏm r-ḏd*) and its transliteration (1958b: 146: *nty twtw r sḏm*); furthermore, line 17 should not be used as an exact model, *wḫȝ*'s actor expression being missing (contrary to *di.f* in line 17). Our restoration remains closer to the preceding line.

future in the apodosis, along with two other forms, instead of the prospective. Compare with the *Armant decree* (line 4) use of the prospective instead of the usual future in the relative clause of the crime's exposition.

- *didi*

* 'Classical' degree 0 forms used: -
* General dialectal features: degree 2.
* Legal terms:

rwi m i3t – classifier: 𓂻 for *rwi* (to expel/deprive from/of office). The classifier represents the superordinate [MOTION] category (metonymic relation) to which the lexeme (implying a transfer) belongs.

rdi r – classifier: ø (to reduce someone to).

* Legal formula: *iw.tw sḏm.f* + *didi r* (expulsion and degradation penalty).

5. Operative part: the crime (part 2 – giving a bribe)

(17) (...) [*ir fȝyw nb it-nṯr nb wʿb nb ẖry-ḥbt nb*] *nty iw.*[*t*]*w* [*r*] *sḏm* [*r*]*-ḏd di.f nkt n pȝ ḥm-nṯr* (17) (...) [As for any porter, any god's father, any *wʿb* priest, any lector] whom o[n]e [will] hear saying that he gave valuables to this prophet,

* Neo-Egyptian characteristics:

- *nty iw.*[*t*]*w* [*r*] *sḏm:* relative impersonal future. Note the absence of resumption of the topicalized syntagm (if the restoration is exact) which may indicate that *r-ḏd* opens an indirect speech, a low priest (offender) reporting that he gave a bribe to a higher priest. It would be the first instance of indirect speech observed in our corpus.
- [*r*]*-ḏd:* opens the illustrative constructed speech texteme.
- *di.f:* past report (delocutive illustrative constructed quoting texteme).
- *pȝ ḥm-nṯr:* perhaps anaphoric, but surely deictic *pȝ* (one can imagine the pointing finger of the accuser) in the speech context.

* 'Classical' degree 0 forms used: -
* General dialectal features: degree 2.
* Legal terms: *nkt* – classifier: × (share, valuables).
* Legal formula: [*ir* + offender + *nb*] + *nty* + *iw.tw r sḏm* + [*r*]*-ḏd* + illustrative constructed speech.

6. Criminal provision: the penalty (part 2)

(17) (...) [*iw.tw rwi.f m*] *iȝt.f didi r iḥwty dit iry.tw pȝ*[*hpw r.f*?]

(17) (...) [one will deprive him of] his office, reduced to (the status of) a cultivator, (and) cause that this [rule?] shall be executed [against him?]

* Neo-Egyptian characteristics:

- *didi:* Helck (1956: 85) sees it as a passive participle.
- *dit:* probably an infinitive due to the ellipsis of the first part of the future, or even as an embryo-conjunctive. See Helck's (1958b: 146) translation: 'der [wird] aus seinem Amt [entfernt], und zum Bauern gemacht, und es wird das [Gesetz (?) angewendet ?]'. Helck and Kitchen's restoration [*rwi.f m*] does not take into account lines 16-17 expression of the penalty (*iw.tw rwi.f*), nor the embarrassing resulting issue of *dit*'s function.
- *iry.tw*: following (Winand 1992: 241-243), in more than 90 % of the cases, *iri* shows the 'double yod final' in the construction *rdi iri.f* (dependent prospective, object of *rdi*) during 19th-20th dynasties.

* 'Classical' degree 0 forms used: -

* General dialectal features: degree 1.

* Legal terms: [*rwi m*] *i3t* – classifier*:* [*Λ?*] for *rwi* (to expel/deprive from/of office).
rdi r – classifier*:* ø (to reduce someone to).

* Legal formula: [*iw.tw sḏm..f*] + *didi r* + *sḏm* (expulsion?, degradation?)

VI. *Elephantine decree*

Rˁmss III's *Elephantine decree* (*KRI* V, 343-345 n. 138B), or at least its three remaining blocks that were found 'built into the quay wall at Elephantine' (Griffith 1927: 207), was first copied by de Rougé; its precise date is a matter of debate (see Kitchen's introductive note, p. 343), and it presumably originates in a temple of *Ḫnmw* (Sethe 1901: 82-84). It is linked by Spalinger (1991: 25-26, 31) to the four inspection decrees and the mission of *Pnp3t3* (see *infra*), as the result of *Rˁmss* III 'temple revision policy' (it may also be covered by *pHarris* I several allusions to decrees organizing the staff of the temples). As for its scope, it protects more than one sanctuary in the country (see line 6 *n3 n rw-prw n it nṯrw nṯrywt nb*, lines 9-10 *n3 n rw-prw*, and line 1 of the third fragment *n ḥwt-nṯr nb*); perhaps the best guess may be that all the *Ḫnmw* temples in the region of the 'Field' (see *infra*) were beneficiaries of the measures in the decree.

The *first fragment* of the preserved text covers what is left of a general preamble (lines 1-3); worth noting are the expressions *smn hpw* (to record, confirm[45] or set laws) and *ḥn* (service/posting) in this background context. Then follows the largest part of the decree legal dispositions, the *second fragment* adding limited information to the first one. The *third fragment* completes the picture with at least one more operative part, followed by an epilogue using the lexeme *ḫwi*.

1. The decree's proclamation to the administration

(3) (…) *wḏt 3wyt m ḥm stp-s3 m hrw pn n ṯ3ty srw smr*[46] *ḳnbwt sḏmyw ḥ3ty-ˁw ṯsw wḥw* […] (4) [*nw šmˁw mḥw k3ḏnw ḥryw iḥw ṯ3y-srywt wˁw n pr ni-swt rmṯ nb h3btw m wpt r sḫty*][47]   (3) (…) Decree proclaimed/issued/handed over in (the) majesty of (the) palace, on this date, to (the) vizier, magistrates/civil servants, courtier(s), courts of hearers, mayors, tribes commanders […] (4) [of Southern and Northern lands, officers, stable masters, standard-bearers, soldiers of (the) king's estate, anybody sent on a mission to (the) Field[48]].

* Neo-Egyptian characteristics: -

45 Grimal (1986: 645).

46 Note the absence of the plural grapheme for this term in the list.

47 Sethe (1901: 83) restores '[und alle anderen königlichen Behörden. Es wird hiermit befohlen, dass die Bewohner des Feldes nicht zu irgendwelchen Leistungen für den Hof herangezogen werden sollen durch]'. Our restoration is based on line 29 of the *Nauri decree* and the next part of the *Elephantine decree* line 4.

48 Sethe (1901: 82-84) 'Dodekaschoinos, das Zwölfmeilenland an der Grenze von Aegypten und Nubien' (the distance from Elephantine to Takompso is 12 miles).

* 'Classical' degree 0 forms used:
  - *wḏt ꜣwyt:* see *Nauri decree*, line 29 (*w{ꜣ}ḏt ꜣwy*[*t*]*w*). Note the difference in spelling.
  - *hrw pn:* anaphoric proximal archaic demonstrative in a formulaic use.
* General dialectal features: degree 0.
* Legal terms: *wḏt* - classifier: (papyrus/leather decree).
  ꜣwy - classifier: (to proclaim, issue).
  ḳnbwt sḏmyw - classifier: ø (courts of hearers).
* Legal formula: *wḏt ꜣwyt* (decree proclamation) + *m* (location) + *m hrw pn* (date) + *n* (list of addressees).

Due to the fragmentary state of the text, the introduction of the content *tꜣ wḏt m ḏd* and the enacting clause *ỉw wḏ.n ḥm.f rdỉt ḥn.tw tꜣ ḥwt* N *ḥr mw ḥr tꜣ* are missing (see *Nauri decree* lines 30-31). Griffith (1927: 207) proposes to restore '[The decree saith: (…) His Majesty hath commanded that ordinance be made for the temples of Chnum Lord of Elephantine (…)]'; for *ARE* IV, § 147, only the last member of the addressees list has to be added, then the preamble *sensu stricto* begins, which is assuredly not in accordance with the textemic analysis of this type of decree.

2. Preamble *sensu stricto* - part 1 (negative intent)

(4) (…) [*tm rdỉt ỉṯꜣ.tw rmṯ nb …ỉ?*]*n wꜥw n pr nỉ-swt rmṯ nb h(ꜣ)btw m wpt r sḫty*[49]
(*r*) *tm rdỉt šnꜥ.tw* boat.*sn ḥr mw ỉn šnꜥy nb*[50]
r tm rdỉt ỉṯꜣ.tw boat.*sny m nḥm r ỉrt wpt nb n Pr-ꜥꜣ ꜥnḫ wḏꜣ snb ỉn rmṯ nb h(ꜣ)btw m wp* [*r sḫty*]
(5) [*…r tm rdỉt ỉṯꜣ.tw*  *ꜥꜣ šꜣ*] *ꜥnḫ tp n ỉꜣwt nb n.sny m nḥm m ḥwrꜥ m r-pw n wstnw ỉn ḥꜣty-ꜥw nb rwḏ nb wꜥw nb hbb* (=*hꜣb*) *m wpt r sḫty*[51]

(4) (…) [to prevent that anybody be seized] by/of soldiers/inspectors[52] of (the) king's estate, anybody sent on a mission to (the) Field;
(to) prevent that be detained their boat on water by any executive force;
to prevent that be seized their boat as commandeered/by order to execute any mission of/for Pharaoh l.p.h. by anybody sent as a messenger [to the Field];
(5) […to prevent that be seized] any [bovine, ass, pig], goat, head of cattle of/from them as commandeered, by robbery, or arbitrarily by any mayors, any agent, any soldier/inspector sent on a mission to (the) Field.

* Neo-Egyptian characteristics:

49 Probably parallel to *Nauri decree*, lines 32-33.
50 Probably parallel to *Nauri decree*, line 33.
51 Probably parallel to *Nauri decree*, lines 34-35.
52 Griffith (1927: 207); see above (*Nauri decree*, line 42).

- *h(3)btw:* for *h3bw* in the *Nauri decree* (lines 30, 34, etc.): see above for a syntagm # *rmṯ nb h(3)btw m wpt r sẖty* # where *sẖty* replaces *Kš* of the *Nauri decree*.
- (*r*) *tm rdit:* omission of the preposition *r*, a common Neo-Egyptian feature. Note the constant use of *rdit* instead of *dit* in this first fragment of the text.
- boat.*sny* and *n.sny:* atypical ending of the suffix pronoun already observed in the *Nauri decree* (line 57). But note before on the same line boat.*sn*.
- *ḥwrʿ:* Neo-Egyptian (*Wb* III, 56).
- *m r-pw:* explicit disjuncter between two adverbial entities # (preposition *m* + noun) *m r-pw* (preposition *n* + noun) #. In the same context, line 35 of the *Nauri decree*, *r-pw* was used as disjuncter.
- *wstnw:* Neo-Egyptian ending. Note that in the *Nauri decree*, line 35, the expression *m sẖtr n wstnw* was used.
- *hb, hbb* (=*h3b*)*: LEG* § 1.6; Winand (1992: 33).

* 'Classical' degree 0 forms used:

- *šnʿ.tw*.N, *iṯ3.tw*.N: dependent prospectives, nominal objects of *rdit*.
- *r irt:* preposition *r* + infinitive, purpose.
- [𓃒 *ʿ3 š3*] *ʿnḫ tp n i3wt nb*: list of the # N N N N *nb* # type, probably composed of [singular hyponyms] + [all-inclusive hyperonym + distributive *nb*] (list of crime objects in Preamble *sensu stricto*, highly cohesive).
- *in ḥ3ty-ʿw nb rwḏ nb wʿw nb:* list of the # N *nb* N *nb* N *nb* # type, comprising [plural or singular hyponyms + distributive *nb*], without hyperonym (or is *wʿw* considered one?) by the end of the list, concerning the offenders presented in hierarchical diminishing progression (less cohesive).

* General dialectal features: degree 1.

* Legal terms: (*r*) *tm rdit* - classifier: ø (to prevent).
šnʿ - classifiers: 𓂻 (to detain). 𓂣 is a 'phonetic determinative'.
šnʿy - classifier: 𓂡 (executive force).
iṯ3 - classifier: 𓍿𓂝 (to seize).
nḥm - classifier: 𓂝 (to commandeer; order).
ḥwrʿ - classifier: 𓂝 (robbery).
n wstnw - classifier: 𓏤𓂡𓂻 (arbitrarily).
rwḏ - classifier: 𓂝 (agent).

* Legal formula: (*r*) *tm rdit* + *sḏm.tw*.N (victim) (+ *m* (method)) + *in* + offender.

3. Operative part: the crime (part 1 - requisition)

(5) (…) *ir p3 nty nb r ir.f*
(5) (…) As for anyone who will commit it (the crime),

* Neo-Egyptian characteristics:

- *ỉr pꜣ nty nb r ỉr.f:* # topic marker + *pꜣ* + relative adjective + colon-enclitic distributive *nb* + preposition + infinitive + object #. Note the junctural openness, see Shisha-Halevy (1981: 318), the use of substantivized *pꜣ,* the absence of feminine ending of the infinitive and the Middle Egyptian adverbial rheme in the relative clause instead of a future.

* 'Classical' degree 0 forms used: -
* General dialectal features: degree 2.
* Legal terms: -
* Legal formula: *ỉr pꜣ nty nb* (offender) + *r sḏm* (crime)

4. Operative part: the penalty (part 1)

(5) (…) *šdw.tw tp n ỉꜣwt nty ỉw.f ỉṯꜣtw.f m-di.f* [...]
(5) (…) (the) head of cattle that he will seize shall be confiscated from him […]

* Neo-Egyptian characteristics:

- *nty ỉw.f ỉṯꜣtw.f:* relative future (omission of the preposition); Neo-Egyptian *tw* ending of the infinitive (the *3-lit.* with *ult.-ꜣ* are masculine infinitives but could acquire a feminine ending during 19th/20th dynasties if assimilated to feminine nouns or to *2-lit.* – see Winand 1992: 91-92).
- *m-di.f*

* 'Classical' degree 0 forms used:

- *šdw.tw*.N: independent modal prospective following the topicalized enunciation of the crime without the *ỉr.tw hpw* modal formula (compare *Karnak decree*, line 16-17 for the absence of *ỉr.tw hpw*).

* General dialectal features: degree 2.
* Legal terms: *šdw* - classifier: (to confiscate).
ỉṯꜣ - classifier: (to seize).
* Legal formula: *sḏm.tw*.N (penalty)

5. Preamble *sensu stricto* (positive intent)?

As Griffith (1927: 208) regarded it, the following paragraph is certainly part of a protective disposition (type *ẖwi-mkỉ*) as in the *Nauri decree*, lines 40-42, that he restores as '[to guard and protect any serfs belonging to these temples, whether men or women, whether……….]'.

(6) [*wp-ḥr wnn.sn ḫwy mky m*?] *wꜣḥw wḥꜥw*[53] *sḥt ḥsmn sḫt ḥmꜣyw*[54] *ꞽrt nb ḥnw.sn r nꜣ n rw-prw n ꞽt nṯrw nṯrywt nbw n rdꞽt ḏꜣ.tw tꜣ r.sn ꞽn rmṯ* [*nb hꜣbtw m wpt r sḫty*?]

(6) [In contrast, it is retained (and) preserved that they will be as?] fishermen, fowlers, natron gatherer(s), salt gatherer(s), all (the ones) who accomplish their service for those sanctuaries of (the) father of all gods (and) goddesses (= *Ḫnmw*)[55], while not allowing that will be interfered against them by [any]body [sent on a mission to (the) Field.]

* Neo-Egyptian characteristics:
  - *ḥsmn:* New Kingdom spelling (*Wb* III, 162).
  - *n rdꞽt:* see *ꞽw nn rdꞽt ḏꜣy.tw tꜣ r.sn* in the *Nauri decree*, line 41. Negator *n* + infinitive, probably a corrupted form of classical circumstantial non-existence *nn rdꞽt;* see *EG* § 307, 1; Gilula (1970: 212 and 210 n.4 *in fine).* In comparison with the *Nauri decree*, the construction used here refers to an older model and is of a lesser degree of Neo-Egyptian.
* 'Classical' degree 0 forms used:
  - *ꞽrt nb ḥnw.sn:* see *ꞽrr nb ḥnwt.f* in the *Nauri decree*, line 40. Participle used substantively as the all-inclusive hyperonym of the list, here without gemination (and prothetic *yod*) but with feminine marker, an unusual feature of a corrupted form. Winand (1992: 362) notes that in the participle 'periphrastic' form, after the beginning of the 19th dynasty, 'rien ne permet de distinguer la graphie de l'auxiliaire [du participe 'imperfectif'] de celle du participe perfectif' (usually with prothetic *yod*). The list is expressed in the form of # [plural or singular hyponyms] + [hyperonym substantivized participle + totalizing determinator *nb* (with plural resumption in *ḥnw.sn* and *r.sn*)] #. The totalizing value of *nb* in the context of a list is new in our corpus.
  - *nꜣ n:* presence of the relator with the plural demonstrative, a classical feature. Anaphoric/cataphoric role of the demonstrative. The relator appears in several instances in our text.
  - *nṯrw nṯrywt nbw:* concord of the determinator *nbw* whose masculine gender covers both feminine and masculine nouns.
  - *ḏꜣ.tw tꜣ:* dependent passive/impersonal prospective, object of *rdꞽt.*
* General dialectal features: degree 1.
* Legal terms: *ꞽrt ḥnw* - classifier: ø (to accomplish a service).
  ḏꜣ tꜣ r - classifier:  (to interfere with/violate).
* Legal formula: [contrast proclitic particle *wp-ḥr* + *wnn.f ḫwy-mky* (protection) + *m*] (activities protected) + *n rdꞽt ḏꜣy.tw tꜣ r.sn* (exclusion of interference) + *ꞽn* (offenders).

---

53 See *Nauri decree*, lines 37, 38, 53 (and the compound, lines 36, 52); Moret (1917: 403); Gardiner (1952: 29).

54 Sethe (1901: 27).

55 Sethe (1901: 27, note 4).

6. Operative part: the crime (part 2 – transgression against temple staff)

(7) [*ir*...] *bityw rmṯ nb n ḥwt nṯr nty iw.tw r thtw r.f ntf ḏd m* (=*in*) *rwḏ mn m r-pw wʿw mn*[56] *thi r.i mntf pw di ḫpr p3 3ḳ ḫprw*

(7) [As for…] honey collectors, anybody of a temple against whom one will commit a transgression and he (= the victim) will say: 'it is an agent so-and-so or a soldier so-and-so who committed a transgression against me; it is he who caused that happened the resulting loss',

* Neo-Egyptian characteristics:
    - *nty iw.tw r thtw:* impersonal relative future (note the infinitive spelling).
    - *nty iw.tw r thtw... ntf ḏd:* 'the missing link' in the conjunctive development, but 'An entirely isolated case, where the scribe has taken it into his head to write the pronoun archaically.' (Gardiner (1928: 95-96); *contra*: Winand (1992: 465) 'graphie fautive'). This form is used to open the direct speech (illustrative constructed quotation texteme), as *mtw*.N *ḏd* in the *Nauri decree* (line 68). See also Kruchten (1981: 70, n. 212). The protasis gives the background information, while the apodosis contains essential elements of the crime: the victim's report of the crime and denunciation of its perpetrator, and the establishment of the causality link between the crime and the loss.
    - *m r-pw:* explicit disjunctive between two nominal entities.
    - *mntf pw di:* # delocutive pronominal focus and rheme + *pw* theme marker + participle belonging to the theme # in a denunciation, an identification cleft sentence (focalization pattern), used in a constructed direct speech, where the participle is not an expansion of the rheme. If the pattern already exists with the locutive independent pronoun in Middle Egyptian (see for instance *The Eloquent Peasant* B1, 21 *ink pw mdw n.k imy-r pr wr pw sḫ3y.k*), it seems that 'only late examples' are to be found with *ntf* (Gilula 1976: 162), for instance in the *Nauri decree*, line 4 (*ntf pw ḳm3 nfrw.f*) or in other texts of *Stḫy* I (*KRI* I, 111.5 and 112.2) (see Ford 1995: 13). For Gilula (1976: 167-168), *ntf* ('the initial pronoun') is always the rheme in this pattern. Note that this focalization pattern follows another one, a participial statement; note also *mntf*'s spelling.
    - *p3 3ḳ:* cataphoric value of the articloid (*ḫprw* is a participle).
    - *m* (=*in*) N *thi:* participial statement, a cleft sentence with focalized initial rheme (*m* (=*in*) N) and participial theme; see the *Kanais decree*, lines 14 and 19.
* 'Classical' degree 0 forms used:
    - *N mn:* see *Nauri decree*, line 105.
    - *ḫpr.N:* dependent prospective, object of *di*.
* General dialectal features: degree 2.

56 Compare the *Nauri decree*, line 105.

* Legal terms:
  thi r – classifiers: (to transgress, commit an abuse against someone).
  3ḳ – classifier: (loss).
* Legal formula: *ir* + nouns (victims) + *nty iw.tw*) *r sḏm* (crime) + *ntf ḏd* + illustrative direct speech.

7. Operative part: the penalty (part 2)

(7) (…) *ir* [*n.sn m-di.f* ?] *pw ṯ3*[*tw*?][57] *nty iw.tw r iṯ3.f m ṯ3tw n t3 ḥwt-nṯr n p3 nṯr ʿ3*

(7) (…) shall act [?] that one will seize as a fine for the temple of this/the great god.

* Neo-Egyptian characteristics:
  - *nty iw.tw r iṯ3.f:* relative impersonal future.
  - *t3 ḥwt-nṯr:* cataphoric use of the determinator.
  - *p3 nṯr ʿ3:* anaphoric or non-phoric use of the articloid referring to *Ḫnmw*.
* 'Classical' degree 0 forms used: -
* General dialectal features: degree 2.
* Legal terms: *iṯ3* – classifiers: (to seize).
  ṯ3tw – classifiers: (fine).
* Legal formula: ?

8. Preamble *sensu stricto* - part 2 (negative intent)

(7) (…) *ḥnʿ tm rdit sḥw* [*n ḥwt-nṯr n ḥnt n ky nṯrw n?*] (8) *n3yw.sn nbw ḥr sk3w n.sn r n3y.sn ḥtpw nṯr*
ḥnʿ tm di iṯ3 imy-r *nb rmṯ nb rwḏw nb n nṯr nb n nṯryt nb r di.f n ky*[58] *m šbt m r-pw m sḫrw ḥwrʿw* [...]

(7) (…) And (to) prevent that be assembled [cattle of (the) temple for (the) service of other gods?] (8) their lords, ploughing for them, for their divine offerings;
and (to) prevent that any cattle overseer, anybody, any agent of any god, of any goddess will seize (it) to put/and that he will put it to/for another in exchange or in plans of (= by premeditated) robbery […];

---

57 A problematic lecture: for Griffith (1927: 208) 'they shall give (?) the…'; for Sethe (1901: 83) 'und er sorge dafür (?, *nwj*), dass der entstandene (*ḫpr*) Schaden (*3ḳ*) wiederhergestellt (*irj*) werde und dass das Erste (?), das heimlich dem Tempel genommen wird'; *ARE* IV, 87 'shall be made good, that the first, which shall be secretly taken from the temple, shall be made good to the god'. The expected sentence would be more like **iw.tw šdw.f m-di.f m iṯ3*.

58 Note that it is used without expansion. Compare this sentence to the *Nauri decree*, lines 74-76.

* Neo-Egyptian characteristics:

- *ḥnꜥ tm (r)di(t): ḥnꜥ* precedes *tm*, omission of the preposition *r* (as already seen above). Following the textemic division of the decree and the lexemic constituency of this segment, it is probably not an embryo-conjunctive. Griffith and Breasted seem to have assimilated *ḥnꜥ* to *m-mitt* as in the *Nauri decree*, lines 86 and 87. See the parallel segment of the *Nauri decree*, lines 58-59. As for *di* that follows *tm*, we have already noted it in the *Karnak decree*, line 16 (a Middle Egyptian feature).
- *nꜣyw.sn, nꜣy.sn:* note the spelling of the first one.
- *ḥr skꜣw:* infinitive with Neo-Egyptian spelling.
- *imy-r [ ] nb rmṯ nb rwḏw nb:* the sequence of the list of offenders is again not exactly the one observed in the *Nauri decree*: # singular hyponym + distributive *nb* + hyperonym *rmṯ nb* + plural hyponym + distributive *nb* (no concord) #. In the *Nauri decree*, the hyperonym always appears last in the sequence.
- *m r-pw:* explicit disjunctive construction between two adverbial adjuncts # (preposition *m* + noun) *m r-pw* (preposition *n* + noun + adnominal expansion in 'loose composition') #.

* 'Classical' degree 0 forms used:

- *iṯꜣ.N:* dependent prospective with an active diathesis.
- *r di.f: r* + infinitive without feminine ending (purpose). See Winand (1992: 84).

* General dialectal features: degree 2.

* Legal terms:

tm (r)di(t) - classifier: ø (to prevent).

iṯꜣ – classifiers: (to seize). The third superordinate taxonomic [MALE HUMAN] category classifier does not usually appear in our corpus.

rwḏw – classifiers: ø (agents).

rdi n ky m šbt – classifiers: [?] (to put/give in exchange to/for another). See the *Nauri decree*.

ḥwrꜥw – classifiers: (robbery).

* Legal formula: *ḥnꜥ tm (r)di(t)* + *sḏm*.N (the crime)

Probably follows a crime disposition of the type ir N/pꜣ nty nb (iw.f) r iṯꜣ N.

9. Operative part: the penalty (part 3)

(9) [… *i*]*w.tw šdw.f m-di.f m iṯꜣ*
(9) […o]ne will confiscate it from him as a fine.

* Neo-Egyptian characteristics:

- [*i*]*w.tw šdw.f:* future (omission of the preposition); see above *Karnak decree*, lines 16-17.

- *m-di.f*

* 'Classical' degree 0 forms used: -
* General dialectal features: degree 2.
* Legal terms: *šdw* – classifiers: (to confiscate).
iṯꜣ – classifiers: – classifiers: (fine). As *tꜣ(wt)*.
* Legal formula: *iw.tw sḏm.f* (penalty).

10. Enacting clause (authority, object) and negative intent

> (9) (…) *m-mitt iw wḏ.n ḥm.f tm rdit nis ṯꜣ[t/i?] nb ḫpr ḫt nb*[59] *ḥr ḥm-nṯr nb n nꜣ n rw-prw m ḥḏ nbw pḳt ḥbsw sg[n]r (= sgnn)* [...(10)...] *pw* (?)
> *mitt*[60] *iṯꜣ.tw nb m-di.sn*
>
> (9) (…) Likewise, his Majesty has decided to prevent that any vizier/seizer[61] existing/to be will request any material property from any prophet of those sanctuaries, consisting of silver, gold, fine linen clothes, unguents […(10)…].
> Likewise every(thing) will have to be seized from them;

* Neo-Egyptian characteristics:
- *m-di.sn*

* 'Classical' degree 0 forms used:
- *m-mitt*
- *iw wḏ.n ḥm.f tm rdit:* interestingly, it is not followed, as in our previous examples, by a positive object (as *rdit ḥn.tw*), but by the negative-preventive *tm rdit*, in a kind of 'raccourci' (coalescence) between the enacting clause and the negative intents preamble *sensu stricto*.
- *nis.N:* dependent prospective, object of *rdit*. The verb *nis* usually takes the preposition *r* or *n* to express the addressee of the request, but here it takes *ḥr* (the addressee is not the proprietor of the goods, but the instrumental agent who brings them to the vizier).
- *nꜣ n*
- *iṯꜣ.tw nb:* independent modal prospective (impersonal or passive diathesis). Note that the object of the requisition is summarized in this sole instance of our corpus by the substantivized *nb* (and not by *ḫt nb*), although '*nb* is the only adjective never used as a noun equivalent' (*LEG* § 5.4).

* General dialectal features: degree 1.
* Legal terms: *wḏ* – classifier: (to decree, command).

59 Note the absence of concord.
60 Apparently without preceding *m*. Note that this sentence may belong to a penalty disposition (prospective, *m-di.sn*) but due to the fragmentary state of the text this cannot be fully ascertained.
61 A clause not present in the *Nauri decree*, as Spalinger (1991: 36) notes. The restoration is uncertain, but it seems that if one compares this disposition to the one in line 11, *ṯꜣi* must be restored.

tm rdit – classifier: ø (to prevent).
ḫt – classifier: ø (material property).
ṯ3[*i*?] – classifier: [?] (seizer).

* Legal formula: *iw wḏ.n ḥm.f* (source of the decree) + *tm rdit* (negative order to the executive power) + *nis*.N (nature of the measure: request) + addressee.

11. Preamble *sensu stricto* (positive intent)

(10) (…) *wpt wn rmṯ nb n n3 n rw-prww*[62] *ꜥḥꜥ mn ḥr st.sn ḥr irt ḥnw.sn n3y.sn nṯrw im* [...]
(11) (…) *iw bn di.i n.f ḫt nb*[w] *ḥr ḳm3?.sn*

(10) (…) In contrast, it is established and maintained in their position, that all people of those sanctuaries are, when carrying out their service of their gods there […]
(11) (…) without my giving him (?) anything from their produce (?)

* Neo-Egyptian characteristics:

- *wpt wn*.N *ꜥḥꜥ mn:* Neo-Egyptian abbreviated version of the formula # *wp-ḥr* + *wnn*.N + binomial statives (here two posture verbs instead of *ḫwy mky*) + *iw*.N *ḥr irt* # of the *Nauri decree*, lines 40-41. Note the short form of the contrast particle, the non-geminated *wn*.N and the absence of thematic *iw*.N (that was part of a nexus whose rheme was *ḥr irt*). Note also the plural reference to *rmṯ nb* in *st.sn, ḥnw.sn, n3y.sn* (again totalizing value of the determinator *nb*).
- *n3y.sn*
- *iw bn di.i:* see *Nauri decree* (lines 60-61, 76) for the discussion of this construction (circumstantial non-existence with that-form, as in *pTurin* P/R 1880, *RAD* 49, 5-6 already quoted in relation to lines 60-61 of the *Nauri decree*). Interestingly, a locutive *di.i* is used in this texteme, perhaps in an illustrative constructed direct speech.

* 'Classical' degree 0 forms used:

- *ḥr irt:* preposition + infinitive in an adverbial adjunct (iterative/durative).
- *ḫt nb*[*w*]*:* probable concord as in line 11 *infra* (*ḫt* viewed as a plural).

* General dialectal features: degree 2.

* Legal terms:

ꜥḥꜥ mn ḥr st – classifier: 𓂻 (for *ꜥḥꜥ*) 𓏠 (for *mn*) 𓉐 (for *st*) (to stand/succeed and be vested in a position). Binomial expression (see in legal English 'establishment and maintenance' noted by Gustafsson 1984: 136). For *mn*, see *Dmḏibt3wy Coptos R decree*, *mn m sr* being understood as to be maintained in the status of a civil servant. The 𓂻 classifier refers to the superordinate [MOTION] category;

62 Note a kind of plural redundancy (each member of the compound noun has the plural mark, as does the compound itself), although it could perhaps be understood as a possessive pronominal suffix (Neo-Egyptian third plural).

the superordinate [ABSTRACT] category classifier may imply the recognition of a right by an official document; the classifier refers to the taxonomic superordinate [HABITAT] category of which it constitutes the prototypical member (a position being neither a house nor a part of a building, relates metaphorically to 'position', understood as a familiar, protecting 'niche'). For metaphorical implications of the classifier, see Goldwasser (1995: 98-99).

ỉrt ḥnw – classifier: (to carry out a service).

* Legal formula: proclitic contrast particle *wpt* + *wn*.N *ꜥḥꜥ mn* (permanence of function) + *ỉw bn di.i* (exclusion).

12. Operative part: the crime (part 4 – requisition of a prophet's property?)

(11) (...) *ỉr ṯꜣỉ nb* [*nty*?] *r* [?] *ḫt nbw nw ḥm-nṯr nb mtw.f di*[*t*] *ḥny sš ḥr*[*.f*?] *ỉr nw šmstw ḥr ỉr šd.tw.f m-di.f* *r-pw ỉr ṯꜣỉ rmṯ n* [...] (11) (...) As for any seizer (?) [who] will [?] any material property of any prophet and cause a scribe to go about [it ?] doing ? a service by acting so that it will be confiscated from him (or penalty: it will have to be confiscated from him); or as for a seizer of people of [...]

* Neo-Egyptian characteristics:

- [*nty*?] *r* [?]... *mtw.f di*[*t*] *ḥny:* full-fledged conjunctive in a relative (?) context. Due to the damaged state of the line, its reading remains a crux. See Griffith (1927: 208) 'and he shall produce writing', apparently taking not as *ḥn* 'go speedily', but as *ḥn* 'to equip, service, allocate, produce' despite the classifier. Compare with the *Armant decree*, line 5 *mtw.f dit ḥny sš*.
- *m-di.f*
- *ḥr ỉr:* probably an adverbial adjunct with Neo-Egyptian spelling of the infinitive.

* 'Classical' degree 0 forms used:

- *ỉr ṯꜣỉ nb* [*nty*?] *r* [?]*:* this is not Kitchen's restoration (*KRI* V, 344: *ỉr ṯꜣỉ nb* [*ḫp*]*r* [*m*] *ḫt nbw;* see Griffith (1927: 208) translation 'If robbery shall take place in regard to any property belonging to any prophet (?), and he shall produce a writing...'). A comparison with a similar sentence of the *Armant decree* (lines 4-5) leads to believe that we have here another topicalized enunciation of a crime, usually comprising a relative clause. The sequence is probably the following: # topicalizer + noun + relative adverbial rheme (as in line 5) #. Furthermore, line 9 probably also refers to a 'seizer' (not a vizier, see above) requesting material property from a prophet, and line 11 to a 'seizer' of temple (?) staff.
- *ḫt nbw nw ḥm-nṯr nb:* note the concord of *nbw* and *nw* (*ḫt* is viewed as a plural), although usually a feminine concord was marked in our decrees.

- *ḥny sš:* dependent prospective object of *dit*.
- *šd.tw.f:* probably dependent prospective with purpose/consequence value, although *šd.tw.f m-di.f* could be understood as the penalty 'it will have to be confiscated from him', an independent modal prospective (note that *m-di.f* appears mostly in the penalty context). Note the singular-masculine resumption for previous *ẖt nbw*.

* General dialectal features: degree 2.

* Legal terms:

ṯ3i – classifier: 𓂡 (the seizer).

ẖt – classifier: ø (material property).

šd – classifier: 𓏴𓂡 (to confiscate). The addition of the crossed sticks classifier to the strong arm implies that the lexeme belongs not only to the superordinate [COERCION] category, but also to the superordinate [UNION/DIVISION] category (separation of the diverted item from its possessor).

* Legal formula: *ir* + noun (offender) + [*nty*] *r* [*sḏm*] (crime)

Very few elements worth noting are to be deduced from the *second fragment*:

13. Preamble *sensu stricto* (negative intent – part 4?)

(2) (…) *m bḥ*[*w?*…] *n3yw.w* (3) […] *r tm* <*rdit*> *m-di iṯ3* 𓃒 *ꜥ3wt* [*š3w ꜥnḫw tp n i3wt*...] (2) (…) by/as a forced labor of ? (3) […] to pre<vent> also that will be seized bovines, asses [pigs, goats, heads of cattle…]

* Neo-Egyptian characteristics:

- *m-di:* used as coordinator.

* 'Classical' degree 0 forms used:

- *r tm* <*rdit*> *iṯ3.N*

* General dialectal features: degree 1.

* Legal terms: - *bḥ*[*w?*] – classifier: [?] (forced labor).
- *r tm* <*rdit*> – classifier: ø (to prevent).
- *iṯ3* – classifier: 𓂡 (to seize).

* Legal formula: *? - r tm* <*rdit*> *m-di* + *iṯ3*.N (the crime)

The *third fragment* belongs to the end of the decree:

14. Operative part: the crime (part 5 – requisition of temple staff?)

(1) [*ir…nb…nty iw.f r iṯ3 rmṯ nb*?] *n ḥwt-nṯr nb r dit tw.f ẖry.f m wp.f nb*

(1) [As for any…who will seize any person?] of any temple to put him under him (= under his control) in any task of his

* Neo-Egyptian characteristics:

- *r dit tw.f:* several interpretations are acceptable, due to the absence of the first part: # preposition *r* + infinitive (purpose) + Neo-Egyptian pronoun (or it may be an unusual spelling of the infinitive with its suffixed object *dittw.f*) #, or a prospective *rdit.tw.f* (passive diathesis) or *rditw.f* (active) (see Winand (1992: 89 and 98-100)).

* 'Classical' degree 0 forms used: -

* General dialectal features: degree 1.

* Legal terms: *ẖry* – classifier: (under, under the control of). The [ABSTRACT] category classifier probably implies an abstract legal dependence that must be recorded in writing.

* Legal formula: [*ỉr* N *nty ỉw.f r iṯȝ*] + *r dit* (purpose)

15. Operative part: the penalty (part 5)

(1) (…) *ỉr.tw hpw r.f diw* […] (1) (…) (the) rule will have to be enforced against him when placed/reduced […]

* Neo-Egyptian characteristics: -

* 'Classical' degree 0 forms used:

- *ỉr.tw hpw*
- *diw*

* General dialectal features: degree 0.

* Legal terms: *ỉr* – classifier: ø (to enforce).
hpw – classifier: (rule, legal norm).

* Legal formula: *ỉr.tw hpw r.f* + *diw* (type of penalty).

16. ?

(2) […] *nfr iṯȝ ẖt nb rmṯ nb m ỉm.sn* (2) […] ? take any material property, anybody among them

Too fragmentary. The following text segment obviously belongs to the epilogue.

VII. Table of the legal register syntactic forms and particularities in protection/criminal law decrees

The following table should be considered as a summary of the forms found in the remaining fragments of our protection/criminal law decrees. The number of occurrences cannot be viewed in a statistical way, most of our texts being too damaged to be of any significance as a means of statistical study. The existing forms should be taken into account when using the list but no weight should be given to a 'significant absence' of some forms in any of the decrees or in the corpus taken as a whole.

Abbreviations:

A = active
Col = colophon
Cr = crimes dispositions
E = eulogy (restricted to the clauses analyzed *supra*)
En = enacting clause
I = introduction of the content
P = preamble *sensu stricto* (positive and negative intents)
Pa = passive
Pn = penalties dispositions
Procl = proclamation
Q = illustrative constructed quotation
x = numerous instances

Form	Degree	***Nauri* 19th d. *Sṯḫy* I**	***Hermopolis* 19th d. *Sṯḫy* I**	***Kanais* 19th d. *Sṯḫy* I**	***Armant* 19th d. *Rˁm.* II**	***Karnak* 19th d. *Sṯḫy* II**	***Elephantine* 20th d. *Rˁm.* III**
*iw sḏm.n.*N (indep. perfect delocutive report, A)	0	4 (En)					1 (En)
sḏm.f (or circ.?)	2	2 (Q)				1 (Q)	
*tht.*N (or circ.?)	2	1 (Q)					
*sḏmw.*N (indep. perfect report, Pa)	2	1? (E)					
sḏm (perfect participle Pa or stative)	0	x (E, P, Cr, Pn)					1 (Procl)
irt (fem.)	0	1 (P)					1 (Procl)
sḏmw (fem.)	1	2 (P, Procl)		2 (P)			
sḏmtw(fem.)	1	1 (Procl)					
sḏmtw (*rmṯ*)	1						2 (P)
sḏm (participle,	0			1 (Pn)			

imperfect, A)							
ḫprw	0						1 (Q)
tmw sḏm	0			1 (Pn)			
didiw (gem. stative/participle)	2	3 (Pn)					
didi	2			1 (Cr)		2 (Pn)	
diw	0	4 (Pn)	1 (Pn)				1 (Pn)
irr (geminating participle, A)	0	1 (P)					
irt							1 (P?)
ḫpr.ty.f(y) (future participle)	0	1 (P)					
sḫnn.t(y).f(y) (gem.)	0			1 (Cr)			
bw tm.n.f sḏm (indep. aorist, A, neg.)	2			1 (Pn)			
bw sḏm.f	2			1 (P)			
nn wn tht.f (indep. prospective non-existence)	0	1 (E)					
nn sḏm (circ. non-existence, prohibition)	0			1 (P)			
n sḏm	1						1 (P)
iw nn sḏm	2	1 (P)					
iw bn sḏm.f	2	2 (P, Cr)					
iw bn di.i	2						1 (P)
sḏm.f (circ. converb, simultaneity, A)	0			1 (P)			
PN *ḏd.f* (present, mark of narrative/direct speech seam, A)	0			1 (Procl)			
sḏm.n.i (indep. perfect abstract that-form, A)	0			4 (P)			
*sḏm.*N	1		1? (Col)				
*ir.n.*N *tm sḏm* (indep. pseudo-archaic perfect that-form, A, neg.)	1	1 (Pn?)					
*sḏm.n.f/*N (rel., durative/anteriority, A)	0	2 (E, P)		1 (P)			
*ḥr-nty sḏm.n.*N (prepositional rel., A)	0			1 (Pn)			
ꜣbb.f (gem. adnominal that-form, A)	0	1 (E)					
sḏm.f (rel.,	0	1 (Pn)					

prospective, A)							
ir ḫpr.N (protasis, prospective eventuality)	0	1 ? (Cr)					
n sḏm.f (prepositional that-form, A)	0			1 (Pn)			
mi wn.sn	1			1 (Q)			
sḏm.f/N (indep. prospective, A, optative/curse)	0			4 (Pn)			1 (Pn)
ir.f sḏm (analytic)	1			1 (Pn)			
m.k + *tw.tw* (indep. prospective, A, hortative + object)	1			1 (Pn)			
sḏm(w).tw.N (indep. prospective, Pa, prescriptive)	0	12 (Pn)	1 (Pn)		1 (Pn)		4 (Pn, En, Cr?)
sḏm.w.N	0	1? (E)					
nn sḏmw.tw.f (indep. prospective, Pa, neg., prohibition)	0	1 (E)					
sḏm.f/N (depend. prospective, object, A)	0	x (Cr, P)		1 (P)	1 (Cr)		4 (P, En, Q)
sḏm.tw(.N) (depend. prospective, object, Pa/Imp.)	0	x (En, P, Cr, Pn)	1 (Pn)			1 (P)	4 (P)
ḥny.tw	1	1 (En)					
tht.tw/*ḥnt.tw*	1	2 (P)				1 (En)	
iry.tw	1					1 (Pn)	
sḏm/*t* (infinitive)	0	x (En,Cr,Pn, Q)	3 (Pn, Col)	x (P,Pn/Cr)	1 (Cr)	2 (En, Pn)	7 (P, En, Cr)
sḏmw	1	3 (Pn)					1 (P)
sḏmtw	1	12 (Cr,Pn,P)		3 (Cr, Pn,P)			2 (Pn, Cr)
sḏm (fem.)/*t* (masc.)	1	3 (Pn)		2 (P, Cr)			2 (Cr, P)
r tm di (neg. purpose)	0					1 (P)	
r tm (r)dit	1	18 (P, Cr)					1 (P)
tm (r)di(t) (preposition omission)	1						3 (P)
st r sḏm (indep. adverbial nexus, imminence)	0			1 (Pn)			
iw.i r sḏm (indep. locutive future, A)	0	1 (Q)					

iw.tw sḏm.f (indep. future, imp, prep. omission, instead of modal prospective)	2					1 (Pn)	1 (Pn)
N *nty sw r sḏm* (rel. adverbial rheme, future, A)	0			1 (Cr)			
N *nty r sḏm*	0	1 (Cr)		1 (Cr)			
N *nty iw.f r sḏm* (rel. future, A)	2	x (Cr)	2 (Cr, Pn)		1? (Cr)	1 (Cr)	2 (Cr, Pn)
N *nty iw.f sḏm* (prep. omission)	2	1 (Cr)					1 (Pn)
N *nty r*.N *sḏm* (nominal actor + prep. omission)	2	2 (Cr)					
nty nb r sḏm (substantivized rel. future, A, open juncture)	0	1 (Cr)					
p3 nty nb r sḏm	1						1 (Cr)
p3 nty iw.f r sḏm (substantivized rel. future, A)	2	4 (Cr)					
p3 nty iw.f sḏm (prep. omission)	2	2 (Cr, Pn)					
p3 nty nb iw.f r sḏm/N (open juncture)	2			2 (Cr)			
p3 nty sḏm.N (substantivized rel. prospective, A)	2				1 (Cr)		
wp(w/t)-ḥr wnn.f/N + stative (contrastive cleft sentence)	0	1 (P)		1 (P)	1 (P)		
wpw-ḥr wnn.N *ḥr ḏrt.f*	0			1 (P)			
wpt wn.N + stative	2						1 (P)
ir ḏr sḏm.N (circ. temporalis protasis in cleft sentence, A)	2	1 (Q)					
iw.N *ḥr sḏm* (dep. adverbial nexus, durative)	0	1 (P)					
apodotic	0	1 (Q)					
N + *iw* + quantifier +	0	4 (Pn)					

prep. + quantifier (circ. adnexal expansion)							
ir.PN *m-sꜣ.f* (indep. adverbial curse performative or prospective A)	2	1 (Pn)		1 (Pn)			
iw.PN *m-sꜣ.f* (circ. curse performative)	0			2 (Pn)			
iw.f n.N (indep. curse performative, possession)	0			1 (Pn)			
nty tw.tw ḥr sḏm (rel. habit., Imp)	2	1 (Cr)					
ḥnꜥ sḏm (coord. of nominal form 'embryo-conjunctive')	1	3 (Pn)					
m-di sḏm	1	5 (Pn)					
ḥnꜥ m-ꜥ sḏm	1	1 (Pn)					
ḥnꜥ ntf sḏm (conjunctive apod.)	2	1 (Cr)		1 (Cr)			
ntf sḏm							1 (Cr)
mtw.f/N *sḏm*		5 (Cr)			1 (Cr)		1 (Cr)
mtw.f tm sḏm (conjunctive apod., neg.)	2	1 (Cr)					
imi sḏm.f (iussive /3rd pers. causative imperative, A)	0			1 (P)			
ink sn (indep. nominal sentence, rhematic possession)	0			1 (Q)			
m (=*in*) N *sḏm.f* (indep. future participial statement)	1			2 (P, Pn)			
m (=*in*) N *sḏm* (indep. past participial statement)	1						1 (Q)
mntf pw + participle (indep. identification cleft sentence)	2						1 (Q)
bw n N + N (indep. nominal nexus,	0			1 (Pn)			

aphorism)							
ḥm.f in locutive context (majestative *enallage*)	0			1 (Pn)			
.sny (delocutive plur. suffix pronoun)	1	1 (P)					2 (P)
.w	1	1 (E)		3 (P, Cr, Pn)			
mntsn (delocutive plur. independent pronoun)	1			1 (Pn)			
st (delocutive plur. dependent pronoun)	1			1 (Pn)			
s3wy (delocutive sing. pronoun)	1				1 (Cr)		
hrw/pr pn, wḏ tn, nn (anaphoric proximal demonstrative)	0	5 (Procl, P, Cr, Pn)		2 (Cr, Pn)			1 (Procl)
pn, nn (cataphoric proximal demonstrative)	0			2 (P, Cr)			
p3y (anaphoric demonstrative)	1	1 (Cr)					
p3y (deictic or possessive)	1	1 (Q)					
p3, t3, n3 (anaphoric articloid)	1	x (I, Cr, Pn)		x (P, Pn)	1 (Cr)	2? (En, Q)	1? (Pn)
p3, t3, n3 (cataphoric articloid)	1	x (En, P, Cr, Pn)	1 (Pn)	x (Cr, Pn, P)		1? (En)	3 (Cr, Q, Pn)
p3, t3, n3 (non-phoric articloid)	1				3? (P)		1? (Pn)
p3, t3, n3 (deictic articloid)	1	6? (Pn, Q)				2? (En, Q)	
n3 n (plural demonstrative)	0		1 (P or Cr/Pn)				2 (P, En)
p3y.f (possessive)	1	9 (P, Cr, Q)					2 (P)
p3.f	1	7 (P, Cr)					
p3	1	1? (Q)					
n3yw.f	1			1 (P)			1 (P)
n3 n.sn	1				1 (En?)		
N *mn* ('so-and-so N')	0	3 (Q)					2 (Q)
p3 mn	1	2 (Q)					
nb value in lists:							
totalizing	0						2 (P)
distributive	0	x (Procl, P,	1 (Cr)	3 (Cr, P)	6 (Cr)		x (P)

		Cr, Pn)					
nb substantivized	1						1 (En)
nbt/*nbw* marked concord	0	x (E, P, Cr)		1 (Procl)			2 (P, Cr)
ḫt nbw	1						1 (P)
lists sequence types:							
N *nb* N *nb* N *nb* (offenders diminishing progression, closing with hyperonym)	0	13 (P, Cr)	1 (Cr)	1 (P)			1 (P) with disturbed sequence
N N N N *nb* (objects, addressees, victims, cohesive group closing with hyperonym)	0	5 (Procl, P, Cr)					2 (P)
n (*nota relationis*)	0	x (E, Procl, P, Cr, Pn, Q)	2 (Cr, Col)	x (Procl, P, Pn, Cr)	x (Cr)		x (P, En, Cr, Pn)
+ marked concord	0	x (En, Procl, Pn, P)					1 (Cr)
ḥnᶜ (coordinator):							
N *ḥnᶜ* N	0	1 (P)					
proclitic	1						2 (P)
embryo-conjunctive	1	4 (Pn)					
conjunctive	2	1 (Cr)		1 (Cr)			
m-di (coordinator)							
enclitic ?	1						1 (P)
embryo-conjunctive	1	5 (Pn)					
r-pw (disjuncter)	0	6 (P, Q)					1? (Cr)
m r-pw	1	1 (Cr)					3 (P, Q)
ir (topicalizer):							
ḫr ir (+ coordinator)	0	6 (Cr)	1 (Cr)	2 (Cr)			
ḫr swt ir (opposition)	1	1 (Pn)					
iw swt ir	1	1 (Cr)					
m-mitt:							
textemic transition	0	3 (En)			1 (En?)		1 (En)
instead of topicalizer	1	5 (Cr)					
instead of other	0	x (Cr)	1? (Col)				
mitt (preposition omission, proclitic)	1						1 (En)
mi (instead of topicalizer)	1	1 (Cr)					
ḫy rᶜ (coordinator + topicalizer?)	1			1 (P)			
m-di.f/N (compound	1	9 (Cr, Pn, Q)			1(En?)	2 (P, Cr)	4 (En, Pn, P,

preposition)							Cr?)
pꜣ-wn + adverbial nexus (cause)	2			1 (Pn)			
ḏd (tagged speech marker)							
m-ḏd	0	1(E)					
r-ḏd	1	2 (Cr)				1? (Cr)	
ntf ḏd (conjunctive)	2						1 (Cr)
mtw.N *ḏd* (idem)	2	1 (Cr)					
PN *ḏd.f* (present)	0			1 (Procl)			
preposition omission	1	7 (Cr. Pn)				1 (Pn)	6 (P, Pn, En)
preposition redundancy	1	4 (Pn, Cr)					
r nḥḥ ḥnꜥ ḏt (binomial)	1			1 (Pn)	1 (P)		
exocentric attributive compounds	0	1 (Cr)		2 (P, Cr)			

Note the total absence of *prothetic yod* forms.

2. Specific endowment decrees

I. Two *Buhen decrees*

Pair of stelae that were standing in a forecourt of Buhen's North Temple, in Nubia, dated *Rˁmss* I's second (and last) year of reign (*Louvre C*57: Champollion 1835: pl. 1, n. 2; *KRI* I, 2 n. 3) and *Stẖy* I's Year 1 (*BM* 1189: Bierbrier (1982: pls. 10-11); *KRI* I, 37-38 n. 18;) which helps to complete *Rˁmss*' stela lacunae. It consists of the 'literary'[1] form of a decree in favor of Min-Amun's cult, establishing an edible offering endowment[2] and comprising very brief prematerial (date, royal titulary, backgrounding/aetiologic texteme), brief normative provisions, a short narrative and *Stẖy* I' titulary (see *RITANC* I, 3). The format is quite close to 12th dynasty *Snwsrt* III *Deir el-Bahari decree*, although the Old Kingdom inherited *wḏ ni-swt n* address is missing here. Endowment decrees of the Old Kingdom usually contain a protection disposition ('reserve') expressed once by the lexeme *nẖt* (in the oldest decree that has survived: *Špssk3f* 4th dynasty *Giza decree*) or *ẖwi* (6th dynasty *Ppy* II *Abydos decree*) being probably specific criminal law decrees that organize both the endowment and its protection. In the New Kingdom and Ramesside period, endowments and protection of foundations are the object of separate documents; on New Kingdom endowment decrees to temples, see Spalinger (1991: 21-39). Here the legal provisions are limited to an enacting clause (authority, object, beneficiary, and applicability), without proclamation, tag clause texteme, general protection clause, or preamble *sensu stricto* and free of any criminal law dispositions or measures to execute (absence of an operative part, the text being a report of what has been decided, without a precise list of offerings to implement in the future). The two versions of the enacting clause (*Rˁmss*' and *Stẖy*'s) are analyzed hereunder.

Legal provisions: enacting clause (authority, object, beneficiary, applicability)

1. *Rˁmss* I stela

(6) *iw w{3}ḏ.n ḥm.f ni-swt bity Mnpḥ(ty)rˁ di ˁnḫ w3ḥ ḥtpw-nṯr n it.f Mnw-Ỉmn ḥr ib [Bhnt tp n w3ḥ].f* (7) *m ḥwt-nṯr.f psn* 12 *bi3t* 100 *ḥnḳt ds* 4 *smw ẖrš* 10

1 For Vernus (1990: 243), the original decree is reduced in its present form to its principal object and the details of the *Ur*-document are lost.

2 For Martin-Pardey (*LÄ* VI: 380), the endowment decrees are not strictly legal dispositions, but productions of the Administration executive function. Nevertheless, it is the royal decree format that is used to convey the original royal command.

m-mitt [mḥ r-pr pn m ḥmw-nṯr] (8) *wʿbw mḥ šnʿ.f m ḥmw ḥmwt nt ḥ3kw ḥm.f ni-swt bity Mnpḥ(ty)rʿ [di ʿnḫ mi Rʿ ḏt nḥḥ]* (6) His Majesty, King of Upper and Lower Egypt *Mnpḥ(ty)rʿ*, given life, has decreed (the) institution of/to establish divine offerings for his father Min-Amun in (the) heart of [Buhen, items/examples/detail[3] of] his [endowment] (7) in his temple (being): *psn* loaf – 12; *bi3t* loaf – 100; beer jar – 4; vegetables bundle – 10; likewise, [(the) filling of/to fill this sanctuary with prophets] (8) (and) priests, (the) filling of/to fill his workshop[4] with male (and) female servants, of captures of his Majesty, King of Upper and Lower Egypt *Mnpḥ(ty)rʿ*, [given life, like Re, for ever and ever].

2. *Stḫy* I stela

(6) *[iw w{3}ḏ.n ḥm.f ʿnḫ] wḏ3 snb w3ḥ [ḥtpw-nṯr n it.f] Mnw-Imn ḥr ib Bhnt tp n w3ḥ.f m ḥwt-nṯr.f psn* 12 (7) *[bi3t* 100 *ḥnḳt ds* 4 *smw ḫrš* 10 *m-mi]tt mḥ r-pr pn m ḥmw-nṯr ḫry-ḥbwt*[5] *wʿbw* (8) *mḥ šnʿ.f m ḥmw ḥmwt m ḥ3kw [ḥ]m.f ʿnḫ wḏ3 snb [ni-swt bity] Mnm3ʿtrʿ di ʿnḫ mi Rʿ ḏt nḥḥ* (6) [His Majesty, L.]P.H., [has decreed] (the) institution of/to establish [divine offerings for his father] Min-Amun in (the) heart of Buhen, items/examples/details of his endowment in his temple (being): *psn* loaf – 12; (7) [*bi3t* loaf – 100; beer jar – 4; vegetable bundle – 10; like]wise, (the) filling of/to fill this sanctuary with prophets, lectors (and) priests, (8) (the) filling of/to fill his workshop with male (and) female servants, as/with[6] captures of his [Majes]ty, L.P.H., [King of Upper and Lower Egypt] *Mnm3ʿtrʿ*, given life, like Re, for ever and ever.

* Neo-Egyptian characteristics:

- *w{3}ḏ:* for the spelling, see above.

---

3 Reconstruction following *Stḫy* I's Buhen decree, line 6. As we have seen with the expression *tp n i3wt* above, the meaning of *tp n* is not easy to ascertain. The issue here is the exhaustive or generic (*'capital, somme'* 'd'où: *compte, bien*' for Moret (1916: 276, n. 3), 'enumeration of', 'details of' for Kitchen (*RITA* I, 2 and *RITANC* I, 5) or paradigmatic exemplary quality ('the best of', 'example of') for Borchardt (1893: 10, note 1) of the list members that follow. The question proves to be crucial when assessing the extent of the staff devoted to the temple's cult by this time (see Kitchen's evaluations and comments in *RITANC* I, 3-4); a general lack of accuracy may be observed in the fact that the endowment periodicity and the extent of the staff are not evoked, a fact that may imply that the decree is a short 'propagandist' version of an original decree. See Vernus (1990: 243).

4 Haring (1997: 194-195, 365), where 'the preparation of food for the offerings took place in the temple'; slaves are commonly appointed to the temple workshops.

5 A category that is probably not mentioned in *Rʿmss* I's decree. Note that the plural is appended to the compound.

6 Note that in *Rʿmss* I's decree, *nt ḥ3kw* appears instead of *m ḥ3kw*.

- *ḥmw ḥmwt nt ḫꜣḳw:* feminine singular marked concord of the adjectival *nota relationis*. The two categories of slaves (male and female) have obviously both the same origin (*ḫꜣḳw*), but the concord is established with the second element only, the feminine one, and only in gender, not in number, characteristics that are not strictly Middle Egyptian.

* 'Classical' degree 0 forms used:

- *ỉw w{ꜣ}ḏ.n ḥm.f:* delocutive report texteme. The enacting clause constitutes almost the unique texteme of endowment and specific commission decrees (with the listing texteme), and it is not preceded by the *tꜣ wḏt m ḏd* introduction formula observed in previous decrees. It is followed by the object of the decree (*wꜣḥ, mḥ*), expressed by substantives or infinitives. Kitchen's past translation of *mḥ* overlooks its object-quality as another measure taken by the king (*RITA* I, 2). The formula is close to Middle Kingdom examples of endowment decrees: see 12th dynasty *Snwsrt* III *Deir el-Bahari decree*, with *ỉw wḏ.n ḥm* (source of decree) + *smnt ḥtp-nṯr* (object = endowment) + *n* (beneficiary) + *m* [*rḫt?*] (list) + *m* (origin) + *m ỉmnyt nt hrw nb* (periodicity) + *m ḥꜣw wnt m-bꜣḥ* (increase) + *ỉr.n ḥm r n mrw srwḏ pꜣwt* (repetition of purpose); for 13th dynasty *Sbkḥtp* IV's *Karnak decree*: *ỉw grt wḏ.n ḥm* (source of decree) + [*wꜣḥ*] *ꜥꜣbt* (object = endowment) + *m mꜣwt* (newly) + *n* (beneficiary) + *r-ṯnw rnpt* (periodicity) + *r m* (...) *n nḥḥ ḥnꜥ ḏt* (term) + *rḫt ỉry* (list) + *ḥr* (origin). For the New Kingdom, see *Ḏḥwtyms* III *Buto decree*: *ỉw wḏ.n ḥm.ỉ* (source of decree) + *rdit* (...) *wꜣḥ.sn ḥtp-nṯr* (object = endowment) + *m* (type) + *m ḥꜣw wnt m-bꜣḥ* (increase) + *m ỉmnyt nt hrw nb* (periodicity) + list; *Ḏḥwtyms* III *Karnak Ptḥ temple decree*: *ỉw grt wḏ.n ḥm.ỉ* (source of decree) + *wꜣḥ ḥtp-nṯr* (object = endowment) + *m mꜣwt* (newly) + *n* (beneficiary) + *m* (short list) + *m ỉmnyt nt hrw nb* (periodicity) + *m ḥꜣw wnt m-bꜣḥ* (increase)*; ꜣḫnitn*'s *Karnak decree*, with [*ỉw wḏ.n ḥm* (…)] + *ḥtp-nṯr wꜣḥ* (object = endowment) + *n* (origin) + *n* (beneficiary) + *m ỉmntw nt hrw nb* (periodicity) + *m* (location) + list.
- *tp n wꜣḥ.f m ḥwt-nṯr.f psn* 12 *biꜣt* 100 *ḥnḳt ds* 4 *smw ḫrš* 10]: listing format constituting a separate texteme, widely used in all kinds of Egyptian texts from all periods, here constructed as: # list title + location/beneficiary of the goods + appellative (sometimes graphically arranged in columns with distanced classifier and plural grapheme as typological marks or taxonomic classifiers) + (unit of measurement) + number (quantity) #, as any table list in modern commercial or administrative documents.
- *m-mitt*: coordination of another object of *w{ꜣ}ḏ*.
- *r-pr pn:* anaphoric use of the archaic proximal demonstrative (although the word previously used referring to the same institution is *ḥwt-nṯr*).
- *di ꜥnḫ:* see *EG* § 303.

* General dialectal features: degree 1.

* Legal terms:

w{ꜣ}ḏ – classifier: 𓏛 (to decree/command).

w3ḥ – classifier: ⟨papyrus roll⟩ (to establish, institute, endowment). See Blumenthal (1970: 120-121) 'seit Pyr als Terminus technicus für Darbringung von Opfern belegt; in der Regel mit direktem Objekt verbunden'. The superordinate [ABSTRACT] category papyrus roll classifier represents a legal institution recorded by a written order. See 6th dynasty *Ppy* II *Coptos G decree*, without classifier.

* Legal formula: *ỉw w{3}ḏ.n ḥm.f* (source of decree) + *w3ḥ ḥtp/mḥ* (object = endowment) + *n* (beneficiary) + *m* (location) + *tp n w3ḥ.f m* (list) + *ḏt nḥḥ* (term).

II. Four *West Silsileh decrees*

Stẖy I's endowment stela to *Ḥꜥpy* is the first of a series of four engraved in recess-chapels in the name of *Stẖy* I, *Rꜥmss* II (Year 1), *Mrnptḥ* (Year 1) and *Rꜥmss* III (Year 6) (*KRI* I, 81-96 n. 44). They comprise a date, # *ẖr ḥm n Ḥr* + the king's titulary #, an introductive invocation, brief normative provisions, a short (only for *Ḥꜥpy* 'this god'[7]) and a long (for all the gods, *Ḥꜥpy* included) offering lists (in *Rꜥmss* III's case, the offering list was never carved), and an epilogue. The four texts being similar, it is *Stẖy* I's version that is given below, with appropriate restorations authorized by the better conserved three other texts (see their parallel versions in Barguet 1952: 50-57). All the preserved endowment decrees have in common the absence of reference to an official charged with organizing the endowment; they must be distinguished from the several commission decrees *infra* (although for Spalinger (1991), *Rꜥmss* III's decree is to be connected with the inspection inscriptions of *Pnpꜣtꜣ* in the general frame of a large 'temple revision policy'). Their engraving commemorates the kings' pious deed and generosity, and their purpose is clearly propagandist. The text below being *Stẖy* I's version of the legal provisions and variance with the other versions being rather minor, variations are indicated in footnotes.

1. Enacting clause (authority, object, beneficiaries, applicability)

(9) *w{ꜣ}ḏ*[8] *ḥm.f wꜣḥ ꜥꜣbt*[9] *n it.f [Ỉmn-Rꜥ ni-swt nṯrw Ḥꜥpy it nṯrw]* (10) *ḏꜣḏꜣt rsy tp n[wy sp sn n rnpt m-hꜣw pꜣ mw] wꜥb n Ḫny*[10] *st ḏsrt*[11] *n wšr*[12] *n nt ḥr.s r ḥꜣp [ḏsrw dwꜣt ḥr ꜥnẖ wḏꜣ snb ni-swt bity nb tꜣwy Mnmꜣꜥtrꜥ sꜣ Rꜥ nb ẖꜥw Stẖy Mrnptḥ*[13] *di ꜥnẖ mi it].f Rꜥ hrw nb irt [mi mꜣꜥ mꜣꜥ nṯr pn m ẖt ẖꜣt*[14] *m* (date) (11) (second date) *m ḥtr n tnw*[15] *rnpt*

(9) His Majesty has decreed (the) institution of/to establish offerings for his father [Amun-Re, king of (the) gods, *Ḥꜥpy*, father of (the) gods,] (10) (and the) divine court of (the) South upon (the) f[lood, twice a year, in the neighborhood of the] pure [water] of Khenyt (= Silsileh), a holy place, without/at (the time of) deprivation of (the) water in it, to cover [(the) sanctity of (the) Netherworld, for (the) life, prosperity, health of (the) King of Upper and Lower Egypt, lord of (the) two lands, *Mnmꜣꜥtrꜥ*, son of Re, lord of crowns, *Stẖy Mrnptḥ*, given life like] his [father] Re, each day, (and) to do [as offering

7 For Kitchen (*RITANC* I, 72), the minor list might be the one offered by the king himself.
8 *w{ꜣ}ḏ{.f} ḥm.f* in *Mrnptḥ*'s version.
9 *ꜥꜣb* in the other versions.
10 *Ḫnwt* in *Mrnptḥ* & *Rꜥmss* III versions (*Rꜥmss* II's version is corrupted).
11 *ḏsr* in the other versions (absence of concord).
12 *whr* in the other versions (see Barguet 1952: 62, n. 2).
13 With appropriate titulary for the other versions.
14 *ꜥꜣbt* in *Mrnptḥ*'s version.
15 *tnw{t}* in *Mrnptḥ*'s version and *n tnw n rnpt* in *Rꜥmss* II and III's versions.

that this god shall be presented with altar goods on (date: beginning of thc inundation) (11) 15th day, (second date: summer low water period)[16], as a due for each year.

* Neo-Egyptian characteristics:

- *w{ꜣ}ḏ*.N: appears instead of *iw wḏ.n ḥm.f* encountered before. It may be either a Neo-Egyptian degree 2 version of the delocutive past report, or an instance of loose composition between two nouns (nucleus + adnominal expansion) so as to give a heading-like, archaic flavor and give authority to the text. Compare with Old Kingdom decrees, where the formula *wḏ ni-swt* (*wḏ* without classifier) is verbal for Goedicke (1964: 34 'the king commanded' and 1967: 10-12), but nominal for Edel (1955: § 87), Blumenthal (1970: 397-400; 1973) and Pantalacci (1985: 248). For Fischer (1977: 58-59), the absence of [ABSTRACT] category 𓏛 classifier for *wḏ* in Old Kingdom decrees may derive from the brevity of the formula, not necessarily because of *wḏ*'s verbal nature). But the fact that the precise Old Kingdom formula is not used (*wḏ ḥm.f* instead of *wḏ ni-swt*) might indicate that a strict parallel cannot be established. Furthermore, one must carefully distinguish the texteme in which these expressions appear: in the Old Kingdom decrees, *wḏ ni-swt* belongs to the heading texteme preceding the addressees; their enacting clause uses a locutive *iw wḏ.n(.i)* or *iw wḏ.n ḥm(.i)* (see *Ppy* I *Coptos A decree*), or *iw wḏ.n ni-swt bity* (*Ppy* II *Coptos B decree)*. Consequently, their *wḏ ni-swt* formula (heading) must be compared to Ramesside decrees proclamation (heading) *w{ꜣ}ḏt ꜣwytw* + addressees (as in *Nauri decree*) or to what must have appeared upon the original decree document but is absent in its lapidary version. Then, if what we have here is an enacting clause, the form *wḏ ḥm.f* must be a degree 2 Neo-Egyptian form of report time ('perfect'). The precise semantic values of *ḥm* and *ni-swt* used in different contexts (heading: *ni-swt*; enacting clause: *ḥm*) in Old Kingdom and posterior decrees are difficult to establish (see *EG*, 74-75; Spiegel (1939: 112-121) 'Gestalt' 'Verkörperung' for *ḥm*; Gardiner (1943: 79) 'servant' for *ḥm*?; Goedicke (1960: 66) the human person for *ḥm* the royal institution for *ni-swt*; *LÄ* III, 478). Furthermore, the situation is far more complicated if one considers the evolution of the heading and the enacting clause formulas:
  - headings:
    Old Kingdom: *wḏ ni-swt*, except for a few cases of king name (+ date) only;
    Middle Kingdom: the practice continues (from the 13th dynasty on, with the addition of the date); but in *Sbkḥtp* IV *Karnak decree* only, *wḏ ḥm.f* is used, followed for the enacting clause by *iw wḏ.n ḥm.i*. It seems that by this time the strictly separated use of *ḥm* and *ni-swt* is fading and that *ḥm* may be employed in both textemes[17];

16 Low water period, see Barguet (1952: 62 & note 2), and *RITANC* I, 70.

17 For Middle Kingdom, see Blumenthal (1970: 23); she also notes during the Old Kingdom the general dynamic role of the king when called *ḥm* in the narrative (with finite syntactic forms; *ḥm* represents

First Intermediate Period: the pre-material formula # date + *ḫr ḥm n ni-swt bity* name + *wḏ ni-swt n* + addressees # is used for the first time (see above);

18th dynasty: several options are found, from sole titulary or the ancient # king + *wḏ ni-swt* + *n* (addressees) # (on the basis of the Old Kingdom formula), to versions close to the 13th dynasty sole case of *wḏ ḥm.f* after the date (with only one sure case of heading, because it is followed by the enacting clause *iw wḏ.n ḥm* in *Ỉmnḥtp* II *Elephantine decree*, the other cases of *wḏ ḥm.f* being either the heading or the enacting clause or a merging of the two textemes). Even a case of *wḏ ḥm.i* appears in *Ḏḥwtyms* III *Karnak Ptḥ temple decree* (followed by the enacting *iw wḏ.n ḥm.i*). Built on the model of 17th dynasty (but without *wḏ ni-swt*!) are some cases of # date + *ḫr ḥm n ni-swt bity* name/complete titulary + *wḏ ḥm.f* # (e.g. *Ḏḥwtyms* III *Heliopolis decree*) or without the final *wḏ ḥm.f* and followed by the enacting *iw wḏ.n ḥm.f* (*Ḏḥwtyms* III *Sai decree*). Finally, a new option appears in *Ḏḥwtyms* IV *decree for Nbimn*, # date + *w{ꜣ}ḏt ꜣwyt* + *tꜣ w{ꜣ}ḏ m ḏd* # which will be adopted during the Ramesside Period.

• Enacting clause:

Old Kingdom: *iw wḏ.n(.i)* or *iw wḏ.n ḥm(.i)* or *iw wḏ.n ni-swt bity* (delocutive, although most examples are locutive ones);

Middle Kingdom: *iw wḏ.n ḥm(.i)* as previously or *wḏ ḥm.i* only in *Ḫwtꜣwyrꜥ Wgf* 13th dynasty decree (preceded by a heading limited to king + date, no addressees but the locutive *ḥm.i* indicates probably an enacting clause).

First Intermediate Period: *iw wḏ.n mwt ni-swt* (the queen-mother replaces *ḥm*, but the form is based on the Old Kingdom model);

18th dynasty: *iw wḏ.n ḥm.i/f* or *wḏ.n ḥm.i* (Neo-Egyptian degree 1 form that lost the thematic *iw*, in *Ḏḥwtyms* IV *decree for Nbimn*), or even *wḏ ḥm.i/f*.

Thus, *wḏ ḥm.f* may be the result of several processes: the enlargement of the scope of the decree, no longer addressed to a limited number of specified persons (decreasing importance of heading limited to *wḏ ni-swt* + addressees); departure from the Old Kingdom lapidary format that was probably graphically close to the papyrus/leather original, New Kingdom lapidary versions of royal decrees gaining a format more adapted to their propagandist role; semantic closeness (or loss of peculiarity) of *ni-swt* and *ḥm* in favor of *ḥm*; and finally Neo-Egyptian syntax (Old Kingdom report time *iw wḏ.n ḥm* is 'translated' into Neo-Egyptian report *sḏm*.N, which is also formally close to ancient *wḏ ni-swt*, a fact that may enhance the appeal of a 'merged' form of header/enacting clause). See also Simpson (1996: 85) for Ptolemaic sacerdotal decrees.

- *pꜣ mw:* cataphoric use of the articloid.
- *n wšr:* circumstantial non-existence (see Middle Egyptian *nn sḏm*). Braguet (1952: 62) sees *n* as the preposition 'à (l'époque où) l'eau y est basse', followed

---

always a living king), *ni-swt* appearing in 'static' descriptive constructions (nominal forms; *ni-swt* may represent a dead or a living king).

by Van der Plas (1986: 146); in *RITA* I, 76, it is translated as the negator '(to be) without lack of water on it'.

* 'Classical' degree 0 forms used:
  - *wꜣḥ, irt:* nominal object (noun or infinitive) of *w{ꜣ}ḏ*.
  - *r ḥꜣp:* purpose expressed by the preposition *r* + an infinitive.
  - *mꜣꜥ nṯr pn:* independent passive prospective *sḏm*.N, prescriptive mode, or prospective that-form.
  - *nṯr pn:* anaphoric archaic proximal demonstrative.
* General dialectal features: degree 1.
* Legal terms: *w{ꜣ}ḏ* – classifier: [sign] (to decree/command).
  wꜣḥ – classifier: ø (to establish, institute, endowment).
  ḏꜣḏꜣt - classifier: ø (divine court). See the *Kanais decree*.
* Legal formula: *w{ꜣ}ḏ ḥm.f* (source of decree) + *wꜣḥ ꜥꜣbt* (object) + *n* (beneficiaries) + *sp sn n rnpt* (periodicity) + *m-hꜣw* (place) + *r* (purpose) + *irt mi mꜣꜥ* (second object) + *m* (object) + *m* (date & periodicity)

2. Operative part: measures to be taken for further offerings

(11) (...) *rḫt n ḥtpw m rnpt ḥḥw*[18] *ḥfnw ni-swt bity nb tꜣwy Mnmꜣꜥtrꜥ sꜣ Rꜥ nb ḫꜥw Sṯḫy Mrnptḥ di ꜥnḫ bḥs wꜣḏ* 1 *r* 1 *smn* 2 *rḫ ꜥꜣbt*[19] *tn nty ḥr mꜣꜥ n nṯrw nbw Nnw hrw*[20] *pf n ḫꜣꜥ mḏꜣt Ḥꜥpy iw sšrw iry ḥr šnwt ḥtp nṯr n Ỉmn-Rꜥ ni-swt nṯrw nb pt ḥkꜣ Wꜣst* (lists arranged in columns)] (11) (...) Amount of offerings for millions (and) myriads of year(s) of (the) king of Upper and Lower Egypt, lord of (the) two lands, *Mnmꜣꜥtrꜥ*, son of Re, lord of crowns, *Sṯḫy Mrnptḥ*, given life: young calf – 1, *r* goose – 1, *smn* goose – 2. List of this offering that is presented to all (the) gods (and) Nun that day of throwing (the) book of *Ḥꜥpy*[21], when (the) grain thereof (is) from (the) granary[22] of divine offering of Amun-Re, king of gods, lord of Heaven, ruler of Thebae: (lists arranged in columns)]

* Neo-Egyptian characteristics: -
* 'Classical' degree 0 forms used:
  - *ꜥꜣbt tn:* cataphoric archaic proximal demonstrative.
  - *nṯrw nbw:* note the concord (*nbw* expresses totality).

18 *ḥḥ* in *Rꜥmss* version.
19 *ꜥꜣb* in *Mrnptḥ* & *Rꜥmss* III versions.
20 *hr{p}w* in *Mrnptḥ* version.
21 Symbolic throwing of offering lists in the Nile (see *pHarris* I 37b: 6 ff. and 54a: 2-3 ff.; Barguet (1952: 63, n. 1); *RITANC* I, 72-73; Van der Plas (1986: 146-147, 181) 'Les dons énumérés ne sont pas offerts *in natura* mais *in scriptura*').
22 See Haring (1997: 195-196). The origin of the goods is also indicated in the *Deir el-Bahari decree* of *Snwsrt* III (see above).

- *hrw pf n ẖꜣꜥ mḏꜣt:* noun + cataphoric distal demonstrative expanded by *nota relationis* (relator + infinitive + its object).
- *bḥs wꜣḏ 1 r 1 smn 2:* first short listing texteme on the model of the *Buhen decrees.*
- lists arranged in columns: second long listing texteme consisting of 5 columns # appellative + color/classifier/*p(f)sw* (: cooking)/others + repetition of the appellative classifier or the color/baking ratio/others + number (quantity)/measure/unit + number (quantity) #.

* General dialectal features: degree 0.

* Legal terms: -

* Legal formula: *rḫt n ḥtpw* (list for the king) + *rḫ ꜥꜣbt... n* (list for the gods) + *hrw pf* (date) + *iw sšrw iry ḥr* (origin) + long list.

III. *Deir el-Medineh decree*

A short endowment decree of *Rˁmss* II (Year 9) engraved upon the limestone statue of the royal scribe *Rˁms* (*Cairo JE* 72000; Bruyère (1952: pl. 12, 35); *KRI* II, 362-363 n. 128) found in Deir el-Medineh. The text begins with the date and royal titulary, adds a brief enacting clause and a list of offerings, and closes with a colophon.

1. Enacting clause (authority, object, beneficiaries)

(3) *w{ꜣ}ḏ ḥm.f ˁn[ḫ] wḏꜣ snb wꜣḥ ḥtp-nṯr n twt [p]n m [t]ꜣ ḥwt[-nṯr] nw Ḥwt-Ḥr* (4) *ḥr-tp Wꜣst m pꜣ ḫr ḫnw ḥtp-nṯr m tꜣ ḥwt Wsrmꜣˁtrˁ Stpnrˁ* (5) *n[ty] ḥr imn Wꜣst*

(3) His Majesty L.P.H. has decreed to institute a divine offering for [th]is statue in [th]e tem[ple] of Hathor (4), chief of Thebae, in the necropolis of (*Rˁmss* II) royal chapel[23], a divine offering from the temple of *Wsrmꜣˁtrˁ Stpnrˁ* (5) w[ho] is on (the) West of Thebae: (list = operative part)

* Neo-Egyptian characteristics:
- *w{ꜣ}ḏ ḥm.f*
- *[t]ꜣ [ḥwt-nṯr]:* cataphoric determinator.
- *pꜣ ḫr ḫnw:* cataphoric determinator.
- *tꜣ ḥwt Wsrmꜣˁtrˁ Stpnrˁ:* cataphoric determinator.

* 'Classical' degree 0 forms used:
- *wꜣḥ:* infinitive object of *w{ꜣ}ḏ*.
- *twt [p]n:* proximal archaic demonstrative.
- *[t]ꜣ [ḥwt-nṯr] nw Ḥwt-Ḥr:* relator (the concord should have been feminine).
- *n[ty] ḥr imn Wꜣst:* relative clause with adverbial rheme.
- list: listing texteme, # appellative + *p(f)sw* (: cooking) + number (baking ratio) + unit (loaves, jars) + number (quantity) #

* General dialectal features: degree 2.

* Legal terms: *w{ꜣ}ḏ* – classifier: (to decree/command).
wꜣḥ – classifier: (to establish, institute, endowment).

* Legal formula: *w{ꜣ}ḏ ḥm.f* (source of decree) + *wꜣḥ ḥtp-nṯr* (object) + *n* (beneficiary) + list (= operative part)

2. Colophon

(6) [...] *ms* (7) *ḫꜣyt.s[n] sš m st mꜣˁt Rˁms* [*iy*] *ḥr.f* (8) *sš ni-swt imy-r niwt ṯꜣt Pꜣ[sr...]*[24] *pꜣ ḥkꜣ* (9) *nfr r* [...] (10) *in sš m st mꜣˁt Rˁms*

23 Bruyère (1952: 56); *RITANC* II, 218.
24 See *RITA* II, 196.

(6) […] who brought? (7) th[eir] altar?, scribe in (the) Place of Truth (= Theban necropolis), *Rꜥms*. It is about him (= it?) that [has come] (8) (the) royal scribe, city governor, vizier *Pꜣ*[*sr*…] the good ruler to (9) […] (10) by (the) scribe in (the) Place of Truth, *Rꜥms*.

* Neo-Egyptian characteristics:

- [*iy*] *ḥr.f sš:* see *Hermopolis decree*. Note the suffix *.f* instead of usual neutral *.s*.
- *pꜣ ḥḳꜣ:* anaphoric determinator.

* 'Classical' degree 0 forms used: -

* General dialectal features: degree 1.

* Legal terms: -

* Legal formula: [*iy*] *ḥr.f* + title and proper noun (responsible) + *r* (purpose)

IV. *Abydos decree*

A short endowment decree from *Rꜥmss* II's Abydos temple (*KRI* II, 515 n.204 A.II) inscribed on the south wall bandeau from the west side door to the east side door. It consists of the royal titulary, a eulogy and a brief enacting clause and is most probably completed by the festival calendar lists that were also preceded by a royal decree (see *KRI* II, 516 n.204 C.2).

Enacting clause (authority, object, beneficiaries and applicability)

(…) *wḏ ḥm.f wꜣḥ ḥtp-nṯr n ỉt.f Wsỉr ḫnty ỉmntyw Ỉst wrt mwt nṯr Ḥr nḫt nḏ ỉt.f Wpwt šmꜥw ḫrp tꜣwy <n> pꜣ sšm ḫw n ni-swt bity Wsrmꜣꜥtrꜥ Stpnrꜥ nṯrw nṯrwt ỉmw ḥwt Rꜥmss Mrỉmn m pr Wsỉr m ỉmnyt nt hrw nb ḥbw nw pt nw tꜣ tp-tr nb ḫpr.t*[*y.f*]*y*

(3) His Majesty has decreed to institute a divine offering for his father Osiris Foremost of (the) Westerners, Isis (the) great, divine mother, Horus (the) protective champion of his father, *Wpwt* of (the) South, controller of (the) Two Lands, <for> the cult image (and its bark) of (the) king of Upper and Lower Egypt *Wsrmꜣꜥtrꜥ Stpnrꜥ* of gods (and) goddesses who are in (the) temple of *Rꜥmss Mrỉmn* in (the) house of Osiris, as daily offerings, festivals of heaven (and) earth, (and) every calendar festival that will occur.

* Neo-Egyptian characteristics:
- *wḏ ḥm.f:* note the Middle Egyptian spelling.
- *pꜣ sšm ḫw:* cataphoric determinator (note the omission of the preposition).

* 'Classical' degree 0 forms used:
- *wꜣḥ:* infinitive object of *wḏ*.
- *nt, nw:* relators with marked concord.
- *ḫpr.t*[*y.f*]*y*: future participle.

* General dialectal features: degree 2.

* Legal terms: *wḏ* – classifier: 𓏛 (to decree/command).
wꜣḥ – classifier: 𓏛 (to establish, institute, endowment).

* Legal formula: *wḏ ḥm.f* (source of decree) + *wꜣḥ ḥtp-nṯr* (object) + *n* (beneficiaries) + *m ỉmnyt* (periodicity).

V. *Medamud decree*

Rꜥmss III donation stela (*IFAO* 5413, *KRI* V, 227 n. 57; Kitchen 1973: 193-200), Year 2. After the pre-material # date + *ḫr ḥm* + royal titulary # begins the enacting clause of the decree.

Enacting clause (authority, object, beneficiary, applicability)

(2) *wḏ n ḥm.f rdit ꜣḥwt ḥnkyt nty* <*sṯꜣt*>50[25] *n pꜣ twt* (3) *n Ỉmn-Rꜥ ni-swt nṯrw ḥnꜥ pꜣ tw(t) n Rꜥmss Ḥkꜣiwnw sꜣ Ỉmn ms n* (4) *Mwt pꜣ nb pꜣ kꜣ m w*[26] *n Prntꜣ ḥr ꜣḥwt Prdwꜣ(t)* (5) *rsy m Prdwꜣt ꜣbtt m Prdwꜣt mḥt m pr Ỉmn imntt* (6) *m pr Mnṯw m wḏ n* (date) *n ni-swt bity nb tꜣwy Wsrmꜣꜥtrꜥ Mrimn* (7) [*iw.w*] *dyt* [*m ḥr n?*] *sꜣw sšw n pr Ỉmn-Rꜥ ni-swt nṯrw Ḫꜥmipt sꜣ Wsir sꜣw sšw* (8) [*idnw*] *n pr-ḥḏ n pr Ỉmn-Rꜥ ni-swt nṯrw Ỉymisbꜣ mꜣꜥ-ḫrw* (*m*) *sꜣ n sꜣ*[*.f*] *iwꜥ n iwꜥ.f n*[*ḥḥ*]

(2) His Majesty has decreed to give endowment fields of 50 <arourae> to the statue (3) of Amun-Re, king of gods, and the statue of *Rꜥmss Ḥkꜣiwnw*, son of Amun, born of (4) Mut, the Lord of the provisions, in (the) district of *Prntꜣ*, on (the) fields of *Prdwꜣ(t)* (5), (the) South being at *Prdwꜣt*, (the) East at *Prdwꜣt*, (the) North at (the) estate of Amun/*Primn*, (the) West (6) at (the) estate of Montu/*Prmnṯw*, according to (the) decree of (date) of (the) king of Upper and Lower Egypt, lord of the Two Lands, *Wsrmꜣꜥtrꜥ Mrimn* (7). [They are] placed [in charge of?] (the) keeper of scripts (= archivist) of (the) estate of Amun-Re, king of gods, *Ḫꜥmipt*, son of the Osiris, (the) archivist, (8) [deputy] of (the) treasury of (the) estate of Amun-Re, king of gods, *Ỉymisbꜣ*, right of acclaim[27], (from) a son to [his] son, a heir to his heir, for[ever].

* Neo-Egyptian characteristics:

- *pꜣ twt:* Neo-Egyptian cataphoric determinator.
- *pꜣ nb pꜣ kꜣ:* cataphoric use of the first determinator; the second is non-phoric (with a notion name).
- *m wḏ n:* see *infra Medinet Habu decree* colophon for the legality/reference/conformity clause, but in the present case the infinitive has no feminine mark. Compare with *Tod and Karnak inspection inscriptions.*
- [*iw.w*] *dyt* [*m ḥr n?*]: Kitchen's restoration (1973: 195-196). In the preceding decree, *ḫr* and *m ḏrt* are used.
- (*m*) *sꜣ n sꜣ*[*.f*] *iwꜥ n iwꜥ.f:* omission of the preposition in the hereditary clause (see *supra*). Note the first instance of suffix appended to the second member of each binomial.

25 See Habachi (1954: 509.b).

26 ×𓏲𓏲 is also found in the similar *decree of Qantir* (see *infra*).

27 Anthes (1954: 21-51).

* ‘Classical’ degree 0 forms used:
  - *wḏ.n ḥm.f*: without thematic *ỉw* as in *Ḏḥwtyms* IV decree for *Nbỉmn w{ꜣ}ḏ.n ḥm.ỉ.*
  - *ḥnꜥ:* coordinator between two identical and determinated substantives.
  - *mꜣꜥ-ḫrw:* exocentric compound attribute.

* General dialectal features: degree 1.
* Legal terms: *wḏ* – classifier: 𓂻 (to decree/command). Highly unusual, probable confusion with *wḏ* ‘to depart’.
  wḏ – classifier: 𓏛 (papyrus/leather decree).
* Legal formula: *wḏ.n ḥm.f* (source of decree) + *rdỉt ꜣḥwt ḥnkyt* (object = endowment) + <*sṯꜣt*> + numeral (surface measure) + *n* (beneficiaries) + *m*/*ḥr* (location) + *m wḏ n* + date (conformity clause) + [*ỉw.w*] *dyt* [*m ḥr n?*] (office holder) + (*m*) *sꜣ n sꜣ*[*.f*] *ỉwꜥ n ỉwꜥ.f* (hereditary clause) + *n*[*ḥḥ*] (unlimited term).

VI. *Medinet Habu decree*

Rˁmss III's decree (*KRI* V, 119 n. 44; *Medinet Habu* III, pls. 139-140) is 'instituting the temple Calendar and the list of new endowments' for the daily service of his funerary temple that was also devoted to Amun (Nelson 1934: fig. 5). It was carved on the sanctuary south wall, and although the carving year is lost, the decree itself was made during the fourth year of *Rˁmss* III's reign (colophon; see Nelson 1934: 15) and may have been based upon the now lost Ramesseum decree preceding its calendar. *pHarris* I 6, 6-7 probably refers to it (see Grandet 1994 II: 30-31 (130)). Again the short enacting clause is followed by the operative part, a list and a colophon.

1. Enacting clause (authority, object, beneficiaries and applicability)

(55) *wḏ ḥm[.f] r wꜣḥ ḥtpw-nṯr n it.f Ỉmn-Rˁ ni-swt nṯrw*[28] *m Ỉpt-st*[29] *n i[t]w.f nṯrw* [or *psḏt?... n*] *pꜣ sšm ḫw n ni-swt bity Wsrmꜣˁtrˁ Mrimn m tꜣ ḥwt* (56) *nt ḥḥ*[*w m*] *rnpw*[*t*] *n ni-swt bity Wsrmꜣˁtrˁ Mrimn ḫnmt* [*m*] *nḥḥ m pr Ỉmn m imnyt nt hrw nb mn wꜣḥ ḏt* [*nḥḥ*]

(55) [His] Majesty has decreed to establish divine offerings for his father Amun-Re, king of (the) gods in Karnak, for his fa[th]ers, (the) Gods [or Ennead?... (and) for] the cult image of (the) king of Upper and Lower Egypt *Wsrmꜣˁtrˁ Mrimn* in the temple (56) of million[s of] year[s] of the king of Upper and Lower Egypt *Wsrmꜣˁtrˁ Mrimn* 'Favored/United [with] eternity in (the) house/estate of Amun', as a daily offering, well established (and) endowed for ever [and ever].

* Neo-Egyptian characteristics:

- *wḏ ḥm[.f] r wꜣḥ:* first encounter with the preposition *r* + infinitive that also appears in line 6 of the *Karnak Year 16 decree* introduction (*iw wḏ.n ḥm.f r wꜣḥ*), although the last construction is fuller (see also the *Edfu inspection decree*). It may reveal a change in the valence of *wḏ* (see *Wb* I, 394: 'Sp.') or that *r wꜣḥ* is conceived as a purpose.
- *pꜣ sšm, tꜣ ḥwt:* cataphoric use of the determinator.
- *tꜣ ḥwt nt ḥḥ[w m] rnpw[t] n ni-swt bity Wsrmꜣˁtrˁ Mrimn ḫnmt* [*m*] *nḥḥ m pr Ỉmn m imnyt:* for the names of memorial temples, see *supra* (*Nauri decree*); obviously here, the concord of *ḫnmt* with *ḥwt* suggests that the proper name *ḫnmt* [*m*] *nḥḥ m pr Ỉmn m imnyt* follows the possessor *ni-swt bity Wsrmꜣˁtrˁ Mrimn.*

28 This is not the first occurrence of the writing of *nṯrw* with a *t* as if it were *nṯrwt* 'goddesses' (see *Rˁmss* II, *Mrnptḥ* and *Rˁmss* III *West Silsileh endowment decrees*; *Karnak endowment decrees*); it could refer to the abstract 'divinity' principle, or to the collective 'gods and goddesses' when the gender marker used is the feminine. In either case, both solutions belong to the same abstract realm.

29 Locative, not an epithet for Haring (1997: 65-74), so that offerings are also made for Amun in Karnak.

* 'Classical' degree 0 forms used:
    - *tꜣ ḥwt nt ḥḥ[w m] rnpw[t]* and *ỉmnyt nt hrw:* feminine marked concord of the adjectival *nota relationis* relators (but note *tꜣ ḥwt n ḥḥw*, line 58).
    - *mn wꜣḥ:* binomial passive participles expanding *ỉmnyt*, or rhematic statives. Note that *ỉmnyt nt hrw nb* is also a binomial expression.
* General dialectal features: degree 1.
* Legal terms: *wḏ* – classifier: 𓏛 (to decree/command).
  wꜣḥ – classifier: ø (to endow, endowment).
* Legal formula: *wḏ ḥm[.f]* (source of decree) + *r wꜣḥ ḥtp-nṯr* (object) + *n* (beneficiaries) + *m ỉmnyt nt hrw nb* (periodicity) + *mn wꜣḥ ḏt [nḥḥ]* (term)

2. Operative part: measures for the endowment

(56) (…) *wꜣḥ n* (57) *[ni-swt bity Wsrmꜣꜥtrꜥ Mrỉmn sꜣ] Rꜥ Rꜥ[mss] Ḥḳꜣỉwnw n ỉt.f Ỉmn-Rꜥ ni-swt nṯrw m Ỉpt-s[w]t ḥnꜥ pꜣ ḫnt[y]*

wꜣḥ n ḥm[.f] m mꜣwt (58) *[n ỉt.f Ỉmn-Rꜥ m ỉmnyt nt hrw n]b ỉw sšrw ỉrw ḥr šnwt*

tꜣ ḥwt n ḥḥw m rnpwt n ni-swt bity Wsrmꜣꜥtrꜥ Mr[ỉ]mn

pr Ỉmn-Rꜥ ni-swt nṯrw

r nḥḥ ḥnꜥ ḏt m ḳ(ꜣ)b [a correction?][30] *wn m-*(59)*[bꜣḥ*

wꜣḥ n ḥm.f ḥtpw-nṯr n ỉt].f šps Ỉmn-Rꜥ ni-swt nṯr[w] ḥr šnꜥw wꜥb n tꜣ wḫꜣt tri n rwh[ꜣ] (60) *[ỉ]w [sš]rw ḥr nꜣ nywt ḥnwt [n pr n] ḥm.f m mꜣwt n ỉt.f Ỉmn-Rꜥ ni-swt nṯrw (list, totals)*

(56) (…) an endowment of (57) [(the) king of Upper and Lower Egypt *Wsrmꜣꜥtrꜥ Mrỉmn*, son] of Re *Rꜥ[mss] Ḥḳꜣỉwnw*, to his father Amun-Re, king of (the) gods in Kar[n]ak, with this offering tab[le];

an endowment of [his] Majesty, newly/anew[31], (58) [to his father Amun-Re, as a daily offeri]ng, when (the) grain thereof is from (the) granary

of the temple of millions of years of (the) king of Upper and Lower Egypt *Wsrmꜣꜥtrꜥ Mr[ỉ]mn*

of the house/estate of Amun-Re, king of (the) gods,

forever and ever, increasing what was (59) be[fore;

an endowment of his Majesty of divine offering to] his august [father] Amun-Re, king of (the) god[s], from (the) pure workshop[32] for the darkness of (the) even[in]g time (60),

30 See Haring (1997: 63, note 3).

31 Caminos (1958: 63) notes that it is impossible to decide if *m mꜣwt* means here anew (*de novo*) or newly (for the first time).

32 See Haring (1997: 86, 117) for *šnꜥ wꜥb*.

[wh]en (the) [gr]ain is from the lands (?) of (the) service staff (?) [of (the) house of] his Majesty, newly/anew, for his father Amun-Re, king of (the) gods *(list, totals)*

* Neo-Egyptian characteristics:

- *t3 wḫ3t, n3 nywt:* cataphoric use of the determinator.
- *p3 ḫnt*[y]*:* anaphoric, deictic (to one of its depictions) or non-phoric referentiality of the determinator (indicating the unique identity of a table, an object not unique in itself, but identifiable because it refers 'to an item which is conventionally held by users of the language to be representative of or especially prominent within its lexical category' (Simpson 1996: 34): the table = the offering table).
- *r nḥḥ ḥnʿ ḏt*
- *m ḳ(3)b wn m-*[*b3ḥ*]*: Wb* V, 9. The form *wn* is a perfect participle. The formula is known from the Middle Kingdom (*Snwsrt* III *Deir el-Bahari endowment decree)* and 18th dynasty (*Ḏḥwtyms* III *Buto decree*, line 9 in fine and *Karnak Ptḥ temple decree*, line 34) as *m-ḥ3w wnt m-b3ḥ,* with feminine antecedentless *wnt;* see Blumenthal (1970: 165). The version of the *Medinet Habu decree* has thus lost the feminine mark and replaced *m-ḥ3w* with *m ḳ(3)b* (but see *Wb Beleg.* V 9,2 <788> *Rʿmss* III *Karnak stela*: *m-ḥ3w wn m-b3ḥ*). Other documents from the time of *Rʿmss* III show the formulation *m wḥm ḥr wn m-b3ḥ* (*Medinet Habu* 184, 8) or *m-ḥ3w* [*m ḳ(3)b*] *ḥr wn m-b3ḥ* (*Karnak Year 16 decree*, see *infra*). *Rʿmss* IV *Cairo stela JE* 48831 (Korostovtsev 1947: 158, 162), line 14 uses *w3ḥ.i ḥtp-nṯr ʿ$3 n k3.k ḳb.i wnw m-b3ḥ m imnyt* (it is not a decree, but it combines in its narrative two kinds of decrees preoccupations in the same sentence, the line being continued with *ḫw.i n mri nt niwt.k mky.i n dmi.k iry.i wḏw r ḥn r-pr.k m sḏ3w nbt* "I have reserved your city's tenants, I have preserved your town, I have done decrees to equip your temple with every treasure").
- *rwh*[*3*]*:* Neo-Egyptian lexeme (*Wb* II, 409).

* 'Classical' degree 0 forms used:

- *w3ḥ n ni-swt/ḥm.f*: either expanded nouns (with relator *n*) or past relative forms with nominal actor (for Haring 1997: 63, note 2), or abstract that-forms (with several candidates for adverbial focused rheme); the first and last options seem more satisfactory because of the change of texteme (see other decrees where the enacting clause closes with the 'eternity' mention).
- list: listing texteme comprising five columns: # appellative + *p(f)sw* (: cooking) and baking ratio + *m ḥk3t* (*per* measure) + unit (loaves, jars) + number (quantity) # followed by totals and provenance.

* General dialectal features: degree 1.

* Legal terms: *w3ḥ* – classifier: ø (to endow, endowment).

* Legal formula: *w3ḥ* + *n* (origin) + *n* (beneficiary) + *m m3wt* (novelty) + *r nḥḥ ḥnʿ ḏt* (term) + *m ḳ(3)b wn m-*[*b3ḥ*] (increase).

3. Colophon (reference to original/verbal order)

<table><tr><td>(60) (…) m w{ꜣ}ḏt n date (61) in ni-swt bity Wsrmꜣꜥtrꜥ Mrimn m ir ḫt n it.f

(60) (…) According to a decree of (date) (61), by (the) king of Upper and Lower Egypt Wsrmꜣꜥtrꜥ Mrimn, acting for his father.</td></tr></table>

* Neo-Egyptian characteristics:
- *m w{ꜣ}ḏt:* Neo-Egyptian spelling. This type of referentiality/legality formulation already appears in the 5th dynasty *Nfrirkꜣrꜥ Abydos decree: m wḏ ni-swt bity Nfrirkꜣrꜥ*.
- *m ir:* note the Neo-Egyptian spelling of the infinitive.

* 'Classical' degree 0 forms used: -
* General dialectal features: degree 1.
* Legal terms: *w{ꜣ}ḏt* – classifier: 𓄛 (papyrus or leather decree). Compare with the preceding.
* Legal formula: *m w{ꜣ}ḏt* (reference) + *n* (date) + *in* (author) + *m ir ḫt n* (beneficiary)

VII. Three *Karnak (Temple of Amun) decrees*

Years 6, 7, and 16 *Rꜥmss* III decrees (*KRI* V, 234-237 n. 70) were carved on the east exterior wall of *Rꜥmss* III temple, visible in Karnak's forecourt of Amun. They are arranged as one text with an 'introduction' concerning the latest of them (Year 16), the three decrees being carved in a chronologically reversed succession (Years 16 – 7 – 6) that unites them closely. This order corresponds to the presentation of the amendment to the two previous decrees. The 'introduction' to the Year 16 decree appears to contain more or less the usual legal dispositions in the format of royal titulary, a 'literary' apparatus with enacting clause *iw wḏ.n ḥm.f*. Then, the text of each decree is reduced to a minimal disposition, probably reproducing the text kept in the temple or the royal administration archives (date, brief enacting clause, list being the operative part).

1. Year 16 decree

1.1 First (general?) enacting clause (authority, object, beneficiary and applicability)

(4) (…) *[i]w w[ḏ].n ḥm.f wꜣḥ ḥtpw-nṯr n it.f [Imn-Rꜥ ni-swt nṯrw]*[33] (5) *m mꜣwt ḥr pꜣy.f ḫnt ꜥꜣ šps wr ḏfꜣw nty mn m-bꜣḥ.f hrw nb ir.n n.f ni-swt bity [nb tꜣ]wy Wsrmꜣꜥtrꜥ Mrimn iw mḥ.n ḥm.f tꜣ šnwt ḥtpw-nṯr n it.f Imn-[Rꜥ] ni-swt nṯrw m šsrw n Kmt ꜥḥꜥw.s* [...]
(6) *iw wḏ.n ḥm.f r ḥḥ* (= *wꜣḥ*) *ḥtpw-nṯr m mꜣwt n it.f Imn-Rꜥ ni-swt nṯrw ḥr pꜣ.f ḫn[t] ꜥꜣ n ḥḏ wr ḏfꜣw ir.n [n.f] ni-swt bity nb tꜣwy Wsrmꜣꜥt[rꜥ] Mrimn sꜣ Rꜥ nb ḫꜥw Rꜥmss Ḥḳꜣiwnw ir.n.f m ḥꜣw [m ḳ(ꜣ)b]* (7) *ḥr wn m-bꜣḥ imnyt nt hrw nb*

(4) (…) His Majesty [h]as de[cr]eed to endow divine offerings to his father [Amun-Re, king of gods] (5), newly/anew, upon his large (and) august offering table 'Great of food' that remains in front of him each day, which (the) king of Upper and Lower Egypt, [Lord of (the) Two L]ands, *Wsrmꜣꜥtrꜥ Mrimn,* has made for him.
His Majesty has filled the granary of divine offerings of his father Amun-[Re], king of gods, with grain of Egypt, its heaps […].
(6) His Majesty has decreed to endow divine offerings newly/anew, to his father Amun-Re, king of gods, upon his large silver offering tab[le] 'Great of food' that (the) king of Upper and Lower Egypt, Lord of (the) Two Lands, *Wsrmꜣꜥt[rꜥ] Mrimn,* son of Re, Lord of crowns, *Rꜥmss Ḥḳꜣiwnw* has made [for him][34], that he made as an increase/it is as an increase that he made (it), [increasing (it)] (7) over what was before, a daily offering.

33 See Nelson (1936: 239).

34 Repetition of the decree's opening sentence; for Haring (1997: 90), it is 'an historical accumulation, or incorporation, of different decrees with the same object.'

* Neo-Egyptian characteristics:

- *p3y.f, p3.f:* Neo-Egyptian possessive determinators.
- *t3 šnwt:* cataphoric use of the determinator.
- *m-ḥ3w [m ḳ(3)b] ḥr wn m-b3ḥ*

* 'Classical' degree 0 forms used:

- *iw wḏ ḥm.f/ iw mḥ.n ḥm.f*: compare the two *Buhen decrees supra*: *iw w{3}ḏ.n ḥm.f* (...) *w3ḥ ḥtpw-nṯr* (...) *m-mitt mḥ* (...)
- *ẖnt* (...) *wr df3w:* noun + exocentric attributive compound (adjective in concord with the preceding noun + noun), on the model of *ẖpn k3w* or *ꜥš3 3pdw*, see Jansen-Winkeln (1994: 53-54). The compound may constitute the proper name of the table, further expanded by two other adjectives (see Nelson 1936: 237-238, n. 13). It is Jansen-Winkeln's contention that the adjective in this kind of compound qualifies the following noun and not the preceding one. It must be added that on the semantic and stylistic levels, there is a certain parallel established in this type of construction between the two nominal elements. The fact that the adjectival element is always in concord with the preceding noun proves that a conceptual link exists between them, as in a *hypallage*; the reversed order and absence of concord in the relation *wr df3w* (instead of **df3w wrw*) also prove that the syntagm *ẖnt wr df3w* is not equivalent to * *ẖnt ḥnꜥ df3w wrw*, for instance. The effect is to create the image of a 'table rich in food' (large table because abundance of food). See *supra*. For a reference to a similar table, see *pHarris* I 5, 12 and Grandet (1994: 229 (118-119) and II: 26-27); Quaegebeur (1994: 167-168).
- *nty mn:* analytic relative construction with stative instead of participle.
- *ir.n* (...) *ni-swt:* synthetic relative active *sḏm.n.*N form, of which the antecedent (*ẖnt*) is the object. Expresses relative anteriority.
- *ir.n.f m ḥ3w:* relative *sḏm.n.f* or abstract that-form with its adverbial rheme/focus. The endowment increase formulation *ir.n.f m ḥꜥw [m ḳ(3)b] ḥr wn m-b3ḥ imnyt nt hrw nb* is close to the one appearing in Middle Kingdom *Snwsrt* III *Deir el-Bahari decree*, although with an inverted order: *m imnyt nt hrw nb* (periodicity) + *m ḥ3w wnt m-b3ḥ* (increase).
- *imnyt nt hrw nb:* note the feminine marked concord of the relator; *nb* has a distributive value.

* General dialectal features: degree 1.

* Legal terms: *wḏ* – classifier: [hieroglyph] (to decree/command).
w3ḥ – classifier: [hieroglyph] (to endow, endowment).

* Legal formula: [*i*]*w w*[*ḏ*].*n ḥm.f* (source of decree) + *w3ḥ ḥtpw-nṯr* (object = endowment) + *n* (beneficiary) + *m m3wt* (newly/anew) + *ḥr* (location) + *ir.n.f m ḥ3w [m ḳ(3)b] ḥr wn m-b3ḥ* (increase) + *imnyt nt hrw nb* (periodicity).

1.2 Brief enacting clause (authority, object, beneficiary)

(8) (date) *wḏ ḥm.f w3ḥ ḥtpw-nṯr n it.f Ỉmn-Rʿ ni-swt nṯrw ḥr p3.f ḫnt ʿ3 n ḥḏ wr ḏf3w ir.*[*n*] *n.f ni-swt bity nb t3w*[*y*] [*Wsrm3ʿtrʿ Mrimn s3 Rʿ nb ḫʿw Rʿmss Ḥk3iwnw di ʿnḫ*] (*lists, total, provenance = operative part*)

(8) (date) His Majesty has decreed to endow divine offerings to his father Amun-Re, king of gods, upon his great silver offering table 'Great of food' that (the) king of Upper and Lower Egypt, Lord of (the) Two Lands, [*Wsrm3ʿtrʿ Mrimn*, son of Re, Lord of crowns, *Rʿmss Ḥk3iwnw* given life], has ma[de] for him: (*lists, total, provenance = operative part*).

* Neo-Egyptian characteristics:
- *wḏ ḥm.f w3ḥ*
- *p3.f:* Neo-Egyptian possessive determinator.

* 'Classical' degree 0 forms used:
- *wr ḏf3w*
- *ir.*[*n*] *ni-swt:* synthetic relative active *sḏm.n.*N.
- list: two columns list comprising # appellative (with qualifier, *p(f)sw*, measure, ratio) + number (quantity) #, total and provenance.

* General dialectal features: degree 1.

* Legal terms: *wḏ* – classifier:  (to decree).
w3ḥ – classifier: ø (to endow, endowment).

* Legal formula: *wḏ ḥm.f* (source of decree) + *w3ḥ ḥtp-nṯr* (object = endowment) + *n* (beneficiary) + *ḥr* (location) + lists, total and provenance.

2 Year 7 decree

Enacting clause (authority, object, beneficiary)

(42) (date) *wḏ ḥm.f w3ḥ ḥtp-nṯr nty ḥr m3ʿ n it.f Ỉmn-Rʿ ni-swt nṯrw ḥr r*[*m*]*n nḫt n p3 twt* (43) *n ni-swt bity nb t3wy Wsrm3ʿtrʿ Mrimn s3 Rʿ nb ḫʿw Rʿmss Ḥk3iwnw nty ḥr-mtr n p3 ḫnt 3ʿt n Ỉmn-Rʿ ni-swt nṯrw* (*list, total, provenance = operative part*)

(42) (date) His Majesty has decreed to endow a divine offering that is sacrificed to his father Amun-Re, king of gods, upon (the) strong arm of (the) statue (43) of (the) king of Upper and Lower Egypt, Lord of (the) Two Lands, *Wsrm3ʿtrʿ Mrimn*, son of Re, Lord of crowns, *Rʿmss Ḥk3iwnw*, that is close to the large offering-table of Amun-Re, king of gods: (*list, total, provenance = operative part*).

* Neo-Egyptian characteristics:

- *wḏ ḥm.f wꜣḥ*
- *pꜣ twt/pꜣ ẖnt:* cataphoric use of the determinator. Note the 'wrong concord' of *ʿꜣt* with *ẖnt* which is masculine.
- *ḥr-mtr:* 'belegt Ende N.R.' (*Wb* II, 171-172).

* 'Classical' degree 0 forms used:

- *nty ḥr mꜣʿ, nty ḥr-mtr:* relative adverbial rhemes.
- list: see above.

* General dialectal features: degree 1.

* Legal terms: *wḏ* – classifier: 𓏛 (to decree).
wꜣḥ – classifier: 𓏛 (to endow, endowment).

* Legal formula: *wḏ ḥm.f* (source of decree) + *wꜣḥ ḥtp-nṯr* (object = endowment) + *n* (beneficiary) + *ḥr* (location) + list and total + provenance

3 Year 6 decree

Enacting clause (authority, object, beneficiary)

(47) (date) *wḏ ḥm.f ḥḥ* (= *wꜣḥ*) *ḥtp-nṯr n ỉt.f Ỉmn-Rʿ ni-swt nṯrw ḥr nꜣ ẖntwy ʿꜣw n ḥḏ nbw* (48) [*ỉ*]*r.n ḥm.f m mꜣwt m pꜣ* [*w*]*bꜣ ʿꜣ n* [...*ḥwt?*] *Ỉmn-Rʿ ni-swt nṯrw* (*list, total and provenance = operative part*)

(47) (date) His Majesty has decreed to endow a divine offering to his father Amun-Re, king of gods, upon the two large silver and gold offering tables (48) that his Majesty [h]as made newly/anew in the great [fo]recourt of [...the temple?] of Amun-Re, king of gods: (*list, total and provenance = operative part*).

* Neo-Egyptian characteristics:

- *wḏ ḥm.f wꜣḥ*
- *nꜣ ẖntwy/pꜣ* [*w*]*bꜣ:* cataphoric use of the determinator.
- [*w*]*bꜣ:* New Kingdom lexeme.

* 'Classical' degree 0 forms used:

- *ỉr.n ḥm.f*
- list: see above.

* General dialectal features: degree 1.

* Legal terms: *wḏ* – classifier: 𓏛 (to decree).
wꜣḥ – classifier: 𓏛 (to endow, endowment).

* Legal formula: *wḏ ḥm.f* (source of decree) + *wꜣḥ ḥtp-nṯr* (object = endowment) + *n* (beneficiary) + *ḥr* (location) + list and total + provenance.

VIII. *Fayum/Herakleopolis decree*

Rˁmss III Fayum donation stela (*KRI* V, 270 n. 89) has only subsisted as fragments (see for details Kessler 1975: 103-134). Its beginning is lost, but may probably be reconstructed as # date + *ḫr ḥm n Ḥr* + royal titulary # (Kessler 1975: 106). The king organizes the cult of a royal statute by endowing lands for this purpose and entrusting the offerings and religious service to a private couple (an officer and his wife) in a brief enacting clause.

Enacting clause (authority, object, beneficiary)

(2) (…) *iw*? (3) *wḏ.n ḥm.f ˁnḫ wḏ3 snb dg3s 3ḥwt ḥnk*[35] *m w*[36] (4) *3ḥ ḳdby 3ḥ smyw n* bovines *n p3* (5) *tw*(*t*) *n Rˁmss Ḥḳ3iwnw s3 Ptḥ mrwt mi Stḫy šmsy.n ḥm.f* (6) *r ḥwt-nṯr Rˁmss Mrimn mri mšˁ.f sšm.f* (?)[37] [*ḥtp-*]*nṯr* (7) *ḥr ˁ3 n twh3yrw Imnḫˁw n p3 nḫt* (8) *n Rˁmss Ḥḳ3iwnw mri mšˁ.f m ḏrt ḥmt.f šmˁ*[*yt*] (9) *n Ptḥ 3st* (*m*) *s3 n s3 iwˁ n iwˁ*
(2) (…) (3) His Majesty L.P.H. has decreed to pace and limit[38] endowment fields in (the) district, (4) *ḳdby*-field, cattle pastures for the (5) statue of *Rˁmss Ḥḳ3iwnw* son of Ptah, popular like Seth. His Majesty has followed (the procession) (6) to (the) temple '*Rˁmss Mriimn* beloved of/who loves his army', so that he would trust (?) (the) divine [offering] (7) under (the control of the) great one of *twh3yrw*-warriors, *Imnḫˁw,* of the fortress (8) of *Rˁmss Ḥḳ3iwnw* beloved of/who loves his army, in (the) possession of his wife, musici[an] (9) of Ptah, Isis, (from) son to son (and) heir to heir.

* Neo-Egyptian characteristics:

- *dg3s:* Neo-Egyptian, see *Wb* V, 501; Kessler (1975: 107-108).
- *ḳdby:* 20th dynasty lexeme, see *Wb* V, 81; Kessler (1975: 109-110).
- *smyw:* 19th dynasty spelling, see *Wb* IV, 119; see *smw n* bovines in the *Nauri decree*, lines 63-64; Kessler (1975: 110).
- *p3 tw*(*t*)*:* Neo-Egyptian cataphoric determinator.
- *twh3yrw:* syllabic spelling of a Semitic lexeme of 18th – 20th dynasty origin, see *Wb* V, 322; Kessler (1975: 112, 117-122 and his references in note 84).
- *p3 nḫt:* cataphoric use of the determinator.
- (*m*) *s3 n s3 iwˁ n iwˁ:* binomials in hereditary clause with omission of the preposition.

35 For the spelling, see *pWilbour* II, 112.

36 Of *Mnnfr*] for Helck (1976: 116).

37 Following Helck (1976: 116) 'zuführen unter die Aufsicht von jemandem'. For Kitchen (*KRI* V, 270), *sšm* is 'unlikely'.

38 The French verb 'arpenter' offers a very interesting parallel with *dg3s*: it is related to 'arpent', acre and signifies 'Mesurer la superficie des terres par toute mesure agraire', but also 'Parcourir à grands pas, à grandes enjambées' (Robert 1987: 102). Surface measuring is of course related to pacing (see the foot as a unit of measurement).

* 'Classical' degree 0 forms used:
  - *ỉw? wḏ.n ḥm.f*
  - *šmsy.n ḥm.f:* motion verb, abstract that-form with adverbial focus *sšm.f* (purpose).
  - *sšm.f (?):* probably a dependent prospective expressing the motivation, here in a past context.
* General dialectal features: degree 1.
* Legal terms: *wḏ* – classifier: (to decree/command).
  ḫr – classifier: ø (under, under the control of). See the *Elephantine decree*, third fragment.
  m ḏrt – classifier: ø (in the possession of). See *m-di* above.
* Legal formula: *ỉw wḏ.n ḥm.f* (source of decree) + *dgȝs ȝḥwt ḥnk* (object = endowment) + *m* (location) + *n* (beneficiary) + *ḫr*/*m ḏrt* (office holders) + (*m*) *sȝ n sȝ ỉwʿ n ỉwʿ* (hereditary clause)

IX. *Qantir decree*

Another *Rʿmss* III donation stela (Cairo *JE* 88879, *KRI* V, 395 n. 174; Habachi 1954: 507-514), found in Qantir. Under the titulary (no # date + *ẖr ḥm* # formula), we find a narrative version of a short enacting clause. Note that in other donation stelae, the enacting (*iw*) *wḏ(.n) ḥm.f* is either erased or absent; see for instance Gauthier (1936: 49, *Rʿmss* II); Helck (1966: 32-41); Gaballa (1973: 109-111, *Rʿmss* III). See also Schulman (1963: 177-184) and *KRI* V, 249-250 n. 74 (*Memphis stela*, University of Pennsylvania Excavations find n. 2882) for a possible publication commission and endowment for the cult of his statue (*Rʿmss* III?)[39].

Enacting clause (authority, object, beneficiary)

(3) (…) *istw wḏ.n ḥm.f rdit* (4) *3ḥt ntw* (=*sṯ3t*) 16[40] *m ḥsyw n ḳrʿw* (5) *ẖ3sty Wsrm3ʿtrʿnḫtw m3ʿ m w n dmit Ḫriw* (6) *wbn.f p3 ḫnm n Smnt3wy*
(3) (…) His Majesty has decreed to give (4) fields of 16 arourae as reward to (the) shield bearer (5) of (the) highland *Wsrm3ʿtrʿnḫtw,* (the) righteous, in (the) district of (the) city of *Ḫriw* (6), his source being the basin of *Smnt3wy.*

* Neo-Egyptian characteristics:
- *dmit:* Neo-Egyptian lexeme (*Wb* V, 456).
- *wbn.f p3 ḫnm: wbn* is Neo-Egyptian (*Wb* I, 294); *p3* is cataphoric. The syntagm is a nominal nexus (# determined theme + determined rheme #), a case that is not identified by Groll (1967) (on page 23, the pattern 'A.f B' is a case of second member absence of determination) but an important pattern in Demotic that also exists in Coptic.

* 'Classical' degree 0 forms used:
- *istw wḏ.n ḥm.f*: independent narrative past form, usually backgrounding, although here at the beginning of the decree (see Junge (1996: 91) for the uses of

39 For the sake of thoroughness, we must add the Neo-Egyptian text (but perhaps pre-Ramesside) of an unknown king Karnak stela found near the third pylon (Helck 1963b: 44-48). The first part is lost; remains of a eulogizing narrative background texteme are followed by a probable enacting clause (lines 6-7: *iw wḏ[.n ḥm.f w3ḥ w3ḥw] m m3wt n n3 ḥʿtw n p3 sšm-ḫw n it.i Ỉmn-Rʿ nb Nswt-T3wy ḫnt Ỉpt-Swt m ḥb.f...* "[His Majesty has] decreed [to endow a garland] newly/anew for the prow of the divine bark of my father Amun-Re, lord of *Nswt-T3wy* in front of *Ỉpt-Swt* during his festival…) (materials used)". Then follows a narrative self-appraisal, the origin of the perpetual endowment, and what looks like a criminal law disposition in case the king's order should not be obeyed (lines 11-12: *ir ḥm-nṯr nb n Ỉmn ḫpr.ty.f(y) nb sẖ.ty.f(y) nb ḥr [wḏ pn ir.n ḥm.i n it].i r tm sw rwḏ.f m mnt m ʿ3t nb šps m ki.f nb ir.n ḥm.f nty m sšw dnw ḥr ʿn ir Ỉmn m ʿḥty ḥnʿ ḥmt.f* "As for any prophet of Amun, anyone who will exist, anyone who will be deaf to [this decree that my Majesty has made for] my [father] to abstain from decorating him daily with all precious stone in any of his form that his Majesty has made (and) that is in paintings upon a drawing board, Amun will make him a cultivator with his wife)".

40 See Habachi (1954: 509.b).

istw, none of which fits our case), instead of *iw wḏ.n ḥm.f*. Probably an erroneous form in an enacting clause.

* General dialectal features: degree 1.
* Legal terms: *wḏ* – classifier: 𓏛 (to decree/command).
* Legal formula: *istw wḏ.n ḥm.f* (source of decree) + *rdit ꜣḥt* (object = endowment) + *sṯꜣt* + numeral (surface measure) + *m* (motivation) + *n* (beneficiaries) + *m w n* (location).

X. Table of the legal register syntactic forms and particularities in endowment decrees

Same remark as for the protection/criminal law decrees table.

Abbreviations:

A = active
En = enacting clause
Col = colophon
DelM = Deir el-Medineh decree
M. Habu = Medinet Habu decree
O = operative part
P = passive
x = numerous occurrences

Form	Degree	Buhen 1 19th d. *Rˁmss* I	Buhen 2 19th d. *Stẖy* I	Silsileh 1 19th d. *Stẖy* I	Silsileh 2 19th d. *Rˁmss* II	Silsileh 3 19th d. *Mrnptḥ*	Silsileh 4 20th d. *Rˁmss* III	DelM 19th d. *Rˁmss* II	Abydos 19th d. *Rˁmss* II	M. Habu 20th d. *Rˁmss* III	3 Karnak 20th d. *Rˁmss* III	Fayum 20th d. *Rˁmss* III	Medamud 20th d. *Rˁmss* III	Qantir 20th d. *Rˁmss* III
iw sḏm.n.N (indep. perfect delocutive report, A)	0	1 (En)									1 (En)	1 (En)		
istw sḏm.n.N	1													1 (En)
sḏm.n.N	1												1 (En)	
sḏm.N	2			1 (En)	1 (En)	1 (En)	1 (En)	1 (En)	1 (En)	1 (En)	3 (En)			
sḏm (perfect participle P or stative)	0	1 (En)	1 (En)		2 (En)	2 (En)	2 (En)			3 (En)	2 (En)	2? (En)	1 (En)	1 (En)
wn (fem.)	1									1 (O)	1 (En)			
sḏmt (masc.)	1									1 (En)				
dyt (masc.)	1												1 (En)	
sḏm (participle, A)	0				1 (En)	1 (En)	1 (En)	1 (Col)				2? (En)		
sḏm.ty.fy	0								1 (En)					
n sḏm (circ. non-existence, prohibition)	1			1 (En)	1 (En)	1 (En)	1 (En)							
sḏm.n.f (indep. perfect abstract that-form, A or relative)	0									3? (O)	5 (En)	1 (En)		
sḏm.N								1 (Col)						

sḏm.N (indep. prescriptive or relative prospective, P)	0				1 (En)	1 (En)	1 (En)							
sḏm.f (depend. prospective, A)	0											1 (En)		
sḏm/t (infinitive)	0	2 (En)	3 (En)	3 (En)	3 (En)	3 (En)	3 (En)	1 (En)	1 (En)	2 (En, O)	6 (En)	1 (En)	1 (En)	1 (En)
sḏm (fem)/*t* (m)	1									1 (Col)				
r sḏm (object of *wḏ*)	1									1 (En)				
N.*f pꜣ* N (nominal nexus)	1													1 (En)
hrw/pr/nṯr pn (anaphoric proximal demonstrative)	0		1 (En)		1 (En)	1 (En)	1 (En)							
pn, tn, nn (cataphoric proximal demonstrative)	0				1 (En)	1 (En)								
pn (deictic demonstrative)								1 (En)						
pf (cataphoric distal demonstrative)	0				1 (En)	1 (En)								
pꜣ, tꜣ, nꜣ	1							2 (En, Col)		1 (O)			1 (En)	

(anaphoric , deictic or non-phoric articloid)														
pꜣ, tꜣ, nꜣ (cataphoric articloid)	1							2 (En)	1 (En)	5 (En, O)	4 (En)	2 (En)	3 (En)	
pꜣy.f (possessive) *pꜣ.f*	1 1										1 (En) 1 (En)			
nbt/nbw marked concord	0				1 (En)	1 (En)								
n (*nota relationis*) + marked concord	0	 1 (En)	1 (En)	3 (En)	x (En)	x (En)	x (En)	 1 (En)	1 (En) 2 (En)	x (En,O,Col) 2 (En)	x (En) 4 (En)	x (En)	x (En)	2 (En)
N *ḥnꜥ* N (coordinator)	0												1 (En)	
m-mitt (proclitic)	0	1 (En)												
preposition omission									1 (En)			1 (En)	1 (En)	
r nḥḥ ḥnꜥ ḏt	1									1 (O)				
exocentric compounds	0										3 (En)		1 (En)	

3. Specific commission decrees

I. Land-survey: *Brooklyn 69.116.1* and *Fayum decrees*

For the sake of thoroughness, one has to mention several short texts that are perhaps not strictly speaking 'decrees' but reminders of royal decrees execution. Because of the nature of the enacting clause texteme in Egyptian royal decrees (a report texteme with a performative flavor, not a 'real' performative utterance, see *supra*), a very fine line separates it from a narrative/report commemorative texteme (see Grandet (1994: 130) concerning the Tod inspection inscription, 'texte commémoratif'). In the two cases presented here, we cannot even talk about narratives. A laconic note upon two 'boundary stelae' (*RITA* I, 152) following a pictorial scene, location coordinates, the pre-material formula # date + *ḫr ḥm n* + royal titulary #, is all one can find upon *Stḫy* I Year 1 (from Kom el-Lufi, *Brooklyn 69.116.1*, Kessler (1983); *KRI* I, 231 n.100) and Year 2 (from the Fayum, Cairo *CG 34502*, *KRI* I, 45 n. 23) stelae. More than enacting clauses, they represent simple mentions (with a slightly more elaborated Brooklyn stela):

Fayum stela

wḏt ḥm.f ỉrt ỉpw Decree of His Majesty to make a land-survey register.

* Neo-Egyptian characteristics:
- *ỉpw*: Neo-Egyptian (*Wb* I, 67 'Art Aktenstück; ob Kataster?').

* 'Classical' degree 0 forms used:
- *wḏt ḥm.f:* nominal lexeme + relational expansion (in 'loose composition') + infinitive object of *wḏt*, this is not a case of a *wḏ ḥm.f* Neo-Egyptian form of report (see the feminine mark of *wḏt* and its classifier in the case of the *Fayum decree*). The reference here is not to the verbal order of the king, but to the administrative-legal document perhaps in the hand of the official accomplishing his mission on the field (see the same form in the second Medinet Habu inscription of the mission entrusted to *Ỉtwy*, *infra*). As these texts appear upon 'boundary stelae', it may be a way of marking the limits of the region covered by the land-survey register. The textual form used is purely nominal and non-nexal, and the texteme represented is a notational one, as a visa of execution.

* General dialectal features: degree 1.

* Legal terms: *wḏt* - classifier: 𓏛 (papyrus or leather decree, the document).
ỉpw - classifier: 𓏛 (land-survey register). Classified by the [BINDING] category classifier.

* Legal formula: *wḏt ḥm.f* + *irt ipw* (object of the document).

Brooklyn stela

(2) (…) *wḏt ḥm.f ꜥnḫ wḏꜣ snb* (3) [*ir*]*t ipw n nꜣ n ꜣḫwt mn wꜣḥ* (4) *rsyt n Pr-Rꜥ mḥtt ḥr-ib n* [...]

(2) (…) Decree of His Majesty L.P.H. (3) to realize a land-survey register of those lands, established and enduring, south of *Pr-Rꜥ* (= estate of *Rꜥ*), north of (the) midst of […].

* Neo-Egyptian characteristics:
- *ipw*: Neo-Egyptian.

* 'Classical' degree 0 forms used:
- *wḏt ḥm.f:* note the absence of classifier of *wḏt* in this case.
- *nꜣ n ꜣḫwt:* deictic determinator (with classical relator) indicating the lands marked by the boundary stela.
- *mn wꜣḥ:* binomial, either participles expanding *nꜣ n ꜣḫwt* (Kessler (1983: 219) 'die Äcker ihr als "bleibend und dauernd" bestä tigt werden'), or adverbial (although the position of the doublet seems to support the first option, Kitchen in *RITA* I, 199 translates 'Decree (…) (to) make a land-register of the fields, it being lasting and permanent'). Note the univalence of the two lexemes ('intransitive').

* General dialectal features: degree 1.

* Legal terms:

wḏt - classifier: ø (papyrus or leather decree, the document).

ipw - classifier: [hieroglyph] (land-survey register). See Kessler (1983: 219). Classified by the [BINDING] category classifier.

mn wꜣḥ - classifiers: [hieroglyph] (*mn*) ø (*wꜣḥ*) (established/vested and enduring/instituted). See above the binomial *ꜥḥꜥ mn* in the *Elephantine decree; Wb* II, 60. The lexeme *mn* appears to be a fecund source of binomial expressions in royal decrees.

* Legal formula: *wḏt ḥm.f* + *irt ipw* (object of the document).

II. Expedition commission: *East Silsileh decree*

Stẖy I's Year 6 rock stela from East Silsileh quarries (*KRI* I, 59-61 n.26) is composed of a pictorial scene, the pre-material formula # date + *ḫr ḥm n* + royal titulary #, a eulogizing aetiologic/narrative background, the enacting clause, a description of the king's largess in food supplies, and an epilogue. Note that commission decrees are in fact designed to commemorate the execution of the king's order and their reference to the actual decree is quite brief; they are sometimes signed by the commissioned official who proclaims, once more, the king's beneficent decision and his own efficient execution of the royal order. The enacting clause is preceded by *ḥḏ tꜣ i*[*w* 2 *n hrw*][1] *ḫpr*[*w*], which gives it a narrative flavor.

Enacting clause (authority, object, beneficiaries)

(6) (...) *iw wḏ*[*.n ḥm.f*] *ꜥnḫ wḏꜣ snb rdit iwt ni-swt wpty n ḥm<.f> ꜥnḫ wḏꜣ snb ḫr-tp ꜥnḫw n mšꜥ s ḫꜣ* (7) *m-mitt* [*ḳmꜣ*? boats] *m iswt* [... *r ẖnt*] *mnw n it.f Imn-Rꜥ Wsir ḥnꜥ psḏt.f m inr nfr rwḏ*

(6) (...) [His Majesty] L.P.H. [has] decreed to cause that will come a royal commissioner of <His> Majesty L.P.H. beside an army corps of a thousand men (7), as well as [to build? boats] with crews [... to transport] monuments for his father Amun-Re, Osiris, and his Ennead, of fine hard stone.

* Neo-Egyptian characteristics: -
* 'Classical' degree 0 forms used:

- *iw wḏ*[*.n ḥm.f*]
- *iwt*.N: dependent prospective object of *iw wḏ*[*.n ḥm.f*]. For its morphology during the 19th dynasty, mostly identical to Middle Egyptian, see Winand (1992: 244).
- *m-mitt:* apparently used as coordinator between the two infinitives, objects of *iw wḏ*[*.n ḥm.f*] (*contra*: Kitchen proposes to restore *ḳmꜣ.n* instead of an infinitive in *KRI* I, 60 note 7^{b-b}). Note that in the larger stela of the *Assuan decree* (*infra*), the enacting clause is followed by another report texteme close to what is left of our stela (*iw ḳmꜣ.f* boat.*w wr*[*w*] *ḥr mrw.sn*/*ẖnt.sn skw mitt.sn ḥr ḫn.sn*/*ẖnt.sn n* (= *m*) *ḫꜣt*); the *East Silsileh decree* should perhaps be restored the same way, although the enacting clauses of the two texts are not exactly similar.
- *ḥnꜥ:* coordinator used between the second and third members of the list of beneficiaries.

* General dialectal features: degree 0.
* Legal terms: *wḏ* - classifier: (to decree).
* Legal formula: *iw wḏ*[*.n ḥm.f*] (source of decree) + *rdit iwt* (object) + *n* (beneficiaries)

1 See *KRI* I, 416 and *RITANC* I, 57, following Helck (1973: 214).

III. Public works of quarrying: *Assuan decree*

Stḫy I two stelae of the same decree (Year 9) were carved into the rock of the quarries on the West (smaller stela) and the East (larger one) sides of the road from Philae to Assuan (Habachi (1973: fig. 1 & 2); *KRI* I, 73-74 n. 36-37). The larger and main stela comprises the formula # date + *ḥr ḥm n* + royal titulary #, a eulogy, an enacting clause and short report; the smaller is extremely brief (same date, royal titulary and enacting clause). See also Davies (1997: 221-224).

1. The larger stela enacting clause (authority, object)

(8) *wḏ ḥm.f ꜥnḫ wḏꜣ snb sḥn kꜣt ꜥšꜣ r irt tḫnw ꜥꜣw wrw twtw ꜥꜣw biꜣw* (9) *ḥr rn n ḥm.f ꜥnḫ wḏꜣ snb*

(8) His Majesty L.P.H. has decreed to commission many works, to execute very large obelisks, great (and) marvelous statues (or statues (and) marvels/produces of quarry) (9) in name of his Majesty L.P.H.

* Neo-Egyptian characteristics:

- *wḏ ḥm.f:* note that after the enacting clause, the decree closes with a background report texteme that does not belong to the enacting clause *sensu stricto*; it describes or commemorates the execution of the royal decree by the king, the eldest prince, and his officials. This texteme reads as follows: *iw ḳmꜣ.f* boat.*w wr*[*w*] *ḥr mrw.sn*/*ḫnt.sn skw mitt.sn ḥr ḫn.sn*/*ḫnt.sn n* (= *m*) *ẖꜣt iw wrw mšꜣkbw ḥr sḥsḫ iw sꜣ.f sms m-ḫft ḥr.sn ḥr irt ꜣḫw n ḥm.f* "when he has formed large boats so as to convey them, ship crews like them so as to transport them from (the) quarry, nobles (and) custom officials hurrying (and) his eldest son being in front of them, doing what is beneficial for his Majesty." The form *iw ḳmꜣ.f* is a circumstantial report tense, and the first part of the sentence very much resembles the preceding expedition commission of the *East Silsileh decree*, but it belongs to a different narrative stage.

* 'Classical' degree 0 forms used:

- *r irt:* preposition + infinitive (purpose).

* General dialectal features: degree 2.

* Legal terms: *wḏ* - classifier: 𓂡 (to decree/command).

sḥn (*kꜣt*) - classifier: 𓂝 (to commission (work)). Coercion is of course used in the commissioning process.

* Legal formula: *wḏ ḥm.f* (source of decree) + *sḥn kꜣt* (object = work commission).

Note that a probable other *Stḫy* I commission decree, found in a fragmentary state in El-Kab, is published by Grandet (1990: 98) who restores [*wḏ ḥ*]*m.f dit m* [*ḥr*] *n* [*i͗my-r ni͗w*]*t* [*tꜣ*]*t Nbi͗*[*m*]*n* […].

2. The lesser stela enacting clause (authority, object)

(1) (…) *wḏ ḥm.f ꜥnḫ* [*wḏꜣ*] *snb r i͗rt tḫnw* (= *twtw*) (2) *ꜥꜣw n km*
(1) (…) His Majesty L.[P.]H. has decreed to execute large statues (2) of black (granite).

* Neo-Egyptian characteristics:
- *wḏ ḥm.f:* note that as in the *Medinet Habu decree* previously analyzed, the object is constructed with the preposition *r*. Here the enacting clause is followed by a narrative form (*ꜥḥꜥ.n gm.n ḥm.f*) obviously belonging to another texteme.

* 'Classical' degree 0 forms used: -
* General dialectal features: degree 2.
* Legal terms: *wḏ* - classifier: ? (to decree/command).
* Legal formula: *wḏ ḥm.f* (source of decree) + *r* + infinitive (object = work commission).

IV. Renewal of festival ritual: *BM 1665 decree*

It is probably another *Sthy* I decree that is mentioned at the base of the *BM 1665* stela (*KRI* I, 231 n.99; Shorter (1933: 60-61)) of which a large part is lost (only the bottom-right part is preserved). Parts are still left of the formula that usually follows the royal titulary (*di ꜥnḫ ḏd w3s mi Rꜥ ḏt*), of the eulogizing aetiologic/narrative background, and what is probably an enacting clause; it closes with the royal titulary (Kitchen in *RITA* I, 199 restores [?on behalf of] before the royal titulary).

Enacting clause ([authority], object)

(8) (…) [*wḏ ḥm*]*.f ir nt-ꜥ ḥb m m3wt nty ḫpr.f* (date) *ḥr W3st* (8) (…) His [Majesty has decreed] to renew (the) ritual of (the) festival that will happen (date) in Thebae.

* Neo-Egyptian characteristics:
- [*wḏ ḥm*]*.f:* note that the object is an infinitive without feminine mark.
- *nty ḫpr.f:* relative clause, probably followed by a prospective form (see the *Armant decree*, line 4).

* 'Classical' degree 0 forms used: -
* General dialectal features: degree 2.
* Legal terms: [*wḏ*] - classifier: ⸗ ? (to decree/command).
* Legal formula: [*wḏ ḥm*]*.f* (source of decree) + infinitive (object = renewal of festival ritual).

V. Publication: *West Silsileh, Bigeh, Armant* and *El-Kab decrees*

Brief decrees constructed (with minor variations) on the following basic scheme: # date + royal titulary + enacting clause + name of the inscription's author #. In other cases, the jubilee publication is limited to its date and mention, without enacting formula. Several short publication orders concerning the numerous *Rꜥmss* II jubilees were inscribed in the above-mentioned sites (see Gomaà 1973: 27-33, 88-90)[2]:

- first jubilee, year 30, West Silsileh inscription by prince *Ḫꜥmwꜣst* (*KRI* II, 377 n. 134.A): # date + royal titulary # + enacting clause (authority, object) [*wḏ ḥm.f*] *sr ḥb-sd m tꜣ r-ḏr.f* "[His Majesty has decreed] to make known (the) jubilee festival in (the) whole land" + colophon (author: *Ḫꜥmwꜣst*);
- second jubilee, years 33-34, West Silsileh inscription by prince *Ḫꜥmwꜣst* (*KRI* II, 384-385 n. 135.C): # pictorial scene + [date + *ḫr ḥm n* +] royal titulary # + enacting clause (authority, object) [*wḏ ḥ*]*m.f rdit* [*m ḥr n sꜣ ni-swt sm Ḫꜥmwꜣst r s*]*r ḥb-sd m tꜣ r-ḏr.f* "His [Ma]jesty [has decreed] to com[mission (the) king's son, *sm*-priest, *Ḫꜥmwꜣst,* to make k]nown (the) jubilee festival in (the) whole land" + narrative;
- third jubilee, years 36-37, Bigeh inscription by prince *Ḫꜥmwꜣst* (*KRI* II, 385-386 n. 136.A): # dates of the 3 jubilees + royal titulary # + enacting clause (authority, object) *rdit*[3] [*ḥm.f m*] *ḥr n sm sꜣ ni-swt Ḫꜥmwꜣst r sr ḥb-sdw m tꜣ r-ḏr.f* "His [Ma]jesty [has decreed] to com[mission (the) king's son, *sm*-priest, *Ḫꜥmwꜣst,* to make k]nown (the) jubilee festival in (the) whole land" + colophon (author: *Ḫꜥmwꜣst*);
- fourth jubilee, year 40, West Silsileh inscriptions by prince *Ḫꜥmwꜣst* (*KRI* II, 390-391 n. 137.A & B) and by the vizier *Ḫꜥy* (*KRI* II, 391 n. 137.C and 393 n. 137.G):
  - n.137C: # pictorial scene + dates of the 4 jubilees + *ḫr* + royal titulary # + enacting clause (authority, object) *wḏ ḥm.f rdi*[*t*] *m ḥr n iry-pꜥt ḥꜣty-ꜥ it-nṯr mr r Nḫny ḥm-nṯr Mꜣꜥt tꜣyty* [*sꜣb imy-r niwt*] *ṯꜣt Ḫꜥy mꜣꜥ ḫrw r* [*s*]*r ḥb-sd*[*w m tꜣ*] *ḏr.f ḫt* [*š*]*mꜥw* [*m*]*ḥw* "His Majesty has decreed to com[m]ission (the) hereditary noble, count, god's father, beloved of (the) god, mouth of *Nḫny*, prophet of Maat, [chief] justice, [city governor], vizier *Ḫꜥy*, right of acclaim, to [ma]ke known (the) jubilee festival[s in (the)] whole [land] throughout [s]outhern and [n]orthern Egypt";
  - n. 137G: enacting clause (authority, object) *wḏ ḥm.f rdit m ḥr n iry-pꜥt ḥꜣty*<*-ꜥ*> *it-nṯr mr r Nḫny ḥm-nṯr* [*Mꜣꜥt*] *tꜣyty sꜣb imy-r niwt ṯꜣt Ḫꜥy mꜣꜥ ḫrw r sr ḥb-sdw m tꜣ ḏr.f ḫt šmꜥw mḥw* "His Majesty has decreed to commission (the) hereditary noble, count, god's father, beloved of (the) god, mouth of *Nḫny*, prophet of [Maat], chief justice, city governor, vizier *Ḫꜥy*, right of acclaim, to make known (the) jubilee festivals in (the) whole land throughout southern and northern Egypt";

---

2 The sole jubilee publications retained here are those comprising an enacting clause.

3 Exceptional and probably faulty.

- fifth jubilee, year 42, West Silsileh inscription by the vizier *Ḫꜥy* (*KRI* II, 394 n. 138.B): # date + royal titulary # + enacting clause (authority, object) *w{ꜣ}ḏ ḥm.f di m ḥr n ṯꜣt Ḫꜥy r sr pꜣ ḥb-sd mḥ* 5 *n* king *m tꜣ r ḏr.f* "His Majesty has decreed to commission (the) vizier *Ḫꜥy* to make known the fifth jubilee festival of (king) in (the) whole land";
- sixth jubilee, year 45, West Silsileh inscription by the vizier *Ḫꜥy* (*KRI* II, 394-395 n. 139.A): # pictorial scene + date + [*ḫ*]*r ḥm n* + royal titulary # + enacting clause (authority, object) *wḏ ḥm.f di*[*t*] *m* [*ḥr*] *n iry-pꜥt ḥꜣty-ꜥ it-nṯr mr tꜣyty sꜣb imy-r niwt ṯꜣt Ḫꜥy* [*r sr*] *ḥb-sdw mḥ* 6 *m tꜣ r ḏr.f ḫt ḏꜣtwt šmꜥw* [*m*]*ḥw* "His Majesty has decre[ed] to com[m]ission (the) hereditary noble, count, god's father, beloved of (the) god, chief justice, city governor, vizier *Ḫꜥy* [to make known] (the) sixth jubilee festivals in (the) whole land throughout southern and northern estates" + praise formula + *in* (colophon: author = *Ḫꜥy*);
- eight jubilee, year 51, Armant pylon inscription (*KRI* II, 396 n. 140.C): badly damaged except for the date;
- ninth jubilee, year 54, Armant pylon inscription by the high steward *Ywpꜣ* (*KRI* II, 396 n. 141.A): # date + *ḫr ḥm n* + royal titulary # + enacting clause (authority, object) *w{ꜣ}ḏ ḥm.f dit m ḥr n sš ni-swt imy-r pr wr m t*[*ꜣ*] *ḥwt Wsrmꜣꜥtrꜥ Stpnrꜥ m pr Imn Ywpꜣ r sr ḥb-sdw mḥ* 9 *n Wsrmꜣꜥtrꜥ Stpnrꜥ* [*m tꜣ r ḏr.f*] "His Majesty has decreed to commission (the) royal scribe, high steward of the temple of *Wsrmꜣꜥtrꜥ Stpnrꜥ* in Amun's estate, *Ywpꜣ* to make known (the) ninth jubilee festivals of *Wsrmꜣꜥtrꜥ Stpnrꜥ* [in (the) whole land]";
- tenth jubilee, year 57, Armant pylon and El-Kab (shorter and damaged) inscriptions by the vizier *Nfrrnpt* (*KRI* II, 397 n. 142A/B; Grandet 1990: 97-98): # date + *ḫr ḥm n* + royal titulary # + enacting clause (authority, object) *wḏ ḥm.f dit m ḥr n imy-r niwt Nfrrnpt r sr ḥb-sdw mḥ* 10 *n* king *m tꜣ r ḏr.f* "His Majesty has decreed to commission (the) city governor *Nfrrnpt* to make known (the) tenth jubilee festivals of (the) king in (the) whole land";
- eleventh jubilee, year 60, Armant pylon inscription by the vizier *Nfrrnpt* (*KRI* II, 397 n. 143): # date + *ḫr ḥm n* + royal titulary # + enacting clause (authority, object) *wḏ ḥm*[*.f*] *di*[*t*] *m ḥr* [*n*] *imy-r niw*[*t*] *Nfrrnpt r* [*s*]*r pꜣ ḥb-sdw mḥ* 11 *n* king *m tꜣ* [*r ḏr.f*] "[His] Majesty has decre[ed] to commissi[on] (the) cit[y] governor *Nfrrnpt* to [ma]ke known the eleventh jubilee festivals of (the) king in (the) [whole] land";
- twelfth jubilee, year 63, Armant pylon inscription (*KRI* II, 398 n. 144.A): date + badly damaged clause;
- thirteenth? jubilee, year 66?, Armant pylon inscription (*KRI* II, 398 n. 144.B): also badly damaged.

The enacting clauses thus contain the following elements:

* Neo-Egyptian characteristics:
  - *wḏ/w{ꜣ}ḏ ḥm.f*
  - *di*: in one case, the infinitive has lost its feminine mark.

- *p3 ḥb-sd mḥ* + numeral: the determinator *p3* appears three times with a cataphoric value.

* ‘Classical’ degree 0 forms used: -
* General dialectal features: degree 2.
* Legal terms: *wḏ* - classifier: 𓏛 /ø (to decree/command).
  rdit m ḥr n - classifier: ø (to commission).
* Legal formula: *wḏ ḥm.f* + (*r*)*dit m ḥr* (object = commission) + *n* (commissioned) + *r sr* (publication purpose) + *m t3 r-ḏr.f* (location).

VI. Public works of carving: *Tanis decree*

The "Year 400" Tanis stela (Cairo *JE* 60539, Montet (1931: pl. XIV); *KRI* II, 287-288 n. 71) was ordered by *Rꜥmss* II in honor of Seth, god of the dynasty. Although it has a religious purpose and content, the disposition expressing the royal command for the production of the stela constitutes an enacting clause belonging to a legal register. The stela begins with a pictorial scene followed by the king's titulary, the enacting clause, the Year 400 date, the god Seth of Ombos titulary, narrative with titles, name and genealogy of *Stẖy* (I when he was only vizier) who pronounces the god Seth's eulogy and presents him with a request. For the actual date of the stela (from Year 34 of *Rꜥmss* II onwards) and bibliography, see *RITANC* II, 168-172. As our analysis concerns only a limited part of the text, the complex stela context will not be discussed hereunder; for a more extensive bibliography and discussion of some controversies concerning the stela, see Goedicke (1981) who qualifies the stela 'less as a historical document than a pseudo-political tractatus in the genre of the "Königsnovelle"'.

Enacting clause (authority, object)

(5) *wḏ ḥm.f irt ꜥḥꜥ ꜥꜣ m inr n mꜣt ḥr rn wr n itw.f*[4] *n-mrwt sꜥḥꜥ rn n it itw.f* (6) *ni-swt Mnmꜣꜥtrꜥ sꜣ Rꜥ Stẖy Mrnptḥ mn wꜣḥ n ḏt mi Rꜥ hrw nb*

(5) His Majesty has decreed to make a great stela of granite stone with (the) great name of his fathers (= *Rꜥmss* ancestors) in order that be erected (the) name of his fathers' father (= the god *Stẖy*?) (6), (and? the) king *Mnmꜣꜥtrꜥ*, son of Re, *Stẖy Mrnptḥ*, established (and) enduring for eternity like Re, every day.

* Neo-Egyptian characteristics:
- *wḏ ḥm.f*

* 'Classical' degree 0 forms used:
- *n-mrwt sꜥḥꜥ rn:* passive prospective that-form *sḏm*.N following the compound *n-mrwt* in a dependent clause expressing purpose (see Polotsky 1944: 189).
- *mn wꜣḥ:* binomial expression, extensively used in legal and religious registers (see the *Brooklyn 69.116.1 decree supra*).

* General dialectal features: degree 2.

* Legal terms: *wḏ* - classifier: (to decree/command)
mn wꜣḥ - classifiers: (established and enduring)

* Legal formula: *wḏ ḥm.f* (source of decree) + *irt ꜥḥꜥ* (object = carving).

4 *Contra*: Goedicke (1981: 33-34) who reads *tfw.f* for probable 'governing functions'.

VII. Perpetuation: *Saqqara, Abu Gorab and Abusir decree*

The short and fragmentary *Rʿmss* II decree (*KRI* II, 873-875 n. 333; Drioton & Lauer (1937: 201-211); Lauer (1957: 114-116); Gomaà (1973: Abb. 2) appears on a few blocks of *Wnis*' pyramid in Saqqara belonging to its south-facing side. It was carved by his royal son *Ḫʿmwȝst*[5] apparently after he had restored the building on the order of *Rʿmss*; his son had also inscribed *Wnis*' name on his pyramid (Kitchen in *RITANC* II, 583 calls the inscription a 'museum-label'). Fragments of similar inscriptions (although lacking their introductory formula) have been found on the sites of:

- *Špsskȝf* Saqqara Mastaba Faraoun (Jéquier 1928: 12-13, fig. 7),
- *Niwsrrʿ*'s sun temple of Abu Gorab (Von Bissing & Borchardt 1905: 72-73, fig. 61),
- *Sȝḥwrʿ*'s Abusir pyramid (Borchardt 1910: 104, fig. 128 & 129),
- *Ḏsr* Saqqara pyramid (Lauer 1939: 449),
- *Wsrkȝf* Saqqara pyramid (Lauer 1955: 121),

the *Wnis* pyramid text is the most complete of the set. It begins with the titulary of both *Wnis* and *Rʿmss* II.

Enacting clause (authority, object)

(1) *wḏ ḥm.f di m ḥr{i}n wr ḫrp ḥm sm sȝ ni-swt Ḫʿmwȝs[t sm]n rn n ni-swt bity Wnis* (2) *is[t] n gm rn.f m ḥr mr.f n-ʿȝ-n mry sm sȝ ni-swt [Ḫʿ]mwȝst smnḫ mnw ni-swt* (3) *bityw ḥr ir.sn nty rwḏ.sn* [*wȝ r*[6] *wȝs*]{*m*}[7] [*s*]*mn.n.f wḏt n ḥtp-nṯr.f ḥr* (4) [...] (*the following part is too fragmentary to permit the identification of the texteme*)

(1) His Majesty has decreed to commission (the) master-craftsman (= high-priest of Ptah at Memphis), *sm*-priest, King's son, *Ḫʿmwȝs*[*t* to perpe]tuate (the) name of (the) king of Upper and Lower Egypt *Wnis,* (2) a[s] his name was not to be found upon his pyramid, inasmuch as (the) *sm*-priest, King's son, [*Ḫʿ*]*mwȝst* wished to restore monuments of kings of Upper and (3) Lower Egypt, because of what they have done, whose resistance [was falling in rui]n[8] ; it is by/because [...] that he has confirmed (the) decree for his divine offering, (4) [...]

* Neo-Egyptian characteristics:

- *wḏ ḥm.f*
- *di m ḥr:* direct object of the preceding (*di* being an infinitive, but without feminine mark), elsewhere appearing as # *rdit* + *m ḥr n* + noun #. Drioton (Drioton & Lauer 1937: 209) notes that *di m ḥr* is followed here by a participial

5 See also *infra* the jubilee *Gebel Silsileh decree.*
6 Following *Špsskȝf*'s version.
7 In *Špsskȝf*'s version, *in sm sȝ ni-swt Ḫʿmwȝst* is inserted here.
8 *Špsskȝf* Mastaba Faraoun version probably ends here with the name of the commissioned prince: *in sm sȝ ni-swt Ḫʿmwȝst* (as in several other commission decrees, see *infra*).

statement instead of a noun + infinitive, so that it has to be understood as '«donner à la face», c'est-à-dire « proclamer, publier », suivi du discours direct' (*contra* : *KRI* II, 874 where Kitchen considers it to be an error for *n*). It is difficult to support Drioton's opinion since too many examples attest to scribal (or carver) error. Already used in *Urk.* IV, 652, 49-51 [*wḏ ḥm.f rdit*] *m ḥr n mšʿ r ḏr.f n* [*ḥm nb.ṯn n-ḫt iwt.tn ḥr*] *m di.ṯn* (...) from *Ḏḥwtyms* III *Annals*.

- *n-ʿ3-n mry*.N: note the spelling of the compound preposition (*n-ʿ3*[*t*]*-n* but *n-ʿ3w-n* in *Špssk3f* inscription version) followed by a nominal non-geminating perfect that-form *sḏm*.N (see *EG* § 181 and Gardiner's example with *n-ʿ3t-n* + geminating *mrr.f* and Polotsky 1944: 82-83).
- *ḥr ir.sn:* preposition + Neo-Egyptian nominal perfect (instead of Middle Egyptian *sḏm.n.f*), a non-geminating abstract that-form. See Frandsen (1974: 166) 'it is only in literary and religious set phrases that we find the syntagm prep + that-form'; Winand (1992: 261) about the perfect that-form 'A partir de la 18e dyn., la forme *sḏm.n.f* a été concurrencée, puis finalement détrônée par une forme sans infixe'; Junge (1996: 107) note that the use of a preposition + nominal *sḏm.f* 'ist im Neuägyptischen sehr weitgehend geschwunden'.

* 'Classical' degree 0 forms used:
  - *is*[*t*] *n gm rn.f:* # non enclitic particle + negator *n* + passive *sḏm*.N #; see *EG* § 422,1 and 424,1; Gunn (1924: 131-133); Gilula (1970: 206). The backgrounding particle *is*[*t*] (*EG* § 231 used 'to describe situations or concomitant facts', introducing sentences 'rendered as independent sentences and sometimes as clauses of time or circumstance.'), an 'auxiliaire d'énonciation (...) qui spécifie le procès comme incident par rapport au fil principal de l'énoncé', permits in a narration 'de poser le cadre general dans lequel l'action a lieu' (Cassonnet 2000: 69). The *n sḏm*.N form is a negative passive perfect form. See above *istw* used in an independent sentence, *Qantir decree*, line 3.
  - *nty rwḏ.sn* [*w3 r w3s*]{*m*}*:* relative sentence with adverbial rheme. The probable New Kingdom orthography *w3s*{*m*} is due to a confusion with *ḏʿm* (*Wb* I, 261). For the origin of the expression *smnḫ... srwḏ... w3s*, see Blumenthal (1970: 118-119).
  - [*s*]*mn.n.f:* Drioton and Gomaà (1973: 63) translate it as an independent past form, perhaps as the 'transitional' form of the perfect report *iw sḏm.n.f*. It may be considered as an abstract that-form with an adverbial focus (*ḥr* [...]).
* General dialectal features: degree 2.
* Legal terms:

  wḏ - classifier: ø (to decree/command).

  di m ḥr - classifier: ø ('to place in sight', to commission someone). Usually translated as 'to charge someone' (see *Wb* II, 468 and *infra*), but literally 'decree of his Majesty to place in face/sight/front of X' (see Caminos 1972: 215, n. 2).

  [*s*]*mn* - classifier: 𓏛 (to confirm). The superordinate [ABSTRACT] category papyrus roll classifier represents the legal measure/document of confirmation and the abstract nature of the act of confirmation.

wḏt - classifier: (decree, the legal document written on a leather or papyrus roll).
* Legal formula: *wḏ ḥm.f* (source of decree) + *di m ḥr* (object = commission).

Colophon (inscription author)[9]

(8) (…) [*in sm s3 ni-swt Ḫ*ʿ*mw3s*]*t ir.f di* ʿ*nḫ*
(8) (…) [by the *sm*-priest, King's son, *Ḫ*ʿ*mw3s*]*t,* may he make 'given life'.

* Neo-Egyptian characteristics: -
* 'Classical' degree 0 forms used:
  - *ir.f:* optative.
  - *di* ʿ*nḫ*
* General dialectal features: degree 0.
* Legal terms: -
* Legal formula: *in* + titles + proper name (author).

9 Restoration following the *Špssk3f* Mastaba Faraoun version: *in sm s3 ni-swt Ḫ*ʿ*mw3st.*

VIII. Unidentifiable commission: *West Silsileh decree*

All that remains of *Mrnptḥ*'s Silsileh (West bank) Year 2 decree (*KRI* IV, 73-74 n. 40) in *Ḥrmḥb*'s Speos is a fragmentary stela, its full text having been quite short (see Champollion's copy 1845: pl. CXIV). It is presented here solely in an attempt to obtain an exhaustive panorama of surviving Ramesside decrees, although the nature of the commission remains unsolved. After a pictorial scene and 'frame texts' presenting the king, his wife, and the vizier *P3nḥsy*[10], the pre-material formula # date + [*ḫr ḥm n*] + royal titulary # the enacting clause is unfortunately badly damaged; it is followed by the brief colophon.

1. Enacting clause (authority, object)

(2) *wḏ ḥm.f rdit m ḥr* [*n*...]
(3) [*w*]*pwt*/[*d*]*pwt*? *t3 ḥwt Wsrm3ʿtrʿ*[*Stpnrʿ*...]
(4) *Ḥr-3ḫty r intw.w r niwt* [...]
(5) man *w*? *p3 ḫr iṯ3* [...]
(6) *swt ʿn m-ḫt tw*? [...]
(7) *nty m Ḫnwyt* [...]
(8) *Mrnptḥ Ḥtpḥrm3ʿt m pr Imn nty* [...]
(9) [...] *ʿ rsyt š3ʿ m* [...]*w p3y.*[*s*]*n* [...]

(2) Decree of his Majesty (or His Majesty has decreed) to commission [...]
(3) inventories/boats? of the temple of *Wsrm3ʿtrʿ*[*Stpnrʿ*...]
(4) *Ḥr-3ḫty,* to bring them to town [...]
(5) ? of this tomb seizing ? [...]
(6) places (and) bring back after? [...]
(7) which is in *Ḫnwyt* (Silsileh) [...]
(8) *Mrnptḥ Ḥtpḥrm3ʿt* in (the) estate of Amun who [...]
(9) [...] Southern province beginning from [...] the[i]r [...]

* Neo-Egyptian characteristics:

- *wḏ ḥm.f*
- *t3 ḥwt:* cataphoric determinator.
- *r intw.w: r* + infinitive with Neo-Egyptian spelling + object suffix pronoun in its Neo-Egyptian form (purpose).
- *p3 ḫr:* due to the fragmentary state of this inscription, the value of the articloid cannot be assessed.
- *p3y.n:* Neo-Egyptian possessive determinator.

10 On *P3nḥsy*, see Weil (1908: 104-105); *LÄ* IV, 662; Helck (1958: 325-326, 458).

* 'Classical' degree 0 forms used: ?
* General dialectal features: degree 2.
* Legal terms: *wḏ* - classifier: (to decree/command).
  rdỉt m ḥr - classifier: ø (to commission).
  ỉṯ3 - classifier: ? (to seize?).
* Legal formula: *wḏ ḥm.f* (source of decree) + *rdỉt m ḥr* (object = commission) + [*n*] (official commissioned)

2. Colophon (inscription author)

(10) *ỉn* (titles) *ṯ3t P3nḥsy*

(10) By (titles), (the) vizier *P3nḥsy*.

* Neo-Egyptian characteristics: -
* 'Classical' degree 0 forms used: -
* General dialectal features: degree 0.
* Legal terms: -
* Legal formula: *ỉn* + titles + proper name (author).

IX. Inspection: *Medinet Habu* and *Deir el-Bahari decree*

The inspection mission entrusted to *Ꞽtwy,* at the time of *Mrnptḥ,* has been recorded as bandeau texts in Medinet Habu (Year 2, Thutmoside temple, bark sanctuary doorway, twin texts, see *KRI* IV, 26 n.9 A/B; Kitchen 1984: 549) and Deir el-Bahari (Year 3, *Ḥ3tšpswt* temple, south side of the granite portal to the upper court, see *KRI* IV, 26 n.10; Kitchen 1984: 550). They probably concern the same mission whose accomplishment extends over several years (two records or 'execution visa' of the same decree). They consist of the pre-material # date + *ḥr ḥm ni-swt bity* royal name # + and the short enacting clause hereunder analyzed for the three texts (on the basis of the Medinet Habu A version), their lacunae being completed with the other versions.

Enacting clause (authority, object)

(1) *wḏ*[11] *ḥm.f dit m ḥr n s*[*š*] *ni-swt* (2) *ḥry-ḥbt*[12] *ỉmy-r pr wr Ꞽtwy r* [*ỉr*]*t* [*s*]*ỉpty wr*[13] *n nṯrw nṯrwt nbw šmꜥ mḥw* (1) His Majesty has decreed to commission (the) royal scri[be], chief lector, high steward *Ꞽtwy* to [mak]e a great inventory of all gods (and) goddesses of Upper (and) Lower Egypt.

* Neo-Egyptian characteristics:
- *wḏ ḥm.f:* in the second Medinet Habu inscription, *wḏt ḥm.f* appears instead, without classifier but surely nominal, as in *Brooklyn 69.116.1* and *Fayum decrees*.

* 'Classical' degree 0 forms used:
- *r ỉrt:* preposition + infinitive (purpose).
- *nṯrw nṯrwt nbw*: concord of the specific determinator (totality) with the masculine gender.

* General dialectal features: degree 2.

* Legal terms:

wḏ/*wḏt* - classifier: 𓏛 (decree – to decree/command). The classifier is absent in the second Medinet Habu text.

dit m ḥr n - classifier: ø (to commission).

sỉpty wr - classifier: 𓏛 (great inventory). See Moret (1912: 80, 96) (*ỉp*) in Old Kingdom *Ppy* II decrees; Redford (1981: 92-94) from the root *sỉp* which, in its 'technical sense (...) means to inspect with reference to an extant inventory, or with an eye to setting up such an inventory' whereas the 'result of such official "stock-taking" was of course an official report to which the noun *sỉpt*,

11 *wḏt* in Medinet Habu B.

12 *ḥry-tp* follows in Medinet Habu B and Deir el-Bahari versions.

13 *wr* and *nṯrwt* are absent in Deir el-Bahari version.

"inventory", could be applied.' He adds that the *sipty wr* 'was in the main a compilation of prescriptions governing the manufacture of divine statues, reliefs, cult paraphernalia, and the performance of rituals'; Grandet (1994: 130 (24)). The inventory implies activities such as counting and comparing, involving abstract notions and methods and written medium (superordinate [ABSTRACT] category). In the Deir el-Bahari bandeau, *ipt* (census) alone is inscribed with the 𓏛 classifier.

* Legal formula: *wḏ.n ḥm.f* (source of decree) + *dit m ḥr* (object = commission) + *n* (official commissioned).

X. Inspection: *Tod, Karnak, Edfu, Elephantine* and *El-Kab decree*

Series of five inscriptions of the same decree, based on an inspection order issued by *Rˁmss* III during his fifth reign year as mentioned in the Tod and Karnak inscriptions (*KRI* V, 232-234 n.65, 67 & 68; Grandet 1990: 97). They were engraved in Tod (on the Northwest exterior wall of an 18th dynasty *Mnṯw* kiosk of *Ḏḥwtyms* III), in Karnak (on the North wing of the Amun temple third pylon; Barguet (1962: 83), in Edfu (upon *Rˁmss* III's pylon, an inscription whose date has been preserved, Year 15), in Elephantine (on a bloc found in the quay) and in El-Kab (block of a chamber that is built East to the great court of the *Nḫbt* temple). Although the Tod text date has not been preserved, it is generally admitted that it may be the same Year 15[14] as for the Edfu inscription (Barguet 1952: 99, n. 3; *KRI* V, 232, n. 65), based on another brief text ('visa d'exécution' as coined by Grandet 1994: 130 (24)) engraved on the Tod kiosk (outside, East face) which is dated the 15th year, and reads # date + *ḫr ḥm n* + royal titulary # *m-ḫt dit m ḥr n ḥry s3wt sšw Pnp3t3 n pr-ḥḏ n Pr-ˁ3 ˁnḫ wḏ3 snb r sip r-prw r-š3ˁ Mnnfr r 3bw* 'after commissioning (the) overseer of documents keepers (= archivists) *Pnp3t3* of (the) Treasury of Pharaoh L.P.H. to inspect temples from Memphis to Elephantine' (Barguet 1952: 99; *KRI* V, 233, n. 66). See also, as noted by Barguet (1952: 99, n. 3), *pHarris* I (25, 8-10; 46, 7 and 57, 6-8 for inventories, restoration, purification of the houses and temples ordered by *Rˁmss* III); Christophe (1958: 19); Spalinger (1991: 22-25); Grandet (1994: 95-98) mentioning also *Rˁmss* III *Karnak Year 20 stela* (*KRI* V, 243-247) describing in great details the inventory ordered during year 5.

A. Tod and Karnak inscriptions

The two inscriptions were presumably identical (the Karnak version is badly damaged). The text below represents the Tod inscription (with mentions of variances with Karnak). The pre-material is lost, except for a partial royal titulary, and is followed by a brief eulogy of the king, the enacting clause and a short legality clause.

1. Enacting clause (authority, object, beneficiary)

(1) (…) *wḏ.n ḥm.f irt spy wr m pr it.f n ni-swt bity nb t3wy Wsrm3ˁtrˁ Mrimn s3 Rˁ Rˁmss Ḥk3iwnw* (2) [*r swˁb r-prw nbw n itw.f nṯrw nṯrwt nbw šmˁw*][15] *mḥw m ˁ rsy mḥtwt p3* 3 *mw ḥnˁ sp n3y.sn prw-ḥm* (= *ḥḏ*) *n3y.sn šnwwt p3.sn ḥtpw-nṯr r swrd n3y.sn r-prw m m3w*

14 *Contra*: Grandet (1994: 129 (23)).

15 For Grandet (1994: 130 (24)), the lacuna is limited to [*nṯrw nṯrwt nbw šmˁw*] instead of the one proposed by Braguet.

r ḳd nty wꜣs{m}w n-mrwt rdit mn rnw n itw.f nṯrw nṯrwt nbw šmꜥw mḥw mi rdi.n.sn n.f ḥfnw m ḥb-sd[16] *ḏt*

(1) (...) His Majesty has decreed to carry out an inventory in (the) house of his father, for the king of Upper and Lower Egypt, lord of the two lands, *Wsrmꜣꜥtrꜥ Mrimn,* son of Re, *Rꜥmss Ḥḳꜣiwnw* (2) [to purify[17] all sanctuaries of his fathers, gods and goddesses, lords of Upper Egypt and][18] (the) Delta, in (the) Southern (and) Northern province(s) (and) the 3 waters ('3 effluents'[19] area), and to inspect their treasuries, their granaries, their divine offerings, to strengthen their chapels aright/anew, to (re)build what was ruined in order to cause that shall remain (the) names of his fathers, gods and goddesses, lords of Upper and Lower Egypt, as they had given to him hundreds of thousands of festivals forever;

* Neo-Egyptian characteristics:
- *wḏ.n ḥm.f*
- *pꜣ* 3 *mw:* geographic proper name, with non-phoric articloid distinguishing a unique entity, the delta portion characterized by three specific Nilotic arms from other waters.
- *irt spy wr... ḥnꜥ sp:* embryo-conjunctive.
- *nꜣy.sn/pꜣ.sn:* Neo-Egyptian possessive determinators (note the prosodic isotopy).
- *nty wꜣs{m}w:* relative clause, instead of a participle, with adverbial rheme (object of *ḳd*), the relative is not preceded by a determinator; see *EG* §§ 201, 328. The probable New Kingdom spelling *wꜣs{m}* is due to a confusion with *ḏꜥm* (*Wb* I, 261), although Peden (1994: 188) views it as a misplacement (*nty m wꜣs*). See line 3 reconstruction in the *Špsskꜣf Saqqara decree.*

* 'Classical' degree 0 forms used:
- *r swrd/ḳd:* preposition + infinitive (purpose).
- *n-mrwt rdit:* compound preposition + infinitive (not as frequent as with *sḏm.f* abstract that-form, see *EG* § 181 and Polotsky 1944: 189).
- *mn rnw: sḏm.*N dependent prospective, object of *rdit.*
- *mi rdi.n.sn:* preposition + *sḏm.n.f* nominal that-form (anteriority).

* General dialectal features: degree 1.

* Legal terms:

wḏ - classifier: ø (to decree/command).

spy wr - classifier: 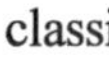 (inventory). This time the lexeme takes the [BINDING] category classifier besides the [ABSTRACT] category classifier observed *supra* (see *(s)ipt (wr)* in the *Medinet Habu & Deir el-Bahari decree*), because the

16 *ḥbw-sd* in the Karnak inscription.

17 Spalinger (1991: 22, n. 5) 'After "purifying" or "cleansing" the temple (of evil, past deeds of a bad nature, etc.), the king then sets up the new regulations.'

18 Barguet (1952: 101) following the *Edfu decree.*

19 They are the 'branches Canopique, Sebennytique et Pelusiaque, dans le Delta' *m itrw ꜥꜣ* (Barguet (1952: 101, n. 4)).

inventory results in a written report/list that has to be archived ([BINDING] category 𓍱 classifier metonymically related to the lexeme).

sp - classifier: 𓏛 (to inspect). The superordinate [ABSTRACT] category classifier may suggest that the mission is accomplished upon a written administrative order or that its results are to be written down. It involves counting and making an inventory of material property, all activities implying abstract notions and methods.

* Legal formula: *wḏ.n ḥm.f* (source of decree) + *irt spy wr… ḥnꜥ sp* (object = inspection) + *m* (location) + *n* (beneficiary) + *r* (purpose).

2. Legality clause (reference, conformity)[20]

(2) (…) *m-ḳnt* (*tp n ir* in Karnak) *mi ḏdwt m* (date)
(2) (…) in force (way/best/beginning of action in Karnak) as (= in accordance with/by virtue of) what was said in (date).

* Neo-Egyptian characteristics: - *ir*: nominal *irt* in Middle Egyptian.
* 'Classical' degree 0 forms used: *ḏdwt:* perfect participle, used as a noun after preposition. Note that *wḏ* is not used here.
* General dialectal features: degree 0.
* Legal terms:

m-ḳnt mi - classifier: *ḳnt* is classified by 𓏛 / 𓀁 (in force as = in force by virtue of). For *m ḳnt*, see *Wb* V, 45 n.16-17; Grandet (1994: 130 (25)) erroneously reads *m ḳnt nḫt*. The expression may be viewed as one that belongs to 'complex prepositional phrases' (preposition + noun + preposition) recognized in modern legal register as a typical legislative writing feature, giving the text a more formal character (Quirk *et alii* 1972: 302; Bhatia 1994: 143; Jackson 1995: 123). On the other hand, *m-ḳnt* may belong to the preceding segment, 'gods and goddesses, lords of Upper and Lower Egypt, as they had given to him hundreds of thousands of festivals forever in force', without any legal connotation (as e.g. in *Urk* IV 648; 895, 15). It is the view adopted by most authors, such as Barguet (1962b: 83), Grandet (1994: 130 (25)), Peden (1994: 1889), although one may ask why the expression follows *ḏt* that usually closes segments (and *tp n irt* is usually a title!). Karnak's adjunction of *tp n ir* is also difficult to understand, as *tp* masks several *signifiés*. In *Wb* V, 267 n.10, one example of *tp n irt* is referred to under 'Art wie etwas zu tun ist', 'von der Überschrift einer List, Berechnung u.ä. (…) c) Med. in der Überschrift (zu folgenden Rezepten)'. Peden (1994: 189) translates it '{a beginning of action}, like that which was commanded in Year

20 Quite different from the Old Kingdom certification formula *ir r-gs ni-swt ḏs.f* (done in the presence of the king himself) in 4th dynasty *Špssk3f Giza decree* for instance (see Goedicke 1964: 35). The legality clause represents a separate texteme in our legal register.

5'). The strong arm classifier represents the [COERCION] category (by force). Note that in Old Kingdom decrees *ḫtf* (*Ppy* II *Coptos B/C/D decrees*: *ir.f ḫt ḫft mdt nt wḏ pn*) or *m* (*Nfrirkꜣrꜥ* and *Tti Abydos decrees*; *Ppy* II *Coptos B/C/G* and *Giza decree*: *m wḏ*) are used to express conformity/legality. Compare also with the formula in the *Stèle juridique de Karnak*, line 12 (17th dynasty): *ir.n.ṯw n.f mi ntt r hp* (it is in conformity with the legal norm that one has acted for him, abstract that-form *sḏm.n.f* + *mi* relative adverbial nexus (focus).

* Legal formula: *m-ḳnt* (*tp n ir*) *mi ḏdwt* (executory and legal) + *m* (date).

B. Year 15 Edfu inscription

See Barsanti (1907: 235); Christophe (1958: 11); *KRI* V, 233, n. 67; Grandet (1994: 130 (24)) for whom it is a simple 'visa d'exécution' of *Pnpꜣtꜣ*'s mission, and who suggests to complete it with *KRI* V, 249, 8-16.

After the pre-material # date + *ḫr ḥm n* + royal titulary #, the decree's legal content is reduced to the enacting clause.

Enacting clause (authority, object)

(1) (...) *iw wḏ.n ḥm.f r swꜥb*[21] *rw-prww*[22] *nbw n šmꜥw r sip prw-ḥḏ šnwwt r ḳ(ꜣ)b ḥtpw-nṯr m ḫꜣw wn [m-]bꜣḥ m-ḫt dit m ḥr n ḥry sꜣwty sšw P(n)pꜣtꜣ mꜣꜥ ḫrw*[23] (1) (...) His Majesty has decreed to purify all sanctuaries of Upper Egypt, to inspect treasuries (and) granaries, to increase divine offerings augmenting[24] what was [be]fore, after commissioning (the) overseer of documents keepers (= archivists) *Pnpꜣtꜣ*, right of acclaim.

* Neo-Egyptian characteristics:

- *r ḳ(ꜣ)b* noun *ḫꜣw wn [m-]bꜣḥ*
- *r swꜥb/sip/ḳ(ꜣ)b:* preposition + infinitives, objects of *wḏ*.

* 'Classical' degree 0 forms used:

- *iw wḏ.n ḥm.f*
- *m-ḫt dit:* compound preposition + infinitive (*EG* § 178 p. 133.3)

* General dialectal features: degree 1.

* Legal terms: *wḏ* - classifier: ø (to decree/command).

21 See Spalinger (1991: 22, n. 5).

22 Again a case of plural compound form with plural marks appended to each member and to the compound.

23 See Anthes (1954: 21-51); Lorton (1974: 109-111), employed also with regard to living persons 'the man's conduct in carrying out his duties was reviewed and approved every year in a juridical setting.'

24 See Christophe (1958: 23) 'doubler'.

sỉp - classifier:  (to inspect).
dỉt m ḥr - classifier: ø (to commission).

* Legal formula: *ỉw wḏ.n ḥm.f* (source of decree) + *r* + infinitive (object = inspection).

C. Elephantine inscription

See *KRI* V, 233, n. 68.

The first part of the text is lost, but the enacting clause is preceded by a eulogy and the clause itself is more elaborated than the preceding inscriptions.

Enacting clause (authority, object, beneficiary, applicability)

(5) *wḏ.n ḥm.f r swꜥb rw-prww*[25] *nbw šmꜥw ḥr bwt*[26] *nb n* [*...m rw-prww n ỉtw.f nṯrw?*] (6) *nṯrw(t?) r sỉp pr-ḥḏ šnwwt r ḫwỉ*[27] *rmṯ.w mnmnt.w* [*m ḳꜣb wn m-bꜣḥ?*[28]*...*] (7) *r sḫpr mꜣꜥt r sḥtm ỉsft r dỉt wn grg m bwt r ḳd* [*nty wꜣs{m}w?...*] (8) *nỉ-swt bỉty nb tꜣwy Wsrmꜣꜥtrꜥ Mrỉmn sꜣ Rꜥ nb ḫꜥw mỉ (Ỉ)tm Rꜥmss Ḥḳꜣỉwnw* [...] (9) *m-ḫt dỉt* [*m*] *ḥr n ḥry sꜣwt sšw Pnpꜣtꜣ n pr-ḥḏ n Pr-ꜥꜣ ꜥnḫ wḏꜣ snb ỉdnw* [*pr? ...*]

(5) His Majesty has decreed to purify all sanctuaries of Upper Egypt of any abomination of [...in (the) sanctuaries of his fathers, gods (and)?] (6) goddesses (?), to inspect treasuries (and) granaries, to reserve their people (and) cattle [increasing what was before ?...,] (7) to create order, to annihilate evil, to cause that falsehood will be in abomination, to (re)build [what was ruined?...] (8) king of Upper and Lower Egypt, lord of (the) two lands, *Wsrmꜣꜥtrꜥ Mrỉmn,* son of Re, lord of crowns, like Atum, *Rꜥmss Ḥḳꜣỉwnw* [...] (9) after com[m]issioning (the) overseer of document keepers (archivists), *Pnpꜣtꜣ* of Pharaoh's treasury L.P.H., deputy [of the house ?...]

* Neo-Egyptian characteristics:

- *wḏ.n ḥm.f r swꜥb:* note the prepositional objects of *wḏ*.
- *rmṯ.w, mnmnt.w*: plural Neo-Egyptian suffixed possessive.
- *r ḫwỉ:* note the infinitive's Neo-Egyptian spelling.

* 'Classical' degree 0 forms used:

- *dỉt wn grg m bwt:* dependent prospective *wn*.N, object of *dỉt*. For similar examples, see *EG* § 118, ex. 2 (*rdỉ.n.s wn.k m nṯr*).
- *m-ḫt dỉt*

25 Again a case of plural compound form with plural marks appended to each member and to the compound.

26 Spalinger (1991: 22-23 and n.6); Grandet (1994: 96) for a comparison with *pHarris* I.

27 There is apparently no trace of a 'summary writing' of the binomial *ḫwỉ mkỉ* (Caminos 1952: 56 (43)).

28 Peden (1994: 190) proposes *r ḳꜣb ḥtpw-nṯr*.

* General dialectal features: degree 1.
* Legal terms: *wḏ* - classifier: ø (to decree/command).
sip - classifier: 𓏛 (to inspect).
ḫwi - classifier: 𓏛 (to reserve).
dit [*m*] *ḥr* - classifier: ø (to commission).
* Legal formula: *wḏ.n ḥm.f* (source of decree) + *r* + infinitives (objects).

D. El-Kab inscription

A brief and fragmentary inscription constituting a 'visa d'exécution' for Grandet (1994: 130 (25)), published by him (1990: 97). Its date is lost, as well as the *ḫr ḥm n* formula and part of the king's titulary.

Enacting clause (authority, object)

wḏ ḥm.[*f*] *rdi*[*t*] *m ḥr n ḥry s3wt*[*y*] *sš*[*w*] *Pn*[*p3t3 n pr-ḥḏ n Pr-ˁ3 ˁnḫ wḏ3 snb r sip r-prw…*]
[His] Majesty has decreed to com[m]ission (the) overseer of archivi[sts] *Pn*[*p3t3* of Pharaoh L.P.H.'s treasury to inspect sanctuaries…]

* Neo-Egyptian characteristics:
- *wḏ ḥm.*[*f*]

* 'Classical' degree 0 forms used: -
* General dialectal features: degree 2.
* Legal terms:
wḏ - classifier: ? (to decree/command).
rdit m ḥr n - classifier: ø (to commission).
* Legal formula: *wḏ ḥm.*[*f*] (source of decree) + *rdi*[*t*] *m ḥr* (object = commission) + *n* (commissioned).

XI. Inventory: *Heliopolis decree*

The *Turin 2682* stela, found in a fragmentary state in Heliopolis, is designed as Old Kingdom decrees (horizontal registers and a vertical (right-side) column with the royal *srḫ* of a lost king. It contains on its recto an inventory of cult objects, with picture, material, measurements and number of items. On the back, the plan of a temple (with legend) mentioned on the recto. Although the year is still visible (year 15)[29], the attribution to a precise reign has been variously proposed: for Ricke (1935: 114) who first published the stela, it could belong to the 22nd dynasty; but for Grandet (1994: 99-100, 132 (64)), *Rᶜmss* III might be a good choice, as *pHarris* I 25, 8 mentions a great inventory, commissioned by the king, of the Heliopolitan *Tm-Rᶜ-Ḥr3ḫty* temple statues, and *Ỉmnmipt* being known as a Great Priest of Heliopolis by the time of *Rᶜmss* II.

Under the royal *srḫ*, three columns comprise a brief enacting clause.

Enacting clause (authority, object)

(1) *wḏ.n ḥm.f rdit m ḥr n it-nṯr ḥry sšt3 Rᶜm3ᶜḫrw s3 Ỉmnmipt n Ḥr-3*[*ḫty pr*] (2) *it-nṯr ḥry sšt3 Nbms s3 Ỉmnmipt n Ḥr-3ḫty pr r ir sipt* [*n ḥwt-nṯr*] (3) *nt mwt.f Ḥwt-Ḥr nb*(*t*) *Ḥtp*(*t*) *t3 dd ḥr sš* [...]
(1) His Majesty has decreed to commission (the) god's father, master of (the) secrets, *Rᶜm3ᶜḫrw*, son of *Ỉmnmipt* of (the) house of *Ḥr-3ḫty* (2) (and the) god's father, master of (the) secrets, *Nbms*, son of *Ỉmnmipt* of (the) estate of *Ḥr-3ḫty* to make an inventory [of (the) temple] (3) of his mother *Ḥwt-Ḥr* mistress of *Ḥtp*(*t*) (and) the *dd* garden in writing [...]

* Neo-Egyptian characteristics:

- *wḏ.n ḥm.f*
- *r ir:* absence of the feminine mark of the infinitive (purpose).
- *t3 dd:* non-phoric articloid in a locality proper noun.

* 'Classical' degree 0 forms used:

- [... *ḥwt-nṯr*] *nt mwt.f:* concord of the relator.

* General dialectal features: degree 2.

* Legal terms: *wḏ* - classifier: ø (to decree/command).
rdit m ḥr - classifier: ø (to commission).
sipt - classifier: ? (inventory).

* Legal formula: *wḏ.n ḥm.f* (source of decree) + *rdit m ḥr* (object = commission) + *n* (official commissioned) + *r ir sipt* (purpose).

29 See Schott (1971: 65-73).

XII. Ritual commission: *El-Kab decree*

Rˁmss III decree engraved in the tomb of *Stȝw* in El-Kab (Gardiner 1910: 47-51, esp. 48), in a text inscribed above a representation of two boats. The decree is probably to be dated to Year 29 of the king's reign (on the basis of a notice in *pTurin* 1880, r° 2,18 recalling the year of the vizier *Tȝ*'s journey); after the lost date and probable *ḫr ḥm n* formula followed by the royal titulary, the mention of *Rˁmss* III's first jubilee and the short enacting clause, a brief report of the vizier's execution of the order and of the royal presence at the bark reception close the inscription.

Enacting clause (authority, object)

(1) (…) *w{ȝ}ḏ.n ḥm.f dit m ḥr n imy-r niwt ṯȝt Tȝ* [*r* (2) *iṯȝ tȝ dpt nṯr n Nḫbt r pȝ ḥb-sd*] *r irt nt-ˁw.s m ḥwwt* (1) (…) His Majesty has decreed to commission (the) city governor, (the) vizier *Tȝ* [to (2) take the divine bark of *Nḫbt* to this sed-jubilee] to carry out her ritual in (the) jubilee temples.

* Neo-Egyptian characteristics:
- *w{ȝ}ḏ.n ḥm.f*

* 'Classical' degree 0 forms used:
- *r irt:* purpose.

* General dialectal features: degree 1.

* Legal terms: *w{ȝ}ḏ* - classifier: 𓂝 (to decree/command).
dit m ḥr - classifier: ø (to commission).

* Legal formula: *w{ȝ}ḏ.n ḥm.f* (source of decree) + *dit m ḥr* (object = commission) + *r irt* (purpose).

XIII. Table of the legal register syntactic forms and particularities in commission decrees

Abbreviations:

A = active

Col = colophon

En = enacting clause

Jubilees = West Silsileh, Bigeh, Armant and El-Kab decrees

L = legality texteme

MH, DelB = Medinet Habu and Deir el-Bahari decree

P = passive

V = visa of execution texteme

x = numerous instances

Form	Degree	Brooklyn..	E.Silsileh	Assuan	*BM 1665*	Jubilees	Tanis	Saqqara…	W.Silsileh	MH, DelB	Tod…	Heliopolis	El-Kab
		19th d.	**19th d.**	**19th d.**	**19th d.**	**19th d.**	**19th d.**	**19th d.**	**19th d.**	**19th d.**	**20th d.**	**20th d.**	**20th d.**
		Sṯḫy I	***Sṯḫy I***	***Sṯḫy I***	***Sṯḫy I***	***Rꜥmss* II**	***Rꜥmss* II**	***Rꜥmss* II**	***Mrnptḥ***	***Mrnptḥ***	***Rꜥmss* III**	***Rꜥmss* III?**	***Rꜥmss* III**
iw sḏm.n.N (indep. perfect report, A)	0		1(En)								1(En)		
sḏm.n.N	1										2(En)		1 (En)
sḏm.N	1			2(En)		x (En)	1(En)	2 (En)	1 (En)	2(En)	1(En)	1(En)	
wḏt ḥm.f (nomin)	0	2(V)				1(En)							
ỉst n sḏm.N (dep. past circ., P, neg.)	0							3 (En)					
sḏm (perfective participle P or stative)	0	2(V)					2(En)						
ḏdwt	0										2 (L)		
wn (fem.)	1										1(En)		
sḏm.f/N (dep. prospective, A)	0		1(En)								3 (En)		
N *nty sḏm.f* (rel. prospective, A)	2				1(En)								
sḏm.n.f (indep. perfect focalizing that-	0							1 (En)					

form, A)													
n-mrwt sḏm.N (prepositional prospective that-form, P)	0						1(En)						
mi sḏm.n.f (prepositional that-form, A, anteriority) *n-ꜥꜣ-n/ḥr sḏm.f*/N	0 1							4 (En)			2(En)		
sḏm/t (infinitive) *sḏmtw* *sḏm*(fem)/*t* (m.)	0 1 1	2(V)	1(En)	3(En)	 1(En)	x(En) 1(En)	2(En)	3(En) 3(En)	1(En) 1(En)	5(En)	x (En) 1(En)	1(En) 1(En)	2 (En)
m-ḫt + infinitive *n-mrwt* + infinitive	0 1										2 (En) 2 (En)		
r sḏm (object of *wḏ*)	1										x (En)		
nty + stative (rel. past object, P)	1										2 (En)		
ḥnꜥ sḏm (embryo-	1										1 (En)		

conjunctive)													
.w (3rd plur. suffix pronoun)	1								1 (En)		2 (En)		
nꜣ n N (plural demonstrative)	0	1(V)											
pꜣ, tꜣ, nꜣ (cataphoric articloid)	1								2? (En)				
pꜣ, tꜣ, nꜣ (non-phoric articloid)	1										1(En)	1(En)	
pꜣy.f (possessive) *pꜣ.f*	1 1								1 (En)		4 (En) 2(En)		
nbt/nbw marked concord	0									3(En)	4(En)		
n (*nota relationis*) + marked concord	0 0	1(V)	2(En)	1(En)			2(En)	2(En)			x(En)	2(En) 1(En)	
m-mitt (coordinator)	0		1(En)										
N *ḥnꜥ* N (coordinator)	0		1(En)										

ḥnʿ in embryo-conjunctive	1									1(En)		

4. Epistolary warning and instruction decrees

I. *pAnastasi* IV. 10, 8 – 11,8

Papyrus Anastasi IV (*BM 10249*) contains diverse texts belonging to *Stẖy* I's reign (*LEM*: 46-47, n. 17; *CLEM*: 176-181). Gardiner calls its lines 10,8-11,8 'A royal rescript of warning and instruction'. It is a personal letter written in hieratic, apparently directly addressed to a royal officer by the king. This document is believed to be a model for a school exercise, based on a real or fictitious letter, the origin of the papyrus being unknown, as is a probable other version of it in *pAnastasi* V.1a; see Erman (1927: 203 n.1); Bakir (1970: 6, 32) 'model letter (...) always lacks an address'; Vernus (1986: 144); Wente (1990: 17). It nevertheless belongs to the sphere of written orders (*wḏ ni-swt*), an expression of the royal command and authority ('lettre d'admonestation' for Vernus 1986: 144 and 1990: 242) that pertains to a different genre (epistolary) and comprises other textemic components (interlocutive; see Sweeney 2001 for her exploration of correspondence and dialogue, letters being (p.1) 'a conversation at a distance'); they are not public normative texts and do not present a legal register. One must note that a parallel schema between personal letters and official decrees is nevertheless the case during the Old Kingdom (see Goedicke 1964: 37), but it might be partly due to the fact that the private decrees that survived were officially authorized tomb versions (see 5th dynasty *Ỉssi*'s letters to *Snḏmib* and *Rʿšpss* and 6th dynasty *Ppy* II's letter to *Ḥrẖwf*), or official personal communications of public relevance (nominations, legally relevant answers to complaints) of which we possess no parallel during the Ramesside Period. See also the Middle Kingdom stelae beginning with an excerpt of a royal decree, followed without marked transition by the stela owner narrative (see *Snwsrt* I decree on *Mnṯwḥtp CG 20539* stela; *Snwsrt* III decree on *Ỉiẖrnfrt Berlin 1204* stela). See also Guieysse (1886: 421-428); also *supra* the Introduction for the inclusion of the epistolary decrees in our corpus.

The three papyrus letters hereby included follow the same scheme: (title and addressee) + introductory formula + object (content) + orders (measures to be taken by the recipient) (+ closing formula + colophon). Note that no 'complimentary preamble' (Bakir 1970: 31) is included before the object of the message in our royal letters corpus (as in any case of a superior writing to a subaltern; see also Goedicke (1948: 46)).

1. Introductory formula

(10,8) (*end of another text*) *r-nt(t/y) in.tw n.k wḏ ni-swt pn n* (10,9) *r-ḏd*

(10,8) (*end of another text*) To (let you know) that it is to you/to say (what follows) that this royal decree has been brought (10,9):

* Neo-Egyptian characteristics:

- *r-nt(t/y)... r-ḏd:* Neo-Egyptian opening and closure of the introductory formula of official letters. As for *r-nt(t/y),* see *EG* § 224-225 *r-ntt* 'without preceding verb (... is) practically untranslatable'; for Hintze (1952: 303) it is principally used in letters; Bakir (1970: 84-85) viewing *r-ḏd* as used for quotations of an original letter, *r-nty* 'may still originate in the relative adjective 'which is, or that is' followed by a sentence functioning as predicate. Thus if *r-nty* is used independently (without any antecedent), an implicit antecedent must be understood, namely the recurring conventional statements (or formulae) that usually precede it in a complete model letter or on ostraca' as 'that is', or 'namely' (note 4); 'direct indicators of syntactic initiality' in *LEG* § 10.10.1; Junge (1996: 93, 227) for whom Neo-Egyptian *r-nty* is etymologically the follower of purpose/cause *r ntt* and in letters 'vorrangig zur Einleitung des eigentlichen Inhalts'. Concerning *r-ḏd,* it introduces the letter content, it is a quotation marker (gerund or converb, a grammaticalization of *ḏd*, the *verbum dicendi*), as in the *Nauri decree* formula *t3 w{3}ḏt m ḏd* (see above). Its value may be a purpose (Sweeney (1986: 339)); for Goedicke (1984: 45-46), about a *Ḥḳ3nḫt* letter opening with *r ḏd* 'according to the saying by', official documents and a superior's address to a subaltern are characterized by the fact that they are 'transcripts' of a verbal dictation, so that 'This independent use of *r* + infinitive has its parallel in the epistolary use of *r-ntt*'. Epistolary decrees from the Old Kingdom that have survived (lapidary versions) follow the public decrees' model, so that the Ramesside introductory formula is based on a scheme that originates in Middle Kingdom/First Intermediate Period:
  - 12th dynasty epistolary decree of *Snwsrt* III in *pBerlin* 10071 ([*wḏ ni-swt n*] + addressee + *ḏd* [*rdit rḫ.*]*k r ntt in.n wḏ n-ḫr ni-swt n.*N "said [to let] you [know] that it is from (the) king that (the) decree has been brought to N"). The address is of the Old Kingdom type, *ḏd* is used to open the quotation of the verbal decree, 𓇋𓈖 is the abstract that-form (relative anteriority) focalizing either *n-ḫr ni-swt* or *n.*N, *r ntt* introducing the object of *rḫ.k* (the preposition indicating purpose has been 'pushed' in front of the relative);
  - 12th dynasty story of *Sinuhe*, version B dating of *Imnmḥ3t* III's reign, where lines 178-179 present a fictional royal letter addressed by *Snwsrt* I to the hero in the format: royal titulary + *wḏ ni-swt n* (addressee) + *m.k in.n(.tw) n.k wḏ pn n ni-swt r rdit rḫ.k ntt* "see that it is to let you know that (...) that this royal decree has been brought to you". The address is of the Old Kingdom type, then the hero is directly addressed by the prospective presentative *m.k*[1], with the following cleft-sentence as its object and focus

1 See David (2000b).

upon the purpose or *n.k*. The purpose expressed by *r rdit rḫ.k* is closed by *ntt* that introduces the object of the decree and of *rḫ.k;*

- two 13th dynasty decrees of *Sbkḥtp* II in *pBrooklyn* 35.1446: again *wḏ ni-swt n* (addressee) + *m.k in.n.tw n.k wḏ pn n ni-swt r rdit rḫ.k ntt*;
- 17th dynasty *Coptos decree* of *Nbḫprwrᶜ ꞽntf*: date + *ḫr ḥm n* + royal titulary + *wḏ ni-swt n* + addressees + *m.tn in.n.tw n.tn wḏ pnn r rdit rḫ.tn r-ntt*, which is an interesting combination of public decrees (it contains criminal dispositions) Old and New Kingdoms features, as well as new modifications to the Middle Kingdom epistolary formula. The direct address loses the *ni-swt* part (previous *wḏ pn n ni-swt*), and *pn* gets its extra *n* for the first time, while *r-ntt* opens the object of the decree and of *rḫ.tn*, although the preposition is also present in front of *rdit*.

For the New Kingdom, see *Ḏḥwtyms* I's *Wadi Halfa* and *Kuban epistolary upon stelae decree* (royal titulary + *wḏ ni-swt n* + addressees + *m.k in.n.tw n.k wḏ pn n ni-swt r rdit rḫ.k ntt*) with a more 'conventional' formula. We may conclude from what precedes that the Ramesside introductive epistolary formula is the product of a Middle Kingdom basis with a 17th dynasty adaptation, *r-ntt* being a neutric 'leftover' from the purpose *r rdit rḫ.tn* (*r*) *ntt*, and *r-ḏd* the actual quotation marker of the decree content, their sequence having been altered since *Snwsrt* III decree.

- *pnn:* see *Wb* I 507, 10 (Beleg.) 'Schreibung mit *pnn* seit D 18. öfters Pap D19/20'. Neo-Egyptian 19th dynasty form of the proximal deictic determinator for Goldwasser (1985: 51 and 2001: 124-125) prominent in 'non-literary' but appearing also in 'literary texts'; Bakir (1970: 86) proposes to see in the *n* doubling a device 'to emphasize pronunciation' (but he notes other instances of the same period with *pn*). Instances of the '*pnn'* demonstrative are apparently to be found in three contexts: our *r-nt(t/y) in.tw n.k wḏ ni-swt pnn (r-)ḏd*, the similar epistolary *r-nty in.tw n.k sš pnn (r-)ḏd* (e.g. *pBologna 1094*, 1,4), and the syntagm # *hrw pnn ḏd/spr ir.n*.N # (e.g. *KRI* III, 554 n.A66), although several examples show *pn*, see Winand 1992: Ex. 999, 1008, 1014-5), as summed up by Goldwasser. # *hrw pnn ḏd/spr ir.n*.N # is a clear case of # *hrw pn* + relator *n* + infinitive + relative form # and cannot be taken as a '*pnn*' occurrence. The origin of *wḏ ni-swt pnn* might be the result of an inversion of the Middle Kingdom formula *wḏ pn n ni-swt* (see above), already in *Nbḫprwrᶜ ꞽnf*'s 17th dynasty decree where *ni-swt* has been dropped to leave *wḏ pn n,* where again one must read *wḏ pn* + relator *n* (+ lost *ni-swt*). As for the *sš pnn* (*r-*)*ḏd* instances (see Caminos (1963: 31-32); *CLEM*, 5 note 1,4 'this writing of speaking'), they are the result of either *sš pn* + relator *n* + *ḏd* infinitive (afterwards, the preposition *r* has been added before *ḏd*) or of Neo-Egyptian *m*/*n* confusion (*sš pn* + *m ḏd*), and further addition of the preposition *r* before *ḏd* when it became the frozen 'that'[2]. See *LEG* § 1.7 about the 'Occasional confusion between the prepositions' *m* and

2 Most of the examples of the formula show *r-nty in.tw n.k sš pn* ***n*** *ḏd*, although a few occurrences of *r-nty in.tw n.k sš pn* ***n m*** *ḏd*, are to be noted (*LEM* 68, 8-9 and 126, 8-9).

n. Note that Caminos (1963: 31-32) adds that all examples of are to be found in 'model letters', which may imply that the 'confusion' has been transmitted again and again but has not entered the 'real letters' register.

* 'Classical' degree 0 forms used:

- *ỉn.tw wḏ:* independent impersonal or passive *sḏm.tw*.N, either a topical abstract relatively past that-form (signaling the beginning of the decree) following *r-nt(t/y)* (see Polotsky 1944: 82), but not in its classical *sḏm.n.tw*.N form (here), with rhematic focus on *n.k* or *r-ḏd*; or a 'perfect' report, retrospective time (see Winand (1992: 310-312) who hesitates between the two options '« Voici pourquoi cette lettre t'a été apportée » (f. emphatique) « on t'a apporté cette lettre à cette fin : » (f. *sḏm.tw* perfective active)'. The first option is, of course, to be retained, as earlier Middle Kingdom epistolary decrees use it in its classical form.

* General dialectal features: degree 1.

* Legal terms: *wḏ* - classifier: (decree, the papyrus/leather document).

* Epistolary formula: *r-nt(t/y) ỉn.tw n.k* (recipient) *wḏ ni-swt pn n r-ḏd* (content of the decree).

2. Content: first object

(10,9) (…) *ỉḫ r r.w m-di.k nꜣ ṯktinꜣ n pꜣ tꜣ n wḥꜣt tw.k ḥr dit ḥnw pꜣy sš tiwy r tft.w* (10,10) *nꜣy.w nyꜣw*
ỉr ḫy rꜥ bn pꜣ Rꜥ bn Ptḥ dit sḏm.tw nkt r ḥr[3] *nꜣy gꜣyrgꜣwtyw nty twtw ḥr* (10,11) *sḏm.w mtw pꜣy ḥꜣty-ꜥ hꜣb r-ḏd ỉṯꜣ.k nꜣ ṯktinꜣ nt(t/y) ḥr smt ỉw.k r-tnw ỉw.k* (10,12) *r pr nym mtw.f hꜣy ḥr tbn.k mi wꜣbwt n šꜥt mtw.tw ỉṯꜣ.k mtw.tw ditw.k ỉm r ṯktinꜣ n hd*

(10,9) (…) What about[4] the watchmen of yours (lit. What about them of yours, the watchmen) of the Oasis[5] land? Do you cause this scribe of yours to go speedily to repulse them (10,10) (and) their *nyꜣw*-troupes?
But if neither the Re nor Ptah is going to/will let something be heard against (= in the) face of those rumors that one hears (10,11) and this mayor will send (a letter) saying: 'you seized the watchmen who scout! Where are you? Whose (10,12) house are you (going) to?', and he will descend upon your head like a dune of sand and one will seize you and reduce you there to (be a) watchman as a sanction?

* Neo-Egyptian characteristics:

- *ỉḫ r r.w m-di.k nꜣ ṯktinꜣ:* accusation mode in an allocutive interrogative texteme to which a delayed response is probably expected, although the question could be rhetorical, composed of # interrogative rheme (*NÄG* § 740) + preposition

3 *CLEM*: 178 ''to counter' or similar; I have no parallel'; could be the preposition *r* (against) + the face ideogram (see the following stroke).
4 Wente (1990: 35) 'What concern do you have with (…) that you should send out'.
5 *CLEM*: 177: Dakhleh and Khargah.

isotopy (*Wb* I, 123: Neo-Egyptian, *iḫ r* 'was ist betreffs'; see Shisha-Halevy 1981: 326 for Coptic ⲁϩⲣⲟ-; on the isotopy, see the *Nauri decree*) + plural suffix + Neo-Egyptian compound preposition (possession) + apposition #. *EG* § 501 notes that the interrogative *iḫ* is rare in Middle Egyptian where it occurs only after prepositions; for *LEG* § 2.7.1, '*iḫ* is to be classified as the equivalent of a bare noun'. Caminos in *CLEM*: 176-177 translates this non-verbal syntagm as 'What concern have you with', and notes that it has 'no exact parallel'. See *pAnastasi* IX, 7 in *KRI* III,16 p 504-8 [*i*]*ḫ r.i tw.i ḥr wḫ3* [*t*]*w*; *pAnastasi* V.22, 5; *Wenamun* 2,65 *iḫ r.k*: 'what is it with you?'. Compare with *Imnḥtp* II epistolary decree upon *Wsrstt* stela, line 9 (*iw.w r iḫ m kft* What for indeed are they?), considered by Helck (1955: 28) as written in a very personal pre-Neo-Egyptian style ('Umgangssprache'). The textemic pace is dynamic, a special type of dialogue with delayed answer.

- *n3 ṯktin3 n p3 t3 n wḥ3t:* cataphoric use of the determinator of *ṯktin3* followed by its nominal expansion (origin relation with relator) and of *t3* (see a similar case above with *p3 t3 n Kš*). *ṯktin3* is also a Neo-Egyptian lexeme (*Wb* V, 411); Albright (1934: 63) 'from Can. *skt*, to pay attention'; *CLEM*: 177 'some class of soldiers of Lybian blood, presumably the Sukkiim of II Chron. 12,3). See *pAnastasi* V.1a, 1; *Mrnptḥ*'s *victory hymn* stela, line 24 in Spiegelberg (1896; 22 (58)).
- *tw.k ḥr dit:* independent durative first present (with interlocutive Neo-Egyptian pronoun). It expresses 'a synchronous, progressive, habitual or repeated action' (Frandsen 1974: 52 with 'transitive' verbs; see also *LEG* § 19.4; Satzinger 1976: 124; Winand 1992: 402-405). Note that the preposition is still retained (see Winand 1992: 414).
- *p3y/n3y:* Neo-Egyptian deictic determinator.
- *tiwy:* Neo-Egyptian interlocutive masculine possessive (*Wb* V, 241 'dir gehört'); in Middle Egyptian, the suffix pronoun would be used when the lexeme is also determined by a demonstrative.
- *tft.w:* Neo-Egyptian lexeme (*Wb* V, 297) with Neo-Egyptian delocutive plural suffix.
- *n3y.w:* Neo-Egyptian possessive determinator.
- *ny3w:* Neo-Egyptian lexeme (*Wb* II, 200 *n3w* 'Art barbar. Truppe?'; *CLEM*: 176-178 who translates it as *nww* 'their hunters'); Vernus (1986: 144): hunting; Wente (1990: 34) 'their reconnaissance patrols'; *Mrnptḥ*'s *victory hymn* stela, line 24 has *n3wt ṯktin3*.
- *ḫy rʿ:* see *CLEM*: 178 and above the *Kanais decree*, line 13, where it is probably parallel to *ḫr ir* (coordinator + topic marker). Here it is preceded by *ir* and may achieve a contrastive coordination in a condition. For Groll (1970: 114, example 248), *ir-ḫy-rʿ* is a compound preposition 'if meanwhile'.
- *ir ḫy rʿ bn* PN *bn* PN_2 *dit:* negative protasis of a conditional sentence composed of # topic marker (condition) + contrastive + [negator *bn* + proper noun] x 2 + infinitive #. The apodosis is inexistent in an open eventuality question (of the

type, for instance, of 'You want to stroll alone in a forest full of wolves? But if they find you and kill you?'). The open question building a possible scenario expresses a covert threat. As for the nature of the form *bn* PN *dit*, it seems to be a negative durative present (omission of the preposition), the negative counterpart to *tw.k ḥr dit;* this is the solution adopted by Groll (1970: 114, example 248) '*bn* precedes each nominal actor expression' and 'may make negative only the noun immediately preceding it'; Winand (1992: 405, example 1022) views it as a first present in a 'proposition indépendante'(he does not note the condition). But neither Frandsen (1974: 76-77) nor Satzinger (1976) mentions in Neo-Egyptian a protasis of a conditional sentence formed with *ir* + first present (see *LEG* § 62.4.2). Another option could be a negative future *bn* (*iw.*)PN (*r*) *dit* whose thematic *iw* is missing, although for *LEG* § 9.3.3 'It seems that *ir* cannot precede a third future formation'. The question remains open.

- *pꜣ Rꜥ*: non-phoric articloid determining a unique entity, prominent proper noun, although it does not appear with the following *Ptḥ*; the reason for this discrepancy could be the fact that *pꜣ Rꜥ* is not to be confused with *rꜥ*, two distinct entities, one being the god, the other the sun in its concrete meaning (there is no possible confusion with *Ptḥ*) or to give preeminence to the supreme divinity. See Groll (1991: 146) and Reiche (1998: 146-147) on *pꜣ Ꞽtn*; for Greek, Rósen (1988: 59) suggests that to establish a distinction between a god and the abstract concept of divinity, the article was used.
- *gꜣyrgꜣwtyw:* Neo-Egyptian *grg* (*Wb* V, 190).
- *nty twtw ḥr sḏm.w:* relative durative present (with Neo-Egyptian delocutive plural suffix and impersonal pronoun).
- *mtw.*N *hꜣb*/ *mtw.f hꜣy*/*mtw.tw iṯꜣ.k*/*mtw.tw ditw.k:* full-fledged conjunctive. It seems that we do not have here a conjunctive form functioning as the apodosis of a conditional/temporal protasis, thus filling the role of a 'main clause' (*LEG* § 42.2.4, on the famous *Wenamun* example – *LES* 67, 13-14 – *iw.k dit n.i n irt.s mtw.i irt.s:* 'If you pay me for doing it I will do it'); for Frandsen (1974: 148-152), the abovementioned example must be understood as a command (related to a condition) 'give me (something) for doing it and I'll do it (too) (lit. you shall give...)'. On another example brought by him – *LEM* 75, 8-9 – *ḫr ir pꜣy.i nb ꜥḥꜥ n pꜣ ꜥꜣ n pr mtw.tw ḥr ḏd n.f:* 'When my lord stood up to the major-domo, one said to him', he admits it is 'difficult to account for'. For Shisha-Halevy (1995: 307), the apodotic role of the conjunctive ('superordinated and rhematic to its protasis', ibid. n. 45) is well-established 'in Late Egyptian, Demotic and some varieties of Coptic (...) by no means restricted to the "conditional apodosis"'. But as previously mentioned, what we have here is an open question, building up a scenario, and the conjunctives again add the main interest to the scenario of which the preceding *ir ḫy rꜥ bn* N, etc. constitutes the backgrounding pre-condition. There is no apodosis to this condition.
- *iṯꜣ.k:* report interlocutive *sḏm.f* in an illustrative constructed pseudo-quotation texteme.

- *nꜣ ṯktinꜣ:* cataphoric use of the determinator with a lexeme further expanded by the relative syntagm *nt(t/y) ḥr smt*.
- *nym:* Neo-Egyptian spelling of the interrogative (*Wb* II, 263 'als Genitiv, z.B.: "wessen Haus"?').
- *tbn*: Neo-Egyptian lexeme (*Wb* V, 261 and *CLEM*: 178-179)
- *wꜣbwt n šꜥt:* Neo-Egyptian lexemes (*Wb* I, 251 and *CLEM*: 179).
- *n hd*: probably for *m hd* (see supra the 'confusion' between *n* and *m*).

* 'Classical' degree 0 forms used:

- *ḥnw*.N*:* dependent active prospective, object of *dit*.
- *r tft.w:* preposition + infinitive (purpose).
- *sḏm.tw nkt:* dependent passive/impersonal prospective, object of *dit*.
- *nt(t/y) ḥr smt:* relative converb.
- *ỉw.k r-tnw:* independent adverbial interrogative nexus in the interlocutive illustrative constructed quotation segment with rhematic focus *r-tnw* and thematic *hic-et-nunc* situational deictic *ỉw.k*; see *EG* § 503; *Wb* V, 373.14 *ỉw.n r-tnw* 'Wohin sollen wir? (scil. uns wenden o.ä.)' and adds for the compound *r-tnw* 'belegt seit Westcar', which means that it is very early Neo-Egyptian; *Medinet Habu* I 28,56 and 46, 35; Grapow (1943: 27); *NÄG* § 710; *CLEM*: 178 and his references, 'ellipsis of a verb of motion before *r* in this sentence and the following'.
- *ỉw.k r pr nym:* independent adverbial interrogative interlocutive syntagm in the constructed quotation segment (*EG* § 496; *LEG* § 61.6), with rhematic focus *r pr nym*.

* General dialectal features: degree 3.

* Legal terms:

di r - classifier: ø (to reduce someone to an inferior position).

hd - classifier: (sanction). See *CLEM*: 180 and *supra*, the *Nauri decree*. Interestingly, apart from the already encountered basic level [ARM MOTION] category classifier (schematic relation), the papyrus roll of the superordinate [ABSTRACT] category appears to classify the lexeme instead of the already observed [COERCION] category classifier. It might suggest that this sanction is always to be registered in writing (*nulla poena sine lege* or written record of the verdict/execution).

* Epistolary formulas: *iḫ r* (complaint interrogation); *ir ḫy rꜥ… mtw.f sḏm* (contrastive open question building scenario) + *r-ḏd sḏm.k* and interrogatives (illustrative constructed speech).

3. Content: second object

(11,1) *mi ḳd pꜣ ky btꜣw ꜥꜣ ꜥꜣ*[6] *i.ir.k m tꜣ wnwt*

6 Adnominal expansion of intensity.

p3 dit i.ir.k iw Pr-ˁ3 ˁnḫ wḏ3 snb r swtwt r Ἰwnw (11,2) *iw bw di.n.k in.tw ḫˁw n p3 ḫpš m grg m-s3 p3y.k nb i.ir.k ir nkt ḳbḥ r iḫ iw bn* (11,3) *ir.kw dit iry.f sw3 is bn dy.tw.k r t3 st n kt-ḫ(t) imy-r pr ḥḏ wnw ḥr sn ḥr ṯktin3* (11,4) *n wḥ3t r ṯftw.f ḥr t3y*[*.f*] *ny3 n3 ḥrw n ḥr ḥr.k*

(11,1) Likewise the other huge crime that you have committed now:
this (fact of) your letting go Pharaoh L.P.H. to stroll to Heliopolis (11,2) without your having caused/although you have (repeatedly) not caused that weapons of the Armory be brought in order/readiness behind your lord. Wherefore is it that you have done something quiet (stupid[7]? apathetic[8]? pleasant[9]?) without (11,3) your letting/although you should not/cannot let him pass/it occur[10]? Is it not that you will be put in the place of other treasury overseers who have been committing/used to commit a transgression concerning a watchman (11,4) of (the) oasis to take him off with [his] *ny3*-troupe[11]? Is that far (of the face) from you?[12]

* Neo-Egyptian characteristics:

- *mi ḳd:* 'vereinzelt Nä auch als Adverb' (*Wb* V, 76), coordinative locution introducing the new object (nominal, heading-like expression). Note that in the 18th dynasty epistolary decree upon stela of *Ἰmnḥtp* II, the second object is introduced by *ky ḏd n.*N (another message/matter to N; see Bakir 1970: 98); in *LRL* 36, 11-12, *kt mdt* is used.
- *p3 ky:* cataphoric use of the articloid.
- *bt3w:* New Kingdom lexeme (*Wb* I, 483-484).
- *i.ir.k:* Neo-Egyptian synthetic active relative form constructed with prothetic *yod.* It is the first instance of prothetic *yod* observed in our corpus, but only in the epistolary decrees genre. For its use during *Stḫy* I's reign, see Winand (1992: 377) who notes that in 'néo-égyptien partiel (principalement dans les documents royaux), les formes relatives gardent la forme sans augment'; obviously not in in all royal documents (but one must keep in mind that the present letter is a school exercise, not an original royal missive).
- *m t3 wnwt:* Neo-Egyptian locution (*Wb* I, 316) with proximal deictic use of the articloid.
- *p3 dit i.ir.k iw.*N*:* 'the causing/letting that you have made that N will go'; verbal thematization without *ir* comprising # determinator (cataphora and anaphora implied by the fact that the syntagm constitutes a nominal elaboration of *bt3*;

7 *CLEM*: 180 ('senseless').
8 Groll (1970: 207, Ex. 445) ; Wente (1990: 35).
9 Cassonnet (2000: 53, ex. 62) '"Dans quel but as-tu entrepris quelque chose d'agréable alors que tu n'es pas capable de la réaliser?" (*lit.* "faire en sorte qu'elle passe")'.
10 Wente (1990: 35) 'when you should not have let him make the journey'.
11 Wente (1990: 35) 'to take him off his reconnaissance patrol'; Vernus (1986: 144) 'jusqu'à le priver de sa chasse'.
12 Cassonnet (2000: 122, Ex. 167) 'Est-ce loin de ton esprit?'; Wente (1990: 35) 'Are you an exception?'.

substantivizer role, see Kroeber 1970: 16) + *dit* (infinitive) + *i.ir.k* (relative form with prothetic *yod*, adnominal expansion of *pꜣ dit*, past reference) + *iw*.N (dependent prospective after *dit;* for the spelling, see Frandsen 1974: 25; *LRL* 19,7-8; Winand 1992: 244) #. See Gunn (1955: 87 & 94, § IX.1), line 38 *ir pꜣy ḏd i.ir.w* 'past infinitive', 'that saying that they have made' or 'As to their having said'; Groll (1970: 182, 184-186) "restricted to past time', *pꜣ dit* and the relative form are an 'accentual unit, i.e. (…) a word group in which one syllable receives prominence through stronger stress', 'not a free construction'; Satzinger (1976: 12) 'präteritale Form', relative construction with closer relation between the infinitive and the relative than between *rdi* and *sḏm.f*; Shisha-Halevy (1978: 53; 1986: 213-214) preterit 'infinitif finitisé (ou personnalisé)'; Winand (1992: 377-378) 'forme relative perfective'. See also *pOrbiney* 17,7 *pꜣ dit i.iri(.ṯ) šꜥd(.tw) pꜣ ꜥš; pBologna* 1094 10,1 *ir pꜣ di i.iri.k iwtw.f.*

- *swtwt: Wb* IV, 77: 18th dynasty.
- *iw bw di.n.k:* Gardiner notes that the form 'seems suspect' (*LEM* 46a, 12a); Cassonnet (2000: 53, 193) sees a rhetorical question (reproach) with *iw bn*. The syntagm is a 'circumstantial' negative referring to the past, perhaps a 'circumstantial' conversion (by the *iw* converter) of the aorist *bw sḏm.n.f* . See Frandsen (1974: 214-216) on the circumstantial negative 'aorist' *iw bw ir.f sḏm.* But one must note that the aorist is atemporal, and the form we have here is clearly related to the past (although the habitual character of the offence may justify the use of the aorist). If what is meant is *iw bw sḏm.f*, then it is a circumstantial past (see Winand 1992: 198 on the past negation 'descendante directe du moyen égyptien *n sḏm.f*', 'perfectif' and he notes the example from *KRI* III, 558 line 11 *iw bw iy*.N 'although N did not come'). See also Junge (1996: 105) on *bw sḏm.n.f* as a form of *bw sḏm.f* (from *n sḏm.n.f*) 'präteritales *bw sḏm.f*'; Satzinger (1976: 180); note that for *LEG* § 10, *bw* is only related to simple present tense (or 'already notion').
- *pꜣ ḫpš:* Neo-Egyptian (*Wb* III, 270), non-phoric use of the articloid (with a noun not referring in itself to a unique object) distinguishing a specific, unique royal administration, context-dependent and recognizable by any official (= the royal armory). Note that *pr ḥḏ* is not determined by the articloid.
- *pꜣy.k/tꜣy*[*.f*]
- *i.ir.k ir... r iḫ:* Neo-Egyptian analytic conditioned nominal abstract that-form (topic initial, auxiliary *iri* + lexical *iri* 'to do') in an interrogative (the question is a complaint, an accusation) cleft sentence focusing the rhematic prepositional interrogative *r iḫ*, in a past context (see Polotsky 1940: 242; Bakir 1970: 115). For Groll (1970: 207), the notion conveyed by the that-form is 'have to' (obligation). Note again the interlocutive interrogative accusation texteme after the nominal enunciation of the crime.
- *iw bn ir.kw dit:* Neo-Egyptian negative adnexal rheme composed of # circumstantial converter *iw* + negator of nominal forms (non-existence) + analytic prospective #, the modal *bn sḏm.f* expressing for Caminos (*CLEM*: 180)

an 'obligation' (interdiction) as in *pBologna* 1094, 6,6 (which presents a very close state of language – see above) and he translates it by 'when you ought not to have caused him to pass'. For Cassonnet (2000: 53, ex. 62 and p. 193), *bw* is meant instead of *bn* (in a rhetorical question implying a 'questionnement argumentatif' for a 'reproche'), which is an unnecessary modification as in the criminal decrees, we have seen that a circumstantial non-existence and prohibition was expressed by *nn sḏm* (degree 0), *n sḏm* (degree 1), *iw nn sḏm*/*iw bn sḏm.f* (degree 2), the last comprising a prospective form; what we have here is another element of the pattern, *iw bn iri.f sḏm*, with an analytic form of the prospective, although not the characteristic *iry.f* morphology of the prospective and a rather strange spelling (see Winand 1992: 212-213). For Junge (1996: 147), the independent prospective does not have a periphrastic form, and the *iri.f sḏm* periphrasis of Demotic concerns only the dependent prospective (but see Winand 1992: 245); concerning the possibility of the use of the auxiliary *iri* with the verb *rdi*, see Kroeber (1970: 182-185), already in *Ḥḳ3nḫt* I, rt. 3, etc. See above the discussion concerning the possibility of an independent prospective to follow the *iw* converter. The meaning is quite obscure due to the use of *ḳbḥ* and *sw3*, and the masculine suffix pronoun of *iry.f*.

- *iry.f sw3:* analytic form of the dependent prospective, object of *dit*. For the morphology of *iri*, see Winand (1992: 241-244); concerning the dependent prospective analytic form of 'causatifs trilitères et les verbes redoublés', see Winand (1992: 245).
- *is bn dy.tw.k:* # particle used in interrogative sentences (*EG* § 491.2; Hintze 1952: 199-200 in Neo-Egyptian 'Reden' 'nur vor Bestätigungsfragen') + negator of nominal forms + passive prospective that-form (theme) # in a rhetorical question expressing a threat. See Winand (1992: 321, ex. 770), opting for an 'emphatic' prospective, Vernus (1986: 144) for whom the negator is the rheme, the theme being the entire subsequent sentence and *dy.tw.k* a perfective or prospective form; Cassonnet (2000: 121-122, ex. 167) for a non 'emphatic' prospective in a rhetorical question. For Shisha-Halevy (1989b: 428-429), second tenses are used in rhetorical questions in Middle, Late Egyptian, Demotic, and Sahidic Coptic (often expressed in Late Egyptian by *is bn i.iri.f sḏm*); see also Polotsky (1944: 50-51, 77-78).
- *t3 st:* cataphoric use of the articloid.
- *wnw ḥr sn:* relative first present # preterit converter *wnw* (participle; the converter is often written *wnw*, see Winand 1992: 410) + *ḥr* + infinitive (*sn* implying a motion, it belongs to Satzinger's (1976: 143-145) category of 'Intransitiven der Fortbewegung' with progressive preterit imperfect value) #, an adnominal expansion of *kt-ḫ(t) imyw-r pr ḥḏ*. Note the presence of the preposition *ḥr* (usually noted during *Stḫy* II's reign, see Winand 1992: 414) and the absence of prothetic *yod* of the participle *wnw*. See also Frandsen (1974: 183); *LEG* § 19.13.8.2 and Ex. 1320; Junge (1996: 171) for the relative first present (past customary activity); Winand (1992: 411-412).

- *r tftw.f*: purpose, with Neo-Egyptian spelling of the infinitive.
- *nꜣ ḥrw n ḥr ḥr.k:* Vernus (1986: 144-145) sees in *nꜣ* the interrogative *ỉn* (see also Junge (1996: 90) for independent sentences being questions for corroboration) and in *ḥrw* the rheme of a nominal phrase with adjectival predicat of the type *nfr* ø 'est-ce loin dans ton esprit?'.

* 'Classical' degree 0 forms used:

- *r swtwt:* purpose.
- *ỉn.tw:* dependent passive *sḏm.tw*.N or impersonal prospective, object of *dỉ.n.k*.
- *kt-ẖ(t) ỉmy-r pr ḥḏ:* first instance in our corpus of the classical plural 'others' (see *EG* § 98), here with a nominal expansion without plural mark.

* General dialectal features: degree 2.

* Legal terms:

ỉr btꜣw - classifier: ×𓅪 (to commit an offence). In addition to the superordinate [INFERIORITY-PERTURBATION] category classifier, the superordinate [UNION/DIVISION] classifier appears in one more contentious and two-sided situation (offender/victim) where it relates metaphorically to the lexeme.

sn - classifier: 𓂻 (to transgress). See *CLEM*: 180. The superordinate [MOTION] category classifier is again used with a lexeme semantically close to *thỉ*.

* Epistolary formulas: *mỉ ḳd* + nominal forms (coordination and introduction of a new object); *ỉ.ỉrỉ.k ỉr… r ỉḫ* (interrogative accusation); *ỉs bn dy.tw.k* (rhetorical question expressing a threat); *nꜣ ḥrw…* (question for corroboration).

4. The orders: measures to be taken

(11,4) (…) *wnn pꜣ wḫꜣ n* (11,5) *Pr-ꜥꜣ ꜥnḫ wḏꜣ snb ḥr spr r.k ỉw.k ḥr ỉr šꜥ*[13] *n pꜣy sš tỉwy ỉ.dỉ.k ḥnw.f r pꜣ tꜣ n wḥꜣt* (11,6) *r-ḏd ỉrtyw ỉrtyw ḥr snn ḥr nꜣ ṯktinꜣ r ỉn rmṯ wꜥtw wꜥtw ỉm.w r-pw* (11,7) *gm.tw.f r.k m btꜣw n mt mtw.k ḥr dỉt tꜣy.k šꜥ m ḏrt wꜥ šmsy*[14] *tỉw mtw.k dỉt ỉwt.f* (11,8) *ỉrm pꜣ sḫs stꜣ stꜣ grḥ*

(11,4) (…) As soon as the present message of (11,5) Pharaoh L.P.H. reaches you, you (are to) compose a letter for this scribe of yours whom you caused that he will go speedily to the oasis land, (11,6) saying: 'Beware, beware of a transgression concerning those watchmen in order to bring even a single one of them, or (else) (11,7) he shall be found (= it shall be reckoned) against you as a capital offense'; and you (are to) confide your document in (the) hand[15] of one attendant of yours, and cause that he will come (11,8) with this courier in a great hurry. End.

13 Bakir (1970: 14-15) designation for personal letters, 'generic term for all kinds of communication in epistolary style'. The king does not use the lexeme *wḏ* as previously.

14 Bakir (1970: 30 and n.3). For the translation of *šms* as 'dispatch-carrier', see Janssen (1961: 31).

15 Like the French 'remettre en mains propres/en personne'? See also Wente 1990: 35.

* Neo-Egyptian characteristics:

- *wnn*.N *ḥr spr... iw.f ḥr ir:* # [*sḏm*.N geminating thematic that-form + rhematic *ḥr* + infinitive for the protasis] + [dynamic circumstantial adverbial nexus in the apodosis] with deontic value (Junge 1996: 290) #. On the macrosyntactic level, *iw.k ḥr ir* and *wnn*.N *ḥr spr* are linked, and the protasis constitutes the topicalized circumstance preceding the focalized and circumstantial main event (Polotsky 1965: note 19), with a 'contiguity' effect ('as soon as', see *supra*), the reception of the order preceding closely in time the writing of the document. Compare with the contrastive *wp(w/t)-ḥr wnn.f*/N (*ḥr*) *sḏm... iw*.N *ḥr sḏm* above and with *ir ḏr sḏm.f... iw*.N *ḥr sḏm* in the *Nauri decree* (we have already discussed the need to analyze within their context the various occurrences of the construction *wnn.f*/N (*ḥr*) *sḏm... iw*.N *ḥr sḏm*). Note that the apodosis is diversely interpreted by Polotsky (1965: note 19) and Junge (1986: 122 and 1996: 223) as a circumstantial first present, by Bakir (1970: 117) as an independent first present, by Groll (*LEG* § 10.12.2 IV a 2 and 40) as a successive non initial main form of the future, and by Frandsen (1974: 192) as a 'third future'. But neither *wnn.N ḥr spr* (formed with a nominal that-form), nor *iw.f ḥr ir* (obviously not the future *iw.f r sḏm*) can have an absolute future value. For Cassonnet (2000: 246, n. 753), the construction is a 'système corrélatif *wnn.f ḥr sḏm* / *iw.f* (*ḥr*) *sḏm*' where a substantivized first present with circumstantial function (protasis) precedes a non-subordinated form (apodosis); close is Bakir's view (1970: 80, 92,117), who adds that the protasis is the 'nominal counterpart of the earlier verbal construction introduced by *ẖft*'; for Junge (1986: 122-124 and 1996: 222-223, 290), it is a 'temporale Abhängigkeitsbeziehung', vestige of a Middle Egyptian balanced sentence. For Goldwasser (1985: 50-56), it is a case of 'slight variation of the frozen' epistolary formula # *wnn t3y.i šꜥt* (*ḥr*) *spr r.k iw.k* (*ḥr*) + infinitive #, a valuable criterion in the identification of a 19th dynasty 'model letter – normative text' or an 'administrative' 20th dynasty text. Note the infinitive *ir* orthography after *ḥr* (no feminine mark). Sweeney (2001: 49-50 (b)) adds that the formula constitutes an 'indirect request' ('explicit statement about some action that the sender would like to see the recipient perform in the future.'). Note that in Middle Kingdom *Sbkḥtp* II decree (*pBrooklyn* 35.1446 (C)), the orders are introduced by *m.k wḏwt irw* 'See the orders pertaining thereto' and in *Nbḫprwrꜥ Intf Coptos decree*, the sole imperative is used.
- *p3 wḫ3:* anaphoric, deictic (the present order, physically in your hand, self-referential) and cataphoric uses of the articloid with Neo-Egyptian lexeme.
- *p3y*
- *tiwy*/*tiw:* Neo-Egyptian interlocutive masculine possessive determinator.
- *i.di.k:* Neo-Egyptian synthetic relative form constructed with prothetic *yod* (anteriority).
- *p3 t3:* cataphoric use of the determinator.
- *r-ḏd:* tagged speech marker, introduces a constructed quotation of a letter to be written. Note that as in previous criminal law/protection decrees, the direct

speech is anticipated and constructed, it is not an actual speech content that is reproduced.

- *ỉrtyw ỉrtyw ḥr snn:* # reiterated imperative (intensivity) + preposition + geminated nominal form (infinitive for *CLEM*: 181, but probably substantive) # in a constructed direct 'speech' (letter content) texteme. Note the Neo-Egyptian spelling of *ỉrtyw* (*Wb* I, 108) that functions as a warning and threat-reinforcing element. Isotopy is used three times in this segment for intensity.
- *nꜣ ṯktinꜣ:* anaphoric use of the articloid determinator.
- *r ỉn:* purpose (note the infinitive without feminine marker).
- *wꜥtw*: Neo-Egyptian spelling (*Wb* I, 278). Adnominal expansion whose isotopy expresses intensive restriction ('even one single').
- *ỉm.w*: Neo-Egyptian delocutive plural suffix.
- *r-pw:* disjunction marker between two nexi (a Neo-Egyptian feature) in the constructed quotation texteme. It belongs to a threat 'beware… or else…' and introduces the penalty in the eventuality of non-compliance, as a negative condition ('ou bien/ou alors/sinon/autrement/faute de quoi' in French). The offense and penalty are thus not expressed by the topicalized enunciation of the crime followed by the prospective penalty, but by a warning and option of penalty.
- *btꜣw n mt:* Neo-Egyptian 'capital offence' (*CLEM*: 181).
- *mtw.k ḥr dỉt/mtw.k dỉt:* full-fledged conjunctives with pronominal interlocutive actor common in Ramesside correspondence after the formula *wnn.*N *ḥr spr… ỉw.f ḥr sḏm* (and again text-rhematic superordination, see Shisha-Halevy 1995: 306 and note 27). See Baer (1965: 138 a); Bakir (1970: 81); Sweeney (2001: 50). Note the alternation of presence/absence of the preposition *ḥr* before the infinitive for stylistic variance.
- *tꜣy.k*
- *ỉrm:* Neo-Egyptian (*Wb* I, 115).
- *pꜣ sḫs:* deictic use of the articloid determinator (the courier who stands in front of you, who brought you this message).

* 'Classical' degree 0 forms used:

- *ḥnw.f:* dependent prospective, object of *ỉ.dỉ.k*.
- *gm.tw.f:* independent passive prospective (modal prescriptive) expressing a threat. *CLEM*, 181 sees the actor as a neutral ('it will be reckoned'), perhaps referring to *snn*, although *.f* must in fact refer to *rmṯ wꜥtw*.
- *ỉwt.f:* dependent prospective, object of *mtw.k dỉt*. It is modified by *sṯꜣ sṯꜣ*.

* General dialectal features: degree 3.

* Legal terms:

wḫꜣ n Pr-ꜥꜣ - classifier:  (administrative dispatch, royal letter containing an order). See Bakir (1970: 15-16) 'embodies an order'. The fact that the [BINDING] category string classifier appears might suggests the fact that it is closed, to be read only by its addressee (metonymic relation with the lexeme).

gmi r m (*bt3w* - classifier: [—]? (to be reckoned against someone as (a crime)). See *CLEM*: 181.

bt3w n mt - classifier: × (capital offense). See Boochs (1991: 62) and his references; *Ḥrmḥb*'s decree, line D6: *bt3w ʿ3 n mt*, with the same classifiers.

snn - classifier: (transgression). See *CLEM*: 180.

* Epistolary formula: *wnn p3 wḫ3 n Pr-ʿ3 ʿnḫ wḏ3 snb ḥr spr r.k iw.k ḥr* + infinitive + conjunctives (the measures to be taken immediately).

II. *pCairo ESP (B)*

This other 'royal rescript of warning and instruction', a personal letter (Helck 1967: 147, 137-140; *KRI* VI, 518-519 n. 17), was directly addressed in Year 2 of *Rˁmss* IX's reign to the first prophet of Amun-Re *Rˁmssnḫtw* and belongs now to the Egyptian Society of Papyrology. It probably comes from Thebae, and pertains to a papyrus roll of 5 documents glued together (possibly for their archiving, see Helck 1967: 135; see also Posener-Kriéger (1985: 195) on the finding of an artificial roll that confirms temple archiving of documents by category during the Old Kingdom). It is regarded as an original document by Helck (1967: 145 and 1974: 120) and Vernus (1990: 244), from a specific service (the treasury?) of the Amun temple in Karnak[16]. The hieratic official chancery script is noted by Helck (1967: 135, 137) and Vernus (1990: 244).

1. Heading and addressee

(22) (royal titulary) *wḏ ni-swt n ḥm-nṯr tpy n Ỉmn-Rˁ ni-swt nṯrw Rˁmssnḫtw* (22) (royal titulary) Royal decree to (the) first prophet of Amun-Re, king of gods, *Rˁmssnḫtw*:

* Neo-Egyptian characteristics: -
* 'Classical' degree 0 forms used: *wḏ ni-swt n*.N: see *supra* for the evolution of the heading and addressees formula. The one used here is close to 12th dynasty formula because of the presence of the preposition *n* before the addressee: # titulary + *wḏ ni-swt* (nominal syntagm in loose composition) + *n* + addressee #. Helck (1974: 121-123) notes that by the end of the 20th dynasty, there is a preference for archaic formulas.
* General dialectal features: degree 0.
* Legal terms: *wḏ* - classifier: 𓏛 (decree, the order). It is the classifier used in most remaining 12th dynasty decrees; see *Snwsrt* I *Abydos epistolary upon stela decree*; *Snwsrt* III *Deir el-Bahari decree*; *Sinuhe* B 180; but in *pBerlin* 10071 epistolary decree, the string classifier 𓍯 is used, and in the epistolary upon stela decree *Berlin* 1204, no classifier appears as for the Old Kingdom decrees.
* Epistolary formula: royal titulary + *wḏ ni-swt* + *n* (addressee)

16 See also Haring (1997: 251).

2. Introductory formula

(23) *r-nty ỉn.tw n.k wḏ ni-swt pnn r-ḏd r-nty*

(23) to (let you know) that it is to you/to say (what follows) that this royal decree has been brought:

* Neo-Egyptian characteristics:
- *r-nt(t/y)... r-ḏd r-nty:* here, the introduction of the decree's content is indicated not only by the quotation marker *r-ḏd*, but also by a second *r-nty* (perhaps because *r-ḏd* is still perceived as the preposition + the *verbo dicendi* and *r-nty* acts as the opening relative expression as in the Middle Kingdom/First Intermediate Period decrees formula ending with *r rdit rḫ.k (r-)ntt*, but here redundantly added to a first *r-nty*).
- *pnn*

* 'Classical' degree 0 forms used:
- *ỉn.tw wḏ*

* General dialectal features: degree 1.

* Legal terms: *wḏ* - classifier: 𓏛 (decree, the papyrus document). This time, the [BINDING] classifier appears instead of the [ABSTRACT] one, which means that it is the document and not the original royal command that is concerned here.

* Epistolary formula: *r-nty ỉn.tw n.k* (recipient) *wḏ ni-swt pnn r-ḏd r-nty* (content of the decree).

3. Content (object)

(23) (…) *hꜣb.ỉ n.k m ḏrt ỉmy-r pr ḥḏ Pr-ꜥꜣ (ꜥnḫ wḏꜣ) snb* (24) *wdpw ni-swt Ỉmnḥtpw r-ḏd ỉmỉ ỉn.tw msdmt nfr nfr*[17] *n* (25) *šꜣwy sḏmw n Pr-[ꜥꜣ] (ꜥnḫ wḏꜣ) snb r pꜣ nty tw.tw ỉm ỉw.k dỉt* (26) *ỉn.tw* 15 *n dbn n msdmt m ḏrt.f ḫr ỉr tw.tw dỉtw.f n nꜣ swnwyw* (27) *n tꜣ st nꜣ swnwyw n Pr-ꜥꜣ (ꜥnḫ wḏꜣ) snb n ḫn r bꜣkw.f* (28) *ỉw.tw gmtw.f m msdmt wỉꜣwỉꜣy ỉw bn šꜣwy* (29) *nꜣ sḏmw n pꜣ bꜣkw n Pr-ꜥꜣ ꜥnḫ wḏꜣ snb ỉm.f wꜥ dbn wꜥty* (30) *n msdmt pꜣw gmyt ỉm.f ptr sw ỉn n.k*

(23) (…) I have sent (a message) to you by (the) hand of[18] (the) Treasury overseer of Pharaoh (L.P.)H.[19], (24) royal butler *Ỉmnḥtpw,* saying: 'Have very good galena be brought (25), fit for (the preparation of) kohl for Phar[aoh] (L.P.)H., to the (place) where One is (= I am).' And so you have caused (26) that be brought 15 *dbn* of galena by his hand. And when it was given to the physicians (27) of Pharaoh's (L.P.)H.

17 Adnominal expansion of intensity.

18 See Bakir (1970: 30).

19 Note the recurring abbreviation of the formula (Demotic).

physicians department of (the) Residence to transform it, (28) one found it as a worthless galena, not fit for (29) the kohl for the use of Pharaoh L.P.H. in it (= to be made from it); only one *dbn* (30) of galena is what was found in it (= in the ore). See it brought to you.

* Neo-Egyptian characteristics:

- *h3b.i*: independent *sḏm.i* (locutive actor) referring to a past action of the king (Neo-Egyptian report form in narrative context); see Bakir (1970: 109-114); Wente (1990: 40). The form is used in a background texteme exposing the circumstances explaining the following order (the reference to or acknowledgment of previous correspondence is already present in 6th dynasty *Tti Abydos decree*, a royal answer to a complaint).
- *š3wy*: Neo-Egyptian lexeme, see *Wb* IV, 404 'Adjektiv' 'auch mit *m* davor', thus the *n* that precedes *š3wy* may be used instead of *m* (a confusion already noted several times in our corpus).
- *p3 nty tw.tw im:* relative clause (preceded by the preposition *r*, an adverbial expansion of *in.tw.s*) with durative adverbial rheme, *p3 nty* being used as a noun, literally 'the (place) that One is (= I am) there' (see *LEG* § 53.6; Shisha-Halevy (1981: 327) for *im*, anaphoric adverbial to *p3* and variants with *t3*/*st* as place names, here without resumptive suffix). Neo-Egyptian impersonal pronoun *tw.tw* is used for *tw.i* in a 'majestative expression' (*enallage*) reinforcing distance and untouchability (see above the *Kanais decree* where delocutive *ḥm.f* replaces *ḥm.i* and *Imnḥtp* III *Medinet Habu decree*, where the pronoun *tw* is consistently used for the king).
- *iw.k dit:* retrodependent, sequential interlocutive narrative following the report *h3b.i* form. See Polotsky (1985: 157-161); Sweeney (2001: 154) 'In both letters and legal texts, the basic narrative form is the chain of past *jw.f ḥr sḏm* forms. This narrative chain often opens with a past active *sḏm.f*'. She adds (p. 87) that 'The positive *jw.f* <*ḥr*> *sḏm* is common in the first or third person when stating that orders have already been executed'. Note the omission of the *ḥr* preposition (Winand (1992: 449) 'A la fin de la 20e dyn., elle est toujours absente'). For Peden (1994: 109), it is a future (omission of the preposition *r*), but this fits poorly the texteme with its background recapitulation of the facts explaining the new message and the following order. For the opposition between report *sḏm.f* and preterit narrative event-chaining *iw.f ḥr sḏm* in Neo-Egyptian, see *inter al.* Shisha-Halevy (2000: 84-85).
- *ḫr ir tw.tw ditw.f... iw.tw gmtw.f:* past temporal with protasis # linking particle *ḫr* (see above) + *ir* topicalizer of temporal clause + first present (omission of *ḥr* and intrusive *w* after the infinitive feminine ending) # and an apodosis consisting of the impersonal retrodependent narrative (omission of *ḥr* and intrusive *w* after the infinitive ending). See Satzinger (1976: 36-40) 'Temporal Sätze' '*ḫr ir* + "Präsens I" | Narrativ (*iw.f ḥr sḏm*)'; Frandsen (1974: 97 and 105) 'closed complex' referring to past time; *LEG* § 9.3.2 a VI ('when the first present is

preceded by *ḫr ir* it is converted to the past tense, and becomes a temporal clause'), §19.4.3 and § 38.2.5; Winand (1992: 408-409) 'élément subordonnant' with first present in a dependent clause; Junge (1996: 274-277) who sees a first present in 'vorangestellten Präpositionalattributs' with '*iw*-Satz (NIMS)' which is a 'non-initial main sentence'; Sweeney (2001: 154 and note 19).

- *n3 swnwyw n t3 st n3 swnwyw n Pr-ʿ3; n3 sḏmw n p3 b3kw n Pr-ʿ3:* cataphoric use of the articloids. Note the abundant use of the relator.
- *wi3wi3y:* Neo-Egyptian lexeme (*Wb* I, 272).
- *iw bn š3wy:* Neo-Egyptian circumstantial non-existence. Note that *š3wy* is not preceded by *n* as *supra*. See Vernus (1985: 166-167) 'qualité abstraite et générale'.
- *wʿ dbn wʿty n msdmt p3w gmyt:* # quantified nominal form (focus) + invariable *p3w* (formal theme) + perfect participle (belongs to the theme) #, a cleft sentence. The function of *wʿty* is to reinforce the focus. The deictic *p3w* may be used as either an independent topicalized and stressed theme of a nominal sentence or before a relative sentence (*oCairo* 25232 *i.irw m p3w i.ḏd.i* 'Do as I say'; *pBeatty* I *BM 10681* r° 8, 5 and 15, 4, *Rʿmss* V, *Horus & Seth, ist bn i.ir.tw m p3w ḏd* N; *pAnastasi* IV 3, 7, *Stḫy* II *p3w ir.k n.k ḏs.k* 'the one which you have built for yourself') or a substantive (*pTurin* P/R 1880 r° 2,5 'Strike Papyrus' *m p3w hrw*). In *LEG* § 3.1.3, the always masculine *p3w* 'may be another form of' *p3y* (in the example provided from *pAbbott* 4, 10, *Rʿmss* IX, *p3w* precedes the participle *ḫpr* 'that which happened'); see also *NÄG* § 120; for Junge (1996: 54), it is used as a substantive or before a relative sentence. The cleft sentence gives the information intended to persuade the addressee that action is needed (see Sweeney 2001: 160-162).
- *ptr sw in:* # imperative ('non-enclitic particle' as *m.k* for *LEG* § 9.6) + dependent pronoun (object of the imperative) + passive perfect participle #. Compare with the extensive use of *m.k* in Middle Kingdom decrees, especially in the introduction, the acknowledgment of receipt, and the conclusion (in *pBrooklyn* 35.1446, for instance).

* 'Classical' degree 0 forms used:

- *imi in.tw:* causative imperative (typical superior to inferior request) + dependent passive or impersonal prospective (object) in a letter quotation marked by *r-ḏd* (for the first time, it is perhaps not a 'constructed' quotation, although it may be a paraphrase of the previous message rather than a literal quotation). Compare with Middle Kingdom 13th dynasty *Sbkḥtp* II decree, in which the order is given by the imperative *imi in.tw.f.*
- *dit in.tw:* causative infinitive + dependent passive or impersonal prospective (object).
- 15 *n dbn n msdmt:* note the use of the relator between the numeral and the measure unit and between the measure unit and the material. The relator is used abundantly in the text in all kinds of appurtenance relationships.

* General dialectal features: degree 3.

* Legal terms: -
* Epistolary formulas: background past reference: *sḏm.i* (report) + *r-ḏd* (quotation of a previous message) + *iw.f sḏm* (chain of events having followed the quoted message).

4. The orders: measures to be taken

(31) *wnn p3w wḫ3 n Pr-ʿ3* (*ʿnḫ wḏ3 snb*) *p3y.k nb spr r.k iw.k šsp* (32) *p3y msdmt inyt n.k mtw.k dit in.tw* 100 *n dbn n msdmt* (33) *nfr nfr nfr nfr n š3wy sḏmw n Pr-ʿ3* (*ʿnḫ wḏ3*) *snb p3y.k nb r* (34) *p3 nty tw.tw im iw.w 3s r iḳry ptr h3b.i r* (35) *iry n.k mtry*

(31) As soon as the present message of Pharaoh (L.P.H.), your lord, reaches you, you (are to) take (32) this galena brought to you and cause that be brought 100 *dbn* of galena (33) 4 times good fit for (the) kohl of Pharaoh (L.P.)H., your lord, to (34) the (place) where One is (= I am), when hurrying very much. See that I have sent (this message) to (35) instruct you (lit. constitute for you an instruction).

* Neo-Egyptian characteristics:
  - *p3w wḫ3 n Pr-ʿ3:* proximal deictic and cataphoric use of the Neo-Egyptian demonstrative *p3w*, instead of *p3* in *pTurin* 1896, line 7.
  - *p3y.k:* with *nb*, as a formulaic apposition to *Pr-ʿ3*.
  - *wnn p3w wḫ3 n Pr-ʿ3 spr r.k iw.k šsp:* note the double omission of the preposition *ḥr*.
  - *p3y*
  - *mtw.k dit:* conjunctive apodosis after *iw.k šsp*.
  - *p3 nty tw.tw im*
  - *iw.w 3s*: Neo-Egyptian delocutive plural suffix in an adverbial circumstantial nexus that reinforces a request from a superior instance to an inferior one (Sweeney 2001: 59-60).
  - *ptr h3b.i:* presentative + relatively past that-form with locutive actor. See Bakir (1970: 111). The formula *ptr h3b.i r iry n.k mtry* recalls 13th dynasty *pBrooklyn* 35.1446 decrees formula *m.k ni-swt dw wḏ3w ib.k m-mitt.*
  - *r iry n.k mtry:* purpose expressed by # preposition *r* + infinitive (see Winand (1992: 74) for *y* ending from *Rʿmss* IX on) + beneficiary + nominal form #. Compare with synthetic *r mtry.k* (*pTurin* 1896, line 14). Reinforcing expression in requests from superior to inferior (Sweeney 2001: 60).
* 'Classical' degree 0 forms used:
  - *inyt:* passive perfect participle; for the characteristic ending, see Winand (1992: 369).
  - *in.tw:* dependent passive prospective (object of *dit*).
  - *nfr* x 2/4 and *r iḳry*: superlative expressions, the first being an adnominal expansion of intensity, the second an adverbial expression.

* General dialectal features: degree 3.

* Legal terms:

wḫꜣ - classifier: (administrative dispatch, royal letter containing an order).

mtry - classifier: (testimony, counsel, instruction). See *Wb* II, 172 *iri mtr*(*t*) 'Auch vom Brief: als Beleg dienen' or 'auch: jemandem einen Brief als Beleg verschappen' 'belegt Nä' (also with classifiers); Sweeney (2001: 236-237) translates it as 'evidence', in an instruction 'to keep the letter for further reference'. *EG*'s T14 classifier is doubled and appears instead of the two vertical fingers (D50) that 'serve as det. accurate'; Gardiner adds (*EG* p. 456, D50 note 2) that 'Possibly two stems *mty* 'precise' and *mtr* 'be present', 'witness' are to be distinguished'. For Moret (1916: 309), it may indicate a specific gesture imposed during the testimony procedure. But note that all kinds of lexemes beginning with *mt-* take the classifier (see for instance *mt* 'duct', *mtrw* 'flood', *mtn* 'reward', *mtr* 'fame') which are not all semantically related in any obvious way; in those cases as in ours, the relationship between the classifier and the lexeme can hardly be assessed, but a phonetic relation is not impossible. Note also the presence of with *ꜥḳꜣ* (precise, exact, straight; rope), *mḫꜣ* (match, adjust, be like), *ḫꜣy* (plumb-line) and *ḫꜣyw* (measurements); in these cases, precise measurement is made by taking into account fine measure units, the fingers (digit, finger breadth).

* Epistolary formulas:

- *wnn pꜣw wḫꜣ n Pr-ꜥꜣ* (*ꜥnḫ wḏꜣ snb*) *pꜣy.k nb spr r.k iw.k* + infinitive + conjunctives (the measures to be taken immediately).
- *ptr hꜣb.i r iry n.k mtry* (intention, purpose).

5. Closing formula

(35) (…) *hꜣb*[20] *pw r rdit rḫ.k r-nty pr ni-swt* (*ꜥnḫ wḏꜣ snb*) (36) *ꜥḏwy snby* (date)

(35) (…) It is a dispatch to let you know that (the) Palace (L.P.H.) (36) is safe (and) sound. (redaction and/or sending date)[21]

* Neo-Egyptian characteristics:

- *hꜣb pw r rdit rḫ.k r-nty pr ni-swt ꜥḏwy snby:* identificative/explicative nominal nexus # verbal noun (rheme) + classic thematic delocutive pronoun, deictic # + # preposition *r* + infinitive (purpose) + dependent prospective (object of *dit*) + *r-nty* + adverbial nexus (with binomial statives) #. Closing formula used during the 19th dynasty, based on a classical Middle Kingdom model, see Bakir (1970: 67-68, 70, 85) for the archaism using *pw* and *rḫ* instead of *ꜥm*. Compare with

20 About the 'sending', see Bakir (1970: 17-18).

21 See Bakir (1970: 70) for the date at the end of the communication; Sweeney (2001: 18, note 125) for the sending date.

12th dynasty *Semnah dispatches* (Smither & Gunn 1945: pl. II-VII; Helck 1974: 119-121) *iw h3w nb n pr ni-swt* L.P.H. *ꜥḏ wḏ3* 'All the affairs of the King's Domain, l.p.h., are safe and sound' and 18th dynasty *Ḏḥwtyms* I *Wadi Halfa and Kuban decrees* (*h3b pw r rdit rḫ.k st ntt pr ni-swt ꜥḏ wḏ3*), perhaps also with 13th dynasty *pBrooklyn* 35.1446 decrees conclusion (although the closing formula is badly damaged in these two instances, see Hayes 1972: 80 and Wente 1990: 25). Note the morphology of the statives (Winand 1992: 114 & 123) and compare with *pTurin* 1896, line 14.

* 'Classical' degree 0 forms used: -
* General dialectal features: degree 1.
* Legal terms: -
* Epistolary formula: *h3b pw r rdit rḫ.k r-nty pr ni-swt ꜥḏwy snby* + redaction/expedition date.

6. Colophon (delivery)

(37) *in m* (date) *m ḏrt ḥry ḥ3p3ti Ḥri*
(37) Brought in (delivery date) by (the) hand of (the) chief of scouts, *Ḥri*.

* Neo-Egyptian characteristics: *ḥ3p3ti:* Neo-Egyptian lexeme. See Helck (1967: 137) 'Oberspäher', and p.139 'Obersten der Kundschafter'. But *ḥ3pytw*/*ḥ3pwty* are for Gardiner (1960: 32) the cultivators of a small plot, whereas for Schulman (1957: 267) and Peden (1994: 109) they are scouts.
* 'Classical' degree 0 forms used: *in:* perfect passive participle. Compare with the formula in the *Stèle juridique de Karnak*, line 11 (17th dynasty): *ir in ḫ3* (…) (done by the office, with participle). Quite different from the Old Kingdom (actually from 6th dynasty on) formula *iw rdi iwt*.N *r.s*; see Goedicke (1964: 36); Helck (1974: 122); Pantalacci (1985: 246-251). Compare also with *pTurin* 1971 in *LRL* 33,6 and Wente (1967: 50) (private document with date + *iw n ḥr*.N) and *Hermopolis decree* delivery colophon *supra*; or with the acknowledgment formula opening a reply in Bakir (1970: 71) *t3y šꜥt tiwt spr r.i m ḏrt* N *m* + date of reception.
* General dialectal features: degree 1.
* Legal terms: -
* Legal formula: *in m* (delivery date) + *m ḏrt* (conveyor name).

III. *pTurin* 1896 r°

This letter to the Viceroy of Nubia *Pȝynḥsy* (Bakir 1970: pls. 24-25; *KRI* VI, 734-735 n. 18) is again a 'royal rescript of warning and instruction', a personal letter expressing the royal command and authority, directly addressed to a high royal official by the king, as was *Stḫy* II's decree in *pAnastasi* IV and *Rꜥmss* IX's message to *Rꜥmssnḫt,* of which the formulas are very close. The letter is dated in its last line to Year 17, and was probably issued in the Thebaid (Peden 1994: 111). The hieratic used is 'typical "literary"' for Goldwasser (2001: 125, noting that it suggests that the writer regarded the letter 'as a "literary" piece'), and again it is impossible to know if the letter is genuine or a copy (although for Bakir (1970: 8) and Helck (1974: 120) because of the address, and for Vernus (1990: 244) because of 'le dispositif, le formulaire et l'écriture de chancellerie', it is an original).

1. Heading and addressee

(Royal titulary) (4) *wḏ ni-swt n sȝ ni-swt n Kšy sš ni-swt n pȝ mšꜥ imy-r šnwwt ḥȝwty Pȝynḥsy n* (5) *nȝ pḏt Pr-ꜥȝ ꜥnḫ wḏȝ snb*

(Royal titulary) (4) Royal decree to (the) King's son of Kush, royal scribe of the army, overseer of granaries, leader of (5) Pharaoh's troops, L.P.H, *Pȝynḥsy*:

* Neo-Egyptian characteristics:

- *pȝ mšꜥ:* non-phoric use of the articloid (specifies uniqueness and importance), 'indicating context-dependent identity' (Simpson 1996: 35), the army being of course meant as the Egyptian army.
- *ḥȝwty:* Neo-Egyptian lexeme (*Wb* III, 29).
- *Pȝynḥsy:* 'This-Nubian', a Neo-Egyptian proper noun constructed with the Neo-Egyptian demonstrative + ethnic noun.
- *nȝ pḏt Pr-ꜥȝ:* cataphoric use of the articloid.

* 'Classical' degree 0 forms used: *wḏ ni-swt n*.N

* General dialectal features: degree 1.

* Legal terms: *wḏ ni-swt* - classifier: 𓏛 (royal decree, the papyrus document). Note that in *pCairo ESP (B)*, the 𓏜 classifier is used.

* Epistolary formula: royal titulary + *wḏ ni-swt* + *n* (addressee)

2. Introductory formula

(5) (...) *r-nty in.tw n.k wḏ ni-swt pnn r-ḏd* {*pnn r-ḏd*}

(5) (…) to (let you know) that: it is to you/to say (what follows) that this royal decree {dittography} has been brought:

* Neo-Egyptian characteristics:

- *r-nty... r-ḏd:* note that the formula does not close with *r-nty* but with a dittography of *pnn r-ḏd* that 'may also point to a frozen archaism' for Goldwasser (2001: 125).
- *pnn*

* 'Classical' degree 0 forms used:

- *in.tw wḏ*

* General dialectal features: degree 1.

* Legal terms: *wḏ* - classifier:  (decree, the papyrus document).

* Legal/epistolary formula: *r-nty in.tw n.k* (recipient) *wḏ ni-swt pnn r-ḏd* (content of the decree).

3. Content (object)

(5) (…) *wḏ.i Ynwsꜣ* (6) *pꜣy ꜥꜣ n pr wdpw n Pr-ꜥꜣ ꜥnḫ wḏꜣ snb didy iwt.f m nꜣ sḥnyw n Pr-ꜥꜣ ꜥnḫ wḏꜣ snb pꜣy.f nb* (7) *wḏy.f r ir.w m ꜥ rsy*

(5) (…) I have sent *Ynwsꜣ* (6), this majordomo, butler of Pharaoh L.P.H., caused that he will come with the commands of Pharaoh L.P.H., his lord, (7) (and) that he will depart to execute them in (the) southern region.

* Neo-Egyptian characteristics:

- *wḏ.i*: independent report *sḏm.i* (locutive actor) referring to a past action of the king that he reports as background to the orders he addresses to *Pꜣynḥsy*; see *Rꜥmss* IX *pCairo ESP (B)* decree, line 23 *hꜣb.i*.
- *pꜣy:* it probably designates the majordomo as carrier of the letter (the addressee has to cooperate with him).
- *nꜣ sḥnyw n Pr-ꜥꜣ:* cataphoric use of the articloid.
- *pꜣy.f*

* 'Classical' degree 0 forms used:

- *didy:* for Frandsen (1974: 28), who transcripts it *dd.tw iwt.f* (although the impersonal pronoun is absent), it is 'the sole example of *dd* expressing "Aussage" in a non-judicial text/context' and considers it a 'perfect passive *sḏm.f*', also Wente's opinion, as his translation (1990: 40) shows, as well as apparently for Peden (1994: 113). For the morphology of the 'perfectif', see Winand (1992: 193-194); one must note that there is no gemination in the examples given by Winand. Furthermore, as there is no sign of the impersonal *.tw* in the text, one could prefer to see a locutive form. Breasted (*ARE* IV, 289) translates *didy* as an imperative, although the imperative form of *rdi* is *imi*. The geminated *didy* form (without prothetic *yod*) might perhaps be better interpreted as a passive imperfect participle or a rhematic stative (the butler is caused to go).

- *ỉwt.f:* dependent prospective (object of *didy*).
- *wḏy.f r ỉr.w:* dependent prospective followed by the preposition *r* + infinitive (purpose; with Neo-Egyptian suffixed object resumptive to the antecedent *sḥnyw* and absence of feminine mark of the infinitive). Translators of the text (Breasted, Peden, Wente) translate *wḏy.f r ỉr.w* as 'which he has set out to execute' (Wente 1990: 40) as if a relative form with the orders for antecedent.

* General dialectal features: degree 2.

* Legal terms: *sḥnyw* - classifier:  (mission, commands). The superordinate [ABSTRACT] category papyrus roll classifier is present as with the lexeme *wḏ* (order, verbal decree), the second classifier being the complete figure of the man with the strong arm (superordinate [COERCION] category).

* Epistolary formula: - background past information: *sḏm.ỉ* (report).

4. The orders: measures to be taken

(7) (…) *wnn pꜣ wḫꜣ n Pr-ꜥꜣ ꜥnḫ wḏꜣ snb pꜣy.k nb spr r.k* (8) *ỉw.k ỉr wꜥ ỉrm.f r dỉt ỉry.f nꜣ sḥnyw n Pr-ꜥꜣ ꜥnḫ wḏꜣ snb* (9) *pꜣy.f nb wḏy.f ỉm.w mtw.k ptrỉ tꜣy fꜣyt n tꜣy nṯrt* (10) *ꜥꜣt mtw.k ꜥrꜥr.s mtw.k ꜣtp.s r* boat *mtw.k dỉt ỉn.tw.s r-ḥꜣt.f r pꜣ nty tw.tw ỉm* (11) *mtw.k dỉt ỉn.tw ḥrst ḫnmt ỉwn ḫwr ỉsmꜣyr ḥꜣrwry kꜣṯỉ* (12) *ḥꜣrwry ḫsbd ḳnw ḳnw r pꜣ nty tw.tw ỉm r mḥ ḏrt n* (13) *nꜣ ḥmwt ỉm.w m ỉr nny n pꜣy sḥny hꜣyby.ỉ n.k* (14) *ptr hꜣby.ỉ r mtry.k*

(7) (…) As soon as the present message of Pharaoh L.P.H., your lord, reaches you, (8) you (are to) cooperate (lit. make one) with him to cause that he will execute the commands of Pharaoh L.P.H., (9) his lord, upon which he departed; and you (are to) see (to) this portable shrine of this great goddess (10), finish (?) it, load it on a boat, cause that it be brought before him to the (place) where One is (= I am), (11) cause that be brought carnelian, red jasper, crystal, corundum, flowers of saffron, (12) flowers of lapis-lazuli, (in) profusion, to the (place) where One is (= I am), to fill (the) hand of (13) the craftsmen with them. Do not fail in this command I sent to you. (14) See that I have sent (this message) to constitute for you an instruction.

* Neo-Egyptian characteristics:

- *pꜣy/tꜣy*
- *pꜣy.f/pꜣy.k*
- *wnn pꜣ wḫꜣ n Pr-ꜥꜣ spr r.k ỉw.k ỉr:* note that *pꜣ wḫꜣ* replaces *pꜣw wḫꜣ* of *pCairo ESP (B)* as in *pAnastasi* IV.
- *pꜣ wḫꜣ:* deictic, anaphoric, cataphoric.
- *ỉr wꜥ ỉrm.f:* # infinitive ('transitive to make' or 'intransitive to be'; note the absence of feminine mark) + quantifier + Neo-Egyptian preposition *ỉrm* + delocutive suffix #.

- *mtw.k pty/mtw.k ʿrʿr.s/mtw.k ꜣtp.s/mtw.k dit:* conjunctives.
- *fꜣyt:* Neo-Egyptian lexeme (*Wb* I, 574).
- *pꜣ nty tw.tw ỉm*
- *ḥrst ẖnmt ỉwn ẖwr ỉsmꜣyr ḥꜣrwry kꜣṯi:* probably all Neo-Egyptian lexemes, syllabic spelling; see Albright (1934: 50 and 60); Wente (1990: 40); Peden (1994: 112-113).
- *ḳnw ḳnw:* Neo-Egyptian lexemes (*Wb* V, 46), expansion of intensity.
- *nꜣ ḥmwt:* either cataphoric (*ỉm.w* acting as an attributive expansion), or non-phoric use of the articloid designating a collectivity belonging to the royal estate, probably considered as a unique organized department of the king's administration or as a class totality.
- *ỉm.w*: Neo-Egyptian delocutive plural suffix.
- *m ỉr nny n:* # imperative of negative verb *imi* as negator (nuclear, preverbal) + 'negative complement' (auxiliary of an analytic form) *ỉr* + negative verb *nny* (infinitive) + relator + determined noun #. See *EG* § 340.2 ('From Dyn. XVIII onward the vernacular replaced the simple vetive *m* by (...) *m ỉr* 'do not make', to which the infinitive was added as object'); Bakir (1970: 81); Frandsen (1974: 263); Sweeney (2001: 45-47) 'periphrastic requests' with encouraging 'double negatives', here summarizing the letter's content.
- *ptr hꜣby.i:* compare *pCairo ESP (B), ptr hꜣb.i.*

* 'Classical' degree 0 forms used:

- *wḏy.f ỉm.w:* # perfect relative form of a motion verb + preposition *m* + Neo-Egyptian plural suffixed resumptive to the antecedent *sḥnyw* #.
- *ỉry.f:* dependent prospective, object of *dit*, with double *yod* (see Winand 1992: 212 for the independent prospective).
- *ỉn.tw.s:* dependent passive prospective (object of *dit*).
- *r-ḥꜣt.f:* Neo-Egyptian compound preposition (*Wb* III, 24).
- *ỉn.tw:* dependent passive prospective (object of *dit*).
- *r mḥ:* preposition *r* + infinitive (purpose).
- *hꜣyby.i:* perfect synthetic relative form, with an uncommon spelling, referring to the antecedent *sḥny*. Note again the absence of prothetic *yod.*

* General dialectal features: degree 3.

* Legal terms:

ỉr sḥnyw - classifier:  (to execute orders). See above.

nny n - classifier: 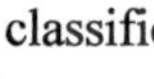 (to fail to, neglect the orders). *EG*'s A7 classifier 'man sinking to ground from fatigue' 'Det. weary, weak' indicates incapacity, powerlessness as for instance the position of the enemy defeated by the king (see Narmer on the recto of the famous *CG* 14716 palette (for the 'abandon, (...) renoncement' meaning of the upturned palms, see Lacau (1954: 15), and the French expression 'baisser les bras', symbolic helplessness gesture). The classifier represents the prototypical attitude of the defeated, a man in a situation that is beyond his capacity, a symbolic image of helplessness; the lexeme is probably a member of the [HELPLESSNESS] category. The superordinate

[INFERIORITY-PERTURBATION] category bird reinforces the negative connotation of the lexeme.

wḫ3 - classifier: (administrative dispatch, royal letter containing an order).

mtry - classifier: (testimony, counsel, instruction).

* Epistolary formulas:

- *wnn p3 wḫ3 n Pr-ʿ3 ʿnḫ wḏ3 snb p3y.k nb spr r.k iw.k* + infinitive + conjunctives (the measures to be taken immediately).
- *m ir nny n p3y sḥny h3yby.i n.k* (request to proceed)
- *ptr h3by.i r mtry.k* (intention, purpose).

5. Closing formula

(14) (…) *h3b pw dit rḫ.k r-nty pr ni-swt ʿḏ snb* (15) (date)
(14) (…) It is a dispatch to let you know that (the) Palace is safe (and) sound. (15) (redaction and/or sending date)

* Neo-Egyptian characteristics:

- *h3b pw dit rḫ.k r-nty pr ni-swt ʿḏ snb:* note that in *pCairo ESP (B)*, we had *h3b pw r rdit* (instead of the present omission of preposition) and the binomials were differently spelled (*ʿḏwy snby*).

* 'Classical' degree 0 forms used: -

* General dialectal features: degree 1.

* Legal terms: -

* Epistolary formula: *h3b pw dit rḫ.k r-nty pr ni-swt ʿḏ snb* + redaction/expedition date.

IV. Table of the syntactic forms and particularities in epistolary decrees

Abbreviations:

A = active
Ad = address
C = content/object
Cl = closing formula
Col = colophon
I = introductory formula
O = orders (measures to be taken)
P = passive
Q = quotation texteme
x = numerous occurrences

Form	Degree	*pAnastasi* IV 19th d. *Sthy* II	*pCairo ESP (B)* 20th d. *Rˁmss* IX	*pTurin* 1896 20th d. *Rˁmss* XI
sḏm.i/k (indep. perfect report, A)	2	1 (Q)	1 (C)	1 (C)
sḏm.tw.N (indep. perfect report or abstract that-form, P)	2	1 (I)	1 (I)	1 (I)
sḏm (perfect participle P or stative) *inyt, gmyt* (fem.) *sḏmy*	0 0 1	1? (C)	2 (C, Col) 2 (C, O) 2 (Cl)	2 (Cl)
didy (gem. participle P or stative)	2			1 (C)
iw bn sḏm (circ. non-existence, prohibition) *iw bn iri.k sḏm*	2 2	 1 (C)	1 (C)	
iw bw sḏm.n.f (circ. past neg.?)	2	1 (C)		
i.iri.k sḏm	2	1 (C)		

(indep. relatively past focalizing that-form, A)				
sḏm.f (non gem. relatively past that-form, A)	0		1 (O)	
h3by.i	1			1 (O)
sḏm.f (rel., perfect, A)	0			1 (O)
h3yby.i	1			1 (O)
i.sḏm.k	2	2 (C, O)		
p3 dit i.iri.k iw.N (past thematized infinitive)	2	1 (C)		
ir ḫy rʿ bn PN *sḏm* (open question, durative present or future?, neg)	2	1 (C)		
gm.tw.f (indep. prospective, P)	0	1 (O)		
sḏm.f/N (depend. object, prospective, A)	0	2 (C, O)	1 (Cl)	1 (Cl)
iwt.f	0	1 (O)		1 (C)
iry.f	0			1 (O)
wḏy.f	0			1 (C)
iry.f sḏm	1	1 (C)		
sḏm.tw(.N/*f*) (depend. object prospective, P/Imp.)	0	2 (C)	3 (C, O, Q)	2 (O)
is bn sḏm.tw.k (indep. rhetorical question with prospective that-form, P, neg)	2	1 (C)		
sḏm/*t* (infinitive)	0	2 (C)	2 (C, Cl)	x (O, Cl)
iry	1			
sḏmtw	1	1 (C)		
sḏm (fem)/*t* (m.)	1	1 (O)		3 (C, O)
N *nty tw.i ḥr sḏm*	2	1 (C)		

(rel. durative first present)				
wnw ḥr sn (rel. preterit-converted first present with participle)	2	1 (C)		
p3 nty tw.tw ỉm (substantivized rel. adverbial clause)	1		2 (Q, O)	2 (O)
wnn.N *ḥr sḏm* ... *ỉw.k ḥr sḏm* (contiguity linked protasis (thematic circ.) & apodosis (circ. first present)) *wnn*.N *sḏm* ... *ỉw.k sḏm*	1 2	1 (O)	 1 (O)	 1 (O)
ḥr ỉr tw.tw sḏm... *ỉw.tw sḏm* (past temporal first present protasis and retrodependent narrative apodosis)	2		1 (C)	
ỉw.N *ḥr sḏm* (indep. or circ first present, durative) *tw.f* (*ḥr*) *sḏm* (indep.)	0 1	 1 (C)	 1 (C)	
ỉw.f (*ḥr*) *sḏm* (retrodependent narrative)	2		2 (C)	
bn N *sḏm* (indep. adverbial nexus, durative, neg)	2	1 (C)		
ỉw.k r-ṯnw/*r*.N *nym* (indep. adverbial	0	2 (Q)		

interrogative nexus)				
mtw.f/N (*ḫr*) *sḏm* (conjunctive apodosis)	2	6 (C, O)	1 (O)	5 (O)
irtyw, *ptr* (iussive imperative, A)	1	2 (O)	2 (C, O)	1 (O)
imi šdm.tw (causative imperative)	0		1 (Q)	
m ir nny (vetive, A)	1			1 (O)
N determined + *p3w* + participle (cleft sentence)	1		1 (C)	
h3b pw r rdit rḫ.k r-nty (nominal nexus, rheme + thematic pron.) *h3b pw dit rḫ.k r-nty*	1 2		1 (Cl)	 1 (Cl)
n3 ḥrw (indep. question for corroboration, adjectival rheme)	1	1 (C)		
twtw for *tw.i* (majestative, *enallage*)	1		2 (C, O)	2 (O)
.w (delocutive plur. suffix)	1	3 (C, O)	1 (O)	3 (C, O)
"*pnn*" (proximal deictic determinator + relator *n*)	1	1 (I)	1 (I)	2 (I)
p3y (deictic deteminator)	1	3 (C, O)	1 (O)	4 (C, O)
p3w (deictic determinator substantivizer or cataphoric)	1		2 (C, O)	
p3, *t3*, *n3* (non-phoric articloid)	1	2 (C, O)		2 (Ad, O)

pꜣ, tꜣ, nꜣ (anaphoric articloid)	1	1 (O)		
pꜣ, tꜣ, nꜣ (cataphoric articloid)	1	7 (C, O)	5 (C)	3 (Ad, C, O)
cata- and anaphoric	1	1 (C)		
cata-, anaphoric, and deictic	1	1 (O)		1 (O)
pꜣy.f (possessive)	1	4 (C, O)	1 (O)	3 (C, O)
tỉw(y) (interlocutive possessive determinator)	1	3 (C, O)		
n (relator)	0	x (C, O)	x (Ad, C, O, Q)	x (Ad, C, O)
r-pw (disjunctor of nexuses)	1	1 (O)		
ỉrm.f (preposition)	1	1 (O)		1 (O)
m-dỉ.f/N (compound preposition)	1	1 (C)		
ḫy rꜥ (contrastive coord.?)	1	1 (C)		
mỉ ḳd (coord. locution)	1	1 (C)		
r-nt(y/t) (introductory purpose marker)	1	1 (I)	3 (I, Cl)	2 (I, Cl)
r-ḏd (tagged speech marker)	1	3 (I, C, O)	1 (I)	2 (I)
ỉḫ r (interrog. rheme + prep.)	1	1 (C)		
nꜣ= ỉn (interrog.)	1	1 (C)		
preposition omission	1			3 (O, Cl)
preposition redundancy	1	1(C)		
n/*m* prepositions confusion	1	1 (C)	1 (C)	

5. Occurrences of classifiers in the Ramesside royal decrees legal register

The number of occurrences in each text is represented by the number in front of the decree's abbreviation in the table. The abbreviation for the decree corresponds to the decree's category (P for protection, E for endowment, C for commission and Ep for epistolary) followed by its chapter number. Note that the definition of the classifier and the name of the category adopted here are exclusively related to the lexemes and categories as they appear in our Ramesside corpus. As for the evolution of the meanings associated with classifiers, see Goldwasser (2002: 13-14).

Abbreviations:

PI = *Nauri decree*
PII = *Hermopolis decree*
PIII = *Kanais/Wadi Abbad* or *Mia/Redesieh decree*
PIV = *Armant decree*
PV = *Karnak decree*
PVI = *Elephantine decree*
EI = Two *Buhen decrees*
EII = Four *West Silsileh decrees*
EIII = *Deir el-Medineh decree*
EIV = *Abydos decree*
EV = *Medamud decree*
EVI = *Medinet Habu decree*
EVII = Three *Karnak (Temple of Amun) decrees*
EVIII = *Fayum/Herakleopolis decree*
EIX = *Qantir decree*
CI = *Brooklyn* 69.116.1 and *Fayum decrees*
CII = *East Silsileh decree*
CIII = *Assuan decree*
CIV = *BM* 1665 *decree*
CV = *West Silsileh, Bigeh, Armant* and *El-Kab decrees*
CVI = *Tanis decree*
CVII = *Saqqara, Abu Gorab* and *Abusir decree*
CVIII = *West Silsileh decree*
CIX = *Medinet Habu* and *Deir el-Bahari decree*
CX = *Tod, Karnak, Edfu, Elephantine* and *El-Kab decree*
CXI = *Heliopolis decree*

CXII = *El-Kab decree*
EpI = *pAnastasi* IV. 10,8 – 11,8
EpII = *pCairo ESP (B)*
EpIII = *pTurin* 1896 r°

Relation classifier/ category	Lexeme classified	Translation	Occurrences in decrees	Alternative
𓍱 - V12 (string) metonymic classifier of [BINDING] basic level categ.	*wḏ(t)*	decree papyrus roll	4 PI; 1 PVI; 1 EVI; 1 CVII; 1 EpI; 2 EpIII; 1 EV; 1 EpII	
	hp(w)	rule, legal norm	5 PI; 1 PVI	𓏛 1 PI; 1 PII; 1 PVI ø 6 PI
	wḫ3	royal letter embodying an order	1 EpI; 1 EpII; 1 EpIII	
	imy-pr	disposition act/title	1 PIII	
	ipw	land survey register	2 CI	
𓏛 - Y1 (papyrus roll) metonymic/metaph. classifier of [ABSTRACT] superordinate categ.	*wḏ*	decree as énoncé d'autorité to decree/command	1 PI; 1 PVI; 1 EI; 2 EII; 1 EVI; 5 EVII; 1 EVIII; 1 EIX; 1 CII; 2 CIII; 4 CV; 1 CVI; 1 CVIII; 2 CIX; 1 CXII; 1 EpII	ø 3 PI; 2 EII; 2 CVII; 3 CX; 1 CXI; x CV 𓂻 1 EV
	ḫt	material property	1 PI; 2 PII; 2 PIII; 2 PIV; 1 PVI	ø 9 PI; 2 PVI
	ḫwy	to retain	1 PI; 1 PIII; 1 CX	
	mky	to preserve	1 PI; 2 PIII	ø 1 PI
	b3kw	work yield, product	2 PI; 1 PIII	
	w3ḥ	to institute, endowment	3 EI; 4 EVII; 1 CVI	ø 4 EII; 1 EVI; 1 EVII
	s3wt sšw	archivist (guardian of scripts)	1 CX	
	sdf	foundation, endowment	1 PIII	
	gmi r m	to be reckoned against s. as (a crime)	1 EpI	
	sp/sip	to inspect	3 CX	
	mn (ḥr st)	to be vested in a position	1 PVI; 1 CVI	
	smn	to establish, confirm	1 CVII	ø 1 PI
	mn w3ḥ	established (and) enduring	1 CI	
	sḫr	plan, premeditation	1 PI; 1 PIII	ø 1 PI
𓍱 + 𓏛	*spy wr*	inventory	1 CX	3 𓏛 CIX
𓂡 - D40 (arm +	*ṯ3w r*	to commit to	1 PI; 1 CX	

stick) metonymic/metaph. classifier of [COERCION] superordinate categ.	*nḥm*	to divert, commandeer	2 PI; 1 PIII, 1 PVI	
	šd	to confiscate	3 PI; 3 PVI	ø 4 PI; 1 PII × 1 PVI
	ḥwrʿ	robbery	1 PI; 2 PVI	
	ꜣwy	to hand over, issue	1 PI; 1 PVI	
	m-ḳnt mi	in force as	1 CX	1 CX
	rwḏ	agent	12 PI; 1 PVI	ø 1 PVI
	kfʿw	by coercion	4 PI	ø 1 PI
	bḥw	by corvée, forced labor	6 PI	? 1 PVI
	pr rwḏ	state agent department	1 PI	
	sḥn	to commission	1 CIII	
+	*(ir) sḥny*	(to execute) orders	3 EpIII	
- A1 (seated man) [MALE-HUMAN] superordinate categ.	*ḳnbt sḏmyw*	court (of hearers)	1 PI	ø 1 PVI
- A1 + B1 + Z2 [BOTH SEXES] superordinate categ. and [PLURAL] superordin. categ.	*wnḏwt*	subjects, dependents (of the 2 sexes)	1 PIII	
+	*šnʿy*	member of the executive force	1 PI	1 PVI
- D40 + D51 (finger) [FINGER ACTIONS] basic level categ.	*iṯꜣ, iṯi*	to seize, abduct, a fine, possession	18 PI; 5 PVI	1PI; 1 PIV 1 PVI
	ṯꜣ(wt)	to seize, a fine	6 PI; 3 PVI	
	ṯꜣi	seizer	1 PVI	ø 1 PVI
- A47 (seated bearded man + stick) [GUARDING] basic level categ. + Y1 + D40	*iry n ʿḥꜣ*	litigant	1 PIII	
- D41 (arm) [ARM MOTION] basic level categ.	*hd*	to assault, drive off, a sanction	1 PI	2 PI 1 EpI
	hd m ḳnbt	to attack in a law court, to convict	1 PI	
- D54 (legs) basic level metaph. classifier of [MOTION] superordinate categ.	*wstnw*	(to deal) arbitrarily	2 PI	ø 2 PI 1 PVI
	rwi m iꜣt	to expel from office	1 PV	
	sn(n)	to transgress, a transgression	2 EpI	

	ꜥḥꜥ (ḥr st)	to succeed in/attend in a position	1 PVI	
	tkn	to approach unto, molest	1 PI	
𓂾 - D56 (leg) metaph. classifier of the [LEG] basic level categ.	thi wḏ	to transgress/violate a decree	1 PI	
𓂻 + 𓂾	thi rmṯ	to lead people astray, to abuse	2 PIII	
	thi r (tꜣš)	to transgress, overstep, trespass, commit an abuse, encroach upon boundaries	9 PI; 1 PVI	𓂻 2 PI 𓂾 ⌴ 3 PI
	šnꜥ	to detain (not let go)	1 PI	𓂾 1 PVI 𓂻 1 PI
𓂾 + ⌴	thm	to interfere	1 PI	
𓉐 - O1 (house) [HABITAT] superord. categ.	(ꜥḥꜥ mn ḥr) st	(to succeed in/attend & be vested in) a position	1 PVI	
𓊛 - P3 (boat) metonymic classifier of [CROSSING] basic level categ.	ḏꜣy tꜣ r	to interfere with, violate, commit an abuse	1 PI; 1 PVI	
× - Z9 (crossed sticks) metaphoric classifier of the [UNION/DIVISION] superord. categ.	wpi	to judge	1 PI	
	iry n wp	opposing party	1 PI	
	iry wpw ḥnꜥ	to execute a verdict against	1 PI; 1 PIII	
	(r)dit m šb(t) n	to give in exchange for/to	1 PI	[×?] 1 PI [𓍱 ?] 1 PVI
	nkt	low quantity/*res*, valuables	1 PI; 2 PV	𓈙 1 PI
× + ⌴	dr m iꜣt	to expel from an office, dismiss	1 PI	
𓅪 - G37 (sparrow) metaphoric classifier of the [INFERIORITY/ PERTURBATION] superord. categ.	ꜣḳ (m ḫt)	loss (of material property)	1 PI; 1 PVI	
	ꜣḳw	to conjure away, disappear, lose?	1 PI	
	btꜣ	crime	1 PIII	
	(mty) bin	evil (witness/advice)	1 PIII	
× + 𓅪	ir btꜣw	to commit an offence	1 EpI	
	btꜣw n mt	capital offense	1 EpI	
𓅪 + 𓀉 - A7 metaphoric classifier of the [HELPLESSNESS] basic level categ.	nny n	to fail, neglect (orders)	1 EpIII	

- F21 (ear) metonymic classifier of the [HEARING] basic level categ.	*sḫ ḥr*	to be deaf to, neglectful, disregard	1 PIII	1 PI
- A40 (seated bearded figure) metaphoric classifier of the [DIVINE] superord. categ.	*ḏ3ḏ3t*	judges	1 PIII	ø 4 EII
- A2 [MOUTH LINKED ACTIVITIES] basic level categ.	*sḫn ḥnᶜ*	to go to law with, plead against, arraign	1 PIII	
	mty (*bin*)	(evil) witness/advice	1 PIII	
× - Z9 + A2	*ir wšb ḥr*	to answer for, defend, protect	1 PIII	
	wšb	to answer, prosecute, a formal arraignment	1 PIII	
for - D50 x 2 (2 fingers) metaphoric classifier of the [CONTROLLED ACTIVITIES?] basic level categ.	*mtry*	testimony, instruction	1 EpII; 1 EpIII	
ø	(*r*) *tm* (*r*)*dit*	to prevent	20 PI; 1 PIV; 1 PV; 5 PVI	
	iri (*r*)	to execute, enforce against	11 PI; 1 PII; 1 PIV; 1 PVI	
	rdi r	to reduce to an inferior position	3 PI; 1 PIII; 2 PV; 1 EpI	
	smi	to complain	1 PI	
	b3rti	(submission?) contract	2 PI	1 PI
	ḥr ḏrt	by (his) own hand, independently	1 PIII	
	ir m-s3	to pursue (of a god)	1 PI; 1 PIII	
	di m ḥr	to place in sight, commission	x CV; 1 CVII; 1 CVIII; 1 CIX; 3 CX; 1 CXI	
	(*iri*) *ḥn*	to attach, allocate (personnel/property), (accomplish) a service, be endowed/equipped with	6 PI; 1 PIV; 1 PV; 1 PVI	1 PIII; 1 PVI 2 PI
	sḏmnw?	hearers/judges?	1 CX	
	gmi ḥr	to catch in the act	2 PI	
	ḫr(*y*)	under (the control of)	1 PVI; 1 CI	1 PVI
?	*st* [*md3wt?*]	[archive] bureau	1 PII	

Conclusions

After he had studied the *Nauri decree* Gardiner (1952: 24) concluded: 'I feel sure that the [Nauri decree] clauses were drafted with the carelessness characteristic of Pharaonic scribes. A pretence of legalistic formulation to meet all contingent cases is certainly paraded, but looking closer we become uncomfortably aware of useless repetitions and important omissions.' He was referring to the incomplete enumeration of staff protected by the decree, the sudden omission of certain categories of personnel, conditions, or misdeeds, the apparent unnecessary duplication of the offenses expression before and in the criminal dispositions, the assignment of the same penalties to a Viceroy and to inferior members of the civil service, a general feeling of penalties blown out of proportion. Although some of these criticisms may be deserved, the general character and formulation of this normative text and of the other normative documents belonging to our corpus show a remarkable homogeneity and constitute a specific linguistic register with a common textemic, pragmatic, and narratologic structure, as well as a coherent syntactic and lexico-semantic usage. The Ramesside decrees belong to two genres: the normative (public sphere) and the epistolary (private sphere), each using a specific dialect and structure that is noticeably opposed to the other (as the format in which they have survived, for official archives have almost disappeared, with only the propagandist 'sacralized' lapidary form of the normative decrees remaining). Furthermore, our main concern (the legal register of the normative decrees) shows a diachronic evolution whose continuity is in itself remarkable, and several common features with modern forensic discourses.

On the textemic level, the corpus studied may be divided into three main categories of decrees: the criminal law/protection decrees, the endowment and commission decrees, and the epistolary decrees (that do not present a legal register). The minimal textemic unit expected in the normative decrees genre consists of the enacting clause, and it indeed appears in all criminal law/protection, endowment and commission decrees (except for minor mentions referring to an administrative legal decree document).

The criminal law/protection decrees are by far the most complex documents in a legal register, constituted of several textemic components, such as the identificative and backgrounding aetiologic texteme (for the pre-material: date, authority formula, narrative background), the heading texteme (for the proclamation) and quotation tag clause (for the introduction of the decree's content), the delocutive report texteme of the enacting clause (for the authority, object, beneficiaries, and applicability), the preamble *sensu stricto* (negative and contrastive positive intents), the function-logic, casuistic texteme (for the crimes and their penalties), and the illustrative, constructed, quotation texteme (for motivation, background, or specific elements of the crime) of the operative part. In some cases, the narrative texteme of the epilogue (not belonging to the legal register) must be added, as well as a technical-legal, formal texteme for the colophon (delivery, copy for archiving). Each of these textemes has specific syntactic, stylistic, and semantic features; the legal register textemes studied have in common the absence of interrogative and dialogic forms (contrary to the epistolary decrees genre); they are mostly delocutive and partly retain formulae whose origin is to be found in Old Kingdom models, with subsequent transformations and adaptations (diachronic continuum, see Shisha-Halevy 1989b: 422). Degree 3 Neo-Egyptian is not realized in this register (see, for instance, the total absence of prothetic *yod* in the normative decrees, as opposed to its presence in one epistolary decree and the major use of phoric determinators, as opposed to a more pronounced use of non-phoric (grammaticalized) articles in degree 3 Neo-Egyptian textemes).

As for the identificative and backgrounding aetiologic texteme, the restricted analysis of a segment of the texteme in the *Nauri decree* has revealed some interesting features, such as the use of passive diathesis or impersonal forms for generalization, of forms 'vestige of an older usage' ('authoritative virtue' of the archaisms, legitimizing effect), of binomials, of deontic modality, of prosodic and lexical parallels, and of classical 'conservative' forms. All these features are equally characteristic of modern forensic discourses (formulaic texts with fixed arrangements of legal dispositions).

The heading texteme consists of a nominal expression with an administrative hierarchy list in a diminishing progression, using hyponyms and a final hyperonym qualified by a distributive *nb* (unspecific and decontextualized value for generality), and an archaic anaphoric expression as in modern legaleses.

The quotation of the content tag clause denotes a process of abstraction that detaches the norm from the royal verbal act; after having being uttered, the decree as a document becomes the origin of the norm.

The enacting clause delocutive report texteme is expressed by an inherited Old Egyptian perfect form, a 'formality' archaism; it is followed by more binomials without explicit coordination, as in poetic texts (prosodic features are characteristic of legal registers).

The preamble *sensu stricto* texteme is composed of a negative intent list marked by cohesive and prosodic isotopy, parallel structures, multinominal sequences enumerating contiguous terms for precision and all-inclusiveness, binomials, archaic concord and anaphora, general terms, specificity expansions, and lists of hyponyms followed by distributive *nb* and also closed by a hyperonym with distributive *nb*. The second part of the preamble *sensu stricto* texteme comprises the positive intent protective contrastive construction, repeated several times in the decrees for cohesive and emphasizing isotopy, and general exclusion of interference.

The operative part function-logic, casuistic (cases description) texteme is constructed on the basis of topicalized categories of offenders (lists for generality, in hierarchical diminishing progression of hyponyms closed by the all-inclusive hyperonym) whose crimes are expressed by an analytic, relative, non-modal future (characteristic of the criminal law register) marking the non-retroactivity of the decree, in a decontextualized and impersonal expression of a condition (eventuality), a hypothetical scenario followed by a necessary punishment. The texteme retains substantivations, use of introductive particles and markers of connectedness with cohesive effect, structural isotopy, prosodic features, a few exocentric compounds, and restricting qualification adjuncts. The penalty is expressed by a modal deontic prospective (ineluctability) in impersonal form (depersonalization, distance, focusing on foreground information), while a coordinating structure deals with the penalty modalities; it also makes use of pseudo-archaisms (contrastive cleft sentence). With the last criminal law decrees, the prospective is sometimes replaced by a non-modal future. All the features observed are characteristic of forensic modern discourse. In a few cases, a performative curse with divine actor is used instead of the usual 'the rule will have to be enforced against…' (see also modern legal discourse poeticization and the 'magic power of words'), or imprecatory prospectives (see the *Kanais decree*). The general aim of the repressive dispositions is anticipative and future-oriented, with a high level of abstraction and distance, minimal context-bound settings and expressions, non-descriptive, impersonal, with all-encompassing formulas, conditional/topicalizing (initial case) structure, and external focalization.

The illustrative constructed quotation texteme (catalysis segment) is a dynamic, concretizing inclusion that provides supplementary information about the crime; the use of such an illustrative texteme is recommended today in the drafting of statutes. It is a locutive texteme, a monologue or direct speech, often using *mn*, the generalizing non-phoric 'so-and-so' instead of a proper name (although in a concretizing context) and explicit alternatives of direct speech. It is not composed in the vernacular variety of language spoken during the same period, and the conscious use of the generalizing *mn* or of explicit alternatives of speech contribute to destroy the illusion of authentic spoken dialect.

The technical-legal, delocutive texteme of the colophon (delivery, copy for archiving) has survived in only one protection/criminal law decree; it is a descriptive, bureaucratic statement signaling the end of the text and the proper execution of formalities. The textemic change is signaled by an 18th dynasty focalization pattern or an infinitive (nominalizations are also frequent in modern bureaucratic formulas).

Endowment and commission decrees are almost exclusively constituted of the pre-material and enacting clause textemes, sometimes followed by an operative part (measures to be taken, listing) and/or a colophon (officials responsible for the execution/inscription of the royal decree, referentiality/legality). Commission decrees are usually of the briefest type, sometimes reduced to the commemoration of the royal order's execution, a laconic mention in a nominal form. The nature of the enacting clause does not vary; it is a delocutive report texteme, sometimes describing an (extensive) series of precisions concerning the endowment/commission (beneficiary, origin, periodicity, increase compared to previous endowments, term, location, conformity, motivation, purpose, measure) and is even followed by a listing texteme of the goods endowed, arranged in a format similar to modern commercial or administrative documents. An evolution is to be noted concerning the report form: contrary to the protection/criminal law decrees, it is often and briefly summarized in a degree 2 Neo–Egyptian form which is also formally close to the Old Kingdom heading of royal decrees. As in the first category of decrees, archaisms are to be noted: feminine marked concord, use of archaic anaphora, passive prospectives, synthetic future participles, prepositions followed by that-forms, prosodic isotopy, exocentric compounds, binomials, and no instance of prothetic *yod*. On the other hand, more occurrences of the non-phoric articloid are to be noted in these decrees. In addition, the colophon is sometimes expressed by a focalizing pattern.

Ramesside epistolary decrees are a totally different type; being literary pieces or actual messages, they do not exhibit a legal register (contrary to examples of Old Kingdom epistolary decrees found in a lapidary form that comprise official communications of public relevance). They present interlocutive (dialogic) textemic components (the object and the orders) after the heading/addressee mention and the introductory formula, and are closed by a specific formula followed by a colophon.

The heading and address texteme has been inherited from the Old Kingdom models, with an adaptation dating to the Middle Kingdom, again due to a marked tendency towards archaism in formulaic contexts.

The introductory formula is based on a Middle Kingdom model that evolved during the Second Intermediate Period; the content of the decree is actually opened by the same kind of quotation marker as in the *Nauri decree*. Other archaisms are to be noted (use of archaic anaphora with probable confusion, of a passive that-form marking the beginning of the decree) as well as redundancy or even dittography of parts of the formula.

The expression of the object (content) of the decree is of an interlocutive nature and uses complaints phrased as questions, contrastive open questions building a scenario, interrogative accusations, rhetorical questions expressing threats, questions for corroboration, illustrative constructed speech/quotation of previous message textemes, background locutive report (followed by preterit event-chaining narrative), and imperatives. It comprises degree 2-3 Neo-Egyptian forms, non-phoric articloids, prothetic *yod*-forms (but not exclusively in *pAnastasi* IV decree), and 'impersonal majestatives'.

The orders (measures to be taken) open with a Ramesside formula linking by contiguity a thematic background circumstance and the main focalized object of the order. Here also, use is made of prothetic *yod*-forms (only in *pAnastasi* IV decree), of constructed quotations of a document to be written, of imperatives, intensity isotopy, periphrastic requests, with offense and penalty being expressed by a warning and an option of punishment (with disjuncter marker) or by passive prospectives. The texteme is sometimes closed by a formula expressing the purpose of the request.

The closing formula of some epistolary decrees consists of an identificative/explicative nominal nexus based on a Middle Kingdom model with archaisms (deictic pronoun, lexical choice, binomials).

The colophon appearing in one epistolary decree deals with the delivery date and official in a Neo-Egyptian degree 1 form.

On a diachronic level, the normative royal decrees have evolved in complex, long, and detailed dispositions with a fixed sequential arrangement, but are still based on archaic models and a formal style, with extensive use of archaisms and features imposed by a repertoire governing the production not only of the normative genre but also of the various religious texts and incantations. The textemic changes in the decrees correspond to specific legal concerns and imply a conceptual division of the normative document that closely parallels composition of modern legal statutes. It is an ordered and fixed sequence of paragraphs that builds the decree and helps the practitioner or any interested party to deal efficiently with a logically conceived text.

On the lexical level, the lexemes used are not specific to the legal register, but there is a marked choice for specific terms and combinations (although binomials, for instance, pervade all kinds of official literature), sometimes a legacy of ancient usage, that permits subtle distinctions akin to modern legal categories (see, for instance, the distinction between property and temporary or illegal possession). An interesting element added to our discussion is due to the Egyptian graphic categorization system of classifiers. Lexemes used to designate legal operations or facts are categorized by a limited number of classifiers, mainly belonging to the [ABSTRACT], [BINDING], [COERCION], [MOTION], [LEG], [UNION/DIVISION] and [INFERIORITY /PERTURBATION] categories. Each category represents a tentative classification of abstract concepts that has features in common with modern legal categories: some of the images used in ancient Egypt are still current in modern lexemic choices to express legal concepts (see 'transgression', עבירה, for example) and their categories may not be far removed from those modern jurists refer to. A painstaking effort is made during the Ramesside Period to accurately render the categorical link, but the choice made is not always unanimous and lasting.

The issue of a specific legal Ramesside technical jargon must now be addressed. Although it has much in common with other forms of speech (in religious genres, for example), numerous features of the decrees legal register are fundamental elements to be found in modern forensic discourses on the syntactic, textemic and narrative, stylistic, prosodic, structural, and lexical levels mentioned above. Having a conventionalized communicative purpose (efficiency in the legal and social spheres), the provisions of the normative decrees share specific constraints. One of these is assuredly to show a sufficient level of authority so as to be perceived as a coercive text emanating from the supreme instance of the social hierarchy, part of the official repertoire. To achieve this purpose, it has to be basically composed in the 'high' dialect of prestige and durability, be publicly displayed in lapidary form (with the appropriate ideological apparatus and backing of the relevant deities), and be strictly enforced. These conditions seem to have been fulfilled by the texts in our corpus.

The prestigious 'high' dialect of the normative decrees postulates the presence of a synchronic vernacular 'low' dialect in Ramesside society, the 'diglossia' or 'heteroglossia' situation previously evoked in the Introduction to the present study. The conservative, 'high' dialect also integrates dynamic, 'low' dialect standardized forms that are legitimized by the governing elite, the power-holders, what Goldwasser (1991: 130) calls 'dynamic canonicity', 'intrusion of new grammatical and lexical forms into texts that already form part of the official repertoire', by a process of 'changes in decorum, or as a result of strong pressures exerted on the canonized culture' or when 'de nouvelles idées entraînent de nouvelles formulations' (Vernus 1996: 557). Jansen-

Winkeln (1995) adds a series of elements influencing the proportioning of Middle Egyptian and Neo-Egyptian in a Ramesside text: medium, subject, part of the text concerned, emotionality, realism, novelty, prestige, and enigmatic reasons of choice. The best example is perhaps the short pseudo-quotations of the illustrative textemes mentioned in the decrees: neither pure 'high dialect' nor spoken language but an 'imitation register of the "written as if spoken" variety, in itself an imitation register' (Goldwasser 1999: 5). This is quite different from more realistic quotations of arraigned persons' depositions using colloquial idioms (Vernus 1996: 555). But almost any texteme of the studied Ramesside decrees uses forms that belong to the degree 1 (adaptation of the Middle Egyptian 'classic dialect') or 2 (innovation of transitory forms added to those adaptations) Neo-Egyptian, which means standardized or canonized 'low' forms, even though degree 3 stage of Ramesside (autonomy of finalized Neo-Egyptian forms) is not reached in the normative decrees. The richness of the syntactic possibilities is considerable. The legal (technical 'Thema' for Jansen-Winkeln 1995: 95-97) register of the Ramesside decrees is Neo-Egyptian, not on the basis of its use of the 'article' that we have seen is still mainly phoric in our corpus, but mainly because of its inclusion of a large range of ancient and new forms. This mixture adds to canonicity the improved clarity of legal dispositions formulated in a dialect closer to the current spoken language and everyday legal practice. The case of the epistolary decrees is also interesting, because the *pAnastasi* IV decree (perceived as a school exercise and dating to the beginning of the 19th dynasty, quite early in comparison with the other two epistolary decrees of our corpus) uses degree 3 prothetic *yod* forms, but the *Rˁmss* IX and XI letters (that may be considered as 'real' royal communications) never use prothetic *yod* forms (although they use participles and relative forms) and incorporate some archaisms. The epistolary decrees are evidently using a more colloquial dialect than the public normative decrees, being in principle not intended for official communication and public exposition. They show 'high' variety formulas, as they emanate from the supreme state instance and are addressed to high officials. But they are perhaps composed or at least used as pedagogic models, and as such, they become what is often called 'literary letters', a new literary genre, 'the normative administrative language of the time' (Goldwasser 1985; 1991: 130-131). They gain the status of standardized academic formulas and *morceaux choisis* in the way that canonic shapes were itemized in Renaissance pattern books. The result is a predominant, degree 3 Neo-Egyptian character, 'written as if spoken', but controlled and infiltrated by archaisms and 'high' dialect elements.

The *social* diglossia situation of Egyptian society that arose from a tension between the 'official language' and the 'other' dialect after the First Intermediate Period (Loprieno 1996: 519) has permitted, from the Amarna Period on, deliberate choices, delicate mixtures of 'high' and 'low' varieties ('Mittelägyptisch und Neuägyptisch in bestimmten "Mischungsverhältnissen"' for Jansen-Winkeln 1995: 92). It became a tool of discrimination between genres and registers, a *cultural* diglossia as Loprieno (1996: 522-523) coined it, 'consciemment utilisée comme procédé stylistique et investie d'une signification particulière' (Vernus 1996: 561). The two varieties of language are studied in the Ramesside schools. Jansen-Winkeln (1995: 106-115) contends that Middle and Neo-Egyptian are already too different during the Ramesside Period to compete as they did during the Middle Kingdom; the tension has disappeared and scribes are taking advantage of their specific value. He refuses to use the term 'diglossia' in these circumstances; but one cannot dismiss the still higher status of the 'égyptien de tradition' model in Ramesside society. Loprieno's distinction between social and cultural diglossia settles the matter in the most appropriate way.

Most of the decrees were probably composed in the administrative capital of the empire by a staff of professional scribes, so that personal and regional influences do not come into play (*contra*: Groll 1987), and we have to deal with an administrative practice and cultural choice rather than with a topolect or an idiolect.

The mixed character of the Ramesside decrees on the linguistic level may reflect the fundamental dual character of the law: 'On the one hand, it claims to be a unified system, a standard accessible to all: law is expressed, for the most part, through (a particular register of) the natural language. To that extent, therefore, even non-lawyers have access to it, as indeed the ideology of the rule of law requires. On the other hand, the law clearly possesses a culture of its own.' (Jackson 1995: 97). This conclusion about modern law applies already to Ancient Egypt's legal texts, their complexity, technical and authoritative character was surely felt to need the offset of a practical approach adapted to the linguistic reality of the citizens, so that the law might be understood (albeit with minimal assistance) to achieve the goal of any propagandist monumental publication. This delicate balance is reflected in the scales, the symbolic image of justice, that we also owe to Ancient Egypt's rich metaphoric world.

Critical devices and bibliography (including abbreviations)

[ ] are used for textual lacuna
( ) are used for textual omission (scribal choice)
(...) are used for textual omission (our choice)
< > are used for textual omission (scribal error)
{ } are used for textual superfluity (dittography, etc.)
are used for delimitating a syntagm

Periodicals, series and collections are referred to as in *LÄ* VII, XIV-XIX

Abydos decree = *KRI* II, 515 n.204A.II

Albright, W.F., 1934. *The Vocalization of the Egyptian Syllabic Orthography*. American Oriental Series 5. New Haven: American Oriental Society.

Allam, S., 1973. *Hieratische Ostraka und Papyri aus der Ramessidenzeit*. URAÄ 1. Tübingen: S. Allam.

— 1973b. *Das Verfahrensrecht in der altägyptischen Arbeitersiedlung von Deir el-Medineh*. Untersuchungen zum Rechtsleben im alten Ägypten 1. Tübingen: S. Allam.

— 1984. La problématique des quarante rouleaux de lois. In *Studien zu Sprache und Religion Ägyptens I: Sprache, Festschrift W. Westendorf*, ed. F. Junge, 447-453. Göttingen: Hubert & Co.

— 1987. Aspects of Law in Ancient Egypt. *Bulletin of the Center of Papyrological Studies* 4: 9-31.

Allen, J.P., 1984. *The Inflection of the Verb in the Pyramid Texts*. BAe 2. Malibu: Undena.

Amada text = Youssef (1964)

Amenemope = Lange (1925)

Amer, A.A.M.A., 1985. Tutankhamun's Decree for the Chief Treasurer Maya. *RdE* 36: 17-20.

Anîbeh inscription = *LD* III, 229c

Anthes, R., 1954. The Original Meaning of *m3ʿ ḫrw*. *JNES* 13: 21-51.

ARE = Breasted (1988)

Armant decree = *KRI* II, 712-713 n.261D

Assmann, J., 1992. When Justice Fails: Jurisdiction and Imprecation in Ancient Egypt and the Near East. *JEA* 78: 149-162.

Assuan decree = *KRI* I, 73-74 n.36-37

Austin, J.L., 1970. *How to Do Things with Words*. New York: Oxford University Press.

3ḫnitn Karnak decree = Saad & Manniche (1971: pl. XXI)

Bacry, P., 1992. *Les figures de style et autres procédés stylistiques*. Collection Sujets. Paris: Belin.

Baer, K., 1965. Temporal *wnn* in Late Egyptian. *JEA* 51: 137-143.

Baines, J., 1999. On Wenamun as a Literary Text. In *Literatur und Politik im pharaonischen und ptolemäischen Ägypten: Vorträge der Tagung zum Gedenken an G. Posener 5.-10. September 1996 in Leipzig*, eds J. Assmann & E. Blumenthal, 209-233. BdE 127. Cairo: IFAO.

Baines, J. & Málek, J., 1981. *Atlas of Ancient Egypt*. Oxford: Phaidon.

Bakhtin, M., 1981. *The Dialogic Imagination: Four Essays* (ed. M. Holquist). Austin: University of Texas Press.

Bakir, A.M., 1970. *Egyptian Epistolography from the Eighteenth to the Twenty-First Dynasty*. BdE 48. Le Caire: IFAO.

Bal, M., 1997. *Narratology: Introduction to the Theory of Narrative*. Toronto: University of Toronto Press.

Barguet, P., 1952. Les stèles du Nil au Gebel Silsileh. *BIFAO* 50: 49-63.

— 1962. Tôd: Rapport de fouilles de la saison février-avril 1950. *BIFAO* 51 : 94-103.

— 1962b. *Le temple d'Amon-Rê à Karnak*. RAPH 21. Le Caire: IFAO.

Barri, N., 1975. Adjectifs antéposés et adjectifs postposés comme signes linguistiques différents. *Folia Linguistica* 7: 209-220.

Barsanti, A., 1907. Rapport sur la découverte à Edfou des ruines d'un temple ramesside. *ASAE* 8 : 233-236.

BD = Naville (1971)

Bedell, E.D., 1973. *Criminal Law in the Egyptian Ramesside Period*. Dissertation Brandeis University.

Beni Hasan I = Newberry (1893)

Bennett, J., 1939. The Restoration Inscription of Tut'nkhamūn. *JEA* 25: 8-15.

Berlev, O., 1975-76. Un don du Roi Rahotep. *OLP* 6/7: 31-41 (= Miscellanea in honorem J. Vergote).

Berlin 1204 = Schäfer (1904: 70-71)

Berlin 1634 = *Urk.* IV, 832

Berlin 13725 = *Urk.* IV, 79-81

Berlin 17500 = Goedicke (1967: Abb. 5)

Berlin 18137 = Dreyer (1998: Abb. 57)

Bhatia, V.K., 1993. *Analysing Genre: Language Use in Professional Settings*. London: Longman.

— 1994. Cognitive structuring in legislative provisions. In *Language and the Law*, ed. J. Gibbons, 136-155. London: Longman.

Biedermann, H., & Cazenave, M. (ed.), 1996. *Encyclopédie des symboles*. La Pochothèque, Encyclopédies d'aujourd'hui. Paris: Librairie Générale Française.

Bierbrier, M.L., 1982. *Hieroglyphic Texts from Egyptian Stelae etc.* X. London: British Museum Publications.

Bilgai stela (*JE* 43341) = *KRI* IV, 341-343 n.2

Blackman, A.M., 1932. *Middle-Egyptian Stories (pBerlin 3022=B, pBerlin 10499=R)*. BAe 2. Bruxelles: Fondation Egyptologique Reine Elisabeth.

Bleiberg, E., 1985-86. Historical Texts as Political Propaganda during the New Kingdom. *BES* 7: 5-13.

Blumenthal, E., 1970. *Untersuchungen zum ägyptischen Königtum des mittleren Reiches. I. Die Phraseologie*. ASAW 61: I. Berlin: Akademie-Verlag.

BM 138 = Robichon & Varille (1936: 2-4)

BM 626 = Goedicke (1967: Abb. 3)

BM EA 1021 = *Urk.* IV, 820-821

BM 1189 = *KRI* I, 37-38 n.18

BM 1665 = *KRI* I, 231 n.99

BM 10052 = *KRI* VI, 767-803 n.25 (= *Great Tomb Robberies*)

BM 10060 = *LES*, 1-9 (= *Doomed Prince*)

BM 10249 = *LEM* 46-47 (= *pAnastasi* IV)

BM 10383 = *KRI* VI, 833-836 n.27 (= *Great Tomb Robberies*)

BM 10403 = *KRI* VI, 828-833 n.26 (= *Great Tomb Robberies*)

Boochs, W., 1991. Religöse Strafen. In *Religion und Philosophie im alten Ägypten: Festgabe für P. Derchain,* eds U. Verhoeven & E. Graefe, 57-64. Leuven: Peeters.

Borchardt, L., 1893. Wie wurden die Böschungen der Pyramiden bestimmt? *ZÄS* 31: 9-17.

— 1910. *Das Grabdenkmal des Königs S'aȝḥu-reᶜ*. I. WVDOG 14. Leipzig: J.C. Hinrichs.

Borghouts, J.F., 1980. Object Pronouns of the *tw*-Type in Late Egyptian. *OLP* 11: 99-109.

— 1980b. Late Egyptian Precursors of Coptic 'Genitival' ⲛⲧⲉ- /ⲛⲧⲁ=. *SAK* 8: 65-78.

Boston 03.1896 = Goedicke (1967: Abb. 2)

Boston 25.632 = *Urk.* IV, 1343

Breasted, J.H., 1988. *Ancient Records of Egypt*. 5 vols. London: Histories & Mysteries of Man.

Brooklyn 69.116.1 = *KRI* I, 231 n.100

Brugsch, H., 1883-91 (new ed. 1968). *Thesaurus inscriptionum Aegyptiacarum*. V/VI. Graz: Akademische Duruck.

Brunner, H., 1939. Das Fragment eines Schutzdekretes aus dem neuen Reich. *MDAIK* 8: 161-164.

— 1980. Immunität. In *LÄ* III: 151-152.

Brunner-Traut, E., 1955. Ägyptische Tiermärchen. *ZÄS* 80: 12-32.

Bubastis Wȝsȝirkn II relief = Van Siclen III (1973)

Budge, E.A.T.W., 1923. *Facsimiles of Egyptian Hieratic Papyri in the British Museum*. II. London: British Museum.

Buhen decrees (*Louvre C* 57, *BM* 1189) = *KRI* I, 2-3 n.3 & 37-38 n.18

Caminos, R.A., 1952. Gebel es-Silsilah no. 100. *JEA* 38: 46-61.

— 1954. *Late-Egyptian Miscellanies*. Brown Egyptological Studies 1. London: Oxford University Press.

— 1958. The Chronicle of Prince Osorkon. *AnOr* 37. Roma: Pontificium Institutum Biblicum.

— 1963. Papyrus Berlin 10463. *JEA* 49: 29-37.

— 1972. Another Hieratic Manuscript from the Library of Pwerem son of *Ḳiḳi* (Pap. B.M. 10288). *JEA* 58: 205-224.

Campbell, L.J. & Holland, V.M., 1982. Understanding the Language of Public Documents Because Readability Formulas Don't. In *Linguistics and the Professions: Proceedings of the Second Annual Delaware Symposium on Language Studies*, ed. J. di Pietro, 157-171. Norwood: Ablex.

Cassonnet, P., 2000. *Etudes de Néo-égyptien: Les Temps Seconds i-sḏm.f et i-iri.f sḏm entre syntaxe et sémantique.* Paris: Cybèle.

CD = Faulkner (1962)

CDL = Martin (1990)

Černý, J. & Gardiner, A.H., 1957. *Hieratic Ostraca*. I. Oxford: Griffith Institute, Oxford University Press.

Černý, J. & Israelit-Groll, S., 1993. *A Late Egyptian Grammar*. StudPohl 4. Roma: Editrice Pontificio Istituto Biblico.

Černý, J. & Peet, T.E., 1927. A Marriage Settlement of the Twentieth Dynasty. *JEA* 13: 30-39.

Černý, J., 1935-51 & 1970. *Catalogue des ostraca hiératiques non littéraires de Deir el-Médineh.* 6 vols. DFIFAO 3-7 & 14. Le Caire: IFAO.

— 1937. Restitution of, and Penalty Attaching to, Stolen Property in Ramesside Times. *JEA* 23: 186-189.

— 1939. *Late Ramesside Letters.* BAe 9. Bruxelles: Fondation Egyptologique Reine Elisabeth.

— 1945. The Will of Naunakhte and the Related Documents. *JEA* 31: 29-53.

CG 34 = Tiradritti (1998: 74)

CG 245 = Tiradritti (1998: 103)

CG 14716 = Tiradritti (1998: 41)

CG 20539 II = Lange & Schäfer (1908: 154-158)

CG 30770 = Petrie (1896: pl. VIII)

CG 34001 = *Urk.* IV, 14-24

CG 34006 = *Urk.* IV, 79-81

CG 34012 = *Urk.* IV, 833-838

CG 34013 = *Urk.* IV, 763-772

CG 34014 = *Urk.* IV, 820-821

CG 34019 = *Urk.* IV, 1287-1299

CG 34025 = Spiegelberg (1896)

CG 35256 = Leahy (1989: 42)

CG 42056 = Legrain (1906)

Champollion, J.-F., 1835-45. *Monuments de l'Egypte et de la Nubie.* 2 vols. Genève: Editions des Belles-Lettres.

Charrow, V.R., 1982. Language in the Bureaucracy. In *Linguistics and the Professions: Proceedings of the Second Annual Delaware Symposium on Language Studies*, ed. J. di Pietro, 173-188. Norwood: Ablex.

Charrow, V.R., Crandall, J.A. & Charrow, R.P., 1982. Characteristics and Functions of Legal Language. In *Sublanguage: Studies of Language in Restricted Semantic Domains*, eds R. Kittredge & J. Lehrberger, 175-190. Berlin: W. de Gruyter.

Chetwynd, T., 1982. *A Dictionary of Symbols.* London: Granada Publishing.

Christophe, L.A., 1958. Le pylône "Ramesside" d'Edfou. *ASAE* 55: 1-23.

Cirlot, J.E., 1962. *A Dictionary of Symbols.* New York: Philosophical Library.

CLEM = Caminos (1954)

Couyat, J. & Montet, P., 1912-13. *Les inscriptions hiéroglyphiques et hiératiques du Ouâdi Hammâmât.* MIFAO 34. 2 vols. Le Caire: IFAO.

Crystal, D. & Davy, D., 1969. *Investigating English Style.* London: Longman.

CT = de Buck (1935-61)

Cumming, B., 1982. *Egyptian Historical Records of the Later Eighteenth Dynasty.* I. Warminster: Aris & Phillips.

Curzon, L.B., 1988. *Dictionary of Law.* London: Pitman.

Danet, B., 1980. Language in the Legal Process. *Law & Society Review* 14 (3): 445-564.

— 1984. (Ed.) Studies of legal discourse. *Text* (special issue) 4-1/3.

— 1985. Legal Discourse. In *Handbook of Discourse Analysis: Disciplines of Discourse*, ed. T.A. Van Dijk, I, 273-291. London: Academic Press.

— 1990. Language and Law: An Overview of 15 Years of Research. In *Handbook of Language and Social Psychology*, eds H. Giles & P. Robinson, 537-559. Chichester: John Wiley & Sons.

David, A., 2000. *De l'infériorité à la perturbation: L'oiseau du "mal" et la catégorisation en Egypte ancienne.* GOF IV. Reihe Ägypten 38. Classification and Categorization in Ancient Egypt 1. Wiesbaden: Harrassowitz.

— 2000b. *m.k* + forme nominale au coeur de la controverse. *LingAeg* 7: 113-123.

— 2003. Review of Borchers, D., Kammerzell, F. & Weninger, S., Hieroglyphen Alphabete Schriftreformen. *BiOr* 60: 569-579.

— 2004. Analyse du discours juridique dans les décrets royaux ramessides. *GM* 199, in press.

— 2004b. Composés attributifs exocentriques, hypallage et métaphore. *LingAeg* 12: 1-7.

Davies, B.G., 1997. *Egyptian Historical Inscriptions of the Ninetheenth Dynasty.* Documenta Mundi Aegyptiaca 2. Jonsered : P. Åströms.

Davis, V.L., 1973. *Syntax of the Negative Particles bw and bn in Late Egyptian.* MÄS 29. München : Deutscher Kunstverlag.

Davison, A., 1980. Linguistic Analysis and the Law. In *Language Use and the Uses of Language*, eds. R.W. Shuy & A. Shnukal, 235-244. Washington: Georgetown University Press.

de Buck, A., 1935-61. (Ed.) *The Egyptian Coffin Texts,* 7 vols. Chicago: Oriental Institute Publications.

— 1937. The Judicial Papyrus of Turin. *JEA* 23: 152-164.

— 1942. De liquidatie van Echnaton's hervormingswerk. *JEOL* II, 8: 569-580.

Deebank, S. *et alii*, 1989. *Harrap's Dictionary of Law & Society.* Bromley: Harrap's Reference.

Deir el-Medineh decree (*JE* 72000) = *KRI* II, 362-363 n.128

Depuydt, L., 1993. *Conjunction, Contiguity, Contingency: On Relationships Between Events in the Egyptian and Coptic Verbal Systems.* Oxford: University Press.

Dmḏibtȝwy Coptos R decree (*JE* 41894) = Goedicke (1967: Abb. 28)

Donadoni, S., 1993. *L'art égyptien.* La Pochothèque, Encyclopédies d'aujourd'hui. Paris: Librairie Générale Française.

Doomed Prince (*BM* 10060 *pHarris* 500 v°) = *LES*, 1-9

Doret, E., 1980. A Note on the Egyptian Construction Noun + *sḏm.f*. *JNES* 39: 37-45.

— 1986. *The Narrative Verbal System of Old and Middle Egyptian.* Genève: Cramer.

Dreyer, G., 1987. Drei archaisch-hieratische Gefässaufschriften mit Jahresnamen aus Elephantine. In *Form und Mass: Beiträge zur Literatur, Sprache und Kunst des alten Ägypten, Festschrift für G. Fecht*, eds J. Osing & G. Dreyer. ÄUAT 12, 98-109. Wiesbaden: Harrassowitz.

— 1998. *Umm el-Qaab I: Das prädynastische Königsgrab U-j und seine frühen Schriftzeugnisse.* AV 86. Mainz: Philipp von Zabern.

Drioton, E. & Lauer, J.-P., 1937. Une inscription de Khamouas sur la face sud de la pyramide d'Ounas à Saqqarah. *ASAE* 37: 201-211.

Ḏḥwtyms I *Wadi Halfa & Kuban decrees to Twri* (*CG* 34006, *Berlin* 13725) = *Urk.* IV, 79-81

Ḏḥwtyms I *Sehel decree* = *Urk.* IV, 89-90

Ḏḥwtyms III *North Karnak decree* to *Snmwt* = Helck (1975: 122-126)

Ḏḥwtyms III *Buto decree* = Klug (2002: 96-105)

Ḏḥwtyms III *Heliopolis decree* (*Berlin* 1634) = *Urk.* IV, 832

Ḏḥwtyms III *Sehel decree* = *Urk.* IV, 814-815

Ḏḥwtyms III *Buhen decree* (*BM EA* 1021, *CG* 34014) = *Urk.* IV, 820-821

Ḏḥwtyms III *Sai decree* = Klug (2002: 191-192)

Ḏḥwtyms III *Karnak Ptḥ temple decree* (*CG* 34013) = *Urk.* IV, 763-772

Ḏḥwtyms III *Annals* = *Urk.* IV, 645-756

Ḏḥwtyms IV *to Nbimn decree* = *Urk.* IV, 1618

East Silsileh decree = *KRI* I, 59-61 n.26

Edel, E., 1955-64. *Altägyptische Grammatik.* 2 vols. AnOr 34/39. Roma: Pontificium Institutum Biblicum.

— 1967. Zur Etymologie und hieroglyphischen Schreibung der Präpositionen ⲙⲛ- und ⲛⲧⲉ-. *Or* 36: 67-75.

Edgerton, W.F., 1947. The Nauri Decree of Seti I: A Translation and Analysis of the Legal Portion. *JNES* 6: 219-230.

EG = Gardiner (1957)

Elephantine decree = *KRI* V, 343-345 n.138B

El-Kab decree = Gardiner (1910: 48)

Epstein, R., 1993. The definite article: early stages of development. In *Historical Linguistics 1991: Papers from the 10th International Conference on Historical Linguistics (Amsterdam, 12-16 August 1991)*, ed. J. Van Marle. Amsterdam Studies in the Theory and History of Linguistic Science, Series IV – Current Issues in Linguistic Theory 107, 111-134. Amsterdam: John Benjamins.

Erichsen, W., 1933. *Papyrus Harris I: Hieroglyphische Transkription.* BAe 5. Bruxelles: Fondation Egyptologique Reine Elisabeth.

Erman, A. & Grapow, H., 1955. (Eds) *Wörterbuch der ägyptischen Sprache,* 6 vols. Berlin: Akademie Verlag.

— 1971 (reprint). *Wörterbuch der ägyptischen Sprache: Die Belegstellen,* 5 vols. Berlin: Akademie Verlag.

Erman, A., 1890. *Die Märchen des Papyrus Westcar.* Berlin: Spemann.

— 1900. Gebete eines ungerecht Verfolgten und andere Ostraka aus den Königsgräbern. *ZÄS* 38: 19-41.

— 1927. *The Literature of the Ancient Egyptians.* London: Methuen & Co.

— 1933. *Neuägyptische Grammatik.* Leipzig: J.C. Hinrichs.

Even-Zohar, I., 1990. Polysystem Studies. *Poetics Today* 11: 1-268.

Fauconnier, G. & Turner, M., 2002. *The Way We Think: Conceptual Blending and the Mind's Hidden Complexities.* New York: Basic Books.

Faulkner, R.O., 1955. The Installation of the Vizier. *JEA* 41: 18-29.

— 1962. *A Concise Dictionary of Middle Egyptian.* Oxford: Griffith Institute.

Fayum decree (*CG* 34502) = *KRI* I, 45 n.23

Fayum/Herakleopolis decree = *KRI* V, 270 n.89A

Ferguson, C.A., 1964. Diglossia. In *Language in culture and society: A Reader in Linguistics and Anthropology*, ed. D. Hymes, 429-439. New York: Harper & Row.

Finegan, E., 1982. Form and Function in Testament Language. In *Linguistics and the Professions: Proceedings of the Second Annual Delaware Symposium on Language Studies*, ed. J. di Pietro, 113-120. Norwood: Ablex.

Finnestad, R.B., 1985. *Image of the World and Symbol of the Creator: On the Cosmological and Iconological Values of the Temple of Edfu*. Studies in Oriental Religions 10. Wiesbaden: Harrassowitz.

Fischer, H.G., 1973. Further Evidence for the Logic of Ancient Egyptian: Diminishing Progression. *JARCE* 10: 5-9.

— 1977. *Egyptian Studies II: The Orientation of Hieroglyphs*. New York: The Metropolitan Museum.

Ford, J.N., 1995. ההקדמה השירית לכתובת של סתי א' מנאורי. MA thesis. Jerusalem.

Frandsen, P.J., 1974. *An Outline of the Late Egyptian Verbal System*. Copenhagen: Akademisk Forlag.

— 1997. On Categorization and Metaphorical Structuring: Some Remarks on Egyptian Art and Language. *CAJ* 7[1]: 71-104.

Gaballa, G.A., 1973. Three Documents from the Reign of Ramesses II. *JEA* 59: 109-113.

Gaballa, G.A. & Kitchen, K.A., 1968. Ramesside Varia I. *CdE* 43: 259-270.

Gardiner, A.H., 1904. An use of the later absolute pronoun. *ZÄS* 41: 135-136.

— 1910. The Goddess Nekhbet at the Jubilee Festival of Rameses III. *ZÄS* 48: 47-51.

— 1911. *Egyptian Hieratic Texts: The Papyrus Anastasi I and the Papyrus Koller, together with the Parallel Texts*. I. Leipzig: J.C. Hinrichs.

— 1912. Review of "Les décrets royaux de l'ancien empire égyptien" by Raymond Weill. *PSBA* 34/4: 257-265.

— 1912b. Notes on the Story of Sinuhe. *RecTrav* 34: 193-206.

— 1912c. The Stele of Bilgai. *ZÄS* 50: 49-57.

— 1923. The Eloquent Peasant. *JEA* 9: 5-25.

— 1928. An Egyptian Split Infinitive and the Origin of the Coptic Conjunctive Tense. *JEA* 14: 86-96.

— 1930. The Origin of Certain Coptic Grammatical Elements. *JEA* 16: 220-234.

— 1932. *Late Egyptian Stories*. BAe 1. Bruxelles: Fondation Egyptologique Reine Elisabeth.

— 1937. *Late-Egyptian Miscellanies*. BAe 7. Bruxelles: Fondation Egyptologique Reine Elisabeth.

— 1941. Ramesside Texts Relating to the Taxation and Transport of Corn. *JEA* 27: 19-73.

— 1946. Second Thoughts on the Origin of Coptic ⲉⲣⲉ-. *JEA* 32: 101.

— 1947. *Ancient Egyptian Onomastica*. I. London: Oxford University Press.

— 1948. *Ramesside Administrative Documents*. Oxford: Oxford University Press.

— 1948b. *The Wilbour Papyrus*. II. Oxford: Oxford University Press.

— 1952. Some Reflections on the Nauri Decree. *JEA* 38: 24-33.

— 1955. A Pharaonic Encomium. *JEA* 41: 30 and 42.

— 1957. *Egyptian Grammar: Being an Introduction to the Study of Hieroglyphs*. Oxford: Griffith Institute.

— 1960. *The Ḳadesh Inscriptions of Ramesses II*. Oxford: University Press.

— 1964. *The Inscription of Mes: A Contribution to the Study of Egyptian Judicial Procedure*. UGAÄ 4. Hildesheim: Georg Olms.

— 1969. *The Admonitions of an Egyptian Sage from a Hieratic Papyrus in Leiden (Pap. Leiden 344 recto)*. Hildesheim: Georg Olms.

Gauthier, H., 1936. Une fondation pieuse en Nubie. *ASAE* 36: 49-71.

Gifis, S.H., 1984. *Law Dictionary*. Barron's Educational Series. New York: Woodbury.

Gilula, M., 1970. Review of Die negativen Konstruktionen im Alt- und Mittelägyptischen by H. Satzinger. *JEA* 56: 205-214.

— 1976. An Unusual Nominal Pattern in Middle Egyptian. *JEA* 62: 160-175.

Goedicke, H., 1960. *Die Stellung des Königs im alten Reich.* ÄA 2. Wiesbaden : Harrassowitz.

— 1964. Diplomatical Studies in the Old Kingdom. *JARCE* 3: 31-41.

— 1967. *Königliche Dokumente aus dem alten Reich.* ÄA 14. Wiesbaden : Harrassowitz.

— 1975. Befehl, Theorie des. In *LÄ* I: 678-679.

— 1981. The "400-Year Stela" Reconsidered. *BES* 3: 25-42.

— 1984. *Studies in the Hekanakhte Papers.* Baltimore: Halgo.

Goldwasser, O., 1980. Hekanakhte and the "Boat Metaphor" (Hekanakhte Papers, I, vs. 2-3). *GM* 40: 21-22.

— 1985. A Late Egyptian Epistolary Formula as an Aid to Dating Ramesside Texts. In *Pharaonic Egypt*, ed. S.I. Groll, 50-56. Jerusalem: The Magnes Press, The Hebrew University.

— 1987. *The Verbal System in Literary Letters of the 19th Dynasty* (Dissertation in Hebrew). Jerusalem.

— 1990. On the Choice of Registers – Studies on the Grammar of Papyrus Anastasi I. In *Studies in Egyptology Presented to Miriam Lichtheim*, ed. S. Israelit-Groll, I, 200-240. Jerusalem: The Magnes Press, The Hebrew University.

— 1991. On Dynamic Canonicity in Late-Egyptian: The Literary Letter and the Personal Prayer. *LingAeg* 1: 129-141.

— 1995. *From Icon to Metaphor.* OBO 142. Fribourg & Göttingen: University Press Fribourg, Vandenhoeck & Ruprecht.

— 1999. "Low" and "High" Dialects in Ramesside Egyptian. In *Textcorpus und Wörterbuch: Aspekte zur ägyptischen Lexikographie*, eds S. Grunert & I. Hafemann. PÄ 14, 311-328. Leiden: E.J. Brill.

— 1999b. The Determinative System as a Mirror of World Organization. *GM* 170: 49-68.

— 2001. Poetic License in Nineteenth Dynasty Non-Literary Late-Egyptian? *LingAeg* 9: 123-138.

— 2002. *Lovers, Prophets and Giraffes: Wor(L)d Categorization in Ancient Egypt.* GOF IV. Reihe Ägypten 38. Classification and Categorization in Ancient Egypt 3. Wiesbaden: Harrassowitz.

Gomaà, F., 1973. *Chaemwese Sohn Ramses' II. und Hoherpriester von Memphis.* ÄÄ 27. Wiesbaden: Harrassowitz.

Gombrich, E.H., 1986 (5th ed., 4th impression). *Art and Illusion: A Study in the Psychology of Pictorial Representation.* Oxford: Phaidon.

Goodrich, P., 1987. *Legal Discourse: Studies in Linguistics, Rhetoric and Legal Analysis.* Houndmills: Macmillan.

Görg, M., 1977. Etymologisch-semantische Perspektiven zu ברית. In *Bausteine biblischer Theologie: Festgabe für G. Johannes Botterweck*, ed. H.-J. Fabry. Bonner biblische Beiträge 50, 25-36. Köln: Peter Hanstein.

Grandet, P., 1990. Un texte historique de Ramsès III à El-Kâb (et autres textes ramessides). *RdE* 41: 95-99.

— 1994. *Le Papyrus Harris I (BM 9999).* 2 vols. BdE 109/I & II. Cairo: IFAO.

Grapow, H., 1911. Zur Bedeutung und Geschichte einer Hieroglyphe. *ZÄS* 49: 116-119.

— 1943. *Wie die Alten Ägypter sich anredeten, wie sie sich grüßten und wie sie miteinander sprachen.* Abhandlungen der Preußischen Akadamie der Wissenschaften 7. Berlin: Verlag der Akademie der Wissenschaften.

Green, M., 1980. Some notes on the words *wšbt* and *šbt*. *GM* 41: 43-50.

Gregory, M., 1967. Aspects of varieties differentiation. *Journal of Linguistics* 3: 177-198.

Griffith, F.Ll., 1889. *The Inscriptions of Siût and Dêr Rîfeh*. London: Trübner.

— 1927. The Abydos Decree of Seti I at Nauri. *JEA* 13: 193-208.

Grimal, N.-C., 1986. *Les termes de la propagande royale égyptienne de la XIXe dynastie à la conquête d'Alexandre*. Institut de France, Mémoires de l'Académie des Inscriptions et Belles-Lettres 6. Paris: Imprimerie Nationale & de Boccard.

Groll, S., 1969. *Iw sḏm.f* in Late Egyptian. *JNES* 28: 184-191.

— 1970. *The Negative Verbal System of Late Egyptian*. London: Oxford University Press.

— 1975. The Literary and the Non-literary Verbal Systems in Late Egyptian. *OLP* 6-7: 237-246.

— 1983. The Egyptian Administrative System in Syria and Palestine in the 18th Dynasty: A model of high integrative level. In *Fontes atque Pontes: Festage für H. Brunner*, ed. M. Görg, ÄUAT 5, 234-242. Wiesbaden: Harrassowitz.

— 1987. The Negative *sḏm.n.f* System in the Kūbban Dialect. In *Form und Mass: Festschrift für G. Fecht*, eds J. Osing & G. Dreyer. ÄUAT 12, 154-166. Wiesbaden: Harrassowitz.

— 1991. Semiotics, Pragmatics and Structuralism as a means to determine the degree of connectedness between utterances. I: *pꜣ*-A versus Ø-A. *LingAeg* 1: 143-153.

— 1992. On the Subject of the Second Tenses in Egyptian and Coptic. *LingAeg* 2: 87-97.

Guastini, R., 1994. Legal Language and Facts. In *The Encyclopedia of Language and Linguistics*, eds R.E. Asher & J.M.Y. Simpson, IV, 2075-2080. Oxford: Pergamon Press.

Guieysse, P., 1886. Réprimande à un fonctionnaire égyptien. In *Mélanges Renier : recueil de travaux publiés par l'Ecole Pratique des Hautes Etudes*, 421-428. Paris: F. Vieweg.

Gunn, B. & Gardiner, A.H., 1917. New Renderings of Egyptian Texts. *JEA* 4: 241-251.

Gunn, B., 1924. *Studies in Egyptian Syntax*. Paris: Librairie Orientaliste Paul Geuthner.

— 1927. The Stela of Apries at Mîtrahîna. *ASAE* 27: 211-237.

— 1955. The Decree of Amonrasonthēr for Neskhons. *JEA* 41: 83-100.

Gunnarsson, B.L., 1984. Functional comprehensibility of legislative texts: Experiment with a Swedish act of parliament. In *Studies of legal discourse*, ed. B. Danet, 71-105. *Text* (special issue) 4-1/3.

Gustafsson, M., 1984. The syntactic features of binomial expressions in legal English. In *Studies of legal discourse*, ed. B. Danet, 123-141. *Text* (special issue) 4-1/3.

Habachi, L., 1973. The Two Rock-Stelae of Sethos I in the Cataract Area Speaking of Huge Statues and Obelisks. *BIFAO* 73: 113-125.

Hafemann, I., 1985. Zum Problem der staatlichen Arbeitspflicht im alten Ägypten: Die königlichen Dekrete des Alten Reiches. *AoF* 12: 3-21.

Haiman, J., 1978. Conditionals Are Topics. *Language* 54: 564-589

Halliday, M.A.K., McIntosh, A. & Strevens, P., 1964. *The Linguistic Sciences and Language Teaching*. London: Longmans.

Hammamat = Couyat & Montet (1912-13)

Hancher, M., 1980. Speech Acts and the Law. In *Language Use and the Uses of Language*, eds. R.W. Shuy & A. Shnukal, 245-256. Washington: Georgetown University Press.

Harari, I.E., 1950. *Contribution à l'étude de la procédure judiciaire dans l'Ancien Empire égyptien*. Cairo: Imprimerie du Scribe Egyptien.

— 1957. La fondation cultuelle de *n.k.wi.ankh* à Tehneh. *ASAE* 54 : 317- 344.

— 1974. Le principe juridique de l'organisation sociale dans le décret de Séti Ier à Nauri. In *Le droit égyptien ancien : Colloque organisé par l'Institut des Hautes Etudes de Belgique, 18-19.3.1974*. Bruxelles: Institut des Hautes Etudes de Belgique.

— 1981-82. Le recrutement de main d'oeuvre dans le décret de Séti Ier à Nauri. *Serapis* 7: 23-32.

— 1987. Les décrets royaux : Source de droit. *Discussions in Egyptology* 8 : 93-101.

— 1987b. Les dispositions juridiques prises par Séti Ier à Kanais. *Discussions in Egyptology* 7 : 88-105.

— 1990. Propriété du roi, dans le décret du roi Seti Ier à Nauri. *BSAK* 4: 226-232 (= *Akten des vierten internationalen Ägyptologen Kongresses München 1985*, ed. S. Schoske, IV. Hamburg: Helmut Buske).

Haring, B., 1997. *Divine Households: Administrative and Economic Aspects of the New Kingdom Royal Memorial Temples in Western Thebes*. Egyptologische Uitgaven 12. Leiden: Nederlands Instituut voor het Nabije Oosten.

Hasan, R., 1973. Code, register and social dialect. In *Class, Codes and Control: Applied Studies towards a Sociology of Language*, ed. B. Bernstein, II, 253-292. London: Routledge & Kegan Paul.

Hayes, W.C., 1946. Royal decrees from the Temple of Min at Coptus. *JEA* 32: 3-23.

— 1955. *A Papyrus of the Late Middle Kingdom in the Brooklyn Museum*. WM 5. Brooklyn: The Brooklyn Museum.

Helck, W. & Otto, E., 1970. *Kleines Wörterbuch der Aegyptologie*. Wiesbaden: Harrassowitz.

Helck, W. & Westendorf, W., 1975-89. (Eds) *Lexicon der Ägyptologie*. Wiesbaden: Harrassowitz.

Helck, W., 1955. Eine Stele des Vizekönigs *Wsr-St.t*. *JNES* 14: 22-31.

— 1955-61. *Urkunden der 18. Dynastie*. Berlin: Akademie Verlag.

— 1956. Zwei thebanische Urkunden aus der Zeit Sethos'II. *ZÄS* 81: 82-87.

— 1958. *Zur Verwaltung des mittleren und neuen Reiches*. PÄ 3. Leiden: E.J. Brill.

— 1958b. Nachlese zu ramessidischen Inschriften. *ZÄS* 83: 145-146.

— 1960. Die Opferstiftung des *Sn-mwt*. *ZÄS* 85 : 23-34.

— 1960b. *Materialen zur Wirtschaftsgeschichte des neuen Reiches*. I. Wiesbaden: Akademie der Wissenschaften und der Literatur in Mainz.

— 1961. *Urkunden der 18. Dynastie*: *Übersetzung zu den Heften 17-22*. Berlin: Akademie Verlag.

— 1963. Der Papyrus Berlin P 3047. *JARCE* 2: 65-71.

— 1963b. Ramessidische Inschriften aus Karnak. *CdE* 38: 37-48.

— 1966. Zum Kult an Königsstatuen. *JNES* 25: 32-41.

— 1967. Eine Briefsammlung aus der Verwaltung des Amuntempels. *JARCE* 6: 135-151.

— 1969. Eine Stele Sebekhoteps IV. aus Karnak. *MDAIK* 24: 194-200.

— 1973. K.A. Kitchen, Ramesside Inscriptions, Historical and Biographical. Vol. I, Fasc. 2; II 6. Oxford, B.H. Blackwell, 1971 (4to). *BiOr* 30: 212-214.

— 1974. *Altägyptische Aktenkunde des 3. und 2. Jahrtausends v. Chr*. MÄS 31. München: Deutscher Kunstverlag.

— 1975. K.A. Kitchen, Ramesside Inscriptions I 4. Oxford, B.H. Blackwell, 1973 (8vo, 32 p.). *BiOr* 32: 18.

— 1976. Einige Bemerkungen zu Artikeln in SAK 2. *SAK* 4: 115-124.

Heliopolis decree (*Turin* 2682) = Ricke (1935)

Hermopolis code (*pCairo JE* 89127-30, 89137-43) = Mattha (1975)

Hermopolis decree = *KRI* I, 125-126 n.67 & VII, 428 n.3-7

Hintze, F., 1950-52. *Untersuchungen zu Stil und Sprache neuägyptischer Erzählungen.* VIO 2 & 6. Berlin: Akademie Verlag.

Hittite Treaty = *KRI* II, 225-232 n.64

Ḥḳ3nḫt = Goedicke (1984)

Hoch, J.E., 1994. *Semitic Words in Egyptian Texts of the New Kingdom and the Third Intermediate Period.* Princeton: Princeton University Press.

Hodge, R.I.V. & Kress, G.R., 1988. *Social Semiotics*. Ithaca: Cornell University Press.

Horus & Seth (*pKahun* VI, 12 r°, *pBeatty* I r°) = *LES,* 37-60

Ḥrmḥb Karnak decree = Kruchten (1981)

Ḫwt3wyrᶜ Wgf Abydos decree (*CG* 35256) = Leahy (1989)

IFAO 3153 = Pantalacci (1985: 247)

IFAO 5413 = *KRI* V, 227 n.57

Iᶜḥms Karnak decree (*CG* 34001) = *Urk.* IV, 14-24

Iᶜḥḥtp Dra Abu el-Naga decree (Cairo) = *Urk.* IV, 45-46

Imnḥtp II *Semneh decree to Wsrstt* (*Boston* 25.632) = *Urk.* IV, 1343

Imnḥtp II *Turah decree* = *Urk.* IV, 1448

Imnḥtp II *Elephantine decree* (*Wien ÄS* 5909, *CG* 34019) = *Urk.* IV, 1287-1299

Imnḥtp II *West Karnak decree* = *Urk.* IV, 1319-21

Imnḥtp III *Medinet Habu 21st dynasty copy of his decree* (*BM* 138) = Robichon & Varille (1936: 2-4)

Imnḥtp III *Turah decrees* = *Urk.* IV, 1680-1

Issi Abusir decree = Posener-Kriéger & de Cenival (1968: pl. LVIII A & LXXII A)

Issi Abusir decrees (*JE* 97348) = Posener-Kriéger (1985)

Issi Giza decrees to Snḏmib = *Urk.* I, 60 & 62

Issi Saqqara decree to Rᶜšpss = *Urk.* I, 179

Jackson, B.S., 1995. *Making Sense in Law: Linguistic, Psychological and Semiotic Perspectives.* Liverpool: Deborah Charles Publications.

Jansen-Winkeln, K., 1993. Das ägyptische Pseudopartizip. *OLP* 24: 5-28.

— 1994. Exozentrische Komposita als Relativphrasen im älteren Ägyptisch: Zum Verständnis der Konstruktion *nfr ḥr* "mit schönem Gesicht". *ZÄS* 121: 51-75.

— 1995. Diglossie und Zweisprachigkeit im alten Ägypten. *WZKM* 85: 85-115.

Janssen, J.J., 1961. *Two Ancient Egyptian Ship's Logs*. Leiden : E.J. Brill.

— 1981. Die Struktur der pharaonischen Wirtschaft. *GM* 48 : 59-77.

JE 41491 = Goedicke (1967: Abb. 9)

JE 41890 = Goedicke (1967: Abb. 4)

JE 41492 = Goedicke (1967: Abb. 10)

JE 41893 = Goedicke (1967: Abb. 8)

JE 41894 = Goedicke (1967: Abb. 28)

JE 41895 = Goedicke (1967: Abb. 17)

JE 43052 = Goedicke (1967: Abb. 11)

JE 43053 = Goedicke (1967: Abb. 18)

JE 43341 = *KRI* IV, 341-343 n.2

JE 48831 = Korostovtsev (1947: 155-173)

JE 51911 = Helck (1969: 199-200)

JE 52453 = Lacau (1949)

JE 60539 = *KRI* II, 287-288 n.71

JE 72000 = *KRI* II, 362-363 n.128

JE 88879 = *KRI* V, 395 n.174

JE 97348 = Posener-Kriéger (1985: fig. A-F)

Jelínková-Reymond, E., 1953. Recherches sur le rôle des "gardiens des portes" (*iry-ʿ3*) dans l'administration générale des temples égyptiens. *CdE* 28: 39-59.

Jéquier, G., 1928. *Le Mastaba Faraoun.* Fouilles à Saqqarah, SAE. Le Caire: IFAO.

Jori, M., 1994. Legal Performatives. In *The Encyclopedia of Language and Linguistics*, eds R.E. Asher & J.M.Y. Simpson, IV, 2092-2097. Oxford: Pergamon Press.

Junge, F., 1986. Das sogenannte narrativ/kontinuative *jw=f ḥr (tm) sḏm*. *JEA* 72: 113-132.

— 1989. *"Emphasis" and Sentential Meaning in Middle Egyptian.* GOF IV. Reihe Ägypten 20. Wiesbaden: Harrassowitz.

— 1996. *Neuägyptisch: Einführung in die Grammatik.* Wiesbaden: Harrassowitz.

Kammerzell, F., 1993. Die altägyptische Negation *w* - Versuch einer Annäherung. *LingAeg* 3: 17-32.

Kanais/Wadi Abbad or Mia/Redesieh decree = *KRI* I, 67-70 n.32C

Kaplony, P., 1963. *Die Inschriften der ägyptischen Frühzeit.* III. ÄA 8. Wiesbaden: Harrassowitz.

Kaplony-Heckel, U., 1971. *Ägyptische Handschriften.* I. Verzeichnis der orientalischen Handschriften in Deutschland 19. Wiesbaden : Franz Steiner.

Karnak (Temple of Amun) decrees = *KRI* V, 234-237 n.70

Karnak decree = *KRI* IV, 263-266 n.18

Karnak Year 20 stela = *KRI* V, 243-247

Kemp, B.J., 1972. Temple and town in ancient Egypt. In *Man, Settlement and Urbanism*, eds P.J. Ucko, R. Tringham & G.W. Dimbleby, 657-680. London: Duckworth.

— 1989. *Ancient Egypt: Anatomy of a Civilization.* London: Routledge.

Kessler, D., 1975. Eine Landschenkung Ramses' III. zugunsten eines "Grossen der *thrw*" aus *mr-mšʿ.f*. *SAK* 2: 103-134.

— 1983. Eine Stele Sethos I. aus Kom el-Lufi (Minia). *SAK* 10: 215-220.

Kevelson, R., 1982. Language and Legal Speech Acts: Decisions. In *Linguistics and the Professions: Proceedings of the Second Annual Delaware Symposium on Language Studies*, ed. J. di Pietro, 121-131. Norwood: Ablex.

Kitchen, K.A., 1968-90. *Ramesside Inscriptions, Historical and Biographical*, 8 vols. Oxford: B.H. Blackwell

— 1979. Egypt, Ugarit, Qatna and Covenant. *UF* 11: 453-464. (= Festschrift für Claude F.A. Schaeffer).

— 1984. A Note on Bandeau Texts in New Kingdom Temples. In *Studien zu Sprache und Religion Ägyptens I: Sprache, Festschrift W. Westendorf*, ed. F. Junge, 547-553. Göttingen: Hubert & Co.

— 1993-2001. *Ramesside Inscriptions Translated and Annoted.* 3 vols. Oxford: B.H. Blackwell.

— 1993-99. *Ramesside Inscriptions Translated and Annoted: Notes and Comments.* 2 vols. Oxford: B.H. Blackwell.

Klug, A., 2002. *Königliche Stelen in der Zeit von Ahmose bis Amenophis III.* MonAeg 8. Turnhout: Brepols.

Korostovtsev, M., 1947. Stèle de Ramsès IV. *BIFAO* 45: 155-173.

KRI = Kitchen (1968-90)

Kroeber, B., 1970. *Die Neuägyptizismen vor der Amarnazeit: Studien zur Entwicklung der ägyptischen Sprache vom Mittleren zum Neuen Reich* (Dissertation). Potsdam: Burkhart Kroeber.

Kruchten, J.-M., 1979. L'évolution de la gestion domaniale sous le Nouvel Empire égyptien. In *State and Temple Economy in the Ancient Near East: Proceedings of the International Conference organized by the Katholieke Universiteit Leuven 10-14.4.78*, ed. E. Lipinski, II, OLA 6, 517-525. Leuven: Departement Oriëntalistiek.

— 1979b. Une révolte du vizir sous Ramsès III à Athribis? *AIP* 23: 39-51.

— 1981. *Le Décret d'Horemheb. Traduction, commentaire épigraphique, philologique et institutionnel.* Bruxelles: Editions de l'Université de Bruxelles.

Kuban stela (Grenoble) = *KRI* II, 353-360 n.126

Kuentz, C., 1929. Sur un passage de la stèle de Naucratis : la lecture du signe . *BIFAO* 28 : 103-106.

Kurzon, D., 1984. Themes, hyperthemes and the discourse structure of British legal texts. In *Studies of legal discourse*, ed. B. Danet, 31-55. *Text* (special issue) 4-1/3.

— 1986. *It is hereby performed...: Explorations in Legal Speech Acts*. Pragmatics & Beyond VII: 6. Amsterdam: John Benjamins.

LÄ = Helck & Westendorf (1975-1989)

Labib, P., 1948. Feudalismus in der Ramessidenzeit. *ASAE* 48: 467-484.

Lacau, P., 1949. *Une stèle juridique de Karnak*. CASAE 13. Le Caire: IFAO.

— 1954. *Sur le système hiéroglyphique*. BdE 25. Le Caire : IFAO.

Lakoff, G., 1986. Classifiers as a Reflection of Mind. In *Noun Classes and Categorization: Proceedings of a Symposium on Categorization and Noun Classification, Eugene, Oregon, October 1983*, ed. C. Craig, 13-51. Amsterdam: J. Benjamins.

Lange, H.O., 1925. *Das Weisheitsbuch des Amenemope aus dem Papyrus 10.747 des British Museum.* Kopenhagen: A.F. Host.

Lange, H.O. & Schäfer, H., 1908. *Catalogue général des antiquités égyptiennes du Musée du Caire: Grab- und Denksteine des mittleren Reichs*. II. Berlin: Reichsdruckerei.

Lauer, J.-P., 1939. Fouilles du Service des antiquités à Saqqarah: Secteur de la pyramide à degrés (11/38-5/39). *ASAE* 39: 447-456.

— 1955. Le temple haut de la pyramide du roi Ouserkaf à Saqqarah. *ASAE* 53: 119-133.

— 1957. Recherches et travaux effectués à Saqqarah (12/54-6/55). *ASAE* 54: 114-116.

LD = Lepsius (1913)

Leahy, A., 1984. Death by Fire in Ancient Egypt. *JESHO* 27: 199-206.

— 1989. A Protective Measure at Abydos in the Thirteenth Dynasty. *JEA* 75: 41-75.

Lefebvre, G., 1955. *Grammaire de l'égyptien classique*. BdE 12. Cairo: IFAO.

LEG = Černý & Groll (1993)

Legrain, G., 1906. *Catalogue général des antiquités égyptiennes du Musée du Caire : Statues et statuettes de rois et de particuliers*. Cairo: IFAO.

LEM = Gardiner (1937)

Leprohon, R.J., 1985. The Reign of Akhenaten Seen Through the Later Royal Decrees. In *Mélanges Gamal Eddin Mokhtar*, ed. P. Posener-Kriéger. BdE 97, II, 93-103. Cairo: IFAO.

Lepsius, C.R., 1913. *Denkmäler aus Ägypten und Äthiopien.* 12 vols. Leipzig: J.C. Hinrichs.

LES = Gardiner (1932)

Lichtheim, M., 1973, 1976 &1980. *Ancient Egyptian Literature: A Book of Readings*. 3 vols. Berkeley: University of California Press.

Liungman, C.G., 1991. *Dictionary of Symbols*. Santa Barbara: ABC-Clio.

Liverpool E 583 = Amer (1985: 18)

Löfstedt, L., 1981. A propos des articles et des articloïdes. In *Logos Semantikos: Studia linguistica in honorem Eugenio Coseriu IV*, eds H. Geckeler, B. Schlieben-Lange, J. Trabant & H. Weydt, 269-279. Berlin: De Gruyter.

Loprieno, A., 1995. *Ancient Egyptian: A linguistic introduction.* Cambridge: Cambridge University Press.

— 1996. Linguistic Variety and Egyptian Literature. In *Ancient Egyptian Literature: History and Forms,* ed. A. Loprieno. PÄ 10, 515-529. Leiden: E.J. Brill.

Lorton, D., 1974. *The Juridical Terminology of International Relations in Egyptian Texts Through Dyn. XVIII.* Baltimore: John Hopkins University Press.

— 1977. The Treatment of Criminals in Ancient Egypt Through the New Kingdom. *JESHO* 20: 2-64.

— 1995. Legal and Social Institutions of Pharaonic Egypt. In *Civilizations of the Ancient Near East*, ed. J.M. Sasson, I, 345-362. New York: Simon & Schuster Macmillan.

Louvre C 57 = *KRI* I, 2-3 n.3

Louvre E 25309 = Peck & Ross (1978: n. 87)

Louvre E 25416a v° = Posener-Kriéger & de Cenival (1968: pl. LVIII G & p. 23)

LRL = Černý (1939)

Lurje, I.M., 1971. *Studien zum Altägyptischen Recht des 16. bis 10. Jahrhunderts v.u.Z.* Weimar: Hermann Böhlaus Nachfolger.

Malaise, M., 1985. La conjugaison suffixale dans les propositions conditionnelles introduites par *ir* en ancien et moyen égyptien. *CdE* 60: 152-167.

Maley, Y., 1994. The language of the law. In *Language and the law*, ed. J. Gibbons, 11-50. London: Longman.

Malinine, M., 1947. Notes juridiques. *BIFAO* 46: 93-123.

Malkiel, Y., 1959. Studies in Irreversible Binomials. *Lingua* 8: 113-160.

Martin, E.A., 1990. *A Concise Dictionary of Law*. Oxford: Oxford University Press.

Martin-Pardey, E., 1986. Tempeldekrete. In *LÄ* VI: 379-381.

Mathieu, B., 1996. *La poésie amoureuse de l'Egypte ancienne: Recherches sur un genre littéraire au Nouvel Empire*. BdE 115. Le Caire: IFAO.

Mattha, G., 1975. *The Demotic Legal Code of Hermopolis West*. BdE 45. Le Caire: IFAO.

McDowell, A.G., 1990. *Jurisdiction in the Workmen's Community of Deir-el-Medîna*. Leiden: Nederlands Instituut voor het Nabije Oosten.

Medamud decree (*IFAO* 5413) = *KRI* V, 227 n.57

Medinet Habu & Deir el-Bahari decree = *KRI* IV, 26 n.9 A/B & n.10

Medinet Habu = The Epigraphic Survey (1930-70)

Medinet Habu decree = *KRI* V, 119 n.44 (3)

Meeks, D., 1979. Les donations aux temples dans l'Egypte du Ier millénaire avant J.-C. In *State and Temple Economy in the Ancient Near East II*, ed. E. Lipinski. OLA 6, 605-687. Leuven: Departement Oriëntalistiek.

— 1980. *Année lexicographique I (1977).* Paris: Dimitri Meeks.

Mellinkoff, D., 1963. *The Language of the Law*. Boston: Little, Brown.

Memphis stela, Univ. of Pennsylvania Excavations find 2882 = *KRI* V, 249-250 n.74

Menu, B., 1971. Le régime juridique des terres en Egypte pharaonique: Moyen Empire et Nouvel Empire. *Revue historique de droit français et étranger* 49: 555-585.

— 1981. Considérations sur le droit pénal au Moyen Empire égyptien. *BIFAO* du Centenaire: 57-76.

— 1990. Méthodes et perspectives pour l'histoire du droit égyptien ancien. *BSAK* 4: 233-237 (= *Akten des vierten internationalen Ägyptologen Kongresses München 1985*, ed. S. Schoske, IV. Hamburg: Helmut Buske).

— 1995. Principes fondamentaux du droit égyptien. *CdE* 70: 99-109.

MMA 14.7.10 = Goedicke (1967: Abb. 11)

MMA 14.7.11 = Goedicke (1967: Abb. 20)

MMA 14.7.12 = Goedicke (1967: Abb. 24)

MMA 14.7.13 = Goedicke (1967: Abb. 19)

MMA 14.7.14 = Goedicke (1967: Abb. 16)

Möller, G., 1909. *Hieratische Paläographie: Die Aegyptische Buchschrift in ihrer Entwicklung von der fünften Dynastie bis zur römischen Kaiserzeit.* I. Leipzig: J.C. Heinrichs'sche Buchhandlung.

Mond, R. & Myers, O.H., 1940. *Temples of Armant: A Preliminary Survey.* 2 vols. London: Egypt Exploration Society.

Montet, P., 1931. La stèle de l'an 400 retrouvée. *Kêmi* 4: 191-215.

Moreno Garcia, J.C., 1999. *Ḥwt et le milieu rural égyptien du IIIe millénaire: Economie, administration et organisation territoriale.* Bibliothèque de l'Ecole des Hautes Etudes, Sciences historiques et philologiques 337. Paris: Librairie Honoré Champion.

Moret, M.A., 1912, 1916 & 1917. Chartes d'immunité dans l'Ancien Empire égyptien. *JA* série 10, 20: 73-113; série 11, 7: 271-341; série 11, 10: 359-447.

Morschauser, S., 1991. *Threat-Formulae in Ancient Egypt: A Study of the History, Structure and Use of Threats and Curses in Ancient Egypt.* Baltimore: Halgo.

Moscow I.1.a.1804 = Berlev (1975-76: 32)

Mrnptḥ's victory hymn (*CG* 34025) = Spiegelberg (1896)

Mrnrꜥ? Giza decree = Goedicke (1967: Abb. 6)

NÄG = Erman (1933)

Naunakhte (*pAshmolean* 1947.97) = Černý (1945)

Nauri decree = *KRI* I, 45-58 n.24 & 416 n.180

Naville, E., 1907. *The XIth Dynasty Temple at Deir El-Bahari.* I. EEF 28. London: Egypt Exploration Fund, Kegan Paul, Trench, Trübner & Co.

Naville, E., 1971. (Ed.) *Das ägyptische Totenbuch der XVIII. bis XX. Dynastie,* 2 vols. Graz: Akademische Druck.

Nbḫprwrꜥ Intf Coptos 'decree' (*CG* 30770) = Petrie (1896: pl. VIII)

Nelson, H.H., 1934. The Calendar of Feasts and Offerings at Medinet Habu. In *Work in Western Thebes 1931-33*, eds H.H. Nelson & U. Hölscher. OIC 18, 1-63. Chicago: University of Chicago Press.

— 1936. Three Decrees of Ramses III from Karnak. *JAOS* 56: 232-241.

Neveu, F., 1985. *La particule ḫr en Néo-égyptien (Etude synchronique).* Mémoire EPHE (IVe section). Paris: Neveu.

— 1988. La particule *ḫr* en néo-égyptien. *SAK Beihefte* 3: 99-110 (= *Akten des vierten internationalen Ägyptologen Kongresses München 1985*, ed. S. Schoske, III. Hamburg: Helmut Buske).

— 1996. *La langue des Ramsès: Grammaire du néo-égyptien*. Paris: Khéops.

Newberry, P.E., 1893. *Beni Hasan*. I. ASE. London: Kegan Paul, Trench, Trübner & Co.

— 1900. The Word  KHA, A "DÎWÂN" or "office". *PSBA* 22: 99-105.

Nfrirk3rʿ Abydos decree (*Boston* 03.1896) = Goedicke (1967: Abb. 2)

Nfrk3wḥr Coptos I, J, O, M, N, Q, S/T decrees (*JE* 43053, *MMA* 14.7.11-3) = Goedicke (1967: Abb. 18-22, 24, 25)

Nfrk3wḥr Coptos K decree = Goedicke (1967: Abb. 27)

Nfrk3wḥr Coptos L decree (*JE* 41895) = Goedicke (1967: Abb. 17)

Nims, C.F., 1936. The demotic Group for 'Small Cattle'. *JEA* 22: 51-54.

— 1948. The Term *hp*, "Law, Right," in Demotic. *JNES* 7: 243-260.

Nordh, K., 1996. *Aspects of Ancient Egyptian Curses and Blessings*. Acta Universitatis Upsaliensis, Boreas: Uppsala Studies in Ancient Mediterranean and Near Eastern Civilizations 26. Uppsala: Uppsala University.

oCairo 25232 = Erman (1900)

oDelM 251 = Černý (1935-51 & 1970: v. IV, pl. 3)

oGardiner 309 = Černý & Gardiner (1957: v. I, pl. XCII, n.2)

oMichaelides 23 v° = *KRI* III, 554 n.A66

Otto, E., 1956. Prolegomena zur Frage der Gesetzgebung und Rechtssprechung in Ägypten. *MDAIK* 14: 150-159.

— 1968. *Egyptian Art and the Cults of Osiris and Amon*. London: Thames & Hudson.

pAbbott (*BM* 10221) = *KRI* VI, 468-481 n. 18 (= *Tomb Robberies*)

pAnastasi I (*BM* 10247) = Gardiner (1911)

pAnastasi III (*BM* 10246) = *LEM*, 20-32

pAnastasi IV (*BM* 10249) = *LEM*, 34-56

pAnastasi IV. 10, 8 – 11,8 (*BM* 10249) = *LEM*, 46-47 n.17

pAnastasi V (*BM* 10244) = *LEM*, 56-72

pAnastasi IX = *KRI* III, 504-508 n.228.2

Pantalacci, L., 1985. Un décret de Pépi II en faveur des gouverneurs de l'oasis de Dakhla. *BIFAO* 85: 245-254.

Parant, R., 1982. *L'affaire Sinouhé: Tentative d'approche de la justice répressive égyptienne au début du IIe millénaire av. J.C.* Aurillac: Parant.

pAshmolean 1947.97 = Černý (1945) (=*Naunakhte*)

pBeatty I r° (*BM* 10681) = *LES*, 37-60 (= *Horus & Seth*)

pBerlin 3022 = Blackman (1932) (= *Sinuhe* B)

pBerlin 3047 = Helck (1963)

pBerlin 3049, v° = Vernus (1979)

pBerlin 10071 = Kaplony-Heckel (1971: 33)

pBerlin 10463 r° = Caminos (1963)

pBN v° 215 = Spiegelberg (1929)

pBologna 1094 = *LEM*, 1-12

pBrooklyn 35.1446 = Hayes (1955)

pCairo ESP (B) = *KRI* VI, 518-519 n.17B

pCairo JE 89127-30, 89137-43 (*Hermopolis Code*) = Mattha (1975)

Peck, W.H., & Ross, J.G., 1978. *Drawings from Ancient Egypt*. London: Thames & Hudson.

Peden, A.J., 1994. *Egyptian Historical inscriptions of the Twentieth Dynasty*. Documenta Mundi Aegyptiaca 3. Jonsered : P. Åströms.

Peet, T.E., 1920. *The Mayer Papyri A and B, Nos. M. 11162 and M. 11186 of the Free Public Museums, Liverpool*. London: Egypt Exploration Society.

— 1928. Two Eighteenth Dynasty Letters: Papyrus Louvre 3230. *JEA* 12: 70-74.

Petrie, W.M.F., 1896. *Koptos*. London: B. Quaritch.

Petrie, W.M.F., Wainwright, G.A. & Gardiner, A.H., 1913. *Tarkhan I and Memphis V*. BSAE 23. London: School of Archaeology in Egypt.

Peust, C., 1996. *Indirekte Rede im Neuägyptischen*. Wiesbaden: Harrassowitz.

pHarris I (*BM* 9999) = Erichsen (1933)

pHarris 500 v° (*BM* 10060) = *LES*, 1-9 (= *Doomed Prince*)

Piehl, K., 1891. Les paroles finales du Papyrus d'Orbiney. *ZÄS* 29: 49-52.

Pintore, A., 1994. Legal Rules. In *The Encyclopedia of Language and Linguistics*, eds R.E. Asher & J.M.Y. Simpson, IV, 2097-2103. Oxford: Pergamon Press.

Pirenne, J., 1934. *Histoire des institutions et du droit privé de l'ancienne Egypte: La Ve Dynastie (2750-2625)*. II. Bruxelles: Fondation Egyptologique Reine Elisabeth.

— 1957. La loi et les décrets royaux en Egypte sous l'Ancien Empire. *RIDA* 4: 2-31.

pLeopold-Amherst (*Brussels E* 6857) = *KRI* VI, 481-489 n.19

pMayer A (*Liverpool* 11112) = Peet (1920)

pMunich ÄS 809 = Spiegelberg (1928)

Polaček, A., 1974. Le décret d'Horemheb à Karnak : essai d'analyse socio-juridique. In *Le droit égyptien ancien : Colloque organisé par l'Institut des Hautes Etudes de Belgique, 18-19.3.1974*. Bruxelles: Institut des Hautes Etudes de Belgique.

Polotsky, H.J., 1940. Une règle concernant l'emploi des formes verbales dans la phrase interrogative en néo-égyptian. *ASAE* 40: 241-245 (= *Collected Papers* 33-37).

— 1944. *Etudes de syntaxe copte*. Le Caire: Société d'archéologie copte (= *Collected Papers* 102-107).

— 1957. The "Emphatic" *sḏm.n.f* Form. *RdE* 11: 109-117 (= *Collected Papers* 43-51).

— 1959. Zur Neugestaltung der koptischen Grammatik. *OLZ* 9/10: 453-460 (= *Collected Papers* 234-237).

— 1964. Ägyptische Verbalformen und ihre Vokalisation. *Or* 33 : 267-285 (= *Collected Papers* 52-70).

— 1965. Egyptian Tenses. *Proceedings of the Israel Academy of Sciences and Humanities* II, 5 (= *Collected Papers* 71-96).

— 1971. *Collected Papers*. Jerusalem: The Magnes Press, The Hebrew University.

— 1976. Les transpositions du verbe en égyptien classique. *Israel Oriental Studies* 6: 1-50.

— 1985. A Note on the Sequential Verb-Form in Ramesside Egyptian and in Biblical Hebrew. In *Pharaonic Egypt*, ed. S.I. Groll, 157-161. Jerusalem: The Magnes Press, The Hebrew University.

pOrbiney (*BM* 10183) = *LES*, 9-29 (= *The Tale of Two Brothers*)

Posener, G., 1956. *Littérature et politique dans l'Egypte de la XIIe dynastie*. Paris: Champion.

Posener-Kriéger, P., 1985. Décrets envoyés au temple funéraire de Rêneferef. In *Mélanges Gamal Eddin Mokhtar*, ed. P. Posener-Kriéger. BdE 97, II, 195-210. Le Caire: IFAO.

Posener-Kriéger, P. & de Cenival, J.-L., 1968. *Hieratic Papyri in the British Museum: The Abu Sir Papyri, Fifth Series*. London: British Museum.

Ppy I *Coptos A decree* = Goedicke (1967: Abb. 4)
Ppy I *Dashur decree* = Goedicke (1967: Abb. 5)
Ppy II *Abydos decree* = Goedicke (1967: Abb. 7)
Ppy II *Assuan decree to Ḥrḫwf* = *Urk.* I, 128-131
Ppy II *Coptos B, C & D decree* = Goedicke (1967: Abb. 8, 9 & 11)
Ppy II *Coptos G decree* = Goedicke (1967: Abb. 10)
Ppy II *Dakhla decree* (*IFAO* 3153) = Pantalacci (1985)
Ppy II *Giza decree* = Goedicke (1967: Abb. 12)
Ppy II *Saqqara decrees* = Goedicke (1967: Abb. 13 & 14)
Prince, G., 1987. *A Dictionary of Narratology*. Lincoln: University of Nebraska Press.
pSallier IV (*BM* 10184) = Budge (1923)
PT = Sethe (1908-22)
pTurin 1875 = *KRI* V, 350-360 n.148 (= *Judicial Papyrus*)
pTurin P/R 1880 = *RAD*, 45-58 (= *Strike Papyrus*)
pTurin 1882 = Gardiner (1955)
pTurin P/R 1887 = *RAD* 73-82 (= *Indictement Papyrus*)
pTurin 1896 r° = *KRI* VI, 734-735 n.18
pTurin 1971 = *LRL* 31-33
pTurin 2021/271 = Černý & Peet (1927)
pTurin 55001 = Brunner-Traut (1955)
pWestcar (*Berlin* 3033) = Erman (1890)
pWilbour (*Brooklyn E* 34.5596) = Gardiner (1948b)
Quaegebeur, J., 1994. La table d'offrandes grande et pure d'Amon. *RdE* 45: 155-173.
Qantir decree (*JE* 88879) = *KRI* V, 395 n.174
Quirk, R., Greenbaum, S., Leech, G. & Svartik, J., 1972. *A Grammar of Contemporary English*. London: Longman.
RAD = Gardiner (1948)
Rʿḥtp decree (*Moscow* I.1.a.1804) = Berlev (1975-76)
Raymondis, L.M. & Le Guern, M., 1976. *Le langage de la justice pénale*. Paris: CNRS.
Reich, N.J., 1933. The Codification of the Egyptian Laws by Darius and the Origin of the "Demotic Chronicle". *Mizraim* 1: 178-185.
Reiche, C., 1998. *Ein hymnischer Text in den Gräbern des Ḥwy3, Iʿḥ-ms und Mry-Rʿ in El-Amarna*. GOF IV. Reihe Ägypten 35. Wiesbaden: Harrassowitz.
Reineke, W.F., 1979. Waren die *šwtjw* wirklich Kaufleute? *AoF* 6: 5-14.
Reinisch, L., 1873. *Aegyptische Chrestomathie*. Wien: Wilhelm Braumüller.
Ricke, H., 1935. Eine Inventartafel aus Heliopolis im Turiner Museum. *ZÄS* 71: 111-133.
Ries, J., 1985. Le signe et le symbolisme de la croix dans les religions non chrétiennes. In *Le symbolisme dans le culte des grandes religions: Actes du colloque de Louvain-la-Neuve 4-5 octobre 1983*, ed. J. Ries. Homo religiosus 11, 295-314. Louvain-la-Neuve: Centre d'Histoire des Religions.
RITA = Kitchen (1993-96)
RITANC = Kitchen (1993-99)
Robert, P., 1987. *Dictionnaire alphabétique et analogique de la langue française Le Petit Robert*. I. Paris: Le Robert.

Robichon, C. & Varille, A., 1936. *Le temple du scribe royal Amenhotep fils de Hapou*. I. FIFAO 11. Cairo: Imprimerie IFAO.

Roeder, G., 1960. *Mythen und Legenden um ägyptische Gottheiten und Pharaonen: Die ägyptische Religion in Texten und Bildern*. Zürich: Artemis.

Rosch, E., 1978. Priniples of Categorization. In *Cognition and Categorization*, eds E. Rosch & B. Loyd, 28-49. Hillsdale: Erlbaum.

Rosén, H., 1994. The definite article in the making, nominal constituent order, and related phenomena. In *Linguistic Studies on Latin: Selected Papers From the 6th International Colloquium on Latin Linguistics (Budapest, 23-27 March 1991)*, ed. J. Herman. Studies in Language Companion Series 28, 129-150. Amsterdam: John Benjamins.

Rosén, H.B., 1984. Composition adjectivale et adjectives composés en hébreu-israélien. In *East and West: Selected Writings in Linguistics – Hebrew and Semitic Linguistics*. II, 121-130. München: Wilhelm Fink.

— 1988. Early Greek Grammar and Thought in Heraclitus: The Emergence of the Article. *Proceedings of the Israel Academy of Sciences and Humanities* 7,2: 21-62.

Saad, R. & Manniche, L., 1971. A Unique Offering List of Amenophis IV Recently Found at Karnak. *JEA* 57: 70-72.

Sander-Hansen, C.E., 1933. *Historische Inschriften der 19. Dynastie*. I. BAe 4. Bruxelles: Fondation Egyptologique Reine Elisabeth.

Saqqara, Abu Gorab & Abusir decrees = *KRI* II, 873-875 n.333

?*Saqqara decree* = Goedicke (1967: Abb. 15)

Satzinger, H., 1976. *Neuägyptische Studien*. Beihefte zur WZKM 6. Wien: VWGÖ.

— 1997. How Good was Tjeker-Baˁl's Egyptian? *LingAeg* 5: 171-176.

Sb3wḫˁ Anibeh tomb = *KRI* III, 130 n.80

Sbkḥtp IV *Karnak decree* (*JE* 51911) = Helck (1969: 199-200)

Schäfer, H., 1904. *Die Mysterien des Osiris in Abydos unter König Sesostris III*. UGAÄ IV (2). Leipzig: J.C. Hinrichs.

Scheepers, A., 1992. Le voyage d'Ounamon: Un texte "littéraire" ou "non-littéraire"? In *Amosiadès: Mélanges offerts au Prof. C. Vandersleyen*, eds C. Obsomer & A.-L. Oosthoek, 355-365. Louvain-la-Neuve: UCL.

Schlichting, R., 1982. Neith. In *LÄ* IV, 392-394.

Schott, S., 1961. *Kanais: Der Tempel Sethos I. im Wadi Mia*. NAWG I, Philologisch-historische Klasse 6. Göttingen: Vandenhoeck & Ruprecht.

— 1971. "Jahr 15" am Rande einer Inventartafel aus Heliopolis. In *Beiträge zur Ägyptischen Bauforschung und Altertumskunde 12, zum 70. Geburtstag von H. Ricke*, 65-73. Wiesbaden: Franz Steiner.

Schulman, A.R., 1957. Egyptian Representations of Horsemen and Riding in the New Kingdom. *JNES* 16: 263-271.

— 1963. A Cult of Ramesses III at Memphis. *JNES* 22: 177-184.

Seidl, E., 1951. *Einführung in die ägyptische Rechtsgeschichte bis zum Ende des neuen Reiches*. ÄF 10. Glückstadt: J.J. Augustin.

Semnah despatches (*pRamesseum* C) = Smither & Gunn (1945)

Sethe, K., 1901. *Dodekaschoinos das Zwölfmeilenland an der Grenze von Aegypten und Nubien.* UGAÄ 2. Hildesheim: G. Olms.

— 1903. *Urkunden des alten Reichs.* Leipzig: J.C. Hinrichs.

— 1908-22. *Die Altägyptischen Pyramidentexte.* 4 vols. Leipzig: J.C. Hinrichs.

— 1927-30. *Urkunden der 18. Dynastie: Historisch-biographische Urkunden,* 4 vols. Leipzig: J.C. Hinrichs.

Shalomi-Hen, R., 2000. *Classifying the Divine: Determinatives and Categorization in CT 335 and BD 17.* GOF IV. Reihe Ägypten 38. Classification and Categorization in Ancient Egypt 2. Wiesbaden: Harrassowitz.

Shisha-Halevy, A., 1974. Protatic ⲉϥⲥⲱⲧⲙ: A hitherto Unnoticed Coptic Tripartite Conjugation-Form and Its Diachronic Connections. *Or* 43: 369-381.

— 1978. Quelques thématisations marginales du verbe en Néo-Egyptien. *OLP* 9: 51-67.

— 1981. Bohairic-Late Egyptian Diaglosses: A Contribution to the Typology of Egyptian. In *Studies Presented to H.J. Polotsky*, ed. D.W. Young, 314-338. Massachusetts: Pirtle & Polson.

— 1985. What's in a Name? On Coptic {ⲡⲁ-} "{he}of -". *Enchoria* 13: 97-102.

— 1986. *Coptic Grammatical Categories: Structural Studies in the Syntax of Shenoutean Sahidic.* AnOr 53. Roma: Pontificium Institutum Biblicum.

— 1987. Grammatical Discovery Procedure and the Egyptian-Coptic Nominal Sentence. *Or* 56: 147-175.

— 1988. *Coptic Grammatical Chrestomathy: A Course for Academic and Private Study.* OLA 30. Leuven: Peeters.

— 1989. Work-Notes on Demotic Syntax, I. *Or* 58: 28-60.

— 1989b. Papyrus Vandier *Recto*: An Early Demotic Literary Text? *JAOS* 109: 421-435.

— 1989c. Review of The Narrative Verbal System of Old and Middle Egyptian. *Or* 58: 247-254.

— 1989d. *The Proper Name: Structural Prolegomena to Its Syntax – A Case Study in Coptic.* Beihefte zur WZKM 15. Wien: VWGÖ.

— 1995. Some Reflections on the Egyptian Conjunctive. In *Divitiae Aegypti: Koptologische und verwandte Studien zu Ehren von Martin Krause*, eds C. Fluck, L. Langener, S. Richter, S. Schaten & G. Wurst, 300-314. Wiesbaden: Dr. Ludwig Reichert.

— 1998. *Structural Studies in Modern Welsh Syntax: Aspects of the Grammar of Kate Roberts.* Münster: Nodus.

— 1998b. A First Structural Grammar of Demotic. *BiOr* 5/6: 587-600.

— 2000. Stability in Clausal/Phrasal Pattern Constituent Sequencing: 4000 Years of Egyptian (with Some Theoretical Reflections, also on Celtic). In *Stability, Variation and Change of Word-Order Patterns over Time*, eds R. Sornicola, E. Poppe & A. Shisha-Halevy, 71-100. Amsterdam: John Benjamins.

Shorter, A.W., 1933. A Stela of Seti I in the British Museum. *JEA* 19: 60-61.

Simpson, R.S., 1996. *Demotic Grammar in the Ptolemaic Sacerdotal Decrees.* Oxford: Griffith Institute.

Simpson, W.K., 1963. Studies in the Twelfth Egyptian Dynasty. *JARCE* 2: 53-63.

Sinuhe (*pBerlin* 3022) = Blackman (1932)

Siut = Griffith (1889)

Smither, P.C. & Gunn, B., 1945. The Semnah Despatches. *JEA* 31: 3-10.

Snwsrt I Abydos decree to Mnṯwḥtp (*CG* 20539 II) = Lange & Schäfer (1908: 154-158)

Snwsrt III Deir el-Bahari decree = Naville (1907: pl. XXIV)

Sottas, H., 1913. *La préservation de la propriété funéraire dans l'ancienne Egypte.* Paris: Champion.

Spalinger, A., 1991. Some Revisions of Temple Endowments in the New Kingdom. *JARCE* 28: 21-39.

Spencer, P., 1984. *The Egyptian Temple: A Lexicographical Study*. London: Kegan Paul International.

Spiegelberg, W., 1896. Der Siegeshymnus des Merneptah auf der Flinders Petrie-Stele. *ZÄS* 34: 2-25.

— 1899. Varia. *RecTrav* 21: 39-45.

— 1906. Demotische Miscellen. *RecTrav* 28: 187-202.

— 1907. Zur Geschichte des Tempels des Harkentechthai zu Athribis. *RecTrav* 29: 53-57.

— 1925. Die neuägyptische Präposition *m-dr* "wegen". *ZÄS* 60: 59-61.

— 1927. Die Konjunktion  *ḫr rꜥ* "zu der Zeit wo, wann, wenn, da, weil". *ZÄS* 62: 42-43.

— 1928. Ein Gerichtsprotokoll aus der Zeit Thutmosis' IV. *ZÄS* 63: 105-115

— 1929. *Die sogenannte Demotische Chronik des Pap. 215 der Bibliothèque Nationale zu Paris nebst den auf der Rückseite des Papyrus stehenden Texten.* ABAW 1. Leipzig: J.C. Hinrichs.

Steindorff, G., 1939. The Statuette of an Egyptian Commissioner in Syria. *JEA* 25: 30-33.

Stèle juridique de Karnak (*JE* 52453) = Lacau (1949)

Sweeney, D., 1986. The nominal object clause of verbs of perception in non-literary Late Egyptian. In *Crossroad: Chaos or the Biginning of a New Paradigm*, eds G. Englund & P.J. Frandsen, 337-373. Copenhagen: Carsten Niebuhr Institute.

— 2001. *Correspondence and Dialogue: Pragmatic Factors in Late Ramesside Letter-Writing.* ÄUAT 49. Wiesbaden: Harrassowitz.

Špssk3f Giza decree = Goedicke (1967: Abb. 1)

Tanis decree (*JE* 60539) = *KRI* II, 287-288 n.71

Tarkhan I = Petrie (1913)

Taylor, J.R., 1989. *Linguistic Categorization: Prototypes in Linguistic Theory.* Oxford: Clarendon Press.

The Admonitions of an Egyptian Sage (*Leyde* I, 334 r°) = Gardiner (1969)

The Eloquent Peasant (*Berlin* 3023, 3025, 10499 r°, *BM* 10274 r°) = Vogelsang & Gardiner (1908)

The Epigraphic Survey, 1930-70. *Medinet Habu,* 8 vols. OIP 8, 9, 23, 51, 83, 84, 93, 94. Chicago: University of Chicago Press.

The Inscription of Mes = Gardiner (1964)

The Installation of the Vizier = Faulkner (1955)

The Instruction of Ptahhotep (*pPrisse*, *BM* 10371/10435, 10509, *Turin* 54014) = Žába (1956)

Théodoridès, A., 1962. Le rôle du Vizir dans la 'Stèle Juridique de Karnak'. *RIDA* (3) 9: 45-136.

— 1964. La stèle juridique d'Amarah. *RIDA* (3) 11: 45-80.

— 1967. A propos de la loi dans l'Egypte pharaonique. *RIDA* (3) 14: 107-152.

— 1970. La notion égyptienne de possession exprimée par la locution prépositive *m-di*. *RdE* 22: 139-154.

— 1971. The Concept of Law in Ancient Egypt. In *The Legacy of Egypt*, ed. J.R.Harris, 291-322. Oxford: Clarendon Press.

— 1972. Mettre des biens sous les pieds de quelqu'un. *RdE* 24: 188-192.

— 1975. Dekret. In *LÄ* I: 1037-1043.

— 1981. Limites à la volonté royale dans l'Egypte pharaonique. In *Atti dell'Accademia Romanistica Costantiniana IV in onore de M. de Dominicis*, 626-643. Perugia: Libreria Universitaria.

— 1982. Une 'charte d'immunité' d'Ancien Empire (24e s. av. J.C.). *RIDA* (3) 29: 71-118.

— 1993. Du rapport entre un contrat et un acte de disposition appelé "imyt-per" en égyptien. *RIDA* (3) 39: 77-105.

The Tale of Two Brothers (*BM* 10183) = *LES*, 9-29

Thiem, A.-C., 2000. *Speos von Gebel es-Silsileh*. I. ÄUAT 47. Wiesbaden: Harrassowitz.

Tiradritti, F. (ed.), 1998. *Egyptian Treasures from the Egyptian Museum in Cairo*. Vercelli: White Star.

Tod, Karnak, Edfu, Elephantine & El-Kab decree = *KRI* V, 232-234 n.65, 67-68 and Grandet (1990)

Trapani, M., 1992. Il decreto regale e l'oracolo divino nell'Antico Egitto. *Annali* (Rivista del Dipartimento di Studi Asiatici e del Dipartimento di Studi e Ricerche su Africa e Paesi Arabi) 52: 1-33.

— 1993. The Royal Decree and the Divine Oracle from the Old to the late New Kingdom: a Compared Research. In *Sesto Congresso Internazionale di Egittologia Atti*, II, ed. S. Curto *et alii*, 537-545. Torino: Societa italiana per il gas.

Tti Abydos decree = Goedicke (1967: Abb. 3)

Turin 2682 (*Heliopolis decree*) = Ricke (1935)

Twtꜥnḫimn Upper Egypt? decree (*Liverpool E* 583) = Amer (1985)

Tyldesley, J., 2000. *Judgment of the Pharaoh: Crime and Punishment in Ancient Egypt*. London: Weidenfeld & Nicolson.

*Urk.*I = Sethe (1903)

*Urk.*IV, 1-16 = Sethe (1927-30)

*Urk.*IV, 17-22 = Helck (1955-61)

Valloggia, M., 1976. *Recherche sur les "messagers"* (*wpwtyw*) *dans les sources égyptiennes profanes*. Centre de Recherches d'Histoire et de Philologie de la IVe Section de l'Ecole pratique des Hautes Etudes II, Hautes Etudes Orientales 6. Genève: Librairie Droz.

Van Siclen III, C.C., 1973. The Accession Date of Amenhotep III and the Jubilee. *JNES* 32 : 290-300.

Van der Plas, D., 1986. *L'Hymne à la crue du Nil*. I. Leiden: Nederlands Instituut voor het Nabije Oosten.

Vandersleyen, C., 1971. *Les guerres d'Amosis*. MRE 1. Bruxelles: Fondation Egyptologique Reine Elisabeth.

Vercoutter, J., 1959. The Gold of Kush: Two Gold-washing Stations at Faras East. *Kush* 7: 120-153.

Vergote, J., 1955. La fonction du pseudoparticipe. In *Ägyptologische Studien, Festschrift für H. Grapow zum 70. Geb.*, ed. O. Firchow, 338-361. Deutsche Akademie der Wissenschaften zu Berlin, Institut für Orientforschung 29. Berlin : Akademie Verlag.

Vernus, P., 1975. Inscriptions de la Troisième Période Intermédiaire (I). *BIFAO* 75: 1-66.

— 1979. Un décret de Thoutmosis III relatif à la santé publique (P. Berlin 3049, v° XVIII-XIX). *Or* 48: 176-184.

— 1980. Inscriptions de la Troisième Période Intermédiaire (IV): Le texte oraculaire réemployé dans le passage axial du IIIe pylône dans le temple de Karnak. *Karnak* VI: 215-233.

— 1981. Formes "emphatiques" en fonction non "emphatiques" dans la protase d'un système corrélatif. *GM* 43: 73-88.

— 1982. Deux particularités de l'égyptien de tradition: *nty iw* + présent 1; *wnn.f ḥr sḏm* narratif. In *L'égyptologie en 1979: Axes prioritaires de recherches* I. Colloques internationaux du Centre National de la Recherche Scientifique 595, 81-89. Paris: CNRS.

— 1982-83. Etudes de philologie et de linguistique (II). *RdE* 34: 115-1128.

— 1983. Review of Le décret d'Horemheb by J.-M. Kruchten. *Revue Historique de Droit Français et Etranger* 61: 73-78.

— 1985. Etudes de philologie et de linguistique (IV). *RdE* 36: 153-168.

— 1985b. "Ritual" *sḏm.n.f* and Some Values of the "Accompli" in the Bible and in the Koran. In *Pharaonic Egypt*, ed. S. Israelit-Groll, 307-316. Jerusalem: Magnes Press.

— 1986. Etudes de philologie et de linguistique (V). *RdE* 37: 139-147.

— 1990. Les « décrets » royaux (*wḏ-nsw*) : l'énoncé d'auctoritas comme genre. *BSAK* 4: 239-246 (= *Akten des vierten internationalen Ägyptologen Kongresses München 1985*, ed. S. Schoske, IV. Hamburg: Helmut Buske).

— 1990b. *Future at Issue. Tense, Mood and Aspect in Middle Egyptian: Studies in Syntax and Semantics*. New Haven: Yale University.

— 1996. Langue littéraire et diglossie. In *Ancient Egyptian Literature: History and Forms*, ed. A. Loprieno. PÄ 10, 555-564. Leiden: E.J. Brill.

— 1997. *Les parties du discours en moyen égyptien: Autopsie d'une théorie*. Cahiers de la Société d'Egyptologie 5. Genève: Société d'Egyptologie.

Villey, M., 1974. De l'indicatif dans le droit. *Archives de Philosophie du Droit* 19: 4-61.

Vogelsang, F. & Gardiner, A.H., 1908. *Die Klagen des Bauern*. Literarische Texte des Mittleren Reiches 1. Berlin: J.C. Hinrichs.

von Bissing, F.W. & Borchardt, L., 1905. *Das Re-Heiligtum des Königs Ne-Woser-Re (Rathures)*. I. Leipzig: J.C. Hinrichs.

W3ḏk3rꜥ? Coptos H decree (*MMA* 14.7.14) = Goedicke (1967: Abb. 16)

Warburton, D.A., 1997. *State and Economy in Ancient Egypt: Fiscal Vocabulary of the New Kingdom*. OBO 151. Fribourg & Göttingen: University Press, Vandenhoeck & Ruprecht.

Wb = Erman & Grapow (1926-57)

Wb Beleg = Erman & Grapow (1971)

Weil, A., 1908. *Die Viziere des Pharaonenreiches*. Leipzig: J.C. Hinrichs.

Wenamun (*Moscow* 120) = *LES*, 61-76

Wente, E.F., 1961. *Ỉwiw.f* in Late Egyptian. *JNES* 20: 120-123.

— 1967. *Late Ramesside Letters*. SAOC 33. Chicago: University of Chicago Press.

— 1990. *Letters from Ancient Egypt*. Atlanta: Scholars Press.

Werlich, E., 1975. *Typologie der Texte*: *Entwurf eines textlinguistischen Modells zur Grundlegung einer Textgrammatik*. Heidelberg: Quelle & Meyer.

Westendorf, W., 1953. Die Wortstellung Nomen + *sḏm.f* als grammatische Konstruktion. *MIO* 1: 337-343.

— 1982. Mund. In *LÄ* IV, 222-223.

West Silsileh (commission) decree = *KRI* IV, 73-74 n.40

West Silsileh decrees = *KRI* I, 81-96 n.44

West Silsileh, Bigeh, Armant & El-Kab decrees = *KRI* II, 384-386 & 390-391 & 393-398 n.135C, 136A, 137A-C & G, 138B, 139A, 140C, 141A, 142, 143A, 144

Whittaker, G., 2001. The Dawn of Writing and Phoneticism. In *Hieroglyphen, Alphabete, Schriftreformen: Studien zu Multiliteralismus, Schriftwechsel und Orthographieneuregelungen*, eds D. Borchers, F. Kammerzell & S. Weninger. Lingua Aegyptia Studia Monographica 3, 11-50. Göttingen: Seminär für Ägyptologie und Koptologie.

Wien ÄS 5909 = *Urk.* IV, 1287-1299.

Wiesmann, H., 1922. Die Determinative des sprechenden Mannes und der Buchrolle in den Pyramidentexten. *ZÄS* 57: 73-77.

Willems, H., 1990. Crime, Cult and Capital Punishment (Mo'alla Inscription 8). *JEA* 76: 27-53.

Wilson, J.A., 1969. Egyptian Rituals and Incantations: Curses and Threats. In *Ancient Near Eastern Texts Relating to the Old Testament*, ed. J.B. Pritchard, 326-328. Princeton: Princeton University Press.

Winand, J., 1991. Le verbe iy/iw: unité morphologique et sémantique. *LingAeg* 1: 357-387.

— 1992. *Etudes de néo-égyptien: La morphologie verbale*. Aegyptiaca Leodiensia 2. Liège: C.I.P.L.

— 1995. La grammaire au secours de la datation des texts. *RdE* 46: 187-202.

Youssef, A.A., 1964. Merenptah's Fourth Year Text at Amada. *ASAE* 58: 273-280.

Žába, Z., 1956. *Les Maximes de Ptahhotep*. Prague: Académie Tchécoslovaque des Sciences.

Index of syntactic forms and technical terms

Index of Egyptian texts and artifacts

Index of main Egyptian lexemes discussed